Fiscal Crisis in
American Cities:
The
Federal Response

Fiscal Crisis in American Cities: The Federal Response

L. Kenneth Hubbell,
Editor

Ballinger Publishing Company • Cambridge, Massachusetts
A Subsidiary of Harper & Row, Publishers, Inc.

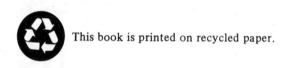
International Standard Book Number: 0-88410-491-5

Library of Congress Catalog Card Number: 79-614

Printed in the United States of America

Library of Congress Cataloging in Publication Data
Main entry under title:

Fiscal crisis in American cities—the Federal response.

   Based on papers presented at a conference held in Washington, D.C. in mid-June 1978.
   Includes bibliographical references.
   1. Intergovernmental fiscal relations—United States—Congresses. 2. Grants-in-aid—United States—Congresses. 3. Revenue sharing—United States—Congresses. 4. Municipal finance—United States—Congresses. I. Hubbell, Loren Kenneth.
HJ275.F553   336.1'85   79-614
ISBN 0-88410-491-5

Contents

List of Figures

List of Tables

Preface

The purpose of this volume is to examine in depth the federal government's response to what recently has come to be referred to as the fiscal crisis of cities. While particular attention is directed at the so-called emergency measures and programs enacted during the economically turbulent years of the mid-1970s, changes in the more established programs from the late 1960s and early 1970s are also scrutinized. Taken together, the assembled papers evaluate the bulk of the federally initiated programs aimed either directly or indirectly at assisting financially troubled cities over the past decade.

Organizationally, the book is divided into three sections. Part I contains three background chapters. Chapter 1, "Federal Policy and the Fiscal Outlook for Cities," by Roy Bahl assesses the fiscal prospect for cities in light of recent events (mid-1960s to 1975) and of current federal policy. Chapter 2, "Localities Under the New Intergovernmental System," is by David Walker. Tracing the federal response to a wide range of fiscal, functional, and socioeconomic pressures on our cities, Walker stresses how the proliferation of federal programs over the past decade has radically altered our federalist system. The last chapter in this section, "Measuring the Regional Economic Impacts of Federal Grant Programs," by Richard Gustely discusses the range of regional economic impacts of federal grant programs as well as the range of methodologies employed in analyzing these impacts. Historical changes in the level and distribution of aid and what this implies for the ultimate distribution of grant impacts are two key issues addressed in his chapter.

In Part II specific federal programs for alleviating the fiscal crunch in metropolitan areas are delineated. To insure uniformity of analysis for comparative purposes, each of the six chapters in this section includes:

1. A brief description of the program and its objectives and goals
2. An empircal evaluation of the effect (in dollars) of the program on recipient cities, including when possible a breakdown of the recipients by city size and region
3. An appraisal of the overall effectiveness as to how well the program met its stated objectives
4. A discussion of the drawbacks, difficulties, deficiencies, and limitations of the program
5. Public policy implications of the program

Ross Stephens in the initial chapter in Part II critically reviews the objectives and performance of General Revenue Sharing program over the past half-dozen years. This chapter is followed by Alan Fechter's assessment of the fiscal implications of social welfare programs, Georges Vernez's and Roger Vaughan's evaluations of counter-cyclical public works programs, Robert Cook's analysis of public service employment. Paul Dommel's chapter on the community block grant program, and John Ross's appraisal of counter-cyclical revenue sharing.

Part III is made up of only two chapters. In an effort to add balance to the total inquiry, this final section considers some possible new directions of federal policy toward cities. Specifically, the widely discussed proposal for a national development bank and alternative tax and wage subsidies to encourage private capital investment in distressed urban areas are examined. The former topic is covered by the editor's chapter, "Development Banking and Financial Incentives," and the latter by Richard McHugh's and David Puryear's contribution, entitled "Tax Credits for Urban Revitalization."

As editor, I am indebted to the Economic Development Administration (EDA) of the U.S. Department of Commerce for granting the funds to support the two-day Washington conference in mid-June 1978, the content of which forms the basis for this book. I am especially grateful to Victor Hausner, Deputy Assistant Secretary for Policy and Planning, EDA, and Dr. Pat Choate of EDA for their advice and counsel about the conference, and to Dr. Paul Braden for acting as conference moderator. Thanks also go to Barbara Newlen and Barbara Howenstine of EDA for their efforts in its organization and presentation.

I would also like to thank the authors who have contributed chapters; their dedication and creative effort actually made the book possible. All of the authors benefited greatly from insightful comments from Harvey A. Garn, Anthony Downs, Peggy Cuciti, Anthony Sulvetta, George Peterson, Harvey Galper, and William Henderson, discussants at the conference. The authors merit additional thanks for adhering so closely to the outlines given them by the editor. This of course means that any structural faults or omissions in the book must be borne by the editor and not the authors.

Finally, thanks are due to Norma Damon for typing the manuscript and Harriette Schultz for assisting in the editing and proofreading of the manuscript.

L. Kenneth Hubbell
Professor of Economics
University of Missouri–
Kansas City

Kansas City, Missouri
Fall 1978

Introduction

In the mid-1960s, considerable attention was drawn to the mounting fiscal problems of many of our larger cities. The disparity in city-suburban public service levels and fiscal capacity, the heavy concentration of the urban poor and of racial minorities in particular in central cities, neighborhood decay and urban congestion, and the deteriorated condition of urban infrastructure were widely discussed topics among city officials, policymakers, and academics. Few believed that these demanding fiscal problems were severe enough, however, to threaten the financial stability of even the most adversely affected cities. Yet by 1974, because of a combination of factors, the size of the deficits for a number of cities had reached the point where financial default was a real possibility.

With the help of hindsight, the desperate condition in which a score of the country's largest cities found themselves may be traced to a combination of factors. For two decades or more the fiscal base of central cities measured either by employment or income had been declining. It is argued that central cities had been losing their hold on manufacturing facilities and their relative attractiveness as places for expansion and new development for the following reasons. (1) Movements in population had caused a shift in markets away from the older, established central cities to the suburban rings and regionally to the Sunbelt states. (2) Technological changes in transportation and communication had diminished the need for business firms to be in close proximity to markets, suppliers, and business services. (3) New production technology had begun employing horizontal production processes, which are very land-intensive and often require special design. (4) Plant and equipment of firms located in the older central cities tended to be outmoded and very costly to maintain and operate. (5) Workers were now so spatially dispersed that firms often found it hard to retain a quality labor force. (6) Adequate land for expansion and growth was unavailable in core areas. (7) Political and socioeconomic conditions were perceived to be less favorable in the central cities than in suburban and exurban locations because of such factors as more bureaucratic red tape, congestion, and crime.

It took the 1974–1975 recession to reveal the full extent of the fiscal decline of many of the older urban areas. As Bahl discusses, the more seriously affected, or those facing an absolute decline in fiscal capacity, were forced to make unpleasant choices. They had either to reduce the quantity or quality of their public services, to increase the real tax burdens imposed on their citizens, or to pursue some combination of the two. The acuteness of the financial crunch was brought home most dramatically when New York City was forced to appeal to the federal government for assistance. In large part, the New York crisis resulted from a prolonged delay in adjusting to a basic service-revenue imbalance. Over the years, New York City's administration had avoided making the hard choice between reduced services or higher taxes by financing current operations from borrowings. In fact, New York had deferred the difficult decisions for so long that it was impossible to adjust immediately to a diminished tax base when the lenders finally became unwilling to roll over (refinance) their existing debt. To rescue the city from the brink of bankruptcy required the involvement of the state and federal governments. To date, no other large city has suffered the degree of financial crisis that New York City has, but some have teetered on the brink and have escaped only by drastically reducing public services or by receiving large amounts of external aid.

Those reviewing the various federal programs for extending assistance to fiscally disadvantaged cities generally agree about several points. First, as Walker shows, the prime federal response has been a fourfold increase in intergovernmental fiscal transfers over the past ten years. Submerged in this extraordinary escalation in dollar outlays, however, are several equally dramatic changes in the system of intergovernmental relations and transfers. Over this short time span there has been a tendency to expand the partnership theme to include practically all local jurisdictions directly and indirectly, a movement by the federal government to strengthen the position of cities and counties, a greater reliance on formulas as opposed to discretionary grants, the development of a tripartite aid system (categoricals, block grants, and general revenue sharing), and the emergence of a maze of substate, generalist, and single purpose bodies as a result of the institutional and procedural strings attached to certain grant programs. The overall impact of these tendencies is the establishment of a "supermarbleized" system of intergovernmental relations that bears little resemblance to the conventional "marble cake" theory. According to Walker, Washington's policy of bypassing the states and their expanding, bilateral links and hosts of substate governments undermines managerial effectiveness and demonstrates the federal government's failure to understand and properly diagnose the long-term fiscal problems of cities.

A second observation related to the first is that a shift is occurring away from the federally run programs that dominated the 1960s to a more flexible system of federal, state, and local programs. The pressure for more decentralized decisionmaking primarily grew out of the dissatisfaction of local officials with the growing federal role in community policy matters and the disillusionment of federal policymakers with the performance of urban renewal, model cities, and various other programs designed to assist disadvantaged cities. Cook points out that granting greater local discretion in the allocation of federal aid does carry with it the possiblity of conflict between federal and local objectives. The emphasis on more local decisionmaking and the increased flexibility on how federal dollars are spent, however, indicate clearly the direction in which national policy is moving.

Third, an integral part of the decentralization and decategorization of federal programs has been the enactment of a series of federal-local programs with substate allocation formulas. Starting with General Revenue Sharing (GRS), the trend has increasingly been to introduce distributional formulas into assistance programs—Public Service Employment (PSE), Community Development Block Grants (CDBG), Anti-Recession Fiscal Assistance (ARFA), and Local Public Works (LPW). Two aspects of this shift in policy are noteworthy. In recognition of the fact that the United States does not have a national urban crisis—but rather that the situation exists wherein a few big cities and a few older and larger suburban cities are experiencing an urban crisis condition—the emphasis in the Carter Administration has been on targeting or channeling federal grants to the most needy cities. This strategy, as Ross, Dommel, and Vernez and Vaughan point out, has not been without its problems. The development of eligibility tests and of targeting systems that concentrate grant funds has resulted in some distortions (initially the bulk of the funds went to a very few cities), required the adoption of exceedingly more and more complex allocational formulas, and created a demand for a new type of policy advisor, the targeting expert.

While targeting is a prominent feature of the Carter Administration's urban policy, the amount of funds allocated under assistance programs that apply eligibility tests, although growing, is small compared to the monies disbursed through general purpose aid programs. Since the advent of GRS, in fact the dominant trend has been to spread federal dollars to literally thousands of local jurisdictions, most of which received little or no outlays previously. This tendency to spread federal funds to virtually all local governments without regard to their respective roles for the responsibility of funding and delivering public services is severely criticized by Stephens.

The fourth and final observation has to do with the urban policy recommendations of the Carter Administration. From President Carter's March 1978 Urban National Policy address, it is clear that new urban-related legislation is to be directed at saving the city as a fiscal and economic entity. The emphasis is on "revitalizing the city" through the improvement of public infrastructure and the extension of subsidies to private firms that elect to expand or relocate within distressed urban areas. Two basic types of incentives are to be offered, capital subsidies and tax incentives (investment credits and employment credits). Both are discussed as general subsidies and as targeted subsidies with an explicit urban focus in the chapters by Hubbell and by McHugh and Puryear.

A conclusion that may be drawn from the chapters in this volume is that the federal government's response to the fiscal crisis of American cities has in general been mixed. On the one hand, it provided immediate fiscal relief for a score or so of the hardest hit cities, but there is equally good evidence to support the proposition that many of the programs were designed without sufficient forethought as to their potential impacts and alternative outcomes. Some, in fact, may actually be counterproductive. To illustrate, the emphasis upon general purpose aids since 1972 clearly has weakened the state role in the federalist system at a time when vigorous state leadership is so desperately needed to deal with the fragmented governmental and financial structures of metropolitan areas. The vast influx of countercyclical aid to several large distressed cities may have staved off bankruptcy, but it has not assisted the cities in adjusting to their diminished fiscal capacities, the major source of their financial difficulties.

Fiscal Crisis in American Cities: The Federal Response

✳ *Part I*

Background and Overview

Chapter 1

Federal Policy and the Fiscal Outlook for Cities

Roy Bahl
Bernard Jump, Jr.
Larry Schroeder

The urban fiscal problem was as popular a topic in 1965 as in 1975, but the nature of the discussion, like the severity of the problem, differed markedly. The burning urban fiscal issues of the mid-1960s were city-suburb disparities in public service levels and fiscal capacity congestion and urban blight, heavy concentration of the poor and badly deteriorated neighborhoods in the central city, and early signs of a worn-out urban infrastructure.[1] Little attention was paid to the possibility that financial problems in some communities could become so severe as to take them to the brink of default. Indeed, as late as 1968 the major rating agencies were struggling with the hypothetical problem of assigning several levels of default probability when all major local government securities were thought to be of investment grade. Some of the urban fiscal issues of the 1960s were even more pressing at the midpoint of the next decade; city-suburb fiscal disparities had widened, poverty in the urban ghettos had deepened, and the urban infrastructure had continued to deteriorate. But by 1975 there were new issues as well. A high rate of inflation and the influence of public employee unions had shifted the pressure on public expenditures away from the demand side—citizen requirements for adequate public service levels—and onto the supply side where costs became the primary consideration. Other notable differences were that a recession had devastated the economies of many old central cities and left some doubt about their future economic roles, regional shifts in economic activity had compromised the financial position of even some state governments, and the financial collapse of New York City had demonstrated that default could indeed occur. The new factors resulted in shifting federal policy emphasis toward short-term financial measures (e.g., CETA, ARFA, Local Public Works) while the more fundamental long-term reforms, particularly public welfare, remained on the shelf.

The purpose of this chapter is to assess the fiscal outlook for cities in light of this history and current federal policy. In the next sections, the events leading to the 1975 crisis are discussed and the outlook is considered in a context of the important federal and local government fiscal responses during the 1975-1978 recovery period. Finally, some principles for a more appropriate federal urban policy are discussed. Because this subject, the urban fiscal problem, is much more commonplace in the Northeast and the industrial Midwest than elsewhere in the country, emphasis is given to the existing situation and prospects for the declining cities in these regions.

THE SOURCES OF THE PROBLEM:
1962-1975

There were three major sources of the urban fiscal problem that led to the crisis conditions for many cities and some states in 1975:[2] the recession that accelerated the decentralization of employment from central cities and from the declining regions; inflation; and public employment and employee compensation growth.[3]

Economic Base Decline

An examination of the New York City case—perhaps the extreme example of the more general problem—underlines the importance of relating the fiscal health of a city to the basic health of its economy. From a peak of 3.8 million in 1969, employment in New York City declined virtually without interruption to a level of 3.4 million by June 1975, an 11 percent drop The employment decline has not been as precipitous since 1975, but the downward trend has continued. During the 1969-1975 period, employment in the nation grew by more than 20 percent and since 1975 has continued to increase. If employment in New York City had grown at the national rate between 1969 and 1978, New York City would have upward of 750,000 more jobs than it now has. The city government revenue loss represented by this job loss is substantial, an amount that would easily eliminate the city's current deficit.[4]

While it must be acknowledged that many of New York City's problems are unique and that New York City's situation is always an exaggeration of what is occurring elsewhere, the problem of a declining economic base is present in many large metropolitan core cities across the country. Those in the Northeast appear to have fared worse than the newer southern and western central cities, but all have experienced employment suburbanization as industries have moved to newer, more spacious facilities closer to their suburban employees. It is difficult to document central city employment trends because no public or private agency collects data on employment in cities. Sacks has adjusted Census Journey-to-Work data to estimate employment in city areas and finds a stereotypic pattern. Between 1970 and 1975, northeastern cities lost employment at an average annual rate of 2.0 percent; midwestern cities declined at 1.6 percent annually. Meanwhile, southern cities grew at 3.2 percent and western cities at 1.6 percent.[5]

One possibility for documenting central city employment decline is the Census Bureau's *County Business Patterns*, but these data limit comparisons among central cities to those ten that are coterminous with county areas.[6] An analysis of these city-county areas for the 1965-1972 period shows that New York, Philadelphia, and St. Louis all experienced employment declines. Between 1973 and 1974, six of the ten were losing employment, and the four gaining counties— Indianapolis, Jacksonville, San Francisco, and Nashville— are conspicuously outside the declining regions.[7] With the recession between 1974 and 1975, all ten counties lost employment. (There are no more recent data to compare these central counties.) The employment situation was only slightly better in the metropolitan areas in which these ten counties are located. During the 1974-1975 recession, eight of the ten metropolitan areas lost employment.

The particular details of this employment decline cannot be carefully documented from available information published by the government even on a county basis. However, there is some evidence that it is not primarily due to interregional firm migration but rather to a much higher death rate than birth rate of firms. Jusenius and Ledebur, using Dun and Bradstreet establishment data for the 1969-1974 period, point out that 20.5 percent of jobs in the northern region were lost because of closure of firms while only 8.9 percent were gained back because of new firm births.[8] The fiscal consequences of lost firms may be even more severe than employment loss due to firm contractions for local governments that rely heavily on the property tax. Property tax assessments probably respond little to employment fluctuations over the business cycle since assessment of such properties is usually made on a reconstruction cost rather than an income basis and since reassessment lags are notoriously long. Firm closures, on the other hand, affect assessments if the property is abandoned or if the use of the building changes substantially.[9]

These data are far from conclusive, but what they show is that the economic base of central counties as well as the base of the metropolitan areas in the declining regions are either growing very slowly relative to the rest of the country or are in absolute decline. One might guess that the situation is even worse for central cities in general. If employment loss is due primarily to firm closure, then a much higher death rate of firms probably occurred in central cities than in suburbs over the 1969-1975 period.

Inflation Impacts[10]

The national economy has experienced a wide variety of inflationary pressures during the past fifteen years. These inflationary pressures can affect the financial fortunes of the state and local sector although their exact impact is not easily estimated. None of the generally available price indexes are designed to measure changes in the cost of providing government services, and as a consequence, such indexes serve only as crude indications of the impact of inflation on the prices of goods and services acquired by governments. Furthermore, there is no regularly published index that takes account of the effect of inflation on revenues although it is clear that a general increase in the level of prices can also inflate the nominal value of many of the tax bases relied on by state and local governments. For example, inflation increases property values, the value of a given quantity of retail sales, and the nominal levels of personal and corporate income.

The years between 1967 and 1972 were marked by a steady but not excessive growth in price levels. Prices paid by state and local governments increased by approximately 23 percent during the period, which is to say that some one-quarter of the growth in state and local outlays could be attributed to inflation. The period was one of substantial expansion in the total size of state and local spending with some of the growth accounted for by increases in real compensation. But a much greater proportion of the increment was due to additions to the work force and enlarged purchases of supplies and materials—both of which imply growth in the level of services provided.

During the period 1972-1976 prices behaved erratically. Between 1972 and 1974 the Consumer Price Index (CPI) for all goods and services rose 17.88 percent, and the Wholesale Price Index (WPI) of all commodities rose a massive 43.42 percent. But as neither the CPI nor the WPI focuses on the effects of inflation at the state and local level, we have computed inflation indexes for state and local government expenditures and revenues for both 1974 and 1976. These are shown in Table 1-1.

The revenue inflation indexes indicate how the own-source 1972 revenue base would have increased solely in response to inflationary pressures. The expenditure inflation index indicates how total expenditures in the several levels of government would need to have grown simply to keep real expenditures at their 1972 levels. For example, if the estimated increase in the nominal values of municipal tax bases between 1972 and 1974 had been taxed at 1972 effective rates, the revenues raised by municipalities would have increased by about 15 percent (revenue inflation index—115.4, see Table 1-1). On the other hand, if municipalities had maintained 1972 levels of services and compensated employees and transfer recipients in accord with increases in the cost of living, expenditures would have increased by about 25 percent (expenditure inflation index—125.4). Similarly, by 1976 the indexes show that the 1972 revenue base for municipalities would have grown 30 percent

Table 1-1. State and Local Governments' Expenditure and Revenue Inflation Indexes, 1972-1976[a]

	Expenditure Inflation Indexes (1972 = 100)		Local-Source Revenue Inflation Indexes (1972 = 100)	
	(1) *1974*	*(2)* *1976*	*(3)* *1974*	*(4)* *1976*
States	125.4	140.8	116.6	128.3
Counties	125.4	140.5	116.7	133.3
Municipalities	125.4	140.6	115.4	130.7
Townships	125.6	141.5	114.8	130.7
School districts	125.0	138.4	119.2	138.8
Special districts	125.7	142.5	113.3	124.2
All state and local	125.3	140.2	116.9	129.6

Source: Roy Bahl, Bernard Jump, Jr., and Larry Schroeder, "The Outlook for City Fiscal Performance in Declining Regions," in *The Fiscal Outlook for Cities: Implications of a National Urban Policy*, Table 6, p. 21.

[a]The indexes were computed using the methods and data sources described in David Greytak and Bernard Jump, *The Effects of Inflation on State and Local Government Finances, 1967-1974*, Occasional Paper No. 25, Metropolitan Studies Program, Maxwell School, Syracuse, New York, 1975. The 1974 entries are slightly different from those in the Greytak and Jump paper because of using revised data here.

over its 1972 level while expenditures would have increased 40 percent over their 1972 levels without even considering any change in level of composition of labor and nonlabor inputs.

Several implications can be drawn from these estimates. (1) As measured by these indexes, the impact of inflation during the 1972–1974 period was nearly equal to that which occurred during the entire previous five years, 1967-1972. (2) Expenditures were much more responsive to inflation than were own-source revenues at both the state and local levels during the 1972-1974 period. (3) While both indexes continued to increase during the 1974-1976 period, the relative cooling of inflationary pressure did allow inflation-induced increases in state-local revenue bases to nearly keep pace with the pressures of inflation on expenditures.

Another way to describe these inflationary effects is to consider the implications for state and local governments' purchasing power. In Table 1-1, division of columns (3) and (4) by (1) and (2) yields estimates of purchasing power indexes based on 1972 revenue bases. For example, relative to 1972 revenue bases, municipal revenues in 1974 would purchase 8 percent less in city government expenditures (index = 115.4/125.4 = 92.03). The calculations show that during the period 1972-1974 the purchasing power index fell nearly 7 percent for all state and local governments. For the 1974-1976 period the overall state and local government purchasing power index remained almost constant. For municipalities even a very slight rise in the purchasing power was noted.[11]

Since both the expenditure and revenue inflation indexes computed here are based upon 1972 expenditure and revenue structures, realization of lowered pressures of inflation on the fisc requires a tax structure capable of producing revenues in accord with the effects of inflation on the tax base while maintaining compensation levels constant in real terms. The reliance upon property taxes, with assessment lags quite common, suggests that the indexes here understate that overall effect of inflation on municipal government revenues. Furthermore, for declining cities it is possible that property values did not keep pace with the general rates of increase in property values experienced throughout the nation, thus adding further to fiscal pressures.

Rising Public Employment and Public Compensation

That public employment costs have been the major source of increase in state and local government expenditures is well documented. Clearly the growth in these costs was a major source of the fiscal problems facing large cities by 1975. While recession had depleted financial capacity, inflation had stimulated increases in public employee compensation. What is not well documented is whether public employee wage and benefit gains were "exorbitant" and a result of union power.

There are two questions pertinent to the argument that public employment compensation increases during the 1960s and early 1970s were out of line. The first is whether the increases were high relative to the private sector and the rate of inflation; the second, whether any differential rates of increase were due to a "catch-up" of public with private sector pay.

The catch-up thesis is based largely on myth since average wage levels in the state and local sectors have for some time exceeded those in the private sector (see Table 1-2). However, the gap has begun to narrow because of a recent acceleration in private sector

Table 1-2. Comparative Levels of Public and Private Compensation (Calendar Years)

	Private Sector	Federal Civilian	State and Local Government
Average wages and salaries per full-time equivalent employee			
1962	$ 5,082	$ 6,239	$ 5,017
1972	8,590	12,676	8,916
1975	10,690	15,195	10,862
1976	11,486	16,201	11,572
Average annual supplements to wages and salary in full-time equivalent employee			
1962	$ 482	$ N/A	$ 431
1972	1,150	1,497	1,110
1975	1,706	2,442	1,619
1976	1,904	2,809	1,848
Total compensation per full-time equivalent employee			
1962	$ 5,564	$ N/A	$ 5,448
1972	9,740	14,173	10,026
1975	12,396	17,637	12,481
1976	13,390	19,010	13,420

Source: U.S. Department of Commerce, Office of Business Economics, *The National Income and Product Accounts of the United States, 1929-1965*, Tables 6-2, 6-4 and 6-7; *Survey of Current Business*, July 1976 and July 1977, Tables 6-5, 6-6, 6-8, and 6-9.

N/A - Data are not available.

compensation. Still the remaining advantage lies in higher average wages and salaries in the public sector, while fringe benefits have tended to remain higher in the private sector during the past decade.[12]

If the increment in public employee compensation cannot be justified on grounds of achieving some parity with the private sector, it seems appropriate to examine these increases in light of the rate of inflation during this period. As may be seen from Table 1-3, the state-local sector increased average wages and salaries at a rate greater than the national inflation rate over most of the decade ending in 1973. Between 1973 and 1975, however, state and local government employees suffered real declines in average wages—even greater than those suffered by all private sector employees. For fringe benefits,

Table 1-3. Indicators of Public Employment Cost Increases

	State and Local	State	Local	Munici- palities
Average annual growth in full-time equivalent employment				
1962-1972	4.5%	5.3%	4.2%	3.2%
1972-1973	3.7	2.4	4.2	3.9
1973-1974	2.9	4.2	2.4	0.9
1974-1975	2.5	3.4	2.2	0.7
1975-1976	1.1	2.0	0.7	-1.7

	All In- dustry	Private Industry	Federal Civilian	State and Local Gov- ernment
Growth in wages and salaries per 1 percent increase in CPI				
1962-1972	1.7%	1.6%	2.2%	1.8%
1972-1973	0.98	0.97	1.05	1.06
1973-1974	0.68	0.73	0.42	0.54
1974-1975	0.93	0.96	0.85	0.87
1975-1976	1.24	1.28	1.14	1.12
Growth in average annual supplements per 1 percent increase in CPI				
1962-1972	2.8%	2.8%	N/A	3.0%
1972-1973	2.5	2.5	2.1%	2.0
1973-1974	1.1	1.1	1.7	1.4
1974-1975	1.6	1.6	2.3	1.4
1975-1976	2.1	2.0	2.6	2.4

Source: Table 1-2 and U.S. Bureau of the Census, *Public Employment in 1976*, Table 2, as reported in Roy Bahl, Bernard Jump, Jr., and Larry Schroeder, "The Outlook for City Fiscal Performance in Declining Regions," in Roy Bahl, ed., *The Fiscal Outlook for Cities: Implications of a National Urban Policy* (Syracuse, N.Y.: Syracuse University Press, 1978).

however, the trend shows increases well above the inflation rate in both the public and private sectors.

It is much more difficult to establish benchmarks for determining whether state and local government wages and salaries were exorbitant. Increases at a rate greater than the private sector may reflect only a changing preference for a greater package of public services or may reflect the productivity differences inherent in the public versus private sector production processes. In any case, the data in Table 1-3 indicate that the public sector grew at a greater rate than the private sector over the decade ending in 1972 and during most of the period thereafter.

Whether these employment and compensation increases are justified or not, it is clear that they placed considerable pressure on state and local government budgets. To the extent that this pressure was due to compensation rather than employment increases—and this would appear to be the case for the 1972-1975 period—the resulting expenditure increase was likely to be much greater than the service level increase.

THE CURRENT FISCAL SITUATION

There have been no more New Yorks in the sense of defaults of federal emergency loan guarantees. Somehow, in the face of declining economic bases, inflation, and rising public employment costs, cities have managed to postpone or avoid financial crisis. The most important of the compensating factors that have allowed even the most distressed cities to remain solvent are national economic recovery, increased direct federal assistance, and a combination of deferred expenditures and cutbacks in the scope of public sector operations.

Economic Recovery

There can be no question but that the recovery of the national economy, with lower rates of both inflation and unemployment, has played an important role in maintaining the fiscal viability of large cities. It is important to point out, however, that even with recovery central cities may not regain former levels of economic activity as rapidly as suburban areas, and that cities in the Northeast and industrial Midwest may gain relatively less and recover more slowly than cities in other parts of the country.

There are a number of a priori reasons why core areas do not share equally in national growth during periods of recovery. During a recession industries with declining employment reduce activities relatively more where operating costs are higher and where physical plant is oldest (i.e., in declining regions generally and in central cities specifically). The process does not reverse itself during the recovery. Expansions have been occurring where comparative costs are lowest—in the growing regions, suburbs, and nonmetropolitan areas. The same pattern appears true for the birth and death of firms. Firms die rapidly in the central city during recession, but new firms open more rapidly in suburbs during recovery. As a result, one would expect central city areas to suffer greater employment losses during a recession and make less employment gain during a recovery than suburban areas. The problem of central city failure to recover is compounded if the city is located in the Northeast or industrial Midwest. The manufacturing-dominated urban economies that face high production costs, particularly for energy, are likely to share least in a recovery.

Unfortunately, any discussion about central city economic performance during the recovery must be heavily speculative. There simply are not adequate data covering the period since 1975 to enable a tracking of the changes in central city employment and income through the most recent recession and subsequent recovery. However, the relatively poorer performance of central cities during a previous recession and recovery is borne out by a study of the 1969–1972 period.[13] Though the 1969–1971 recession was less severe and the 1971–1972 recovery not as sustained as the latest recession-expansion, the results of this study support the basic premise that private sector employment in core areas declines more during recession and recovers less during expansion. The results show that only core counties[14] had absolute losses in employment during the 1969–1971 period and that during the recovery they gained employment at about half the rate of other counties (i.e., other central counties, suburban counties, and nonmetropolitan counties). Even these results likely overstate the relative performance of central city economies since the central county often contains suburban areas that are growing more rapidly than the central city. In sum, the lesson from the last cycle is that core areas do gain in the absolute from national growth but continue to fall behind relative to the rest of the country.

While core areas generally will benefit least from the recovery, some central cities will benefit a great deal less than others during such a recovery. Particularly those central cities in growing regions and those with areawide boundaries (county or metropolitan areas) should benefit proportionately more. Again referring to the Oak Ridge study, core counties in the northeastern and midwestern census regions fared worse in the last recession *and* recovery. These regions encompass a majority of the most "distressed" American cities.

Ideally, we would trace the pattern of core areas through the present cycle to determine if the thesis that core areas in the Northeast and Midwest regions recover least and slowest is valid. Data are not available for such an analysis, but as noted above, employment in ten central counties and their Standard Metropolitan Statistical Areas (SMSAs) fits this pattern for the recession period; during the recovery the SMSA employment trends also fit the pattern. Though this is only superficial evidence, it is alarming because it suggests that the most distressed cities and areas are sharing least in the present recovery.

Direct Federal Assistance

A major reason large central cities have performed above expectations is the massive inflow of direct federal aid to cities. The Advisory Commission on Intergovernmental Relations (ACIR) reports that in many cases direct federal grants now account for more of the financing of total current expenditures than do own-source revenues.[15] For example, the ratio of direct federal aid as a percentage of own-source revenue averages 57.3 percent for St. Louis, Newark, Buffalo, Cleveland, and Boston and 51.8 percent for Baltimore, Philadelphia, Detroit, Chicago, and Atlanta (1978 estimates).

Most of this increase in direct aid is the Carter Administration's Economic Stimulus Package, the key elements of which are Anti-Recession Fiscal Assistance (ARFA), Local Public Works (LPW), and Public Service Employment (PSE). A recent U.S. Treasury report describes the aid flow under these three programs to forty-eight large city governments, classified by degree of fiscal strain, and shows a high degree of targeting in the distribution of funds.[16]

Such data leave little doubt about the critical importance of these programs to the basic financial health of large city governments. To say that they are being relied on to finance current operations is a gross understatement. Their curtailment, in money or real terms would seriously compromise the financial position of these governments.

Service Level Cutbacks and
Expenditure Deferrals

A third reason for the relatively strong performance of central cities during the past three years has been their willingness to attempt to maintain costs at a consistent level and even to try to cut back public service levels. This has taken a number of forms, including reductions in public employment, elimination of certain programs, and the deferral of capital facility maintenance and replacement.

Examination of employment trends during the last few years reveals a slowdown in the number of employees added to state and local government payrolls, which is in sharp contrast with most of the post-World War II period when nonfederal public employment expanded at rates greatly above those for private industry and the federal government. For example, annual employment growth between 1962 and 1972 averaged 4.5 percent for the state-local sector compared with a private industry growth rate less than one-half that rate (see Table 1-3).

Since 1972, however, the reins appear to have been drawn on state-local government job expansion. Average annual employment growth between 1972 and 1976 fell to about one-half the rate for the ten years preceding, and in 1976 state and local government employment grew by only 1 percent. Even more drastic than the curtailment of job growth for all nonfederal governments has been the abruptness with which municipalities have clamped down on the growth of their work force. After growing at an average annual rate of 3.2 percent between 1962 and 1972 and another 3.9 percent in 1973, employment by municipalities grew by quite modest amounts in 1974 and 1975, actually declined by 1.7 percent in 1976, and at the end of 1976 stood at a lower absolute level than in 1973.

Anyone familiar with the enormous job cutbacks carried out by New York City might assume that the New York City employment reductions were swamping the employment statistics for all municipalities, producing a statistical aberration. Yet inspection of the employment records for large cities shows that actual reductions in large city work forces are not uncommon and have not been for several years. But though the phenomenon of shrinking municipal government work forces has been manifesting itself in several major cities for longer than just the last couple of years, 1976 (the last year for which data are available) was a noteworthy year in that more than half of the twenty largest cities in the United States reduced the number of employees on their payrolls.

Although it would require a detailed analysis city by city to determine why the number of large cities involved in employment reductions has increased, it seems logical on an a priori basis to infer that this reflects attempts to compensate for the combined effects of economic base deterioration and the fiscal pressures brought about by abnormally severe inflation and a recession. It is virtually axiomatic that many of the country's largest cities have long been struggling to keep their budgets under control as they witness an exodus by employers and higher income residents. It is reasonable to suspect that inflation and recession hit the public sectors of larger cities harder than they did other types of government, thereby adding another reason for municipal employment carrying a relatively larger burden of adjustment than state and local public employment generally.

Another kind of expenditure deferral is the postponement of replacing obsolete capital stock, or even the discontinuance of adequate maintenance. This is especially serious in the most fiscally pressed central cities where the capital stock is older and investment has lagged.[17]

While such deferral measures temporarily enhance the fiscal health of these cities, they also mean that the most dependent segments of the population receive fewer or less adequate public services and that the cities will have to contend later with even more obsolete and deteriorated capital stock.

THE OUTLOOK

Detailed and useful quantitative projections of the fiscal health of state and local governments simply have not been made. However, in line with the discussion above, the four general factors that will shape the likely course of events are the state of the national and regional economies, the likelihood of continued substantial infusions of federal aid, the ability of governments to continue to cut services through employment reduction and capital expenditure deferrals, and the resurgence of a movement back to the city together with a changing composition of the urban population. Two other factors could affect the outlook: the possibilities of a taxpayer revolt and the role that state governments choose to play in dealing with the urban fiscal problem.

State of the Economy
Two major determinants of the fiscal health of a local government are expansion in the level of economic activity in the area and the rate of increase in prices. It is not clear that the future course of either factor will work to the advantage of distressed regions and governments. While such federal policies as tax cuts may stimulate the national economy enough to sustain economic growth into the early

1980s, whether the large cities in the declining regions can share fully in this growth seems doubtful in the absence of other more region-specific stimulative policies. There seems no reason to believe that general economic growth will reverse or even slow the flow of employers and population from the "Snowbelt" to the "Sunbelt." Furthermore, as noted above, general economic expansion is unlikely to increase the relative attractiveness of large cities as sites for private employment vis-à-vis suburban or outlying areas.

On the other hand, if continued economic expansion stimulates the economy enough to set off a new surge of inflation at rates close to those experienced in the early part of the decade, there seems to be little doubt that the distressed governments will be able to avoid "sharing" in such inflation. As has been shown, during the previous inflationary period public sector expenditures were more responsive to price level increases than were own-source revenues. Thus one could argue that while the expansionary macroeffects are unlikely to produce uniform benefits across regions or across central city and noncentral city areas, the effects of price increases are likely to be uniformly distributed across regions and subregional areas.

This implies that continued national recovery, while it may improve the fiscal position of Northeastern and Midwestern local governments by stimulating employment and income, will probably have an even more favorable effect on the local government fisc in the growing regions. Hence continued growth in the economy over the next three to five years will likely result in pressuring governments in the declining region to reduce their public sectors to a size more in conformity with the taxpaying ability of their private sector resources. If the rate of inflation does not increase, this may mean tax reduction, but if prices rise, any savings from employment reduction may be offset by an acceleration of compensation rate increases.

Federal Aids

Probably the major factor influencing the fiscal performance of governments in the declining region is continuation of the inflow of direct federal aid to cities. In 1978, Comprehensive Employment and Training Act (CETA), local public works, and countercyclical grants were distributed in above average per capita amounts to governments in the northeastern and midwestern regions. To give some idea of the current importance of these programs, the Treasury Department estimates for the forty-eight largest cities show that withdrawal of all three programs would call for a tax increase equivalent to 16 percent of own-source revenue or for an equivalent reduction in expenditures.[18]

The entire stimulus program is due to expire at the end of September 1978 although its expiration is not a realistic possibility. It is realistic, however, to expect that the package will not continue to produce revenue increases at the same rate as during the past three years. The programs were enacted as part of an economic stimulus program for the national economy and the need for such stimulus is now largely gone.[19] Moreover, a combination of large state-local sector surpluses and a federal deficit is not likely to result in congressional sympathy to expand the program.

The Potential for Service Level Reductions

If the pattern of the past three years were to continue, local governments would continue to reduce employment, postpone capital spending, and cut back services. If inflation rates do not accelerate much, tax cuts may also follow. State and local policymakers are becoming increasingly sensitive to the charge (substantiated or not) that a major cause of the relative decline of the region is due to the relatively high taxes already borne by residents and firms.[20] While tax bases may expand as the general economic condition of the region improves, it is unlikely to expect that these policymakers will further increase tax rates. The recent California vote has made discretionary tax increases all the more unpopular and unlikely. The real issue had been whether expenditure growth could be controlled enough to permit tax reduction; it may now be how much expenditure increase will be permitted by tax ceilings.

On the expenditure side there are major dilemmas in the face of fiscal pressures. While cutbacks in public employment levels constitute one option that apparently is being used, unless major increases in the productivity of the remaining employees can be achieved the quantity or quality of public service outputs are likely to suffer. Furthermore, this policy option ignores the resistance from public employee organizations to further cutbacks in the levels of such employment and to relatively low increases in compensation. There is also the major public policy question of the equity effects of such cutbacks since the primary beneficiaries of such services, especially in the central cities, tend to be economically disadvantaged.

Some observers hope decreased expenditures can be achieved via decreased or smaller increments in compensation levels. But this too seems unlikely in the near future, especially if inflationary pressures or increases in real wages are experienced in the private sector. Even if some public employee organizations appear to have moderated their demands recently in response to fiscal pressures, it is unlikely that such restraints can continue for very long.

Finally, some nonlabor expenditures, especially capital spending, might be further delayed; however, the effectiveness of such restraints is questionable. Deterioration of capital facilities such as public transportation, bridges and highways, sanitation facilities, and water production facilities not only have deleterious effects on service levels but also may tend to speed up the exodus of the economic base from the cities. Likewise, price increases in nonlabor inputs, which most likely have low elasticities of demand, tend to make even current nonlabor expenditures difficult to cut back.

Central City Growth

Some would argue that there are factors at work that will improve the relative fiscal capacity of the city. Higher energy and housing costs may make cities more attractive residential locations and more childless couples and singles are potentially city dwellers. There is, however, little evidence that such a movement back to the city is taking place.

There is also the absolute decline in city population and employment that should provide some possibilities for expenditure reduction. Again, the realization of the possibilities in declining cities is not so clear. Peterson found that declining cities spend 60 percent more on a per capita basis for a common set of functions than do growing cities.[21] Muller reached similar conclusions when comparing public employment levels.[22] Peterson also noted that over the 1964–1973 period, city employees per capita increased by 41 percent while population was declining by 10 percent. Per capita employment in growing cities increased by 10 percent over the same period.[23]

A DIRECTION FOR FEDERAL POLICY

The Carter Administration's Urban Policy Statement was intended to be a set of principles for a national policy toward urban problems.[24] The statement was weak, however, in two important respects. It was so general that it did not even imply the approaches to be taken in dealing with urban problems, and it suggested a "spreading" rather than a "targeting" approach to allocating assistance. The first shortcoming probably illustrates a combination of unwillingness to give up the present package of programs and agency responsibilities that in fact constitutes "an urban policy" and an absence of new ideas and approaches. The second weakness is well described by Nathan: "A special benefit to everyone is a special benefit to no one."[25] Unfortunately, we still do not have a national policy toward urban policy; it is therefore not surprising that even the newest federal initiatives may have uncertain and possibly detrimental effects on urban areas.

It is obviously difficult to formulate policy to deal with issues as difficult as those surrounding the urban fiscal problems. If there were magic solutions, they would have appeared long before now. It would therefore not seem inappropriate to propose another set of principles for national urban policy, but to do so in light of some current trends that seem irreversible and in light of the current outlook for urban governments.

Fiscal Adjustment by State and Local Governments

An underlying objective of any policy designed to deal with the fiscal problem of cities should recognize the need for retrenchment in public sector activity in some states. Clearly, federal policy should encourage state and local governments to bring about a better balance between expenditure requirements and taxpaying capacity. In some states in the declining regions the public sector has become "overdeveloped" in the sense that the quality, quantity, and cost of public services provided exceed financing capacity, resulting in taxes that are high, possibly inordinately high, relative to the rest of the nation. Since the economy in these states is growing slowly, the financing gap will continue to widen.

The federal government faces two policy options in such cases. The first is to subsidize the public sector in these states through an increased flow of grants and subsidies. But since these states generally have among the highest public service levels in the country, such a policy would not work toward national equalization of fiscal capacity. It would enable states like New York and New Jersey to maintain high levels of services at the expense of deferring the upgrading of lower service levels in states like Mississippi and Alabama.

The second avenue open is to encourage, reward, and assist the process of fiscal adjustment. State governments in particular must assume leadership in defining a livable fiscal equilibrium between the public and private sectors. During the past decade, personal income in the northern tier of states grew at a rate from one-third to one-fourth slower than that in the southern tier, but revenues raised from their own sources grew at about the same rate in both regions. Either there was no sense of having to match expenditures with resources or expenditures are largely uncontrollable. A better fiscal balance is clearly in the national interest since it may avoid the need for emergency measures of the New York City type, which may be formulated on an irrational basis in haste. On the other hand, the federal government must play a role in cushioning the effects of this retrenchment on the low-income population by targeting aid to distressed cities and by assuming more financial responsibility for the redistribution functions.

There are other desirable features of the fiscal adjustment process, the most important of which is a reexamination of public sector activities and costs. State and local governments have discovered that at least some fiscal retrenchment can be accomplished without serious public service declines. If government payrolls are over-inflated and increasing public expenditures have not brought improved public services, then much of the increased expenditures may be primarily a transfer from taxpayers to public employees. Since state and local tax systems tend to be proportional at best and usually regressive and since state and local government employees have average compensations above the private sector, such a transfer would not seem justified on redistributive grounds.

Compensating and Reinforcing Existing Trends

The federal government must play the role of complementing as well as compensating for current demographic and economic trends. Population, employment, and income decline are not necessarily undesirable, and federal policy ought not to focus on reversing or even stopping these trends. Neither is a shrinking public sector undesirable. Indeed, federal policy should encourage some urban governments to reduce the scope and magnitude of public services and public expenditures. Wherever technically efficient, capital grants should encourage repair and maintenance rather than new construction, and current grants should not be designed to stimulate expenditures with local matches or mandates or to encourage local governments to "buy into" new programs. Wherever possible, federal grants should reward public sector reduction in the overdeveloped region.

At the same time it must be recognized that a reduction in public sector activity may have undesirable redistributive effects, particularly as social services are cut back. A major role of the federal government in this case is to compensate central cities during the transition period. This suggests priorities in a national urban policy of shifting financial responsibility for redistributive services away from the local governments and of even more targeting of federal monies to the distressed cities.

Revitalization

A second important principle has to do with the issue of revitalizing central cities. if revitalization means restoring the central city manufacturing base, this simply is not a reasonable expectation. There are good economic reasons for manufacturing decentralization, and federal policies are not likely to reverse this trend. This is not to say that cities should be abandoned or that they no longer have a useful economic function. Rather it is to say that the economic future of central cities does not lie with the productive sector but with the service sector—hardly a novel idea—and, more importantly, that a waiting period is necessary before this economic revitalization can begin. The key to the length of the waiting period is the viability of the local public sector, especially the improvement of education services.

The cycle of suburbanization that lowered fiscal capacity that lowered public service levels that induced more suburbanization that further lowered public service levels simply went too far. The poor education services in central cities may well be the major deterrent to residential relocation in the city, and revitalization of that service— even if it were a focus of national policy—would take a considerable time.

There is another element implicit in the revitalization strategy. By arguing that blue-collar jobs should be held in the city and by targeting employment subsidies in central areas, it is implied that the low-income and unskilled should be held in the central city. This may encourage an industry and employment pattern for the city that is far from its best long-term interest. It is not likely that core cities can continue to retain so large a share of the poor and underprivileged and become truly revitalized.

The Role of State Government

A final proposition is that a national urban policy ought to define the role of state government toward local government fiscal problems. A major mistake of the past has been a failure to coordinate federal and state programs for aiding central cities. Federal programs were structured to take into account two important considerations: (1) the fragmented governmental and financial structures of metropolitan areas and (2) the assignment of expenditure and financing responsibility between the state and its local governments. Yet fragmented local government structure is at the very heart of the urban problem, particularly in the Northeast and industrial Midwest where one would presume the most significant amount of urban aid will be targeted. To provide such aid to these regions without insisting on a better balance between taxpaying capacity and expenditure requirements of local governments in metropolitan areas would be a mistake. It would implicitly reward suburban jurisdicttions that have refused to share taxpaying wealth with central cities. Put another way, it would in effect constitute a penalty to governments elsewhere in the country that have taken positive steps toward the solution of urban problems through tax-base sharing, regional financing, or areawide governance.

A working part of federal policy toward cities should be the requirement of a state government urban policy. Two elements of such a state program are important. The first is provision for regional financing of certain important local services. The objective of income redistribution through provision of higher quality services in central cities is not compatible with high-income suburbs and low-income cities, each financing its own services. Changed annexation laws, tax-base sharing, regional financing, or state government direct assumption with financing based on progressive income taxation are all ways to achieve this redistribution. It is important to note that the above reforms would require legislation initiated at the state government level. Second, with the redistribution objective in mind, there needs to be better coordination among direct federal aid to cities, federal aid that passes through state governments by mandate to local governments, and state aid programs in order to distribute the entire assistance package in a reinforcing and more effective way.

CONCLUSIONS

The most distressed urban governments have avoided emergencies like that in New York City since 1975. But the factors that have led to this measure of fiscal health—national recovery, increased federal assistance, and expenditure cutbacks and deferrals—cannot be relied on indefinitely. This rather bleak fiscal outlook for distressed cities raises four critical issues that might be viewed as central to the formulation of a national urban policy.

The first is the prospect for increases in federal aid to local governments of the same magnitude as during the past three years. Such increases are highly unlikely because there is less need for grants as a national economic stimulus and because the growing surplus in the state-local sector—whether a meaningful measure or not—will not encourage Congress to increase grant assistance from a deficit federal budget. The implications of reducing this aid flow or even slowing the rate of increase are particularly serious for the larger so-called distressed cities that have become dependent on such funds. CETA monies are at least partially substitutive for local resources, and many older cities have become heavily dependent on the counter-cyclical public works program to finance their regular capital works programs.

The second important issue is targeting the largest allocation of funds to the most distressed communities and whether this targeting is a major feature of the Carter Administration's urban policy. While the Carter plan does not contain specifics that would make it possible to evaluate its distributional features, there are early signs that its targeting emphasis might be diluted by increasing the number of eligible jurisdictions.

A third issue is whether national urban policy will be focused on urban revitalization (i.e., trying to reverse population decline and to hold the manufacturing sector in the city) or on facilitating fiscal adjustments to population and economic decline. The size of future federal subsidies is not likely to reverse or even appreciably effect the economic decline of cities in the older industrial areas. While the national recovery of the past three years has improved the fiscal position of even the most distressed cities, it is clear that these cities do not share proportionately in the economic recovery. Though the administration's program is not specific on an economic development strategy for urban areas, the tone of the program suggests a revitalization approach. Little attention seems to have been paid to the possibility of using federal policy to assist local governments in declining areas in making fiscal adjustments during the transition period. Indeed, there are some hopeful signs even for the most distressed cities. Population and school enrollments are declining, thereby lowering service costs and infrastructure requirements, at the same time that the energy crisis and housing costs increase the relative attractiveness of central city residential location. The growing proportions of singles and childless couples in the national population may also improve the comparative advantage of central cities. Even the decrease in the number of manufacturing jobs is not completely negative since it reduces congestion and infrastructure needs.

The federal government's policy ought to reinforce these positive trends. Increased targeting to improve public service levels in hardship cities is one important area of reinforcement, a grant system that subsidizes capital stock maintenance as well as expansion is another, and a recognition that many cities' economic futures are not best served by a program of subsidy to attract and hold manufacturing activities is a third. Such a strategy would concentrate heavily on compensation of the declining central cities and their residents during the adjustment process. The fourth issue is whether these principles of a national urban policy suggest yet another new federalism. There are at least hints that they may. Nathan sees the beginnings of a shift back toward categorical aid and more federal strings and away from revenue sharing and the decentralization themes of the early seventies,[26] while others are concerned about the absence of a plan for an increased and more meaningful role for state governments. The administration's plan mentions the importance of state governments, but the wording is cautious. Finally, there is no firm indication that the federal government will play a role in inducing change in the fragmented pattern of metropolitan government that is at the heart of the fiscal problem of many northeastern cities.

An inescapable conclusion is that the fiscal outlook for cities *and* the effects of the administration's urban program will be largely dictated by the performance of the national economy. And irrespective of that performance, cities, particularly distressed cities, will be caught in the middle. If national recovery continues, these cities will not share proportionately, and they will likely be the big losers as the countercyclical aid programs are phased down. If national growth slows, their economies are likely to be hardest hit, their tax bases most reduced, and their social service expenditure requirements hardest pressed. Such an untenable position would seem to underline the need for an urban policy based on compensation and adjustment rather than revitalization, and on targeting rather than spreading.

NOTES

1. For a good discussion of the problems of that period, see Alan Campbell and Seymour Sacks, *Metropolitan America* (Glencoe, Ill.: The Free Press, 1967).

2. We at the Maxwell School have developed most of these points in more detail in Roy Bahl, Alan Campbell, David Greytak, Bernard Jump, Jr., and David Puryear, *The Impact of Economic Base Erosion, Inflation and Employee Compensation Costs of Local Governments,* Occasional Paper No. 23 (Syracuse, N.Y.: Metropolitan Studies Program, Syracuse University, 1975); and in Roy Bahl, Bernard Jump, Jr., and Larry Schroeder, "The Outlook for City Fiscal Performance in Declining Regions," in Roy W. Bahl, ed., *The Fiscal Outlook for Cities: Implications of National Urban Policy* (Syracuse, N.Y.: Syracuse University Press, 1978).

3. Financial mismanagement, often cited as the major cause of the difficulties experienced by many cities, was more a response to these underlying pressures on city budgets and to an overassignment of local public services.

4. We have estimated that the loss of a job due to firm closure costs the

New York City government approximately $800. See Roy Bahl, Alan Campbell, and David Greytak, *Taxes, Expenditure and Economic Base: A Case Study of New York City* (New York: Praeger Publishers, 1974); and Roy Bahl and David Greytak, "The Response of City Government Revenues to Changes in Employment Structure," *Land Economics* 52, 4 (November 1976).

5. Seymour Sacks, "Estimates of Current Employment Trends and Related Information for Large Cities," paper presented to the National Urban Roundtable, Washington, D.C., March 1978.

6. These data also have the disadvantage that they exclude government and proprietorship employment. Furthermore, there is a substantial publication lag of approximately three years.

7. The remaining three cities-counties are Baltimore, Denver, and New Orleans.

8. Carol Jusenius and Larry Ledebur, "Documenting the Decline of the North," paper presented at the 1977 Conference of the Committee on Taxation Resources and Economic Development, Cambridge, Massachusetts, October 1977.

9. See Roy Bahl and David Greytak, "The Response of City Government Revenues to Changes in Employment Structure."

10. This analysis of inflation impacts is drawn from the work of David Greytak and Bernard Jump, Jr., *The Effects of Inflation on State and Local Government Finances, 1967-1974*, Occasional Paper No. 25 (Syracuse, N.Y.: Metropolitan Studies Program, Syracuse University, 1975); and Greytak and Jump, *The Impact of Inflation on the Expenditures and Revenues of Six Local Governments, 1971-1979* (Syracuse, N.Y.: Metropolitan Studies Program, Syracuse University, 1975); and Greytak and Jump, "Inflation and Local Government Expenditures and Revenues: Method and Case Studies," *Public Finance Quarterly* 5, 3 (August 1977); and from some extensions in Roy Bahl, Bernard Jump, Jr., and Larry Schroeder, "The Outlook for City Fiscal Performance in Declining Regions."

11. It is, of course, impossible to conclude from these aggregate indexes that individual cities realized inflation-induced increases in both revenues and expenditure similar to those found for all municipalities. Only city-level studies could attempt to answer that. For examples of the use of estimates of the impact of inflation on individual units of government, see David Greytak and Bernard Jump, *The Impact of Inflation on the Expenditures and Revenues of Six Local Governments, 1971-1979* (Syracuse, N.Y.: Metropolitan Studies Program, Syracuse University, 1975), and Edward M. Cupoli, William A. Peek, and C. Kurt Zorn, "An Analysis of the Effects of Inflation on Finances in Washington, D.C., 1972-1975" (Syracuse, N.Y.: Metropolitan Studies Program, Syracuse University, forthcoming).

12. Of course, these averages are not "cleaned" for occupational or educational background differences of state-local versus private sector workers. To the extent workers in the state-local sector are on the average more productive than those in the private sector, these statistics may be consistent with a "catch-up" argument.

13. Kathryn Nelson and Clifford Patrick, *Decentralization of Employment*

During the 1969-1972 Business Cycle: The National and Regional Record (Oak Ridge Tenn.: Oak Ridge National Laboratory, June 1975, p. 15).

14. Core counties are metropolitan counties (a) containing the central business district of a central city and (b) located in SMSAs with population in excess of 100,000.

15. Advisory Commission on Intergovernmental Relations, *Intergovernmental Perspective* (Winter, 1976).

16. *Report on the Fiscal Impact of the Economic Stimulus Package on 48 Large Urban Governments* (Washington, D.C.: U.S. Department of the Treasury, Office of State and Local Finance, January 23, 1978).

17. For a discussion of the problems of urban capital obsolescence, see George Peterson, "Capital Spending and Capital Obsolescence: The Outlook for Cities," in Roy W. Bahl, ed., *The Fiscal Outlook for Cities: Implications of a National Urban Policy,* (Syracuse, N.Y.: Syracuse University Press, 1978).

18. *"Report on the Fiscal Impact of the Economic Stimulus Package on 48 Large Urban Governments"* (Washington, D.C.: U.S. Department of the Treasury, January 1978).

19. Robert Reischauer, "The Economy, the Federal Budget and the Prospects for Urban Aid," in Roy W. Bahl, ed., *The Fiscal Outlook for Cities: Implications of a National Urban Policy* (Syracuse, N.Y.: Syracuse University Press, 1978).

20. An example being the recent move by the New York State legislature to decrease income tax rates, especially in the upper income brackets in hopes of encouraging executive decisionmakers to remain within the state.

21. George Peterson, "Finance," in William Gorham and Nathan Glazer, eds., *The Urban Predicament* (Washington, D.C.: The Urban Institute, 1976), pp. 48-50.

22. Thomas Muller, *Growing and Declining Urban Areas: A Fiscal Comparison* (Washington, D.C.: The Urban Institute, 1976), pp. 39-40.

23. Peterson, "Finance," p. 50.

24. "New Partnership to Conserve America's Communities," Office of the White House Press Secretary, March 27, 1978.

25. Richard P. Nathan, "The Outlook for Federal Grants to Cities," in Roy W. Bahl, ed., *The Fiscal Outlook for Cities: Implications of a National Urban Policy* (Syracuse, N.Y.: Syracuse University Press, 1978).

26. Ibid.

✳ *Chapter 2*

Localities under the New Intergovernmental System

David B. Walker

The United States has developed over the past decade a new system of intergovernmental relations—one that differs markedly from its predecessor of the mid-1960s and drastically from that of the 1950s. This new network has been shaped heavily by the pressures on America's localities, especially her cities, and by the kinds of responses to these pressures of the federal government and the states. And the future course of local government, if not that of the system itself, hinges heavily on what kind of long-term impacts these higher level responses will have on local units and their respective electorates.

These are the propositions that will be probed in this chapter. In analyzing them, the author relies heavily on the Advisory Commission on Intergovernmental Relation's (ACIR) six-volume series on *Substate Regionalism and the Federal System* (1973–1974) and on its recently completed fourteen-volume study of *The Intergovernmental Grant System: An Assessment and Proposed Policies.*[1] The latter examines developments in federal and state aid over the past decade. Out of the array of facts, findings, and attitudes that these volumes delineate, certain major trends emerge.

THE EMERGENCE OF A SUPERMARBLEIZED SYSTEM

When viewed from a historical as well as a contemporary perspective, these trends combine to suggest that a new, "supermarbleized" system (nonsystem would be a more appropriate term) of multiplying intergovernmental relationships has emerged. Never have the funding, functioning, administration, and personnel of so wide a range of state and local services particularly been as "intergovernmentalized" as they are today. Moreover, current developments indicate no tapering off of this "intergovernmental imperative." What happened over the past decade and a half to bring this about?

Federal Aid Trends

From the federal level, ten current trends—all of them relating in one way or another to assistance programs—need to be traced.

1. Those eligible for federal aid now include all governmental units from the Johnson era—the federal government, all of the states, some special districts, some larger cities and counties, some school districts, and some nonprofit units—as well as a whole range of new units such as all other local general governments, including towns and townships, almost all school districts, some additional special districts and authorities, and over 1,800 substate regional units. Because of the eligibility and entitlement provisions of General Revenue Sharing (GRS), the Comprehensive Employment and Training Act (CETA), and the Community Development Block Grant (CDBG)—to mention only the more obvious—the concept of "partnership" has been greatly expanded, and President Carter's urban policy holds the promise of extending that partnership even further.

2. The power position of these participants in Washington is more blurred today than it was in the 1960s. The states are in a somewhat less important yet still powerful position (receiving about 70 percent of all federal aid to states and localities), while cities, counties, and school districts now play a more significant role than ever before. Direct assistance to them rose from 10 percent of the total of federal aid in 1965 to over 30 percent in fiscal year 1978, largely because of GRS (1972), CETA (1973), CDBG (1974), and the three countercyclical programs (1976-1977)—all of which either bypassed the states or left them with less influence. Random impressions suggest that this shift in influence is partly reflected in the relationship between and among the various public interest groups representing the states, counties, and cities in Washington. Meanwhile the federal government still plays a senior partner role fiscally, but its administrative capacity, collaborative intentions, and program purposes now are being questioned by the states and localities with considerable vigor.

3. More grant dollars (about 75 percent) are now distributed in conformance with congressionally mandated formulas than was true a decade ago. GRS and most of the funds under all of the five block grants as well as all the aid of formula-based and open-ended categoricals are included in this group. A major factor in this development was the designing for the first time in the 1970s of substate allocational formulas for the newer forms of aid going directly to units of local general government. In turn, this prompted a new style of "grantsmanship"—wherein energetic efforts are mounted to help fashion the formulas and to effect the eligibility provisions. Scattered aid dollars—save in the case of some of the countercyclical programs—enhanced regional and public interest group competition, and strenuous attempts to generate better figures to gauge "need," "effort," and so on, have been other byproducts of this trend.

4. Functionally, all major endeavors of intergovernmental and national significance—welfare, health, hospitals, transportation, and education—are assisted by federal grants, and people-related programs have witnessed the greatest dollar and proportionate gains since 1965. Activities that a short time ago would have been considered state or local responsibilities also are aided now: rural fire protection, car pool demonstration projects, jelly fish control, estuarine sanctuaries, juvenile justice, libraries, and solid waste disposal. In some cases, federal grants have stimulated wholly new servicing roles among some recipient governments, especially local governments, as illustrated by community development and manpower services in certain cities and urban counties. A similar step toward the growing servicing marbleizing was taken when the federal government assumed financial responsibility for the adult welfare categories in 1972, although this move was not total since state "add-ons" were permitted.

5. Federal aid to states and their localities has expanded dramatically since 1966 with conventional types of categoricals (296 project, 36 project-formula, 106 formula, and 4 open-ended in fiscal year 1975) together with at least five block grants and general revenue sharing. Categoricals accounted for 70 percent of the 1977 federal aid package, block grants 12 percent, and GRS 9 percent. In dollars, local governments, especially cities and counties, have benefited more from the emergence of GRS, two of the block grants, and the countercyclical programs (only one of which is really categorical in character) (see Table 2-1). The states, on the other hand, are involved more with the

Table 2-1. Federal Grants to Local Governments: Fiscal Years 1968 and 1977 (estimated in millions)

	1968	1977
General revenue sharing:	—	$4,436[a]
General support aid:	—	1,133[a]
Block grants:		
CETA—Title I		1,083[a]
Community Development	—	2,089
Categorical grants:		
Local Public Works	—	577
CETA—Titles II and VI	—	2,467- 3,242[a]
Other	$2,318	4,634
	$2,318	$16,419-17,194
Percent of total federal grants	12.5	24.0-25.1

Source: ACIR staff calculation using data from U.S. Office of Management and Budget, *Special Analysis H., Federal Aid to State and Local Governments*, January 1978, and from U.S. Department of Labor.

[a]Four items listed here did not go exclusively to local governments but it was possible to separate out the local portion (estimated), which is shown here. The four are General Revenue Sharing, General Support Aid (ARFA), CETA—Title I, and CETA—Titles II and VI. GRS and ARFA were split two-thirds local, one-third state.

categoricals though they also share in some of the newer forms of aid.

6. Recipient discretion is greater with general revenue sharing than with the other types of aid; when block grants are broad in functional scope and funded adequately, they provide greater discretion than do the categoricals. Of greater significance, however, is the servicing and fiscal discretion that results from receiving a large mix of federal aid—categoricals, block grants, and GRS. And if the proportion is heavily weighted in favor of GRS and block grants, as it is for larger cities and counties, random evidence suggests that even greater discretion is, in fact, required.

7. Conditions, however, now accompany all forms of federal aid, despite earlier claims that GRS and block grants are essentially "no strings" and "few strings" assistance programs. The civil rights, citizen participation, and auditing requirements that were added to GRS in 1976 and the tendency of most block grants to add new constraints over time have resulted in more procedural strings. Moreover, an array of national purpose, across the board requirements in the equal rights, equal access, environmental, handicapped, historic preservation, and personnel areas now applies to practically all federal assistance, giving rise to a new level of federal regulation. These conditions

are much more complicated, more intrusive, and more pervasive than the programmatic strings of the 1960s. They have been especially burdensome for smaller local jurisdictions and have produced nearly as much litigation as implementation.

8. Gauging the fiscal impact of federal aid is more difficult today than in the past. Earlier studies tended to agree that federal aid stimulated greater state and local outlays, either in the aided program area or overall. Recent analyses, though less than comprehensive, are not certain of this effect. Some indicate that the impact is merely additive or even substitutive—especially with the newer forms of aid and for larger jurisdictions involved with several federal aid programs. Another dimension of federal and fiscal impact is the degree to which federal aid to localities is targeted to jurisdictions with supposedly greater needs. ACIR studies show that the countercyclical programs with their stress on unemployment have, in conjuction with GRS, CDBG, CETA, and the categoricals, indeed distributed more funds per capita to distressed cities than to healthier local jurisdictions; federal aid is sometimes equal to half what the cities raise from their own revenue sources (see Table 2-2).

9. Institutionally, a clear attempt has been made for over a decade to favor general governments and generalists. State executive branches have been strengthened greatly since the early 1960s, but direct links between this development and the growth of federal aid during the same period are tenuous. Recent efforts by state legislatures to strengthen their positions regarding expenditures by state agencies relate to this rapid growth and to the belief that executive branches have been bolstered by the rising tide of federal aid. Many of the newer direct federal programs to localities, particularly community development programs, have emphasized the role of elected officials and a mutual approach to program implementation. Yet only meager evidence can be found to suggest that many basic management changes within recipient local jurisdictions have resulted.

10. From the substate (and some would add, the multistate) angle, the campaign to strengthen generalists and build general governments has been understandably unsuccessful. More than a score of federal aid programs, enacted largely since 1966, have encouraged the establishment of more than 1,800 single purpose, multicounty planning bodies. Though multipurpose, generalist-dominated regional units (usually Councils of Governments or COGs) have benefitted from the A-95 review and comment process, these bodies have not always been authorized to carry out the functions of the other federal regional programs. The busy

Table 2-2.   Direct Federal Aid as a Percent of Own-Source General Revenue, Selected Cities and Fiscal Years 1957–1978

City	Fiscal Years				Exhibit: Per Capita Federal Aid[c]	
	1957	1967	1976	1978 Estimated	1976	1978 Estimated
St. Louis	0.6%	1.0%	23.6%	56.1%	$ 86	$228
Newark	0.2	1.7	11.4	64.2	47	291
Buffalo	1.3	2.1	55.6	75.9	163	239
Cleveland	2.0	8.3	22.8	60.3	65	190
Boston		10.0	31.5	30.2	204	219
Unweighted Averages	0.8	4.6	29.0	57.3	113	233
Baltimore	1.7	3.8	38.9	46.4	167	225
Philadelphia	0.4	8.8	37.7	53.8	129	204
Detroit	1.3	13.1	50.2	76.8	161	274
Chicago	1.4	10.9	19.2	42.1	47	117
Atlanta	4.3	2.0	15.1	40.0	52	167
Unweighted Averages	1.8	7.7	32.2	51.8	111	197
Denver	0.6	1.2	21.2	25.9	90	150
Los Angeles[a]	0.7	0.7	19.3	39.8	54	134
Dallas	0		20.0	17.8	51	54
Houston	0.2	3.1	19.4	23.8	44	71
Phoenix[b]	1.1	10.6	35.0	58.7	57	117
Unweighted Averages	0.5	3.1	23.0	33.2	61	105
Unweighted Average of 15 Cities	1.1	5.2	28.1	47.5	95	179

Source: ACIR staff computations based on U.S. Bureau of the Census, *City Government Finances in 1957, 1967, and 1976.* Estimated city own-source general revenue for 1978 based on annual average increase between 1971 and 1976. Direct federal grants to each city for fiscal 1978 based on (a) ACIR staff estimates of the federal stimulus programs for 1978 and (b) Richard Nathan's estimates for all other federal aid in fiscal 1978 as set forth in his testimony before the Joint Economic Committee on July 28, 1977.

[a]Percentage based on federal aid excluding general revenue sharing. Funds withheld pending judicial determination.
[b]Less than .05%.
[c]Based on 1975 population.

substate regional scene, therefore, is primarily a product of procedural and institutional strings attached to federal aid programs enacted over the past fifteen years. Yet the institutions produced by these programs—whether generalist or specialist dominated—are not authoritative, legally or politically.

State Aid Trends: Fiscal and Functional

For a better understanding of the impact of recent intergovernmental initiatives on local government, state undertakings as well as federal actions must be considered. For example, general trends at the state level should be examined for their effect on local governments.

State assistance programs more than doubled between 1969 and 1975, reaching the $50.5 billion mark; a state's reputation as the prime fiscal supporter of local governments is therefore upheld. Yet when the one-fifth of the overall state aid that is "pass through" federal grant money (nine-tenths of it going for welfare and education) is subtracted from the state figure and added to the direct federal to local amount (roughly $40.5 billion state aid vs. $34.5 billion federal aid in fiscal year 1977), this state position is not as dominant as a decade ago. Unlike the federal aid package, state efforts are focused more on function, with seven-eighths of the 1972 total channeled into four program areas: education, welfare, highways, and health-hospitals. While the states' theory of partnership is almost as inclusive as the federal government's, certain local partners enjoy a different status under most state aid arrangements. For example, school districts and counties tend to be more favored recipients, while cities occupy a preferred position only in the 10 percent of state aid channeled into revenue-sharing programs. In grant design, nine-tenths of state aid, compared with three-fourths of federal aid, is distributed in conformance with allocation formulas. But like federal aid, about nine-tenths of it is conditional, with the cost-sharing approach among the more prominent grant design features. State aid, then, is both similar and dissimilar to the federal effort.[2]

Aid to education stands out as the prime focus of state attention in the 1970s. Between 1970 and 1977, over half the states moved to change fundamentally their funding programs to public schools. In eighteen of these, state financing rose from 39 percent of the total to over 50 percent. Accompanying these greater fiscal efforts and a corresponding reduction in dependence on local property taxes, however, have come attempts to reduce educational outlays by legislating budget restrictions, general educational controls, and tax limits on local school districts.

State fiscal efforts can also be seen in the direct assumption by a state of program responsibilities heretofore local or of new ones that could be assigned to local units. A 1976 ACIR survey of cities and counties found that the functions most often shifted to the state level were public health, public welfare, municipal courts, pollution abatement, property tax assessment standards, building codes, land use regulations (including coastal zones and wetlands), and regulation of surface mining.[3] These shifts, it should be noted, were mandated by the states, though usually with local support.

Property tax relief has been another component of state efforts to aid local governments. By 1977 all states had taken action on such relief with nineteen raising the level of funding for this purpose. Twenty-six states have "circuit breaker" provisions, which, as in electrical systems, "interrupt when there is an overload" of the property tax relative to family income, particularly the income of the elderly.

Still another approach is to diversify the local revenue base by authorizing levies other than the property tax. By 1977, thirty-two states authorized some or all of their cities or counties to assess either a local sales or earnings tax. And Minnesota has sanctioned a modest "share the growth" regional tax arrangement for its seven county "Twin Cities" area.

Of all the state approaches, however, the assistance and direct functional assumption options have been the most significant. By 1976, four-fifths of the states had assumed the senior partner role in their respective state-local revenue systems, which account for 50 percent or more of the combined state-local tax revenues. On the expenditure side, this is reflected in the increased aid programs and in the assumption of new or transferred program responsibilities. On the revenue side, this is accounted for by the fact that forty-one states now have a broad-based income tax; forty-five a sales tax; thirty-seven both; and only one has neither. Not to be overlooked, however, is the influence of federal aid on state expenditures and revenues. After all, the states still receive seven-tenths of all federal assistance funds but these federal-state programs, far more frequently than federal-local programs, have matching or other cost-sharing requirements.

Along with these state efforts to aid their localities both fiscally and functionally are other actions, frequently more constraining and costly. State mandating of local governmental services and programs has increased over the past decade, justified as an effort to achieve uniform policies, to upgrade service performance (especially in heavily aided program areas), and to upgrade local revenue raising efforts and fiscal management. But many such mandates constitute arbitrary actions inspired by special interest groups that localities bitterly resent. Overall by 1976, twenty-two states had enacted thirty-nine or more mandates, or more than half of the total number noted in an ACIR survey.[4] Yet only seventeen states required that a fiscal note accompany any legislation imposing additional fiscal burdens on local governments, and only six of the "heavy mandating" states were among the seventeen taking such action.

On related fronts, by 1977 fourteen states provided no form of compensation to local governments for tax-exempt state property. Eight states recently moved beyond the traditional curb on property tax rates to limit the property tax levy, while one has enacted an explicit lid on overall local expenditures.[5] Finally, the fact that nineteen states make low use and nine make no use of their income tax indirectly conditions state-local financial and functional relations— usually in an adverse way.

STATE TRENDS: JURISDICTIONAL
AND INSTITUTIONAL

As significant as state moves on the fiscal and functional fronts are for local governments, no discussion of the state role would be complete without some mention of the jurisdictional-institutional issue. Indeed, finances and functions cannot be considered apart from these jurisdictional and institutional factors. The states, as the architects of the local jursidictional map, have paramount power in determining the internal structure of their localities. Overall, the record can only be described as mixed.

On the positive side, by the 1960s almost all states had moved to permit their municipalities to determine their own legislative, executive, and administrative structures; nine-tenths of the cities today have either a mayor-council or council-manager form of government. Moreover, by the end of 1977, only nine states had failed to give their counties comparable discretion. In some instances, these omis-. sions appeared justified, given the minor role played by counties in some states. On a less formal level, county commissioners in twenty-four states now have the right to hire personnel to help them discharge their official duties because of recent state legislation, state judicial decisions, or state attorney generals' rulings.[6] And in a marked departure from traditional practice, two states over the past year and a half, Arkansas and Tennessee, have mandated reorganizations of all counties. This latter action is particularly significant because voluntary initiatives by local governments, especially counties, which are subject to voter approval, face severe political and legal obstacles. Typically, only one out of every three county charter proposals is approved by the voters.

Fragmentation continues to be a dominant trait of the local governmental map with the nonmetropolitan areas of the county facing almost as severe jurisdictional challenges as the urban. These nonmetropolitan areas comprise a majority of the land area, but only one-quarter of the population. They encompass 85 percent of the counties, two-thirds of the special districts, 70 percent of the independent school districts, 80 percent of the towns and townships, and 70 percent of the municipalities. At the same time, the real servicing and viability dimensions of local governmental fragmentation are revealed by the number of units employing no, one, or two to five full-time employees (see Table 2–3).

For urban areas, the typical metropolitan area in 1972 was "governed" by eighty-five units—two counties, thirteen townships, twenty-one municipalities, eighteen school districts, and thirty-one special districts. Because of generally permissive municipal incorporation practices in the past, about one-third of all urban municipalities had fewer than 1,000 residents, and half encompassed less than one square mile of land. Only one-ninth had a population that exceeded 25,000, and less than 1 percent covered twenty-five square miles or more.

This jurisdictional atomization in both urban and rural America has fiscal and functional implications that cannot be overlooked, especially when long-term solutions to problems are sought. With counties as potential, if not actual, middle-tier governments, another set of problems arises. Only about 100 of our 281 metropolitan areas are basically single county in nature. If all of these 100 assumed all of the functional, fiscal, and structural traits of "marbleized" county

Table 2-3. Number of Local Governments by Number of FTE Employees, 1977

Local Governments	Number of FTE Employees, 1977				Totals
	Zero	One	2–5	6 or More	
Counties	N.A.	N.A.	N.A.	N.A.	3,042
Municipalities	4,420	1,211	2,773	10,452	18,856
Towns/Townships	7,267	1,300	1,113	7,142	16,822
Special Districts	9,204	1,304	1,248	14,384	26,140
School Districts	N.A.	N.A.	N.A.	N.A.	15,260
(Totals)	(20,891)	(3,815	(5,134)		80,120

Source: Special Tabulation for ACIR by the Bureau of the Census.

governments, a basic mismatch would still exist between the geography of certain servicing problems and the geographic reach of the general local governments in a majority of the metropolitan areas. Changing county boundaries, exclusively a state prerogative, is rarely a part of any effort to reform this unit of government, although county-county mergers are legally authorized in twenty-one states.

Thus annexation, consolidation, and other reorganization approaches are left as possible options, all falling wholly within the province of state legislation. Recent annexation has not proved to be effective as a basic restructuring mechanism, largely because of restrictive state annexation laws and the absence of unincorporated areas bordering older cities. At the same time, more annexation took place between 1960 and 1970 than in the previous two decades. Almost two-thirds of all urban municipalities annexed territory during the 1960s, and over six million people were affected by such actions. This trend continued in the 1970s with 300,000 people affected in 1974 and 220,000 in 1975.[7] Yet most of these actions occurred in the South and West and involved only small parcels of land. In only a few cases—Oklahoma City in 1959, for example—have de facto areawide governments been achieved by this process. Yet the current strength and vitality of most cities in the South and West are due in part to these earlier annexation actions.

Recent State Reorganization Models

The consolidationist approach has acquired some renewed popularity over the past two decades. More city-county consolidations— thirteen—occurred between 1962 and 1977 than during the previous century and a half. At the same time, out of every four attempts at such mergers an average of only one has won approval, and most of these have been in the Southeast and rural western states. Moreover, four of the six most recent attempts between 1974 and 1975 were unsuccessful.[8] Of the thirteen successful consolidations mentioned earlier, only six involved mergers with metropolitan central cities. Each involved less than complete consolidations with some smaller municipalities and some special districts remaining outside the merger. Generally, these new units have been more successful than the previously separate governments in receiving federal funds. They also have developed a more professional managerial capacity and have improved public services. Consolidation has usually led to higher local government costs although not necessarily to higher tax rates. While these units have not yet achieved fundamental shifts in the collection and distribution of local tax revenues, they have sought and obtained federal assistance for programs of a redistribution character. For state action, however, only one of the major consolidations—that of Indianapolis-Marion County—was achieved by legislative mandate; the rest resulted from local initiative and voter approval.

The formal two-tier, federative option is best epitomized by Miami-Dade County. The "modernized county" provides a less formal approach to two-tier reorganization, but in Miami, the relations between the levels are much more clearly spelled out in the charter. A revitalized county government with significant new powers was set up in 1957 by popular vote in conformance with special state-authorized legislation. Yet the existing municipalities are guaranteed continuity as governmental units and are authorized to enact more stringent zoning, servicing, and other regulations than those enacted by the metropolitan government. At the same time, the latter has full authority to perform all municipal services and acts as the prime provider for the county's unincorporated areas. Over time, fiscal and other pressures have prompted the municipalities to take advantage of the charter provision that permits them to transfer functions to the metropolitan government when such services have assumed countywide significance. Governmental costs have risen under the new system, but so has the level of services and of professionalism. Some elements of redistributive politics have emerged. Urban renewal, public housing, and community development programs are partly metropolitan responsibilities, and the cost of services are now spread more evenly across the county. The dominant role of the metropolitan government in community development programs, it should be noted, has been undercut somewhat by the impact of HUD's Community Development Block Grant, with both the metropolitan government and the cities receiving funds under the program. Overall, however, most of the earlier doubts about this reorganizational experiment have now disappeared; indeed many would judge it a success.

Another two-tier approach, which could be three-tier when two or more counties are involved, is provided by the metropolitan servicing authority device. At least four states now authorize such units, but few metropolitan areas in these states have taken advantage of the legislation. The Municipality of Metropolitan Seattle still stands after twenty years as the prime example of this reorganizational approach, but it exercises only two of the six functional roles that could be assigned to it: sewage disposal and transit, the latter having been approved by the voters only a few years ago. The municipality's performance in these two areas has won widespread commendation. Efforts to establish a comparable unit in the Denver area were rejected by the voters four years ago, but an alternative proposal is to be put to referendum this year; Portland's voters approved such an option in May.

The most innovative of these reorganizational approaches and the first example of a three-tier unit came with the launching in 1968 of the Metropolitan Council in Minnesota's Twin Cities area. This state-supported, multipurpose unit has responsibility for developing areawide plans, authoritatively coordinating the major areawide functional agencies operating in its region, and guiding metropolitan development. In 1974, the state legislature expanded the role and powers of the council. It is now directed to prepare policy plans for regional functions, which in turn will serve as a basis for the drafting of development programs by the special districts (commissions), counties, and other bodies that actually run the regional programs. For the first time, the council is empowered to review and suspend for one year local governmental and private sector projects that are inconsistent with its development guide. The council also is authorized to appoint the members of nearly all the metropolitan special districts. Over the past six years each house of the Minnesota legislature has voted to make the council elective (it is now composed of gubernatorially appointed members), but to date they have failed to act jointly during the same session. Finally, with the enactment of a strong state-regional-local planning process in 1976, the council is now in an even stronger posture vis-à-vis the land use decisions of its constituents that have potential spillover effects. The appeal of this Minnesota experiment prompted the Georgia legislature to set up a somewhat similar, but far less authoritative, unit for the Atlanta area in 1971. Others have also more recently probed the Twin Cities' record to determine whether a state-supported regional council is suitable for their respective metropolitan areas.

These three reorganization approaches—one-, two-, and three-tier urban governmental arrangements—are thus valid options today. It is also apparent that local initiative and referenda, combined with permissive state authorizing legislation, have been the dominant means of achieving these reforms. Only rarely in this century have states moved on their own to effect basic jurisdictional change. This, in turn, suggests that only a partnership approach to the question— involving the federal government and the states acting in concert— will suffice, assuming, of course, that the fragmentation issue is perceived by both to be a fundamental impediment to effective, efficient, and strong local governments.

The chief example, therefore, of this kind of partnership approach involves state-established substate districts. Partly in response to state concerns with strengthening the basis for multicounty planning and development efforts, but more particularly in light of the strong federal encouragement that emerged after 1967, forty-five states have delineated over 530 substate districts and helped to organize about 95 percent of them (compared to 56 percent in 1973)—usually following a council of governments format.[9] Most of these districting organizations have been charged with regional planning, development, coordination, and, in some cases, operational functions. A few are designed to facilitate the decentralization of state services, and all are intended to provide at least a common geographic framework for federally assisted areawide programs. Indeed, a 1973 ACIR survey indicated that the boundaries of then existing substate districts were adhered to by about one-third of the federally encouraged areawide units operating within the districts.[10] Moreover, districting organizations were utilized directly by these federal programs only about one-sixth of the time. Such figures and later data on individual programs suggest continuing problems in achieving conformance in federal and state districting efforts.

These, then, constitute the incremental attempts by state governments with federal encouragement to provide a multipurpose, generalist-dominated counterpoint to the proliferation of single purpose planning districts and operating authorities at the substate regional level. These efforts have obviously been less than successful, but confederal bodies that are asked to perform coordinative managerial functions are fraught with problems.

Against this backdrop of state-established substate districting efforts and of largely locally engineered reorganization efforts must be placed the continued growth of special districts and authorities. They have become the major cause of growing fragmentation at the local level and of much of the jurisdictional proliferation of the regional tier. These single purpose units increased in number by 18 percent between 1967 and 1977, passing the 26,000 mark in the latter year. Two-thirds of these units are in nonmetropolitan areas, but the remainder are urban based and include more than 1,000 countywide or multicounty districts that account for a major proportion of overall metropolitan outlays in their respective functional areas, especially in public health, hospitals, transportation, sewage, and utilities.[11]

The boundaries of three-quarters of the 26,000 coincide neither with those of a city nor a county. One way or another, all of them trace their origins to state legislation—whether they are created by local units, in a few cases by the electorate itself, or quite clearly by a state. Their popularity, then, is undeniable. They avoid civil service regulations, permit a circumvention of state limits on local indebtedness, allow local tax rates to escape the burden of a new service, and above all achieve a match between the boundaries of a servicing challenge and those of the unit(s) that are attempting to cope with it. In short, they present the least threat to the jurisdictional, political, and fiscal status quo while not ignoring the need to do a job on a multijurisdictional basis. The likelihood is that they will grow in strength and in numbers, but organizational and accountability questions remain and only the states can provide authoritative answers to them. The chief response to date has been the creation in seven states of local boundary commissions at the state level, at the substate regional level, or simply in certain metropolitan areas. Although the evidence is fragmentary, there are some indications that these bodies have curbed the growth of special districts and, in some cases, have brought about their merger with general local governments.

State-Local Interaction

What does this overall state record on local affairs suggest? From the local vantage point, it seems to suggest (and this by no means is intended to ignore the variations and diversity among the fifty):

—More financial aid, but still largely in traditionally assisted program areas and without a major urban or city focus

—Much greater recognition by a majority of states that in fiscal terms, at least, income, sales, and property taxes are but three angles of one revenue triangle and that the property tax angle has been much too large

—A growing state tendency to assume directly the responsibilities for new responsibilities and to mandate an upward shift of certain local functions, but with most of these actions being carried out in an ad hoc fashion and with no attempt to formulate an overall servicing assignment policy

—A continuing practice in nearly half the states of mandating service levels, the conditions of employment, and some functions, with "fiscal note" warnings frequently missing

—Much more local discretion being granted to enable cities and counties to adopt alternative forms of government, to enter into interlocal contracts and agreements, and, to a lesser degree, to transfer functions, although complex procedural requirements and limited structural options often impede their use

—Only modest shifts toward granting all cities and counties all functional powers not denied by state constitutions or by state laws, toward liberalizing annexation laws, toward discouraging special district formations, and toward authoritatively strengthening substate districts

—No real change, essentially, from the traditional state policy of leaving basic restructuring issues to permissive legislation and to hard to achieve local initiatives and referenda

—No real effort to link systematically the fiscal and functional challenges to both state and local governments, despite numerous recent study commissions dealing with the local institutional (and jurisdictional) issue

In short, the states, like the federal government, have scrapped any pretense of adhering to a dual federalist theory in their local relations and instead have developed their own theory of cooperative federalism. Again, like the federal government, their current theory bears little resemblance to its predecessor of a decade or so ago. Through a broad combination of inducements—conditional financial aid and permissive authorizing legislation, mandates, and statutory constraints and limits—the states have markedly conditioned the finances, functions, form, and generally fragmented character of their local governments. Despite some efforts to sort out functions by devolution or state assumption and despite the expansion of local structural discretion, the dominant theme seems to be one of a growing state role in local finance, including management, service standards, and personnel. This trend applies as often to cities as to school districts and counties. In a way that combines—to a much greater degree than the federal government's approach—intergovernmental fiscal transfers, conditions, mandates, and direct statutory constraints as well as inducements, the states have fashioned their own heavily marbleized theory of intergovernmental relations.

HOW DID IT GET THIS WAY?

How did we get to the point where both the federal government and most of the states now adhere to a "supermarble cake" theory?

Initial Federal Responses

In one sense, Washington's intergovernmental relations today are merely a logical, almost inevitable outgrowth of President Johnson's "Creative Federalism." The expansive definition of the partnership principle, the emphasis on direct federal ties with local governments (especially cities), the growing urban and human resources focus in aid programs, the move into servicing areas formerly deemed to be the responsibility of states or localities or even of the private sector, and especially the tendency to enunciate highly ambitious national policy goals while at the same time relying on conditional grants to a range of subnational units—not just the states—to implement them —are all traits of the current federal approach to intergovernmental relations that were present in the Creative Federalism efforts of the mid-1960s. The present is therefore clearly linked with the past and especially with the Johnson years.

Another set of contemporary federal tendencies clearly may be traced to the Nixon-Ford era. Out of the conflicting initiatives and compromises between the two political branches of the national government emerged a series of paradoxes.

For example, a conscious presidential effort was made to check the proliferation of categorical programs through proposed mergers and special revenue sharing as well as by impoundments, vetoes, and so forth. Yet the number of categorical grants grew by at least a hundred during this period, largely because of congressional actions.

In addition, a serious presidential drive was mounted to devolve greater decisionmaking authority to state and local general governments. One of these efforts involved general revenue sharing, which, by its statutory formula, allocated funds to states and to all local general governments (whether genuinely general or not) and to which certain potentially intrusive procedural strings now are attached.

Another aspect of this presidential effort to devolve authority was special revenue sharing and its proposed merging of 126 categorical and block grants into six broad grants with few program or administrative strings attached. Out of these efforts and after congressional action, three block grants emerged—Social Services-Title XX, Comprehensive Employment and Training Act of 1973 (CETA), and the Community Development Block Grant (CDBG)—with more national direction and more strings than the special revenue sharing format contemplated, but with more recipient discretion than was so with previous categorical programs. Each of the three grants and the Safe Streets program, however, are now struggling to resist the tendency to accumulate additional conditions and related categoricals.

A strong presidential campaign was mounted to streamline the grants management process through the Federal Assistance Review task force within the Executive Office and more forceful management circulars. At the same time, however, the piecemeal enactment of various measures that applied certain national purpose requirements on an across the board basis to practically all federal assistance programs generated new administrative confusion, heavy paperwork, and uneven implementation.

A preferred position ostensibly was accorded to elected officials and general governments by both the president and Congress as general revenue sharing, the special revenue sharing proposals, the three block grant enactments, and many management circulars demonstrate. Yet it was also during this same period that federal substate regional programs became most active. More than 1,800 separate units were created under more than a score of separate programs. Many see this as a victory for the program specialists despite the presumed ascendency of local officals and despite efforts to strengthen generalist-dominated councils of government (A-95 units). One major HUD effort in 1972 to develop a coherent federal policy that would favor a single generalist-dominated, multipurpose unit in each metropolitan area was rejected by the White House, presumably as a potential threat to local general governments "from above."

Finally, the Nixon Administration with its proposed special revenue sharing measures (as well as the Family Assistance Plan) and Congress with its "federalization" of the adult welfare categories made some moves in the direction of sorting out functions. Still extended marbleization, not demarbleization, was the dominant trend in the servicing assignment areas because of GRS, the block grants (especially the two federal-local ones), the continued heavy reliance on categoricals, the expansion of direct federal-local contracts, the expanded range of recipients, and the emergence of "creeping conditions."

These paradoxical results of the Nixon-Ford era clearly are prime conditioners of the contemporary system. But the attempts by Congress in 1976 and 1977 and by President Carter in 1977 to fashion a cluster of aid programs that would help bolster the national economy as well as the operations of state and local governments also must be considered. It was, after all, this federal response to the earlier recession and the subsequent ragged recovery that currently serves as the dominant determinant of the present federal aid system.

More Recent Initiatives

A new "tripartite countercyclical initiative" was launched with the Local Public Works Program (authorized by Title I of the Public Works Employment Act of 1976 and expanded by the Intergovernmental Anti-Recession Act of 1977), the Anti-Recession Fiscal Assistance Program (established by Title II of the 1976 omnibus legislation and extended as part of the 1977 measure), and the major expansion of public service employment programs (Titles II and VI) of the Comprehensive Employment and Training Act of 1973 (with enactment of the Carter Administration's proposals in June 1977). This countercyclical program is having a crucial impact on the whole pattern of intergovernmental relations as well as on recipient governments. It is distinctive because substantial amounts of money ($13.9 billion from November 1976 to November 1977) are involved, and most of it bypasses state governments and is substituted for local revenues. Moreover, it has attained a degree of targeting to hard-pressed central cities with heavy unemployment that previous aid programs have rarely achieved. In grant devices, it involves a mix of general support (countercyclical revenue sharing), block grants (CETA Titles II and VI, in practice if not in form, tend generally to conform to most of the traits of this grant device), and categoricals (Local Public Works)—all under a basic policy of relying on state and particularly local governments as agents of a national economic stabilization effort.

The strategy, implementation devices, relationships with other aid programs, and uncertain impact of this novel countercyclical program, in effect, add up to making this the single most important factor shaping current federal-state-local relations. Efforts to devise a new federal-urban strategy should not ignore the fact that one already is in place. When the outlays of this program are added to regular expenditures under GRS, CETA, and CDBG, the result amounts to the most costly urban undertaking the federal government has ever launched. The temporary nature of the countercyclical program partially explains the unawareness of its urban and local governmental significance. Yet while the Carter Administration was identifying the components of a possible new strategy in 1977 and launched its "New Partnership" policy in March 1976, Congress and the Carter Administration, in effect, had adopted one already.

The debate continues as to how and when the present Washington approach to intergovernmental relations was really shaped. This observer believes that the present system has been fashioned by the cumulative actions of Creative Federalism, the New Federalism, and the Congress. Each has had its distinctive impact, but the trends that have produced the present, almost mystifyingly marbleized setup reflect their combined impact.

WHY DID THE SYSTEM GET SUPERMARBLEIZED?

Some Reasons for Washington's Behavior

The complex reasons that explain Washington's recent intergovernmental initiatives are even more difficult to understand than the evolving, confusing pattern of pressures and responses. Yet a comparison of the forces, ideas, and attitudes that condition national policymaking today with those of a decade and a half ago helps to uncover some of the reasons accounting for Washington's behavior.

Among the more significant are the political changes that have occurred in Congress and in the political parties as well as among the interest groups. In Congress, the ascendancy of southern hierarchs has nearly come to an end, and despite recent reforms and new and aggressive leadership, the forces of dispersion within the two chambers are perhaps stronger than ever. In purely party terms, cohesion —while rarely strong—is now at a low ebb. For interest groups, the number of lobbying efforts has grown considerably with new social, single issue, and strongly activist public interest groups (representing governors, legislatures, counties, and cities) providing the major new actors and with the specific program people and private sector economic and social interests constituting a perennial, but steadily growing sector of this richly pluralistic pressure group scene. In short, there is hardly an interest, a public issue, or a jurisdictional grouping that does not have its champion in Washington at the present time; in fact the fractured condition of the national parties and the Congress is in part a result of this development.

In legal terms, the last genuine efforts to debate and define national purposes and aid programs in a constitutional context took place in the late 1950s and early 1960s. The 1964 presidential contest was the most recent event in which such questions were raised and the specific character of the national canvass, along with its result, ended the need to defend, rationalize, or attack a new federal grant program referring to the expressed (or implied) powers cited in Article I, Section 8 of the Constitution. For a much longer period, no federal court has handed down a decision disputing Congress' right to involve the national government in any grant-in-aid activity it has authorized. National purpose, then, has become defined in wholly political terms.

Fiscally, the recent recession provided a short-term reason for some of the current major federal aid efforts. Moreover, the countercyclical programs more than the earlier federal-local efforts broadened the tendency to bypass the states. In addition, this effort to actually utilize subnational governments as major agents of the federal government in achieving national economic recovery is a basically new strategem although the concept is old. The long-term fiscal reasons for seeking out the federal government for assistance, of course, relate to the rigidities of local revenue systems, the late development of the states as major revenue raisers, the comprehensive reach and productivity of the federal income tax, and Washington's authority to run deficits. From these factors have emerged certain myths: the illusion that the federal income tax is a cornucopia for ever-increasing aid programs and the feeling that federal budgets (unlike those of most states and practically all localities, in practice) need never to be balanced.

Bureaucratically, the vertical linkages between and among program administrators at the federal-state-local levels should not be discounted when seeking explanations for Washington's tendency to intergovernmentalize nearly every functional area. Major efforts in wholly new functional areas reflect this relationship less than the expansion of existing programs and the development of new grants that fall within the program areas. Moreover, events of the Nixon years suggest that these functional groupings can be controlled, though at some cost politically and administratively. The continued dominance of categoricals, however, reinforces these vertical functional linkages. In addition, while so-called single agency requirements are somewhat less prevalent than they were a decade ago, variations on the theme persist in assuring a direct chain of command for an aided program within individual state-local administrative systems. Not to be overlooked is the evidence from opinion surveys that state administrators of aided programs exhibit a strong tendency toward divided (between federal and state) loyalties, and the same no doubt would hold for local program managers. Bureaucratic, if not technocratic, developments, then, have served as a contributing factor to the further intergovernmentalization of the system.

Questions of equity and of "righting ancient wrongs" are also part of the process. Washington has perenially served as the chief adjudicator of the claims of the dispossessed, disadvantaged, and those who feel they are deprived—whether it be through the courts or the political branches, or both. In the past, the closed political systems of various states and localities helped develop this attitude. Today, the pervasive role of federal assistance provides a new means of correcting real or alleged injustices at the other levels. The technique, of course, is to apply nondiscriminatory conditions on an across the board basis to all assistance programs. With the growing popularity of so-called equity politics in and out of Congress, this technique has become a major new feature of recent grant legislation and administration, ushering in a new era of federal regulation.

As much of the foregoing suggests, there has been a marked change in political attitudes both in Washington and throughout the country. The dominant point of view of most decisionmakers at all levels is some variation of what might be termed "interest group pragmatism." In part, it is a by-product of the emergence of the constitutional relativism noted above. In part, it is reflected in the growing number of groups who have entered the game of grantsmanship. In part, it is observed in the evolution of an expanding federal role in major functional areas wherein a range of grant programs are enacted, sometimes separately and over time, sometimes in an omnibus bill, but always with a goal of accommodating the conflicting claims of diverse interests within one program area. Questions of fiscal effort, of real need, of jurisdictional capacity, and of state-local or local-local servicing relationships tend to be given cursory attention when this accommodating, or co-opting, process is at work. Finally, the pragmatic norm is reflected partly in the hyperresponsiveness of Congress to the myriad pressures that swirl around it. This view, it should be noted, bears little resemblance to the traditional American pragmatism since it is largely concerned with whether something can be worked out for the moment. The long-term, practical intergovernmental effects—institutionally, managerially, pragmatically, and even fiscally—are rarely examined or discussed.

These, then, are some of the underlying reasons for the federal government's present role in our federal system. They help explain the addiction to the intergovernmental imperative in Washington, and they combine to raise basic questions about the future direction of the American federal system

Why the State Shifts?

If the reasons for Washington's recent intergovernmental initiatives are difficult to discern, those prompting the bewilderingly broad and more varied actions of the states almost defy analysis. Yet when one draws back and views state behavior today in contrast to that of the early 1960s, certain causal factors are suggested.

The political and legislative processes of an overwhelming majority of the states are much more open and competitive now because of the reapportionment decisions of the U.S. Supreme Court (*Baker* v. *Carr*, 1962, and *Reynolds* v. *Simms*, 1964, in particular) and to a strengthening of the socioeconomic bases of two partyism in many heretofore one-party states. These developments clearly have intensified the basis for greater activism at the state level.

The strengthening of the states' executive branches over the past decade and a half through the assignment of greater powers to governors, reorganization and mergers of departments and agencies, and improved personnel systems; the slower, but discernible process of casting off many of the shackles that were placed on state legislatures a century ago; and the fairly dramatic reforms that have taken place in the fifty state-local judicial systems all add up to a state institutional image and capacity that are infinitely more positive and problem oriented than was true a short decade and half ago.

While the political and decisionmaking processes have become more open and representative and while the institutions of state government have become better organized, the political parties within the states became significantly more pulverized because of a number of developments that cannot be explained here. Meanwhile, much of the void left by the parties' inability to play the role of authoritative arbiter among competing interests has been filled by a growing power and even greater pluralism among the interest groups, both private an public, that have begun to focus on state capitals nearly as much as on Washington.

Two very different sets of interests generally came into their own in state capitals over the past decade or so. One includes the growing number of functional trends that are also common to the Washington scene. With the growth in federal conditional grants and the new activism of the states, the legislative-administrative-private sector alliances to protect, preserve, and extend specific programs became nearly as active at the state level as they did at the federal. In addition, the vertical linkages between these functional groupings at the two levels (and frequently extending downward to the local level as well) helped to generate and sustain their efforts. Not to be overlooked here is the fact that the states employ about a million and a half more civil servants than does the federal government.

The second clustering that became prominent comprised the local public interest groups. State municipal leagues, county commissioners associations, and organizations of local school officials and teachers began generally in the mid-1960s and continue today to make much more vigorous representational efforts in state capitals than they did previously. The same, of course, can be said of their counterparts at the national level.

The role of state courts cannot be overlooked in any investigation of changing state-local relations. In educational finance, their role has been a critical factor for change and for a more authoritative state role—whether in California, Connecticut, Washington, or Ohio. Although dramatic, this is but one area of state judicial activism. With the growing body of state law in environment, land use, taxation, and local government—to cite only the more obvious areas—the courts of the fifty states have had to expand their traditional view of the law and enter into unfamiliar territory, sometimes with meager statutory or case precedents for rendering decisions. All this underscores the legal significance of state law and of state courts in the eyes of local governments, their officials, and the citizenry.

Finally, the impact of federal actions on state governments must be counted as one of the half-dozen basic reasons for many of the changes in state-local relationships over the past fifteen or more years. On the one hand, the federal government still adheres to the traditional federal-state partnership approach for distributing 70 percent of its funds (and the proportion was much higher a decade ago, as was noted earlier). Insofar as these programs involved local governments, either the substate allocation and the conditions attached were left to the states according to their own internal servicing arrangements or pass through requirements were attached. In welfare, education, public health, libraries, criminal justice, and highways, to cite only the more obvious, federal aid to states has had a significant indirect impact on state-local relationships in these functional areas. In federally encouraged regional efforts, the institutional strings appended to a score of federal-state grant programs generated the 1,800-odd districts referred to earlier. In numerous other areas, from personnel to matching requirements, to budgeting, to new programs of joint concern, federal grants, both categorical and block, have impacted heavily on the state and have frequently had fallout effects on local governments.

But there is another partnership principle in the present federal approach to intergovernmental relations: the direct federal-local partnership. This relationship has been getting stronger in recent years for reasons cited previously. What the real effect of bypassing is on the states and on state-local relations generally is difficult to gauge. Yet it certainly does not facilitate a strong state middleman's role in urban affairs, and it ignores the institutional implications of many local servicing challenges. Nevertheless, it is a fact of contemporary intergovernmental relations, a fact that confronts the federal government and the states as well as the affected localities with a series of fundamental questions about the long-term implications of what amounts to a federal theory of dual partnership.

IMPLICATIONS OF THE NEW SYSTEM FOR LOCAL GOVERNMENTS

These trends at the federal and state levels and the underlying factors supporting them combine, in my opinion, to establish in effect a new American federal system—one with a dramatically changed, bewilderingly complex, and heavily overloaded network of intergovernmental relations.

The newness of this system, however, has largely gone unnoticed. After all, the dynamics that shaped it have been largely piecemeal, partial (in the sense of moving incrementally in individual program areas), heavily pluralistic (in inputs and outputs), and still poly-centric (with the states as well as the federal government acting independently as well as jointly). In short, the process at first glance was and is the traditional one in our system. This, of course, helps to conceal the full impact of the range of recent incremental inter-governmental initiatives. Yet the volume, variety, pervasiveness, and pace of the recent initiatives, as well as the fact that all governments now are caught up in the intergovernmental labyrinth, suggest non-traditional tendencies for the most part. And these are the basic reasons for concluding that the system today is substantially dif-ferent from its predecessor of only a decade ago.

Looking ahead, it is not so much the newness as the basic impli-cations of the present system that need to be understood. Unfortu-nately, a consensus position has not yet emerged about how these exchanges should be interpreted. Some find that the overriding tendency, reflected in most of the recent trends, is toward a greater centralization in Washington. The extraordinary growth in the size of federal aid and as a proportion of state-local revenues, its involve-ment in practically every kind of state and local activity, its contact with nearly every subnational government, its increasingly conditional character, and its new role as a regulatory device combine in the view of these decentralists to present a specter of Washington ascendancy that was inconceivable even at the heights of the Great Society.

Most of these critics feel that this centralizing tendency probably will continue, given the absence of any real judicial capacity to curb it, the continuing strength of the functional triads at the national level, the growing muscle in Washington of the public interest groups —especially those representing local governmental units—the weakness of the political parties—particularly the state parties—the inability of the states to effect a common front in defense of their potential middleman's role as coordinative managers, the hyperresponsiveness of Congress, and the renewed focus on equity issues—not to mention the nationalizing effects of grappling with a ragged economic re-covery, energy, and the environment. In their view, the steady cen-tralization of real decisionmaking, the new habitual state and local pandering for additional federal funds, the growing federal intrusion into the internal operations of state and local governments, the overlooking of the state's legal and potentially facilitative role in the system, the general ignoring of basic and varied state-local fiscal-functional relationships, and the stark inability to come to grips with the local jurisdictional question are some of the more corrosive results of this continuing tendency to centralize in Wash-ington. The more alarmed among these critics feel, then, that a neounitary form of government has, in fact, emerged.

A second group sees other tendencies in the present system that suggest that what is apparently centralizing need not actually be so. The federal bureaucracy, these realists emphasize, has grown at only a glacial pace in view of the manifold assignments given it. Subnational governments still are the basic implementors of federal domestic programs, and Congress' reluctance to expand the federal bureaucracy, despite its willingness to enact more and more aid programs, is as strong, if not stronger, than ever. Supervision, monitoring, and assessment of aid programs, they point out, frequently become much less stringent in practice than in principle. The Administration and Congressional tendency to institute grant conditions and then to constrain or cut agency manpower has not disappeared. They stress, newer behavioral traits must be added to it by national policymakers. That is, an eagerness to legislate high moral principles, on the one hand, and an abiding capacity to tolerate a wide gap between these principles and actual practice, on the other. All of these practical administrative constraints have special meaning for America's localities. After all, they question, how does one monitor over 80,000 local governments?

The kind of program and fiscal discretion that receipients currently acquire as a result of participating in a range of federal aid programs also is part of their argument. This benefit, of course, does not flow to all receipient jurisdictions, and yet nearly all of the larger local ones reap the reward. Few in Washington have pondered this decentralizing effect of the new aid system, they claim, because most deal with separate programs and not the aggregative impact of the whole aid package on single jurisdictions. If this were done, many of the outer signs of centralization—program constraints, skewing of receipient priorities, fiscal stimulation, and so on—would be put in a questionable light. A de facto decentralizing tendency, then, is very much a by-product of the intricacies of current intergovernmental relations to those who investigate the fiscal impact of current federal aid programs.

Finally, some of these realists point to the more assertive state role in local affairs as another basic factor supporting the traditional decentralizing trait of our system. They would concede that many recent state actions on the regulatory conditions attached to aid, mandating, functional shifts, and expenditure limits fronts appear to local governments as merely another form of centralization. But they argue that only with these and other state actions can the principle of polycentric decisionmaking be sustained. The realist group would argue that the states should go even further and mount an aggressive drive to sort out the servicing assignments of state and local governments and to reorganize the local and regional units in light of the servicing and financial needs at the local, regional, and state levels. Such actions, they emphasize, more than anything else would dramatically underscore the constitutional principle that under our system the formal powers, functions, and forms of local governments are exclusively a matter of state law. State assertiveness, then, either actual or potential, is another dimension of noncentralization.

The third group of critics, dominated largely by pragmatists, focuses less on the centralizing and decentralizing themes and concentrates on the growing malfunctioning of the overall system. The intergovernmentalizing of nearly every domestic American governmental activity, they feel, has produced a dangerous overloading of the system and a vast muddling of the appropriate fiscal, administrative, and servicing roles of the various governments in the system.

The growing Washington tendency to bypass the states and its expanding bilateral links with a host of substate governments undermine managerial effectiveness, they contend, and reflect a basic federal failure in diagnosing long-term solutions to local problems. Only the states, they stress, possess the legal power and the political sensitivity to help remedy the interjurisdictional, structural, fiscal managerial, and developmental difficulties that face many localities in rural as well as urban America.

The nature of any contemporary federal aid programs also figures prominently in the pragmatists' explanation of this malfunctioning. Poor design features, unrealistic expectations, airy assumptions about implementation, and a basic ignorance about the workings of intergovernmental relations in general and of recipient jurisdictions in particular have been prime factors producing the poor performance ratings of many grant programs. These critics also maintain that the popular practice of using grants as regulatory vehicles for achieving an expanding list of broad social and moral goals has only compounded the problems of program implementation since it typically ignores the manpower, fiscal, and judicial (if not the complex moral) implications of their implementation. Wide gaps between promise and performance have been the general result together with an undermining of the ethical base of the federal contract and the administrative base for effective intergovernmental relations.

Institutionally, the pragmatists claim that federal efforts at the substate regional level reflect faulty notions about planning, legitimate governmental power, and the persuasiveness of the federal purse. State efforts in this crucial institutional area, they note, have been no more productive although for different reasons. Managerially, the thrust of most of the recent federal-local endeavors suggests a coodinative management capacity at the recipient level that in most cases simply is not there. Some of this, the group argues, is due to the heavily pluralistic structure of most county and city governments. Some of it rests with the impossible expectations of federal policymakers about local program efforts that, in fact, have major private sector, interlocal, and interlevel spillover effects; and some with the foolish notion that the states have no real role practically or potentially in these undertakings.

As much as anything, this third school of opinion emphasizes that the fractured concept of public responsibility spawned by the federal government's intrusion in local government affairs has contributed as much as anything else to contemporary federalism's feeble functioning. The extent of fiscal-functional marbleizing has nearly obliterated any really clear lines of accountability. At the federal level, the newer concept of treating recipient governments as mere agents of national policies, the cumulative effect of conditions, the numerous citizen participation requirements, along with the auditing provision in GRS, the pragmatists maintain, are but a few of the most recent developments that have squeezed much of the real meaning out of the traditional concepts of administrative and elected official responsibility at the recipient levels. While the states have been as much affected by these developments as the localities, they have applied their own interventionist policy to state-local relations and have for the most part failed to address the local institutional, fiscal, and functional reforms that alone can bring a halt to the intergovernmentalization imperative. When these federal and state interventionist thrusts are combined with the older vertical linkages between and among specialized sectors of the bureaucracies at the different levels, so their argument runs, a multifaceted notion of official responsibility emerges at the local level with several upward, often downward, and some outward dimensions to it.

Theories of offical accountability, the pragmatists concede, have never been simple under our system. But present arrangements have generated a degree of "buck passing," not so subtle (fiscal) subterfuges, and sham campaign rhetoric that would have been unthinkable a generation ago. None of this contributes to the proper functioning of a federal system under heavy pressure or to the strengthening of local government. In the final analysis, they warn, a pervasive pattern of divided responsibility undermines effective program implementation, undercuts the position of elected officials and their generalist allies, and enervates the vitality and legitimizing effects of the electoral process.

In short, the centralizing and decentralizing tendencies in the present pattern of intergovernmental relations, for these critics, combine to produce a nonfunctioning or feebly functioning federalism despite massive funding. They note that more and more officials at all levels—including the President, some academicians, certain governors, various local leaders, and the public at large—have singled out various facets of this basic feature in the current system for criticism or cynical comment.

A RETURN TO GENUINE PRAGMATISM

To confront this dilemma (and the author is convinced it must be confronted) is to pose the basic question that pragmatic Americans always pose: Does it work? The "it" here may mean a single program, a cluster of services in a particular functional area, an administrative agency, a political branch of government, a local government, a pattern of so-called metropolitan governance, or even the whole system. In a very real sense, it makes little difference which of these are addressed for a probing analysis of the formal and informal operations of any one of them will lead to the conclusion that galloping intergovernmentalization is an ineffective way to solve public problems in a vast, richly heterogeneous society such as ours.

This, in turn, should prompt a principled investigation of the legal, fiscal, and functional roles of the three traditional governmental levels with a view toward clearly assessing the various factors that constrain and enhance the power position of each. Any such assessment would indicate that ours is still a recognizably federal system—not a quasi-unitary one—and that various factors (legal, political, bureaucratic, and attitudinal) continue to hinder the emergence of one governmental, political, and administrative system. The residuals of the older federalism are still there, and as has been noted, a new but not necessarily constructive force—fiscal fungibility—has been added to the arsenal of state and local weaponry.

But a crusty concern with results would puncture the politics of posturing and of pretense. It would underscore the limits of each level's actual capacity as well as the potential contributions of all. It would underscore the futility of a near exclusive reliance on intergovernmental fiscal transfers and piecemeal functional shifts as a means of meeting the pressures on America's local governments. It inevitably would focus heavily on questions of governmental structure, especially local governmental structure, and it might well lead some to ponder what conventional wisdom tells us is impossible—should and can we "demarbleize" the system, at least to some extent. And if this topic is explored at any length, it soon would become apparent that without local government reorganization, no effort of this kind is likely to succeed. The heavy fragmentation of local government, its functions and fiscal bases, is, after all, the prime reason for higher level initiatives and intrusion. Reorganization, of course, would not end these thrusts from above. But it would provide local governments with the capacity to achieve some sense of independence in an era of growing interdependence, and it would curb the need to resort continually to federal or state intergovernmental solutions to what, in essence, are wholly local or substate regional-local problems. Above all, perhaps it would restore some meaning to the concept of accountability at the local level (as well as the others) and permit a lightening of the heavy load the contemporary intergovernmental system is forced to bear.

The system, then, is "between a rock and a hard place." On the one side is the political rock that makes it nearly impossible to even approach the structural reorganization issue; political forces at local and state levels, as well as some at the federal level, have put that rock into place. On the other side is the hard fact that an unsystematic and steadily increasing intergovernmentalization of the finances and functions of America's subnational governments, especially her localities, produces an unmanageable, unresponsive, and basically irresponsible system. When the electorate and the decisionmakers recognize just how hard these facts are perhaps the rock of reorganization may not be as difficult to displace as it now appears to be.

NOTES

1. Advisory Commission on Intergovernmental Relations, *Substate Regionalism and the Federal System, Volumes I-VI* (Washington, D.C.: U.S. Government Printing Office, October 1973); Advisory Commission on Intergovernmental Relations, *The Intergovernmental Grant System: An Assessment and Proposed Policies* (Washington, D.C.: U.S. Government Printing Office, March 1977).

2. See Advisory Commission on Intergovernmental Relations, *The States and Intergovernmental Aids* (A-59) (Washington, D.C.: U.S. Government Printing Office, February 1977).

3. Advisory Commission on Intergovernmental Relations, *Pragmatic Federalism: The Reassignment of Functional Responsibility (M-105)* (Washington, D.C.: U.S. Government Printing Office, July 1976), p. 37.

4. Advisory Commission on Intergovernmental Relations, *State Mandating of Local Expenditures (A-67)* (Washington, D.C.: U.S. Government Printing Office, July 1978), pp. 45–46.

5. Advisory Commission on Intergovernmental Relations, *State Limitations on Local Taxes and Expenditures (A-64)* (Washington, D.C.: U.S. Government Printing Office, February 1977), pp. 2–4.

6. Advisory Commission on Intergovernmental Relations, "A Tilt Toward Washington, Federalism in 1977," *Intergovernmental Perspective* 4, 1 (Winter 1978), p. 21.

7. See Advisory Commission on Intergovernmental Relations, *Regionalism Revisited (A-66)* (Washington, D.C.: U.S. Government Printing Office, June 1977), p. 28.

8. Ibid.

9. Ibid., pp. 9–10.

10. Advisory Commission on Intergovernmental Relations, *Regional Decision-Making: New Strategies for Substate Districts (A-43)* (Washington, D.C.: U.S. Government Printing Office, October 1973), p. 342.

11. Ibid., pp. 19–48.

 *Chapter 3*

Measuring the Regional Economic Impact on Federal Grant Programs

Richard D. Gustely

In March 1978, the report of President Carter's Urban and Regional Policy Group outlining a national urban policy was made public. The basic aim of the policy was made explicit in the preface to that report:

> Our goal must first be to provide immediate assistance to the most troubled cities and communities. Beyond this, our goal must be to help all cities offer their residents decent services, adequate jobs, sound neighborhoods, good housing and healthy environments. Our efforts should be directed, to the maximum extent possible, at helping cities help themselves.[1]

A basic component of the policy as recommended in that report is to determine how and to what extent federal programs affect urban areas:

> The Administration should develop the capacity to evaluate the impact on cities of all key federal actions (including those not directly related to cities). The Administration should be willing to amend, change or abolish government actions not consistent with national urban policy.[2]

The traditional approach to assisting urban areas and the one emphasized in the report cited above is federal grant-in-aid programs. Since 1950, total federal grant-in-aid programs have grown thirtyfold. Over that same period, the composition of that aid has also changed; while 63 percent of the aid outlays were payments to individuals in 1950, only 34 percent went for this purpose in 1977. This period was also characterized by marked increases in direct federal aid to urban areas.

Accompanying these changes in the level and distribution of federal aid has been increased research into questions relating to grant impacts. The research in this area has employed a variety of methodologies in analyzing a wide range of impacts for a wide range of programs.[3] However, while such divergent approaches are often necessary for analyzing these complex questions, policy conclusions across previous studies have sometimes been difficult to draw. Accordingly, the purpose of this chapter is to place the grant impact research in perspective by discussing the range of regional economic impacts, the range of methodologies employed in analyzing these impacts, and by identifying questions in need of further research.

The remainder of this chapter is divided into four sections. In the first, the discussion focuses on historical changes in the level and distribution of aid and what this implies for the ultimate distribution of grant impacts. This is followed in the next section by a discussion of the range of grant impacts. A description of the range of methodologies employed for measuring impacts is presented next, followed by a discussion of some of the important unresolved research issues in the succeeding sections.

Before proceeding, several caveats should be mentioned. While the specific focus of this chapter is on the regional economic impact of grant programs, it should be noted that the formulation of an effective urban policy requires that similar attention be placed on the analysis of other federal tax, expenditure and regulation policies and their regional impacts. Such consideration, however, is beyond the scope of this chapter.[4] Furthermore, mention should also be made of the fact that the aim is not to document all grant impact studies, but rather to identify representative approaches that have been employed in order to suggest directions for future research. Finally, it should be emphasized that the focus here is on the economic impacts of grants on regions as opposed to cities. While some of the methodologies discussed in this chapter may be successfully applied to cities, data limitations restrict the implication of the more sophisticated behavioral models to a larger region of which the city is a part.

OVERVIEW OF TRENDS IN FEDERAL AID

As the figures in Table 3-1 clearly show, federal grants have increased substantially in both absolute and relative terms. It should also be noted that a substantial portion of this growth has occurred since 1970 with the introduction of such programs as General Rev-

Table 3-1. Trends in Federal Grant-in-Aid Outlays (Fiscal Years)

| | | *Federal Grants as Percentage of* | |
	Total Grants (millions of Dollars)	*Federal Outlays*	*State and Local Expenditures*
1950	$ 2,253	5.3	10.4
1955	3,207	4.7	10.1
1960	7,020	7.6	14.7
1965	10,904	9.2	15.3
1970	24,018	12.2	19.4
1971	28,109	13.3	19.9
1972	34,372	14.8	22.0
1973	41,832	16.9	24.3
1974	43,308	16.1	22.7
1975	49,723	15.2	23.2
1976	59,037	16.1	24.7
1977	68,396	17.0	26.4
1978[a]	80,288	17.4	27.5

Source: *Budget of the United States Government Fiscal Year 1979, Special Analysis*, p. 184.
[a]Estimate.

enue Sharing and the assorted economic stimulus programs enacted in 1977. Over this 1970-1978 period, federal grants have increased by over 230 percent ($56.27 billion) in absolute terms, and by about 40 percent relative to both total federal outlays and total state and local expenditures.

While state and local government reliance on federal aid has increased substantially over the years, it should also be noted that local reliance has increased by more than that for states. As indicated by the figures presented in Table 3-2, growth in direct federal grants as a percentage of state expenditures has increased by only 13 percent since 1970, while reliance on direct federal aid by local governments has increased by almost 160 percent. Furthermore, if account were taken of the fact that these figures do not reflect the grants distributed under the economic stimulus program of 1977-1978 and that a portion of grants to state governments are passed through to local governments, growth in local reliance on federal aid since 1970 would be still greater.

One result, then, of the increasing aid distributed to local governments is that some cities have become heavily dependent upon federal aid as a source of revenue. For example, it is estimated that in 1978, both Cleveland and Detroit will receive direct federal assistance equal to about 70 percent of their own-source revenues, or about 40 percent of their expenditures.[5]

Table 3-2.   State and Local Government Reliance on Grants-in-Aid (Calendar Year)

	Direct Federal Grants as Percent- age of State Expenditures	Direct Federal Grants as Percent- age of Local Expenditures	State and Federal Grants as Percent- age of Local Expenditures
1960	22.2%	1.7%	28.8%
1965	23.7	2.3	31.7
1970	25.9	4.3	39.3
1971	26.7	4.9	40.1
1972	30.6	6.5	42.3
1973	27.3	8.8	45.2
1974	26.3	8.6	44.6
1975	28.8	9.9	45.2
1976	29.2	11.1	46.6

Source: Bureau of Economic Analysis estimates published in *Survey of Current Business* (May 1978), pp. 16, 17.

In addition to the changes in the distribution of federal aid mentioned above, the geographic distribution of aid has shifted substantially since 1969. As indicated in Table 3-3, per capita grants to the more urbanized northeastern and north central states (Regions I, II, III, and V) have grown more rapidly than per capita grants to the less densely populated southern and western states (Regions V, VII, VIII, and IX). Although per capita grants in some of the less densely populated states are still larger than those for the more populous ones, the trend is clearly in favor of the latter. The net effect of this trend is apparently toward equilization of per capita grants.[6]

In addition to the changes in the level and distribution of federal aid, marked changes in the character of federal aid have taken place since 1970. As indicated by the data in Table 3-4, aid in the general purpose and broad-based categories has increased substantially since 1972. Specifically, while these two categories of aid represented about 10 percent of total aid in 1972, they are estimated to represent about 26 percent of total aid in 1978. Such an increase is the direct result of the introduction of such aid programs as General Revenue Sharing (GRS), Anti-Recession Fiscal Assistance (ARFA), Community Development Block Grants (CDBG), Comprehensive Employment Training Act (CETA), and Local Public Works (LPW). Such programs represent a significant departure from the specific purpose grants that characterized federal aid programs prior to 1972.

Several implications of these trends in federal aid for future studies of grant impacts are important to mention here. First, the increasing

Table 3-3. The Geographical Distribution of Federal Grant Outlays (Fiscal Years)

Region	Total Grants (Millions of Dollars) 1977[a]	Per Capita Grants		Percent Change 1969-1977
		1969	1977	
I. Maine, Vermont, New Hampshire, Massachusetts, Connecticut, Rhode Island	$ 4.2	$102	$344	237
II. New York, New Jersey, Puerto Rico, Virgin Islands	10.9	103	375	264
III. Virginia, Pennsylvania, Delaware, Maryland, West Virginia, District of Columbia	8.3	94	341	263
IV. Kentucky, Tennessee, North Carolina, South Carolina, Georgia, Alabama, Mississippi, Florida	10.4	101	288	185
V. Illinois, Indiana, Michigan, Ohio, Wisconsin, Minnesota	12.7	77	277	260
VI. Arkansas, Louisiana, Oklahoma, New Mexico, Texas	6.0	111	262	136
VII. Iowa, Kansas, Missouri, Nebraska	2.8	88	238	170
VIII. Colorado, Montana, North Dakota, South Dakota, Utah, Wyoming	2.1	136	328	141
IX. Arizona, California, Nevada Hawaii, other territories	8.4	116	320	176
X. Idaho, Oregon, Washington, Alaska	2.6	117	359	207
United States	68.4	99	311	214

Source: *Budget of the United States Government Fiscal Year 1979, Special Analysis,* p. 183.
[a]Preliminary data.

historical role of federal aid as a prime agent of urban policy suggests the importance of research into the impacts of these aid programs on urban areas. This research is required to insure that existing and proposed programs are producing effects consistent with national policy. Second, the historical shifts in the geographical and government level distribution of aid imply a need for further attention to questions relating to variations in grant impact between levels of government and among regions. Third, the increased historical importance of general purpose and broad-based aid categories relative to specific purpose grants suggests the need to analyze a broader range of direct

Table 3-4. Trends in General Purpose, Broad-Based, and Other Grants-in-Aid (Fiscal Years)

	Outlays in Millions of Dollars				
	1972	1975	1976	1977	1978[a]
General purpose aid:					
General revenue sharing	—	$ 6,130	$ 6,243	$ 6,758	$ 6,827
Other general purpose fiscal assistance and TVA	516	878	907	2,748	2,996
Subtotal, general purpose aid	516	7,008	7,150	9,506	9,823
Broad-based aid:					
Community development block grants	—	38	983	2,089	2,584
Comprehensive health grants	90	82	128	104	94
Employment and training	—	1,333	1,698	1,756	1,820
Social services	1,930	2,047	2,251	2,534	3,246
Criminal justice assistance	281	577	519	580	500
School aid in federally affected areas	602	577	558	719	744
Local public works	—	—	—	577	2,286
Subtotal, broad-based aid	2,903	4,654	6,137	8,359	11,274
Other aid	30,953	38,061	45,750	50,531	59,191
Total	34,372	49,723	59,037	68,396	80,288

Source: Budget of the United States Government Fiscal Year 1979, Special Analysis, p. 187.
[a] Estimate.

and indirect impacts of federal aid programs. This is due to the fact that such broad-based grants are likely to have impacts on a wider range of economic activity than specific purpose grants.

A DISCUSSION OF THEORETICAL
GRANT IMPACTS

For the purpose of discussing the likely economic impact of federal grant-in-aid programs, it is helpful to divide their effects into four basic categories: regional fiscal effects, regional microeconomic effects, regional macroeconomic effects, and interregional effects. While these categories of effects are interrelated, they do provide a useful starting point for the discussion. The focus of this section is on a discussion of grant impacts subsumed under each of these categories.

Regional Fiscal Impacts
Of all grant impacts, the area given the most attention in the literature is regional fiscal impacts. Grants are typically divided into three categories—open-ended matching, lump sum, and closed-ended matching grants. Open-ended matching grants are of unlimited size and must be spent together with a prespecified amount of local funds on a particular program. Lump sum grants are of limited size and may be spent with or without additional local funds on any program. Closed-ended matching grants are of limited size and must be spent together with a prespecified amount of local funds on a particular program.

The effects of each of these types of grants on the receiving government's budget line are indicated in Figure 3-1.[7,8] As shown there, open-ended matching grants produce a change in the slope of the budget line at all levels of expenditures. Lump sum grants shift the budget line but leave relative prices unchanged; closed-ended matching grants change the slope of the budget line for expenditures to the limit of the grant at which point relative prices revert to their pregrant levels. At least three variations of these grants can also be identified. First, a closed-ended grant for which the donor government requires no matching by the recipient produces a horizontal budget line to the limit of the grant at which point relative prices revert to their pregrant levels. Second, an open-ended matching grant limited to incremental expenditures produces a change in relative prices only after a minimum expenditure level has been achieved. Third, a closed-ended matching grant limited to incremental expenditures produces a change in relative prices after a minimum level of expenditures has

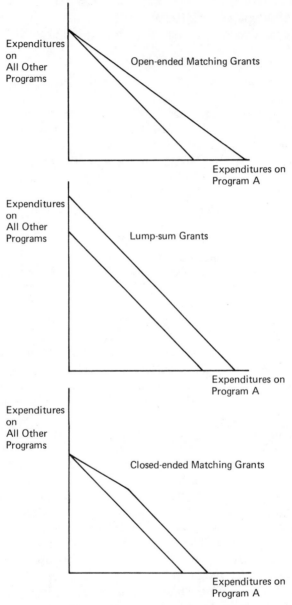

Figure 3-1. Effect of Particular Grants on Recipient Government's Budget Constraint

been achieved but only to the limit of the grant at which point relative prices revert to their pregrant levels.

Although the exact effect of each of these grants depends on the price and income elasticities of demand for the recipient government's expenditures as well as on the extent to which the grant is used to increase government cash balances, it is possible to make some statements about the relative effects of these grants on expenditures.[9] First, open-ended matching grants are likely to increase total spending more than similar size lump sum grants since part of the latter may be used for tax reduction. Furthermore, closed-ended matching grants are likely to stimulate total spending more than lump sum grants (because of the change in relative prices) but less than open-ended matching grants (because the extent of the grant is limited). Finally, closed-ended matching grants limited to incremental expenditures may in fact increase spending by more than open-ended matching grants (since a minimum amount of locally financed expenditure must be maintained in the former case), while open-ended matching grants limited to incremental expenditures will stimulate spending more than similar closed-ended grants.

The above discussion has focused on the relative expenditure effects of several "pure" types of grants assuming given price and income elasticities. Several difficulties arise, however, when these theoretical relationships are employed in the analysis of actual grant programs.[10] First, the specific provisions of many grant-in-aid programs are such that it is often difficult to place them in a single grant category. Second, variations in price and income elasticities among government programs, types of governments, and geographical areas are often substantial enough to produce expenditure effects different from those suggested by the theoretical analysis. Both of these considerations suggest that the determination of the expenditure effects of actual grants is basically an empirical question although the above analysis does point out the important parameters that need to be analyzed.

In addition to the possible effects of grants on total expenditures, such forms of aid are likely to affect the recipient's fiscal situation through their impact on the wage and employment decision.[11] For example, if the increased spending that results from a grant-in-aid is due to an increase in wages paid to existing employees, then the grant will likely have little impact on the recipient government's service level. On the other hand, if the grant results in the hiring of new employees or the purchasing of equipment, the service level of the recipient government is more likely to rise. Such a consideration of the composition of the expenditure change and its effect on the level of service is especially necessary if the impact of the grant is to be traced throughout the remainder of the regional economy.

Although the discussion in this section has focused primarily upon expenditure impacts, grants-in-aid are likely to have significant revenue impacts.[12] The most basic is the effect of the grant on the willingness of the recipient government to raise revenues locally. The general conclusion discussed above was that grants with matching provisions, especially those that apply to incremental expenditures, are more likely to stimulate additional taxation locally than are lump sum grants. In addition, grant programs can directly increase the tax base by raising consumer and business taxable incomes. For example, a grant that is used to finance construction activity will enhance the income, property, and sales tax bases by raising the profits of the construction firms, wages of the workers, and assessed value of the property owners involved in the project. Finally, federal grants-in-aid can indirectly enhance the local tax base by encouraging the provision of local public services that make particular areas more attractive to prospective businesses and residents.[13] Specifically, the provision of high quality public services such as police, fire, sanitation, transportation, and education, especially when accompanied by low local tax rates, can stimulate the immigration of population and business, thereby increasing the income, sales, and property tax bases.

Regional Microeconomic Impacts

In addition to their fiscal effects, federal grants can produce significant impacts on the regional labor, capital, and land markets.[14] In this presentation, it is useful to distinguish between the likely effects of two types of assistance: general purpose fiscal aid and specific purpose aid.

Focusing first on general fiscal assistance, the impacts on the consumer and business sectors should be noted. To the extent that the aid results in higher consumer after-tax incomes, the effect is to increase consumer purchases of goods and services. Such increases can result in an increased demand by businesses for land, labor, and capital inputs as well as increased prices for these factors of production. In addition, such increases in consumer after-tax income can directly impact on the land market by raising the demand for space as well as its price, although grant programs would have to be substantial for this effect to be significant. To the extent that the aid results in lower tax payments by businesses, the effect is also to lower production costs and product prices and to increase the input demand of these businesses.

Turning to specific purpose aid, the likely effects on individual markets are easier to identify. For example, programs that result in increasing the recipient government's demand for labor can impact on the local labor market by bidding up wage rates and making it more difficult for firms to obtain employees locally. Of course, if there is substantial slack in the local labor market, this effect will probably be less significant.

A similar result could occur in the land market. For example, aid programs that support the purchase of land result in an increased demand for this factor, thereby producing pressure on prices in this market. If there are substantial quantities of vacant or underutilized land in the area, price pressure may not be great. However, even in this case, land prices in surrounding areas may be affected as the displaced businesses or residents may bid for alternative locations.

Often opposing forces are likely to be at work in determining the effect of specific purpose grants on the regional capital market. If the recipient government undertakes capital investment that can be viewed as a substitute for private capital investment, the net effect of the grant may be to limit the development of private sector productive capacity and to inhibit growth. On the other hand, if the recipient government undertakes capital investment that can be viewed as complementary to private investment, the result in the capital market is more likely to be increased overall investment.

Regional Macroeconomic Impacts

Significant regional macroeconomic impacts can also occur as a result of federal grant programs.[15] These impacts can be viewed as falling into one of four areas of effects: consumer expenditures, government and private investment, direct government purchases, and government employment and wages. As in the previous section, it is useful to distinguish between the likely effects of general purpose fiscal aid and specific purpose grants.

Focusing first on general purpose fiscal aid, the pattern of impact differs depending upon whether the direct result is an expenditure increase or a tax cut. For an expenditure increase, the effect of the grant will depend upon the extent to which the expenditures were used to increase government wages, employment, transfer payments, or purchases of goods and services from the private sector. The size of the resulting multiplier will then depend upon the marginal propensities to consume locally of each of these groups. If, for example, the government employees, transfer recipients, or supplying firms rely heavily upon products imported into the region, the regional macroeconomic impact of a grant-in-aid program would be less substantial than might otherwise be the case. This kind of impact leakage is a particular problem when the recipient government is a single jurisdiction (perhaps the central city) in a large metropolitan area. In this case, it is quite possible that a substantial portion of the stimulative effects of the grant on the macroeconomy may be felt outside the recipient jurisdiction's boundaries.

If, in fact, the result of the grant were a reduction in taxes, the impact is somewhat different. For example, if taxes were cut for individuals, the extent of the stimulative effect on the macroeconomy would depend, at least in part, upon the marginal propensity of the affected group to consume locally. Similarly, if taxes were cut for businesses, the extent of the stimulative effect would depend, at least in part, upon the marginal propensity of the affected group to invest locally. The relative size of these propensities, then, is a measure of the relative macroeconomic stimulus provided by such cuts to businesses as opposed to consumer groups.

As was the case for microeconomic impacts, the macroeconomic impacts of specific purpose aid programs are more easily characterized than those for general purpose aid programs. For example, the macroeconomic impact of a federal grant program on labor subsidies would depend upon the number of employees added to the work force as a result of the program, the amount of any wage supplement provided, and the marginal propensity of the recipients to consume locally. For a federally sponsored capital investment program, the macroeconomic impact would depend upon the extent of the investment expenditure, its effect on private investment, and the extent to which the investment expenditure resulted in purchase of locally produced goods and services.

Interregional Impacts

While the focus of this section has previously been on the impact of grant programs within a given region, emphasis here centers around the interregional impacts of federal grant programs. At issue here is the extent to which the impact of a grant to a particular region produces impacts in neighboring regions. While some of these effects have been discussed in previous sections specifically in terms of city versus suburban impacts, the focus of this subsection is on the existence of broader intermetropolitan and interstate effects of grant-in-aid programs. Specifically, the discussion here centers around the interregional fiscal, microeconomic, and macroeconomic effects of federal grants-in-aid.

Focusing first on interregional fiscal effects,[16] grant programs that result in tax reductions for one region relative to another can have the effect of encouraging both businesses and individuals to alter locational decisions based upon these differences. The resulting migration could then produce the secondary result of expanding the business and residential tax base in the recipient region to the detriment of the other region. If increased expenditures result from the grant, the effect could be the same, with individuals and residents altering locations as a result of the grant, thereby affecting the tax base in each region.

Turning to the consideration of interregional microeconomic effects,[17] grant programs that produce changes in regional labor and capital markets can have the result of producing both capital and labor flows between regions. For example, if a grant to jurisdictions in one area were used to enhance labor employment or wage opportunities in that region, one result could be the inmigration of prospective employees to take advantage of the interregional differential. A similar result is possible for the capital market, where a grant that was used to increase capital investment in one region provided an incentive for further capital flows from adjacent regions.

Finally, in terms of interregional macroeconomic impacts,[18] the inflow of capital and labor into an area as a result of federal grants would affect that region's overall economy. Specifically, the increased investment spending could stimulate the local production of goods and services that would further increase the economic growth of the recipient regions, while any outflow of capital and labor from neighboring regions would diminish their growth.

In sum, the analysis of grant impacts needs to be viewed in terms of their overall effect on all regions of the economy. While much can be learned about grant impacts by the detailed analysis of particular areas, such analysis is incomplete when the implicit assumption is made that each region is economically autonomous. A more complete analysis of grant-in-aid impacts, therefore, requires recognizing that geographical variation in the distribution of grants is likely to alter interregional economic relationships, thus inducing interregional flows of factors.

METHODS FOR ANALYZING GRANT IMPACTS

While the purpose of previous sections has been to analyze changes in the level and distribution of federal grants-in-aid and their expected impacts, the focus here is on a discussion of alternative methods that can be used to measure these impacts. Specifically, this section focuses on methodologies that can be used for analyzing regional fiscal impacts, regional microeconomic impacts, regional macroeconomic impacts, and interregional impacts.

Measuring Regional Fiscal Impacts

The simplest and most straightforward method that can be used to analyze the fiscal impacts of grant-in-aid programs is the descriptive statistical approach.[19] Data relating to expenditures and revenues are gathered by direct survey methods, from census publications, from national income and product tables, or directly from the budgets of recipient governments. These data can be compared for periods before and after the receipt of the grant or with similar data for governments not receiving the grants to identify trend differences that might be associated with the introduction of the grant program. These trends might also be compared with those of general economic indicators such as employment and personal income in an attempt to sort out the differential impact of the grant program on the revenue and expenditure patterns of the recipient government. However, while this method does provide general descriptive information about relative growth levels of regional public and private sectors, it cannot provide a quantification of grant impacts since other factors affecting expenditures and revenues have not been considered.

A more sophisticated form of the above approach has been employed at the Brookings Institution in the monitoring of the impacts of a variety of federal aid programs.[20] Such a methodology requires the identification of a representative sample of recipient jurisdictions, the continuous collection of a wide range of fiscal and economic data, and the interviewing of public officials of the recipient jurisdictions. This detailed information is then analyzed to determine the extent to which local government decisions were affected by the receipt of federal grants-in-aid.

This method represents an improvement over the descriptive statistical approach since it attempts to associate changes in aid with changes in recipient government expenditure and revenue decisions for a large number of jurisdictions. It has the added advantage of being relatively easy to update after the network is formulated. However, there is one significant problem associated with such a methodology. This problem relates to the fact that the quantification of impact is imprecise because it does not allow for the direct determination of grant impact holding other factors constant.

A more precise methodology, although it is more costly and time-consuming to implement, relies on the formulation of a behavioral model of the recipient government's revenue and expenditure determination process.[21] These models range in sophistication from single equation models, used for analyzing grant impacts in one program area, to simultaneous equation systems that consider interrelationships among types of expenditures, revenues, and the economic structure of the region. These models can be constructed for individual cities or levels of government using time series or cross-sectional techniques, depending upon the nature of the question being addressed.

The virtue of these models is that they can provide direct estimates of grant impacts, holding other factors constant. For this purpose, they may be viewed as superior to either the descriptive statistical or monitoring approaches. However, because they are often costly to implement and because the aggregate data used in their estimation sometimes mask important variation, the results of studies employing this methodology should be interpreted in conjunction with more detailed data on actual government decisions. Such a blending of monitoring and modeling methodologies would, therefore, seem appropriate for analyzing the regional fiscal impacts of grants.

Measuring Regional Microeconomic Impacts

As was the case for fiscal impacts, the simplest method for analyzing regional microeconomic impacts relies on descriptive statistics.[22] For example, the determination of the effect of an aid program designed to encourage hiring of unemployed would focus on statistics relating to the number hired under the program, their wage rate relative to that of similar workers employed in the private sector, and the duration of their employment and general economic trends, including the unemployment rate before and after the institution of the program. A comparative analysis of these data would permit the formulation of a qualitative statement of grant impacts. A quantitative statement would require a more detailed analysis of causation than this methodology allows.

A monitoring methodology similar to that described under fiscal impacts can provide a more detailed assessment of microeconomic impact than is possible using the descriptive statistical approach.[23] For example, for job creation programs, the acquisition of specific information on skill levels of participating employees, descriptions of the kinds of jobs they are performing, and determinations of the extent to which job displacement from the public or private sector has occurred allow for a more specific quantitative statement to be made regarding grant impact than is possible with the descriptive statistical approach.

The most detailed quantification of the microeconomic impact of grant programs is possible when behavioral models are applied.[24] The analysis of microeconomic impacts of a job creation program using such models could simply focus on effects of the program on labor demand or wage rate determination, or simultaneously analyze its effects on labor market supply and demand. The basic difference between this approach and the previous ones is that the former provides a measure of impact based upon a behavioral model, while the latter relies heavily upon descriptive statistics. While descriptive statistics can lend credence to empirical estimates based upon behavioral models, only such models can provide specific empirical estimates of grant impacts.

Measuring Regional Macroeconomic Impacts

While the use of descriptive statistics might be appropriate for identifying general grant impacts in the fiscal and microeconomic area, their usefulness for measuring macroeconomic impacts is severely limited. This conclusion is based upon the fact that macroeconomic impacts of grants are more likely to be indirect while fiscal and microeconomic impacts are more likely to be direct.

The measurement of regional macroeconomic impacts of grants requires the estimation of output, employment, or income multipliers. These can then be used to translate the increased spending directly related to the grant into estimates of the resulting effect on the overall economy. Three basic modeling approaches can be used to generate estimates of these multipliers: simple economic base models, econometric models, and input-output (I-O) models.

The economic base approach relies upon estimates of the historical relationship between the key sectors of the regional economy.[25] This technique requires the identification of the relative importance of these key industries (typically those that produce goods primarily to satisfy demands external to the region) in the total regional economy. As viewed within this framework, regional growth is a function of growth in these key sectors. Increased federal grant spending in the regional economy, then, can be viewed as an external demand for regional production, the result of which is to stimulate regional spending by the multiple estimated from historical data. While this method might enable a rough estimate of overall regional macroeconomic impact of grant programs to be made, this estimate is not likely to be very accurate since the model does not take into account the complex interrelationships among sectors in the regional economy.

A more sophisticated approach to estimating regional macroeconomic impacts relies on econometric models.[26] While most regional econometric models rely on relatively simple economic principles, they focus specifically on interindustry differences in economic activity. Furthermore, not only do these models typically produce estimates of multipliers for a large number of sectors, but they also focus upon the interrelationships among regional output, employment, wages, and personal income. While such detail is useful in providing a better estimate of the overall macroeconomic impact of grant programs than is possible using simple multiplier models, it also allows for an identification of sectoral differences in impact. However, because these models are often very large, it may be difficult to rely upon them for obtaining such estimates of impact when such models are not already constructed.

Input-output type models represent a still more detailed method of analyzing the macroeconomic impacts of grants.[27] Such models typically identify industrial interrelationships in much more detail than either of the two previous methods, and they can therefore be more useful than either in aiding the estimation of the industrial distribution of grant impacts. As with econometric models, specific region I-O models would not seem appropriate for measuring grant impacts except in those areas for which such models already exist. However, techniques for obtaining indirect estimates of I-O multipliers have been developed, thus enabling a more universal application of this methodology for grant impact estimation. For example, one such approach, the Regional Industrial Multiplier System (RIMS), can produce I-O type multipliers for any county or combination of counties for any combination of industries included in the national I-O table.[28] Such a technique is quite useful in that it allows fairly detailed and accurate region specific impact estimates to be made for a small fraction of the cost of constructing a regional specific model.

Measuring Interregional Impacts

Several approaches can be employed in the analysis of interregional impacts of federal grant policy. The most elementary, descriptive statistical approaches rely heavily on the analysis of data relating to the geographical distribution of grant funds.[29] However, while this approach is useful in identifying regional differences in aid payments, it sheds little light on the interregional impacts of federal grant policy on the economy.

Two approaches to modeling interregional economic behavior for estimating grant impacts are worthy of note here. One approach relies on econometrically estimated relationships between economic activity in one region and all other regions. These relationships can be estimated either by analyzing each region's share of national economic activity[30] or by linking a system of regional models together and aggregating to produce national totals.[31] Both types of econometric models relate the level of regional economic activity to the proximity of that region to neighboring regions.

The other general interregional modeling approach is based upon input-output relationships within and among regions.[32] In this approach, national input-output relationships are first adjusted to reflect the industrial composition of each region and are then further adjusted to reflect interregional commodity trade flows.

Based upon such behavioral models, it is possible to provide estimates of the interregional impacts of a range of grant policies. For example, using such models, it would be possible to determine how changes in the geographical distribution of aid for capital investment would differentially affect the level and distribution of economic activity in each region within the nation. Similarly, such models could be used to determine the extent to which the impact of grant-induced tax relief in some regions would spill over into other regions.

PROMISING AREAS FOR FUTURE GRANT IMPACT RESEARCH

Previous sections of this chapter have dealt with a discussion of the range of grant-in-aid impacts and the methodologies that seem appropriate for analyzing these impacts. The focus of this section is on a discussion of some of the more promising areas of grant impact research. As in previous sections, regional fiscal impacts, regional microeconomic impacts, regional macroeconomic impacts, and interregional impacts will be discussed.

Regional Fiscal Impact Research Issues

Of all the areas of grant impact research, the most extensively analyzed have been regional fiscal impacts. Numerous studies have been undertaken to analyze the fiscal impact of individual programs and combinations of programs on individual jurisdictions and combinations of jurisdictions. The focus of these studies has typically been upon aggregate government expenditures and revenues. The research issues that remain in this specific area have been discussed elsewhere and will not be reiterated here.[33]

However, while analysis of grant impacts on expenditures and revenues has been extensive, relatively little research has been conducted into the effects of grants on the composition of government expenditures in terms of wage rates, employment levels, and purchases of supplies and equipment. If, for example, grant funds are used to pay higher wage rates to public employees, the result of the grant program is much less likely to increase public output than if these funds had been used to hire additional employees or to purchase additional equipment or supplies. Since the aim of grant programs is often to stimulate the provision of local public services, not just to increase expenditures, such research would appear useful for policy purposes.

An additional related issue concerns the extent to which cutbacks in aid programs have fiscal effects different from aid increases. For example, while aid increases may be used to finance wage increases for public employees, it is unlikely that aid cutbacks will result in wage cuts for these employees. Such analysis is particularly appropriate given the likely realignment of some aid programs over the next few years.

Regional Microeconomic Impact
Research Issues

Much of the research into the microeconomic impacts of grant programs has been of the descriptive statistical variety. While much can be learned about impacts from such descriptive analysis, it is clear that additional research is needed. Specifically, emphasis on modeling the local labor market and its relationship to local public sector wage and employment decisions and grants-in-aid would seem warranted. Similar analysis of the local capital market, particularly as it is affected by federally funded local government capital investment programs, appears appropriate. Finally, additional analysis on the effects of federal grant programs on the local land market would be fruitful, particularly when the aid program subsidizes the direct purchase of land by the local government.

In addition to the areas mentioned above, it would seem appropriate to further analyze the indirect effects of government grant programs on the land, labor, and capital markets. For example, to what extent do grant-induced increases in public employment raise wage rates in the private sector? Similarly, to what extent do the grant-induced increases in public investment raise the cost of capital to the private sector? These and other issues relating to the indirect effects of grant-induced government action warrant further consideration.

Regional Macroeconomic Impact
Research Issues

Relatively few analyses of the regional macroeconomic impacts of federal grant programs have been undertaken. A basic reason for this neglect is that such research often requires regional macroeconomic models that are very costly to develop. However, over the past ten years, an increasing number of regional econometric models have been constructed. In addition, methods have been developed that make the generation of regional I-O multipliers relatively inexpensive. At this point, it appears that greater use of existing models can be made.

A basic issue here is the extent to which different types of aid programs impact on the various sectors of the regional macroeconomy. For example, what are the differential regional macroeconomic effects of grant programs that produce decreases in general taxation, increased employment of the disadvantaged, and increases in business investment? In addition, research needs to be focused on both the overall stimulative effects of these programs and their effects on the distribution of economic activity. For example, aid programs that stimulate business investment are likely to affect the manufacturing sector and perhaps the willingness of marginal firms to relocate. On the other hand, aid programs that stimulate personal consumption (e.g., public employment programs) are more likely to affect the trade and service sectors by encouraging their continued expansion relative to manufacturing. Clearly, more research is called for in this area.

Interregional Impact Research Issues

As was true for the analysis of macroeconomic impacts of federal grant programs, little research has been done on interregional impacts. Again, this is so because relatively few such interregional models exist. Still, even with existing models, it is possible to focus on some important areas of research.

The most basic research questions that existing models can be used to address relate to the effects of changes in the geographical distribution of federal aid. Specifically, what would be the national and regional economic implications of changing aid formulas so that greater proportions of aid flowed to some regions as opposed to others? Furthermore, to what extent might the benefits of particular kinds of aid to particular regions spill over into adjacent regions? Finally, to what extent are interregional capital and labor flows affected by changes in the distribution of federal aid? While none of these questions has as yet been adequately addressed in the impact literature, current models are available from which specific estimates could be obtained.

A CONCLUDING NOTE

It is clear from the report of the Urban and Regional Policy Group that a determination of the impact of federal grant programs on urban areas is an important part of President Carter's Urban Policy. Accordingly, the purpose of this chapter has been to discuss the range of economic impacts of grant programs and the methodologies that can be employed in their estimation in order to make suggestions about future research directions in this area.

In conclusion, it should again be noted that much research has been undertaken in the estimation of the economic impacts of federal aid programs. Clearly, however, more needs to be done in order to provide policymakers with the information necessary to make decisions about aid programs. In addition to the specific research issues addressed above, impact analysis needs to be coordinated so that the results of impact studies on a variety of programs can be compared and evaluated. Such coordination will likely be difficult given the large number of researchers in the field. However, it is necessary for effective policy formulation because, without such coordination, grant policy will likely continue to be characterized as a patchwork quilt of programs working at cross-purposes with one another.

NOTES

1. President's Urban and Regional Policy Group, *A New Partnership to Conserve America's Communities: A National Urban Policy* (Washington, D.C.: U.S. Department of Housing and Urban Development, 1978), p. P-4.

2. Ibid., p. III-6.

3. Only recently has a common methodology been utilized for analyzing the impacts of several aid programs for a range of jurisdictions. See Richard P. Nathan and Charles F. Adams, *Revenue Sharing: The Second Round* (Washington, D.C.: The Brookings Institution, 1977); and Richard P. Nathan, Allen D. Manvel, and Susannah E. Calkins, *Monitoring Revenue Sharing* (Washington, D.C.: The Brookings Institution, 1975).

4. For a discussion of these factors, see Stephen M. Barro, *The Urban Impacts of Federal Policies, Vol. 3, Fiscal Conditions* (Santa Monica, Calif.: Rand Corporation, 1978); and Roger J. Vaughan, *The Urban Impacts of Federal Policies: Vol. 2, Economic Development* (Santa Monica, Calif.: Rand Corporation, 1977).

5. Richard P. Nathan, "The Outlook for Federal Grants to Cities," presented at conference sponsored by U.S. Conference of Mayors, Syracuse, April 1978, p. 5.

6. U.S. Government, *Budget of the United States Government Fiscal Year 1979, Special Analysis* (Washington, D.C.: U.S. Government Printing Office, 1978), p. 132.

7. Some analyses focus upon the tradeoff between grant-aided goods and all other goods although this does not change the basic conclusions derived. See Edward M. Gramlich, "The Effect of Federal Grants on State-Local Expendi-

tures: A Review of the Econometric Literature," *Proceedings of the Sixty-Second Annual Conference on Taxation* (Boston: National Tax Association, 1970).

8. Ibid., these effects are discussed in more detail.

9. For another discussion of these points, see Stephen M. Barro, *The Urban Impacts of Federal Policies, Vol. 3, Fiscal Conditions.*

10. Some of these issues are identified in Edward M. Gramlich and Harvey Galper, "State and Local Fiscal Behavior and Federal Grant Policy," *Brookings Papers on Economic Activity*, 1 (1973), pp. 15-65, 18-19.

11. For a more detailed presentation of these issues, see Roy W. Bahl and Richard D. Gustely, "Wage Rates, Employment Levels and State and Local Government Expenditures for Health and Education: An Analysis of Interstate Variations," in Selma J. Mushkin, ed., *State Aids for Human Services in a Federal System*, Part II of *Services to People, State and National Urban Strategies* (Washington, D.C.: Public Services Laboratory, Georgetown, University, May 1974).

12. These considerations are also discussed in Stephen M. Barro, *The Urban Impacts of Federal Policies, Vol. 3, Fiscal Conditions*, ch. 5.

13. Roger Vaughan, in *The Urban Impacts of Federal Policies: Vol. 2, Economic Development*, analyzed the extent to which federal policies have encouraged migration to the suburbs and the Sunbelt.

14. A more detailed consideration of the effects of federal policies on the land, labor, and capital markets can be found in Roger Vaughan, *The Urban Impacts of Federal Policies: Vol. 2, Economic Development*, ch. 6. The results of some empirical studies relating to the employment impacts of public works programs are presented in Roger Vaughan, *Public Works as a Countercyclical device: A Review of the Issues*, ch. 5.

15. For a discussion of the effects of federal policies on the demand for goods and services, see Roger Vaughan, *The Urban Impacts of Federal Policies: Vol. 2, Economic Development*, ch. 5.

16. Some of these effects are discussed in Stephen M. Barro, *The Urban Impacts of Federal Policies, Vol. 3, Fiscal Conditions*, pp. 89-90.

17. Some of the interregional microeconomic effects of public works and public employment programs are analyzed in Roger Vaughan, *The Urban Impacts of Federal Policies: Vol. 2, Economic Development* (Santa Monica, California: Rand Corporation, 1977), pp. 94-96.

18. Roger Vaughan in *The Urban Impacts of Federal Policies: Vol. 2, Economic Development*, pp. 120-123, discusses some of these effects for selected federal programs.

19. Studies employing this type of methodology include F. Thomas Juster, "A survey of the Impact of General Revenue Sharing," *General Revenue Sharing Research Utilization Project: Summaries of Impact and Process Research, Vol. 2* (Washington, D.C.: National Science Foundation, 1975), pp. 35-48; Catherine Lovell and John Korey, "The Effects of General Revenue Sharing on Ninety-Seven Cities in Southern California," *General Revenue Sharing Research Utilization Project: Summaries of Impact and Process Research*, Vol. 2 (Washington,

D.C.: National Science Foundation, 1975), pp. 81-96; and John P. Ross and Richard Gustely, "Changing the Intrastate General Revenue Sharing Formula: A Discussion of the Issues," *Public Administrative Review* 36(6) (November-December, 1976), pp. 655-660.

20. This methodology has been used in Richard Nathan and Charles Adams, *Revenue Sharing: The Second Round* (Washington, D.C.: The Brookings Institution, 1977); Nathan et al., "Monitoring the Block Program for Community Development," *Political Science Quarterly* 92, (2) (Summer, 1977), pp. 219-244; and Richard Nathan et al., *Monitoring Revenue Sharing* (Washington, D.C.: The Brookings Institution, 1975).

21. For examples of this approach, see Thomas J. Anton, "Understanding the Fiscal Impact of General Revenue Sharing," General *Revenue Sharing Research Utilization Project: Summaries of Impact and Process Research,* Vol. 2 (Washington, D.C.: National Science Foundation, 1975), pp. 23-53; Roy Bahl et al., *Taxes, Expenditures and the Economic Base: A Case Study of New York City* (New York: Praeger, 1974); Roy Bahl and Richard Gustely, "Wage Rates, Employment Levels and State and Local Government Expenditures for Health and Education: An Analysis of Interstate Variations," in Selma Mushkin, *Services to People, State and National Urban Strategies* (Washington, D.C.: Public Service Laboratory, Georgetown University, May 1974); Richard Gustely, *Municipal Employment and Public Expenditure* (Lexington, Mass.: Lexington Books, 1974); and Edward Gramlich and Harvey Galper, "State and Local Fiscal Behavior and Federal Grant Policy," *Brookings Papers on Economic Activity*, Vol. 1 1973, pp. 15-65.

22. For analyses of this sort, see Roger Vaughan, *Public Works as a Countercyclical Device: A Review of the Issues* (Santa Monica, Calif.: Rand Corporation, 1976); and Robert Reischauer, "The Economy, the Federal Budget and the Prospects for Urban Aid," paper presented at conference sponsored by U.S. Conference of Mayors, Syracuse, April 1978, pp. 14-16.

23. See Richard Nathan et al., "Monitoring the Block Program for Community Development," *Political Science Quarterly* Vol. 92 No. 2 (Summer 1977), pp. 219-244; and Nathan et al., *Monitoring the Public Service Employment Program* (Washington, D.C.: The Brookings Institution, 1978).

24. Such models have been employed by Michael Borus and Daniel S. Hamermesh, "Study of the Net Employment Effects of Public Service Employment—Econometric Analysis," unpublished paper prepared for National Commission for Manpower Policy, 1977; and Georges Vernez et al., *Regional Cycles and Employment Effects of Public Works Investments* (Santa Monica, Calif.: Rand Corporation, 1977).

25. A discussion of the structure of these models is included in Charles M. Tiebout, *The Community Economic Base Study Committee for Economic Development*, Supplementary Paper No. 16 (New York: Committee for Economic Development, 1962). For examples of such studies, see R.L. Barrows and D.W. Bromley, "Employment Impact of the Economic Development Administration's Public Works Program," *American Journal of Agricultural Economics* 57 (February, 1975), pp. 46-54; and Consad Research Corporation, *A Study of the*

Effects of Public Investment, prepared for Office of Economic Research, Economic Development Administration (Washington, D.C.: U.S. Department of Commerce, May 1969).

26. A discussion of the utility of regional econometric models is presented in Norman Glickman, *Econometric Analysis of Regional Systems* (New York: Academic Press, 1977). For the application of such large-scale models, see Richard Gustely, *Forecasting Regional Economic Activity: The Tennessee Econometric Model (TEM II)* (Knoxville, Tenn.: Center for Business and Economic Research, University of Tennessee, 1978); and Georges Vernez et al., *Regional Cycles and Employment Effects of Public Works Investments* (Santa Monica, California: Rand Corporation, 1977).

27. For a discussion of the structure of such models, see Walter Isard, *The Philadelphia Region Input-Output Study* (Philadelphia: Regional Science Research Institute, Mimeo, 1967); and Karen R. Polenski, *Techniques of Multiregional Input-Output Research,* 5 vols. (Lexington, Mass.: Lexington Books, 1971).

28. This model is presently being used by the Regional Economic Analysis Division of the Bureau of Economic Analysis. The methodology is described in Ronald L. Drake, "A Short-Cut to Estimates of Regional I-O Multipliers: Methodology and Evaluation," *International Regional Science Review* 1, 2, 1976 pp. 1-17; and U.S. Department of Commerce, *Industry Specific Gross ·Output Multipliers for BEA Economic Areas* (Washington, D.C.: U.S. Government Printing Office, 1977).

29. Such descriptive analysis has been employed by *National Journals,* June 26, 1976, pp. 821-824; F. Thomas Juster, "A Survey of the Impact of General Revenue Sharing," *General Revenue Sharing Research Utilization Project.* Vol. 2 (Washington, D.C.: National Science Foundation, 1975), pp. 35-48; and John Ross, "Countercyclical Aid: Performance and Prospects," presented at Annual Meetings of The Allied Social Science Association, New York, 1977, pp. 12-22.

30. Two such models are described in R.J. Olsen et al., *Multiregion: A Simulation-Forecasting Model of BEA Economic Area Population and Employment* (Oak Ridge, Tenn.: Oak Ridge National Laboratory, 1977), and Curtis C. Harris, *The Urban Economies,* 1985 (Lexington, Mass.: Lexington Books, 1973).

31. Such a model is being developed by the Regional Economic Analysis Division of the Bureau of Economic Analysis. For a discussion of its theoretical structure, see Kenneth Ballard and Norman Glickman, "A Multiregional Econometric Forecasting System: A Model for the Delaware Valley," *Journal of Regional Science* 17, 2 (1977) pp. 15-27.

32. One such interregional model is described in Karen R. Polenski, *Techniques of Multiregional Input-Output Research.*

33. For a review of this literature, see Edward M. Gramlich, "The Effect of Federal Grants on State-Local Expenditures: A Review of the Econometric Literature," *Proceedings of the Sixty-Second Annual Conference on Taxation* (Boston, Mass.: National Tax Association, 1970).

✳ *Part II*

Established Federal Programs

Chapter 4

The Great Reform in Federal Grant Policy or What Ever Happened to General Revenue Sharing?

G. Ross Stephens

BACKGROUND AND APPROACH

General Revenue Sharing (GRS), the State and Local Fiscal Assistance Act of 1972 (P.L. 92–512), as amended in 1976 (P.L. 94–488), is designed to provide general financial assistance to states and general purpose local governments. It was and is a radical departure from the more common form of categorical federal aids. With its long legislative history, many different, sometimes incompatible, objectives are put forth as its basic purpose.[1] More verbiage, scholarly and otherwise, has been uttered about revenue sharing than any other federal grant program, perhaps more than about all other federal aids combined. As a consequence, this chapter will not be a survey of the literature but will focus instead on the overall effects of revenue sharing and how well it is meeting some of the broader objectives claimed when the program was first enacted.

This chapter is divided into three sections. First, a general or macro approach analyzes the background and objectives of General Revenue Sharing, how it fits into the system of federal aids, and the general effect of GRS on recipient levels, state and local. The second section looks specifically at the effects of GRS on the largest city in each of the fifty states for the roles played by the city, its overlying local units, and the state government. There is also a brief description of the vast differences among the fifty states in how state and local governments interact and operate. The concluding section summarizes findings of the first two about how well GRS has met its objectives, how well it is targeted, policy implications of the findings, and prospects for the future.

General Revenue Sharing is important because at the time it was approved, it was the largest single grant program ever enacted in the United States, distributing nearly $56 billion in the succeeding years. (Only Medicaid has turned out to be larger with the passage of time.) At the time of its enactment, it represented a radical departure in the way federal aids were distributed in terms of formula as to direct recipients of the money and eligibility.[2] Moreover, the same formula is being used to distribute countercyclical aids under the Anti-Recession Fiscal Assistance Act of 1976 (ARFA) and under President Carter's proposed "new ARFA" program.[3] Traditional federal project grants give the federal administrator involved a high degree of discretion as to whether or not a project will be funded; the program focus (recipient's discretion) is very narrow; performance conditions (intrusiveness, specificity) are quite explicit. The situation for GRS is just the opposite—entitlement is automatic, the recipient's functional spending discretion is almost completely unrestricted, and performance conditions are virtually nonexistent.[4]

GENERAL REVENUE SHARING OBJECTIVES

The basic GRS program has distributed approximately $6 billion a year to states, counties, municipalities, townships, Indian Tribes, and Alaskan Native Villages.[5] One-third of the money goes to the states, with the rest distributed to local recipients using formulas that include population size, urbanization, population weighted inversely for per capita income, state income taxes, and general tax effort.[6] For most recipients, population is the critical variable.[7] The formulas are both complex and multiplicative.

There are four basic objectives of GRS: general purpose support, increased discretionary funds, (horizontal) fiscal adjustment, and increased aid to large cities.[8] Before 1972 very few and very minor federal aids fell in the general support category; that is, 1 or 2 percent of all federal grants. A basic GRS objective was to provide more money for the general support of state and local governments. GRS was designed as a steady source of federal aid not subject to minute specifications or the whim of some federal administrator.

The second objective, increased discretionary funds, thus more state and local autonomy in the way these funds are expended, decentralized decisionmaking and service priorities. Many supporters saw GRS as the wave of the future and hoped that larger proportions of federal monies would be distributed on this basis over time. It provides an alternative to categorical aids and one that gives recipient governments much wider spending latitude.

Thirdly, it was to provide some (horizontal) fiscal adjustment (balance) among state and local governments and curb undue state and local dependence on highly specific federal categorical aids, to benefit poor governments more than rich ones, and to help all recipients become more financially independent. Finally, related to this was the objective of providing more money to needy central cities with large dependent populations—central cities more than the affluent suburban entities that surround them. Apparently, there are also a number of subsidiary objectives. These include: aiding native Americans, helping state and local governments that help themselves financially, and providing something for nearly every local government, no matter how small, as long as it is a so-called general purpose entity.

The General Revenue Sharing formula set the pattern for later formulas in the allocation and distribution of federal aid under countercyclical and block grant programs and represented a distinct break with the past:

1. A shift in direct recipient from state to local, an arbitrary state-local division of funds, or the allocation of all monies to local governments
2. An automatic entitlement and formula allocation among governments
3. The insertion of sometimes real, sometimes proxy measures of need, service delivery, and financial responsibility in the formula (much of these data was not originally collected for the purpose of allocating funds among governments)
4. The allocation of funds to local governments on the basis of nomenclature; that is, using names to determine eligibility—counties, municipalities, and townships
5. The elimination of matching fund requirements (though not all categoricals had this)
6. Assured funding levels over a period of years, but not necessarily assured amounts to individual governments

Though revenue sharing is only one example, formula allocations of federal aid now account for 75 percent more funds than a decade ago.[9]

MACRO ANALYSIS

Distribution Over Time

General Revenue Sharing provides nonspecific aids to named types of local governments, those called municipalities, townships (or towns), and counties. Over time, the amount of money distributed has increased very gradually. After fiscal year 1973, the proportion of federal aid in GRS has declined annually, the exception being when ARFA is included for fiscal years 1977 and 1978. Because of the way funds are distributed, the amount of money going to states has increased slightly faster than that going to local units. In per capita terms, GRS monies declined from 1973 through 1976 and then rose slightly over the past two years.[10] The hope of some proponents that this form of aid would become the principal federal subsidy has not materialized.

If GRS is viewed in constant dollars, using implicit price deflators for the adjustment, the purchasing power of these funds has declined from one-quarter to one-third, depending on whether it is viewed totally or in per capita amounts. Congress has never been overly enthusiastic about GRS; its passage was principally the result of extreme political pressure on Congress by the intergovernmental lobby. The public interest groups (PIGs), representing local governments, mounted a massive campaign to secure both the initial passage and renewal of GRS. One interpretation of the failure of Congress to increase funds significantly is that they do not really like the program and are letting it "twist slowly in the wind" of inflation. In any case, it is now a much smaller part of the federal aid package than when first passed, and there is little indication that Congress is going to increase funding in the foreseeable future.

General Revenue Sharing is, by virtue of the two-thirds local/one-third state (arbitrary) division of the funds, at least twice as important to local as to state governments. As a percentage of direct general expenditures, it presently (fiscal year 1978) pays for only 2.0 percent of state-local costs. For all local units, this proportion is 2.3 percent while for recipient local governments it is 3.9 percent. This represents a decline of about 40 percent in the proportion accounted for by GRS funds from fiscal year 1973 to the present; that is, from 3.3 percent state, 3.9 percent total local, and 6.6 percent for recipient local governments. The same is true when GRS is measured against total general revenues and general revenues from own sources—decline of proportionate support is in the 40 to 50 percent range.

GRS and Other Federal Aids

Not only is the proportion of state and local finances covered by revenue sharing on the decline, but it is now also declining as a percentage of federal aids to state and local governments. Block grants, something in between special revenue sharing and categoricals, became prominent in the mid-1970s. Block grants are functionally specific, giving fairly wide discretion to the recipient government within a particular function. They, too, seem to be leveling off as a portion of federal aid.[11] Categoricals or highly specific grants, for example, project grants, still make up over 72 percent of federal aid.[12] The argument that GRS would make state and local governments less dependent on categorical aid, even when block grants are taken into account, does not hold up. State and local governments are as dependent on categoricals as ever and perhaps more so. For example: Between 1972 and 1977, categoricals increased by 60 percent and are estimated to more than double for the 1972–1979 period. Even in constant dollars, they rose 10 percent between 1972 and 1977, the period in which GRS and most of the block grants were instituted. In real terms, categoricals are expected to go up another 13 percent between 1977 and 1979. Categoricals have thus not been replaced by GRS and block grants and are still, by far, the most important type of federal subsidy.

	Fiscal Years		
	1972	*1977*	*1979 (estimated)*
Categorical Aids:			
In Current $ (Billions)	$31.0	$50.5	$64.6
In Constant $ (Billions)*	46.0	50.5	57.0

*Using implicit price deflators for state and local government purchases.

Types of Recipients

Owing in large measure to the arbitrary state/local split and the use of nomenclature to designate general purpose local governments, the payout of GRS monies does not fit well with either financial responsibility for state and local public services (as measured by own-sources revenues) or service delivery (as measured by direct expenditures). States get less than 34 percent of the GRS funds, take in 53.5 percent of general revenues, and spend directly 37.5 percent of the state-local total. The average state deviates from these percentages because of the high degree of variability in state/local systems and the fact that large states tend to be much more decentralized than small ones.[13] Large decentralized states skew national data totals downward, making it appear that most states are highly decentralized, which is in fact not true.

The proportions of GRS funds received by different types of local governments are not consistent with the roles they play in state/local systems. County governments receive 25.5 percent of GRS entitlements although they account for only 10 percent of own-source revenues and less than 14 percent of direct expenditures. Municipalities get 35.5 percent of the total GRS funding while comprising 16.5 percent of general own-source revenues and 20.7 percent of direct general expenditures. Townships account for only 2 percent of revenues and expenditures while receiving 5 percent of GRS funds. Native Americans get only one-tenth of 1 percent of this grant program; schools and special districts are excluded altogether from GRS.[14]

As a result of the passage of time and the institutionalization of the proceeds of GRS, it is no longer possible to determine the impact of these funds on state and local governments. Because they lack specificity as to functional purpose, revenue sharing monies are highly fungible, especially when mixed in with own-source revenues, state aids, and other federal grants. It is virtually impossible to know how these funds are actually spent. It is possible, however, to determine how the distribution of federal aids among types of local governments has changed since the enactment of revenue sharing.

Between 1972 and 1976 significant changes in direct recipients of federal aid have occurred. In fiscal year 1972, direct federal aid to local governments went mostly, 56 percent, to municipalities; 18 percent to special district governments; 16 percent to school districts. By fiscal year 1976, after the implementation of GRS and some of the block grants, municipalities still received 55 percent of direct federal aids and special districts received 14 percent, but the allocation to other types of local entities changed appreciably. Counties increased their proportion from less than 9 to more than 21 percent, and townships tripled theirs from 1 to 3 percent, while school districts' proportions dropped from over 16 to less than 7 percent. These distribution changes occurred during a four-year period when direct federal-to-local aid more than tripled. Stated differently, in current dollars municipalities received three times as much direct federal aid in 1976 as in 1972; school districts only 1.3 times as much (actually less in constant dollars); special districts, 2.3 times; counties, 7.9 times; and townships, 8.5 times. The influence of GRS can be seen in these figures relative to changes in emphasis for counties, townships, and school districts.

Emphasis relative to types of local recipients for state aids had not altered appreciably during the 1972–1976 period. Close to half of all state aids went to local schools with about one-fourth each to counties and municipalities. Special districts and townships got very little state support compared to other local entities.

Large Cities

One thing GRS accomplishes is that it distributes larger payments to larger municipalities (see Table 4-1).[15] Places and townships with populations of less than 500 receive an average of less than $2,000 annually while those over 150,000, an average of $7.8 million. In fact, the 97 places with 150,000 or more people, representing only 0.4 percent of municipalities and townships, received 35 percent of the $2.2 billion that went to places and townships in 1975. The 13,790 units of under 500 inhabitants with 38 percent of the recipient units, on the other hand, received only 1 percent of this allocation. Typically, GRS provides far more per capita to the nation's major central cities than to rich suburban communities. These central cities get from 1.5 to 3 times as much as their suburban municipalities.[16]

FEDERALISM, CITIES, AND GENERAL REVENUE SHARING

In order to analyze the effects of revenue sharing on cities, we must look at the roles played by large cities in our federal system. More specifically, we must study the different roles played by cities in our

Table 4-1. Allocation to Places (Municipalities) and Townships, Fiscal Year 1975 (EP-5)

Population of Unit	Number of Units	Percent of Units	Allocation ($ Millions)	Percent Allocation	Average Allocation ($ Thousands)
Under 500	13,790	38%	$ 27	1%	$ 2.0
500 to 2,499	13,806	38%	149	7%	10.8
2,500 to 9,999	5,573	16%	284	13%	49.2
10,000 to 49,000	2,393	7%	571	27%	238.6
50,000 to 149,999	368	1%	376	17%	1,021.7
150,000 or more	97	a	756	35%	7,793.8
	36,207	100%	$2,163	100%	$ 59.7

Source: Stanford Research Institute, General Revenue Sharing Data Study, vol. 2, Menlo Park, Calif., August 1972, p. 20.
[a]Less than 1 percent.

fifty diverse state/local systems. If we take the largest city in each state as an example, the city proportion of state and local general own-source revenues for fiscal year 1972 varies (as Table 4-2 shows) from 15 percent in Cheyenne to 55 percent for New York City and 100 percent in Washington, D.C. The city share of direct general expenditures ranges from 13 percent in Cheyenne to 68 percent for New York City and nearly 100 percent for the District of Columbia. The role of the state and other local governments varies inversely with these proportions. Overlying local units account for from 0 percent in several states to 37 percent in Omaha in revenues and from 0 percent in several cases to 51 percent in Los Angeles for expenditures. The state share of revenues ranges from 0 percent in Washington, D.C. to 37.5 percent in St. Louis and 75.5 percent in Honolulu. The figure for San Juan, P.R., is almost 91 percent. The state share of direct general expenditures varies from 0 percent for Washington, D.C., to 29.5 percent in Cleveland and 80 percent in Honolulu. For San Juan, P.R., the proportion is 87 percent. Therefore, when we compare cities in different states we are comparing very unlike entities.

State/Local Systems

General Revenue Sharing, as well as some of the block grants, ignores vast differences among the fifty states in the way individual state/local systems interact and operate. Some states are highly centralized and others highly decentralized. An arbitrary one-third state to two-thirds local division of the funds as in GRS, or all local recipients as with some of the block grants, simply does not fit the state/local-fiscal/service complex for most states. There are many different state (legal-structural) systems of local government, and each state has unique structural characteristics. Moreover, the way each state interacts with its political subdivisions in a policy/financial/ service delivery sense is another differentiating characteristic. Though not a focus here, there is a fourth dimension to state/local systems: political characteristics.

State Centralization. The average state is more important vis-à-vis its local governments than national data totals lead us to believe. Large states tend to be much more decentralized than small ones. They also tend to have more complex systems of local government with both overlying and discrete jurisdictions. Smaller states are more centralized with simpler local governmental structures. Highly decentralized states in a fiscal/service sense include New York, New Jersey, Ohio, and California; the most centralized state/local

Table 4-2. Per Capita Distributions of Own-Source General Revenues, Direct General Expenditures, and General Revenue Sharing for Tiered Governments, 1972.

State System of Local Government	State	City	Items	Percent Distribution of Per Capita Items			
				City	Overlying Local Units	Total Local	State
I. State-County	Hawaii	Honolulu	ROS[a]	24.5%	—%	24.5%	75.5%
			DGE[b]	20.3	—	20.3	79.7
			GRS[c]	65.3	—	65.3	34.7
	Puerto Rico	San Juan	ROS	9.4	—	9.4	90.6
			DGE	13.0	—	13.0	87.0
			GRS	—	—	—	—
II. State-Municipal	Alaska	Anchorage[d]	ROS	54.4	—	54.4	45.6
			DGE	47.0	—	47.0	53.0
			GRS	66.9	—	66.9	33.1
III. Southern	Maryland	Baltimore	ROS	42.8	—	42.8	57.2
			DGE	72.6	—	72.6	27.4
			GRS	72.8	—	72.8	27.2
	Virginia	Richmond	ROS	51.5	—	51.5	48.5
			DGE	73.5	—	73.5	26.5
			GRS	72.1	—	72.1	27.9
	Tennessee	Memphis	ROS	28.5	22.3	50.8	49.2
			DGE	52.7	15.3	68.0	32.0
			GRS	46.7	27.4	74.1	25.9
	N. Carolina	Charlotte	ROS	24.3	18.9	43.2	56.8
			DGE	33.0	35.3	68.3	31.7
			GRS	52.1	24.5	76.6	23.4

Table 4-2. continued

State System of Local Government	State	City	Items	Percent Distribution of Per Capita Items			
				City	Overlying Local Units	Total Local	State
IV. New England Town	Massachusetts	Boston	ROS	56.8	0.9	57.7	42.3
			DGE	64.5	1.0	65.5	34.5
			GRS	74.2	—	74.2	25.8
	Connecticut	Hartford	ROS	52.0	e	52.0	48.0
			DGE	63.3	e	63.3	36.7
			GRS	71.8	—	71.8	28.2
	Rhode Island	Providence	ROS	41.9	—	41.9	58.1
			DGE	51.1	—	51.1	48.9
			GRS	71.8	—	71.8	28.2
	Maine	Portland	ROS	52.8	—	52.8	47.2
			DGE	59.3	—	59.3	40.7
			GRS	69.9	3.1	73.0	27.0
	N. Hampshire	Manchester	ROS	47.5	8.0	55.5	44.5
			DGE	50.8	1.8	52.6	47.4
			GRS	68.6	5.2	73.8	26.2
	Vermont	Burlington	ROS	18.0	22.6	40.6	59.4
			DGE	14.6	26.7	41.3	58.7
			GRS	66.0	1.3	67.3	32.7
III/IV. Southern Conventional	Alabama	Birmingham	ROS	30.2	11.8	42.0	58.0
			DGE	27.9	24.8	52.7	47.3
			GRS	56.7	21.4	78.1	21.9

State	City					
Florida	Miami	ROS	24.6	29.8	54.4	45.6
		DGE	22.2	47.8	70.0	30.0
		GRS	52.0	28.0	80.0	20.0
Georgia	Atlanta	ROS	34.2	26.4	60.6	39.4
		DGE	37.8	31.8	69.6	30.4
		GRS	37.5	37.0	74.5	25.5
Louisiana	New Orleans	ROS	27.4	10.2	37.6	62.4
		DGE	28.8	21.9	50.7	49.3
		GRS	74.0	—	74.0	26.0
Mississippi	Jackson	ROS	21.2	31.7	52.9	47.1
		DGE	25.1	29.2	54.3	45.7
		GRS	52.9	18.2	71.1	28.9
Kentucky	Louisville	ROS	32.9	10.6	43.5	56.5
		DGE	30.7	17.4	48.1	51.9
		GRS	55.0	23.6	78.6	21.4
Nevada	Las Vegas	ROS	15.8	35.6	51.4	48.6
		DGE	21.2	46.1	67.3	32.7
		GRS	31.8	41.0	72.8	27.2
S. Carolina	Columbia	ROS	17.1	23.1	40.2	59.8
		DGE	29.3	29.5	58.8	41.2
		GRS	51.9	26.9	78.8	21.2
Utah	Salt Lake City	ROS	24.8	16.8	41.6	58.4
		DGE	19.3	27.7	47.0	53.0
		GRS	47.9	28.0	75.9	24.1
W. Virginia	Charleston	ROS	33.7	3.8	37.5	62.5
		DGE	31.0	13.9	44.9	55.1
		GRS	57.2	18.2	75.4	24.6
New Jersey	Jersey City	ROS	45.4	11.3	56.7	43.3
		DGE	60.1	9.2	69.3	30.7
		GRS	53.8	20.3	74.1	25.9

IV/V. A. Town-Con-
ventional

Table 4-2. continued

State System of Local Government	State	City	Items	Percent Distribution of Per Capita Items			
				City	Overlying Local Units	Total Local	State
IV/V. B. Town-Township-Conventional	New York	New York City	ROS	55.3	3.7	59.0	41.0
			DGE	68.2	12.8	81.0	19.0
			GRS	73.6	—	73.6	26.4
	Pennsylvania	Philadelphia	ROS	37.8	12.9	50.7	49.3
			DGE	39.0	26.8	65.8	34.2
			GRS	73.1	—	73.1	26.9
	Wisconsin	Milwaukee	ROS	18.9	32.1	51.0	49.0
			DGE	24.3	47.0	71.3	28.7
			GRS	45.8	25.4	71.1	28.9
V. A. Conventional without townships	Arizona	Phoenix	ROS	19.3	25.7	45.0	55.0
			DGE	23.3	40.7	64.0	36.0
			GRS	41.8	25.8	67.4	32.4
	Arkansas	Little Rock	ROS	25.3	15.7	41.0	59.0
			DGE	22.2	30.7	52.9	47.1
			GRS	61.2	14.0	75.2	24.8
	California	Los Angeles	ROS	22.0	33.4	55.4	44.6
			DGE	21.3	50.7	72.0	28.0
			GRS	38.2	33.8	72.0	28.0
	Colorado	Denver	ROS	34.9	24.0	58.9	41.1
			DGE	43.6	23.3	66.9	33.1
			GRS	69.8	—	69.8	30.2

Delaware	Wilmington	ROS	37.8	4.0	41.8	58.2
		DGE	53.9	5.2	59.4	40.9
		GRS	52.7	27.7	80.4	19.6
Idaho	Boise	ROS	17.0	24.0	41.0	59.0
		DGE	19.8	31.6	51.4	48.6
		GRS	51.5	20.2	71.7	28.3
Iowa	Des Moines	ROS	20.5	32.0	52.5	47.5
		DGE	25.4	41.0	66.4	33.6
		GRS	43.9	28.4	72.3	27.7
Montana	Billings	ROS	20.2	30.1	50.3	49.7
		DGE	19.3	29.3	48.6	51.4
		GRS	40.6	28.9	69.5	30.5
New Mexico	Albuquerque	ROS	19.8	11.6	31.4	68.6
		DGE	31.2	23.9	55.1	44.9
		GRS	55.2	20.1	75.3	24.7
Oregon	Portland	ROS	22.3	36.6	58.9	41.1
		DGE	20.6	41.2	61.8	38.2
		GRS	54.4	22.6	77.0	23.0
Oklahoma	Oklahoma City	ROS	23.8	19.2	43.0	57.0
		DGE	26.2	24.7	50.9	49.1
		GRS	57.3	14.0	71.3	28.7
Texas	Houston	ROS	24.4	28.2	52.6	47.4
		DGE	22.5	39.1	61.6	38.4
		GRS	51.0	20.0	71.0	29.0
Washington	Seattle	ROS	23.8	25.4	49.2	50.8
		DGE	29.2	32.8	62.0	38.0
		GRS	53.1	20.0	73.1	26.9
Wyoming	Cheyenne	ROS	14.6	26.0	40.6	59.4
		DGE	13.2	33.8	47.0	53.0
		GRS	24.4	34.7	59.1	40.9

Table 4-2. continued

State System of Local Government	City	State	Items	Percent Distribution of Per Capita Items			
				City	Overlying Local Units	Total Local	State
V. B. Conventional Declining Townships							
	St. Louis	Missouri	ROS	38.5	24.0	62.5	37.5
			DGE	36.5	31.7	68.2	31.8
			GRS	70.9	—	70.9	29.1
	Omaha	Nebraska	ROS	20.6	37.3	57.9	42.1
			DGE	24.7	37.0	61.7	38.3
			GRS	51.4	19.8	71.2	28.8
V. C. Conventional Midwestern Townships							
	Chicago	Illinois	ROS	23.3	32.6	55.9	44.1
			DGE	29.6	34.4	64.0	36.0
			GRS	63.1	10.1	73.1	26.9
	Indianapolis[d]	Indiana	ROS	40.4	9.9	50.3	49.7
			DGE	52.0	16.3	68.3	31.7
			GRS	67.6	—	67.6	32.4
	Wichita	Kansas	ROS	23.2	26.3	49.5	50.5
			DGE	30.9	35.8	66.7	33.3
			GRS	46.2	19.3	65.5	34.5
	Cleveland	Ohio	ROS	26.4	34.7	61.1	38.9
			DGE	28.0	42.5	70.5	29.5
			GRS	58.3	17.8	76.1	23.9
	Fargo	N. Dakota	ROS	19.3	25.5	44.8	55.2
			DGE	25.3	29.2	54.5	45.5
			GRS	42.0	23.2	65.2	34.8

S. Dakota	Sioux Falls	ROS	23.7	27.8	51.5	48.5
		DGE	23.7	26.4	50.1	49.9
		GRS	52.3	18.2	70.5	29.5
V. D. Conventional Classified Townships						
Michigan	Detroit	ROS	29.6	21.3	50.9	49.1
		DGE	34.0	32.3	66.3	33.7
		GRS	63.1	12.2	75.4	24.7
Minnesota	Minneapolis	ROS	21.0	28.4	49.4	50.6
		DGE	24.6	47.5	72.1	27.9
		GRS	45.8	25.9	71.7	28.3

a General Revenues from own sources (ROS) fiscal year 1972.
b Direct general expenditures (DGE) fiscal year 1972.
c General revenue sharing (GRS) EP-9.
d Adjusted for change in local governmental structure.
e Less than 0.1 percent.

systems are found in Hawaii, Alaska, Vermont, and West Virginia. Nearly all states are more centralized in financial responsibility than in service delivery. Depending upon the measure used, New York local governments deliver from three-fourths to four-fifths of the state/local package of public services while the state of Hawaii delivers between 75 and 80 percent of the service package. The average state, however, has a more balanced state/local division of service and financial responsibilities with state government assuming a somewhat larger share of both.[17]

State/Local-Fiscal/Service Interaction. State/local-fiscal/service interaction is directly related to state centralization, mentioned above, and to state systems of local government discussed in the following pages. Though the research is not yet complete, it appears that there are at least five basic patterns of state/local-fiscal/service interaction.[18] At one extreme are states like New York, where more than half of the state/local own-source revenue is local, the state heavily subsidizes local governments, the bulk of the services are locally delivered, and local units set much of the public policy. This is labeled a "local policy, local delivery" type. At the other extreme are states like Hawaii, where the state sets basic policy and pays for and delivers the bulk of public services. This is a "state policy, state delivery" type of arrangement. Wisconsin and Minnesota are examples of an arrangement where the state sets the basic public policies and funds most public services while service delivery is left to the political subdivisions. This is labeled "state policy, local delivery." Another way to interact is by means of a "layer-cake" model where each level, state and local, has its own revenue sources and package of public services, and each sets basic policies pertaining to them. New Hampshire is the only clear-cut present example of this pattern although it was a fairly common arrangement twenty or thirty years ago. (When education is excluded as a public service, several states still fit this pattern.) Finally, there is the shared function or "marble-cake" arrangement where a mixture of state and local activity exists in the same functional areas as well as some sharing of the same tax base or tax sources. This is becoming a more common pattern of which Arizona is a fairly good example. Many states do not fall clearly into any of these patterns but are a mixture of models. Moreover, there are different ways to handle state/local affairs within a particular model. For example, Alaska and Hawaii, both "state policy, state delivery" types, have very different administrative and service delivery arrangements.

State Systems of Local Government. General Revenue Sharing passes monies to named types of local governments on the assumption that they are "general purpose" local entities because the Governments Division of the Census Bureau so classifies them. But states use the same nomenclature for very different kinds of local governments called counties, municipalities, and townships. Of the 80,000 local governments, nearly 21,000 are so small that they do not have even one full-time equivalent (FTE) employee. These include 4,420 municipalities and 7,267 townships.[19] A quick perusal of GRS data for Entitlement Period 9 reveals that 94 percent of the townships without any employees and 95 percent of municipalities lacking even one FTE employee receive GRS monies.[20] Moreover, another 2,600 municipalities and townships have only one FTE employee, and yet nearly all are GRS recipient units.

County governments range from insignificant or nonexistent in New England to the most important unit of local government in Maryland and the only unit of local government in Hawaii. Similar disparities exist for towns and townships with the range from generally very minor roles for Midwestern townships to dominant roles in New England. Even more extreme divergences exist for entities classed as municipalities. For many of these classifications, vast differences exist within as well as between states, although intrastate differences are somewhat fewer than those among the fifty states except for municipalities. Municipalities range from 4,420 without any employees to New York City, which spends more money directly than any of the fifty state governments.[21]

There are at least five basic state systems of local government, three combined types, ten subtypes, and up to seven variants, as may be seen in Figure 4-1.[22,23] The basic types are the *state/county* system in Hawaii; *state/municipal* arrangement, Alaska; *New England town* pattern; six states; *Southern* system, four states; and the *conventional* model utilized in twenty-four states. Ten states combine the Southern and conventional pattern; New Jersey combines New England town and conventional patterns; three other states combine the town pattern with Midwestern type townships and the conventional system.

GRS, as well as many other federal aids, does not recognize that not all counties, townships, or even municipalities can be classified as general purpose local governments. The Census Bureau classification of local governments ignores too many differences among local units and forces divergent entities into a common mold whether or not they fit. A county in one state is simply not the same as what is

Figure 4-1. Typology of State Systems of Local Government, 1977

I. STATE/COUNTY, Hawaii.

State is highly centralized with three counties and one city-county. Puerto Rico is similarly organized with 76 municipios, but the Commonwealth is even more highly centralized than Hawaii.

III. SOUTHERN, four states.

Counties and large cities or city-counties, with dependent school systems, are the important local governments. No minor civil subdivisions and, with one exception, few special districts. These states are fairly decentralized.

↓

III/V. SOUTHERN/CONVENTIONAL, ten states

Falls in between the Southern and Conventional systems with the use of coterminus school district governments. No township or other minor civil subdivisions. Use of special district governments is varied.

II. STATE/MUNICIPAL, Alaska.

State is also highly centralized. 140 municipalities perform local services where they exist. The seven regular boroughs (counties) are heavily state funded. There are three city-boroughs, and one borough that is really just a school district. Local services provided directly by the state throughout much of the area (23 unorganized borough areas).

IV. NEW ENGLAND TOWN, six states.

The town, an incorporated entity, is the principal unit of local government. Most cities are towns with a more urban character that choose to call themselves cities. Relatively little use is made of special district governments. Counties are unimportant or non-existent.

↓

IV/V.A. TOWN/CONVENTIONAL, New Jersey.

A conventional system where all towns (townships) have broad municipal powers.

IV/V.B. TOWN-TOWNSHIP/CONVENTIONAL, Pennsylvania, New York, and Wisconsin.

A conventional pattern with a number of New England type towns and Midwestern townships. The towns have municipal powers, but the townships do not.

↑

V. CONVENTIONAL, Twenty-four states.

Consists of a miscellany of discrete and overlying jurisdictions; i.e., counties, municipalities—often of several different classes, school districts, and special districts and authorities.

↑

V.a. Without Townships, fourteen states.

Either without townships at all or what exists are mere vestiges of former minor civil subdivisions.

V.b. Townships Declining, Missouri and Nebraska.

Midwestern type townships with limited powers exist in fewer than one-third of the county areas of the state.

V.d. Classified Townships, Michigan and Minnesota.

Two or more classes of townships, a few with municipal powers usually located in urban areas.

V.c. Midwestern Townships, six states.

Midwestern type townships with limited authority exist in most or all county areas of the state.

Source: R. Stephens and G. Olson, "Policy Implications of State Pass-Through of Federal Grants-and-Aids," (Preliminary Report.) *NSF Grant APR7700348,* September 1, 1978, p. 40.

called a county in another; a town in one state frequently differs from that in another. For example, most Midwestern type townships (towns) do almost nothing while many New England towns provide virtually all services of local government. Counties are the most important local unit in several states and useless appendages in others. One way to minimize this difference and the resulting problems would be to require recipient governments to spend a specified minimum amount per capita for each of five services from a list of eight or ten activities considered to be common services of general purpose local governments. This would eliminate many present recipients and limit participation to those local units that have some general governmental characteristics.

Of Politics and PIGs.   Political parties, representational arrangements, interest groupings, and influence structures vary widely from one state to another and are interrelated with the character of the state/local-policy/financial/service delivery system. But in many states the character and influence of public interest groups (PIGs), the intergovernmental lobby, are related to the character of the state/local system and vice versa. With the decline and fall of political parties in the United States, PIGs have become a substitute for political parties insofar as intergovernmental relations are concerned. PIG influence with Congress has had a great deal to do with the passage of GRS and other more general federal aids as well as with the state/local division of funds. The states have not fared as well as local governments in getting federal money for newer grant programs. Congress is used to counting the opinions it receives; that is, it plays the "numbers game." In the battle for federal largesse, the states are only fifty entities with about 10,000 elected officials and 2.9 million employees compared to 80,000 local governments, about 500,000 locally elected officials, and 7.5 million employees.[24]

Tiering of Revenue Sharing and Fiscal-Service Responsibility

In order to analyze how well GRS is targeted, it is necessary to delineate the roles played by the city, its overlying local governments, and the state level. It is, of course, impossible to do this kind of analysis for all cities. For comparison, this study looks at the largest city in each of the fifty states and compares GRS per capita allocations with general own-sources revenues and direct general expenditures for the city, its overlying units, and the state government.

If we make the assumption that GRS is supposed to be used for general support of state and local governments and that such support is purportedly for those units that have financial and service delivery responsibility for general governmental activities, then one way to see how well it is targeted is to look at GRS allocations to the largest city in each state, to overlying local units (counties), and to the state government. GRS allocations are then compared to the distribution of general own-source revenue and direct expenditures for each city, the county area (less the central city and other municipalities and townships in the county area), and the state. This is only one method by which GRS can be judged, but it is important if revenue sharing is supposed to be general purpose aid. How else can one measure general governmental activities and compare up to 39,000 recipient units?

Formula elements of population, tax effort, and relative income indicate this assumption is reasonably valid. The inclusion of state aids (up to one-third) of total adjusted taxes (local taxes plus aids) indicates that both financial and service delivery responsibilities are parts of the allocation process among recipient governments. The problem with determining eligibility by fiat—making all local units that are called counties, municipalities, towns, and townships eligible for GRS allocations—has already been discussed in some detail. Units classified as the same type are simply not comparable, a fact that raises questions about how well these funds are targeted for general governmental activities of subnational governments. Comparing per capita general revenue sharing allocations for the largest city in each state, the county in which it is located, and the state government with similar per capita distributions for direct general expenditures and general revenues from own-sources is as close as we can come with the data available to estimating differences in fiscal/service responsibility for (tiered) recipient governments. Furthermore, the last year for which sufficient data are available, at this writing, is 1972.[25]

Tables 4-2 and 4-3 provide such comparisons. Using as examples the data for Honolulu, Hawaii, and Memphis, Tennessee, the tables were developed in the following manner: Honolulu and the state of Hawaii divide per capita own-source revenues $197/$608 (city/state) or 24.5 percent/75.5 percent; the division of expenditures is $235/$922 or 20 percent/80 percent, whereas that for revenue sharing is $26/$14 or 65 percent/35 percent. The city of Honolulu thus receives 167 percent more revenue sharing proportionately relative to its own-source revenues and 222 percent more proportionately relative to its share of state and local direct general expenditures. There are no overlying local units of government in Honolulu. This means

Honolulu, Hawaii	Largest City	Overlying Local Units	State Government
Per Capita:			
General Revenue Own Sources	$197.15	—	$607.66
Direct General Expenditures	235.37	—	921.51
General Revenue Sharing	26.25	—	13.95
Percent Distribution:			
General Revenue Own Sources	24.5%	—	75.5%
Direct General Expenditures	20.3	—	79.7
General Revenue Sharing	65.3	—	34.7
Targeting:			
GRS divided by GROS20[26]	+166.5%	—	-54.0%
GRS divided by DGE[26]	+221.7	—	-56.5

Memphis, Tenn.	Largest City	Overlying Local Units	State Government
Per Capita:			
General Revenue Own Sources	$166.64	$130.27	$288.19
Direct General Expenditures	417.80	121.05	253.16
General Revenue Sharing	18.23	10.70	10.14
Percent Distribution:			
General Revenue Own Sources	28.5%	22.3%	49.2%
Direct General Expenditures	52.7	15.3	32.0
General Revenue Sharing	46.7	27.4	25.9
Targeting:			
GRS divided by GROS[26]	+63.9%	+22.9%	-47.4%
GRS divided by DGE[26]	-11.4	+79.1	-19.1

that relative to general activity Honolulu is getting more than it should and Hawaii less than half of its fair share judged by these criteria. The situation is more complex but a little better targeted for Memphis, its overlying county, and the state of Tennessee. GRS targeting is very poor for both the city and the state for revenues, but only 23 percent off for the county. For direct expenditure comparision, it is much better for the city and the state and much worse for the county government. Targeting comparisions for the largest city in each state were calculated in this manner.

In this sample, selected to show the position of the largest city in each state, the average city gets 93 percent more than its "fair share" relative to own-source revenues and 81 percent more relative to its responsibility for the delivery of public services. This, of course, assumes that a fair share is an amount proportionate to the role played by state or local governmental units in general governmental activities.

Table 4-3.   Proportionate Fit of Per Capita General Revenue Sharing with the Per Capita Distribution of State and Local Revenues and Expenditures for the Largest City in Each State.

GRS Proportion Over or Under re General Revenue of Direct General Expenditure	Percent Distribution of Per Capita General Revenue Sharing[a] Divided by Percent Distribution of:							
	Per Capita General Revenue Own Sources[b]				Per Capita Direct General Expenditures[b]			
Fit	Largest City Share	Overlying Local Units	Total Local Share	State Share	Largest City Share	Overlying Local Units	Total Local Share	State Share
Bad: −50.1 to −100.0%	—	8	—	15	—	11	—	8
Poor: −25.1 to −50.0%	—	10	—	34	—	15	—	19
Fair: −10.1 to −25.0%	—	5	—	1	2	4	1	12
Good: 10.0 to 10.0%	1	6	—	—	5	4	17	10
Fair: +10.1 to +25.0%	2	3	7	—	3	1	11	—
Poor: +25.1 to +50.0%	7	3	26	—	6	3	15	1
Bad: +50.1 to +100.0%	14	4	14	—	17	1	5	—

Worse: +100.1 to +200.0%	23	1	3	—	15	2	—	—
Miserable: +200.1 or more	3	3	—	—	2	2	1	—
Number of cities	50	43	50	50	50	43	50	50
Average City	+93.3%	+14.1%	+54.0%	-44.3%	+81.1%	-6.9%	+27.0%	-27.6%
Average Dispersion	+93.3%	±72.1%	+54.0%	-44.3%	±82.2%	±77.1%	±28.4%	±29.6%
Range: From	+9.6%	-100.0%	+13.4%	-66.3%	-11.4%	-100.0%	-19.6%	-64.0%
To	±266.7%	+592.5%	+166.5%	-22.4%	+352.1%	+432.7%	+221.7%	+39.8%
From	Atlanta GA	6 Cities	St. Lou. MO	Wilm. DE	Memphis TN	6 Cities	Fargo ND	Albuq. NM
To	Boise ID	Wilm DE	Hono HA	St Lou MO	Burl VT	Wilm DE	Hono HA	New Y NY

a EP-9.
b Fiscal year 1972, the last year for which sufficient data are currently available.

Allocation of more money to larger cities was one of the objectives of some proponents of revenue sharing. While targeting gives more money to these cities, it is erratic. In other words, there is no consistency in the average given to large cities among the sample studied.

Table 4–3 summarizes the results of this study for the sample of fifty cities, their overlying local units, total local, and the state share. The classifications into ranges is arbitrary and assumes that if the relative share for GRS is within ± 10 percent, targeting is good; between ± 10 to 25 percent, targeting is fair; between ± 25 and 50 percent, it is poor; and so on. The first vertical column in Table 4–3 shows that only one city falls within ± 10 percent in the comparison of the relative proportion of GRS with the relative share of state and local own-source general revenues; two cities fall in the +10.1 to +25.0 percent range; seven from 25.1 to 50.0 percent; fourteen are out of line by from 50.1 to 100.0 percent; twenty-three cities are off by between 100.1 and 200.0 percent; and three are off the mark by more than 200.0 percent. The average city gets 93 percent more GRS funds proportionately than its relative share of own-source revenues with a range from +9.6 percent in Atlanta to +266.7 percent in Boise. All cities studied received relatively more GRS per capita than would be expected if the allocation were based on governmental activity as measured by general own-source revenues.

Targeting of GRS Allocations for Fifty Cities

Summarizing the results from Table 4–3, targeting is good (±10.0 percent) for only one city for revenues and five for expenditures; it is *fair* (±10.1 to 25.0 percent) for two cities relative to revenues and five cities relative to expenditures; *poor* (25.1 to 50.0 percent) for seven cities for revenues and six cities for expenditures; *bad* (50.1 to 100.0 percent) for fourteen cities for revenues and seventeen for expenditures; *worse* (100.1 to 200.0 percent) for twenty-three cities relative to revenues and fifteen relative to spending; and *miserable* (200.1 percent or more) for three cities for revenues and two for spending. In these terms, GRS is very poorly targeted according to what municipal governments are doing. It is even more erratic for county governments relative to general governmental responsibilities.

GRS targets only slightly better for the total local share (city plus overlying local units) with local governments averaging 27 to 28 percent too much relative to spending and 54 percent too much for revenues. The range is from minus 20 to plus 222 percent for spending and plus 13 to plus 167 percent for revenues. Thirty-nine states get considerably less than they should in direct expenditures; ten receive what they should, and only New York gets more than it should relative to direct expenditures. The state share of own-sources revenues is less than it should be for all fifty states. The range is from a 22 percent shortage in Missouri to -66 percent in Delaware.

The only conclusion one can draw from these data is that General Revenue Sharing is very poorly targeted in relation to the general purpose activities of state and local governments. Generally speaking, the allocation of funds is better for cities and local governments in states with decentralized service delivery systems. In a haphazard manner, GRS gives more proportionately to large cities, but in neither case is the distribution altogether satisfactory.

One addition to this analysis of targeting. Because counties in some states provide fewer services inside cities, it is sometimes argued that cities should receive relatively more GRS funds per capita. In some ways this is a valid argument, but it is also difficult to deal with except in the negative, that is, is the targeting of GRS monies any better for cities without overlying local governments or without any significance? Table 4-4 looks at the targeting of GRS allocations for eleven cities of this type. The answer is that the targeting is not any better when compared to the total local figures for the fifty states.[26] If anything, the targeting is slightly worse:

	Total Local	
	11 Cities	*50 Cities*
General Revenue Own Sources:		
Average City	62.3%	54.0%
Range—from	23.0%	13.4%
—to	266.7%	266.7%
Direct General Expenditures:		
Average City	35.6%	27.0%
Range—from	-1.9%	-19.6%
—to	+221.7%	221.7%

Total local figures are used for comparison because cities without overlying local governments are considered totally local in this analysis.[27] The average city of the eleven receives a larger relative proportion of GRS money than the average for the fifty cities for both financial and service delivery responsibilities. Moreover, the eleven exhibit almost the full range of variation among the fifty cities included in this study.

Table 4-4.   Targeting of GRS for Eleven Largest Cities in States Lacking Significant Overlying Local Governments and Overlying Local Recipients

Fit for Largest City	Comparison of Total Local Allocation[a] with			
	General Revenues from Own Sources		Direct General Expenditures	
Good:				
± 10.0%			Virginia	-1.9%
			Indiana	-1.0%
			Maryland	0.3%
Fair:				
10.1 to 25.0%	Alaska	23.0%	Connecticut	13.4%
			Massachusetts	15.0%
			Maine	17.9%
Poor:				
25.1 to 50.0%	Massachusetts	30.6%	New Hampshire	35.0%
	Maine	32.4%	Rhode Island	40.3%
	New Hampshire	33.0%	Alaska	42.3%
	Indiana	34.4%		
	Connecticut	38.1%		
	Virginia	40.0%		
	Tennessee	45.9%		
Bad:				
50.1 to 100.0%	Maryland	70.1%		
	Rhode Island	71.4%		
Miserable:				
200.1% or more	Hawaii	266.7%	Hawaii	221.7%
Average for Eleven States		62.3%		35.6%

Source: Data derived from data used to develop Tables 4-2 and 4-3.

[a]Comparison is made for total local because overlying units are either insignificant or nonexistent relative to revenues, expenditures, and general revenue sharing.

FINDINGS AND CONCLUSIONS

Summary of Objectives

The basic objective of General Revenue Sharing is to provide continuing general purpose financial support to state and local governments without matching fund or program requirements such as discretionary monies. It was promoted as a means of deemphasizing categorical aids. The objective of horizontal equalization among states and within states among local governments is a part of the formula given allocation factors of population, need (lower per capita income), tax effort, and fiscal/service responsibility (taxes plus state aids, i.e., adjusted taxes). Related subsidiary objectives include helping governments that help themselves and those units with an unusually large proportion of poor people as well as giving more money to big cities. A final objective is helping native Americans, Indian tribes, and Alaskan native villages.

Appraisal

General Revenue Sharing distributes discretionary financial support on a regular and continuing basis to general purpose local governments and to many local governments that are not general purpose. There are no matching requirements, very little is required in reporting, the payments are automatic, and the funds are almost completely fungible, that is, discretionary. But neither GRS nor block grants is replacing categoricals, and at this writing such a development appears unlikely in the foreseeable future. In fact, after the initial dispersals, GRS has represented a declining proportion of federal aid while categoricals continue to increase substantially in both current and constant dollars. Congress was subjected to major political pressures at the time of its passage and has never been entirely satisfied with the concepts involved. It is presently letting GRS "twist slowly in the wind" of inflation.

Horizontal equalization is largely a failure if only because the amount of money involved is far too little to accomplish anything, but there are many other reasons as well. GRS represents only a small portion of state and local revenues and expenditures. It does allocate more direct federal aid to big cities, but larger cities have always received more federal aid. The substantial increases in proportionate federal aid went to counties and townships after the passage of GRS. In fact, municipalities now receive a slightly smaller proportion of total direct federal aid than they did prior to the passage of GRS. With 39,000 recipient governments, there has never been a longer line at the "pork barrel."

Although there are formula factors aimed at horizontal equalization, the formula itself has several constraints that abrogate horizontal equalization: the 20 percent floor and 145 percent ceiling on per capita allocations to local entities; a 50 percent limit for counting state aids as a proportion of adjusted taxes for the recipient unit; and the one-third state to two-thirds local arbitrary division of the funds. No matter how rich, a community receives 20 percent of the amount earmarked for that type of unit; no matter how poor, a recipient government can receive only 145 percent of the average. The 50 percent limitation circumscribes the amount a local entity can receive if it is heavily supported by aids from larger governments. The one-third state/two-thirds local division of GRS monies does not conform at all to the state/local division of responsibility of paying for and delivering public services. In 1972, the average state paid for three-fifths of the state/local share of state and local general expenditures with a range from 44.5 percent to 79.2 percent. Also for service delivery, this ratio does not conform. Only for New York, California, and Minnesota is the state proportion of direct general expenditures one-third or less, and the average state delivers half of the public services directly. The range for the other forty-seven states is from 36 to 81 percent.[28]

Horizontal equalization among the states that results from GRS is minimal at best and applies only to ten states with the lowest per capita income insofar as any significant difference is concerned.[29] Horizontal equalization among local units is difficult to assess without better data than are currently available. The tax effort data utilized are not really tax effort, but rather tax resource data, and tend to reward wealthier communities where they have unusually large tax bases. It should also be noted that helping governments with large proportions of poor people or helping poor governments do not necessarily help poor people.

The inclusion of native Americans as recipients is an anomaly. There is little doubt that the federal government should provide such aid, but GRS is an extremely poor vehicle for doing so. Allotments have little or no relationship to the needs of the groups involved. They are whipsawed back and fourth by factors affecting interstate and intrastate allocations. Surely, some better mechanism can be found that would provide more reasonable distributions of funds to native Americans.[30]

Targeting

There are some who think GRS funds are well targeted. But if it is assumed that general purpose aid should go to the governments responsible for paying for and delivering general governmental services, then the targeting is poor. When judged by tiered proportionate distributions monies, there are very few places where the proportions are appropriate:[31] The targeting is only slightly better for expenditures than for revenues, but in neither case can it be considered good.

The two basic reasons for the failure of GRS targeting are (1) the state/local split and other formula constraints and (2) the use of nomenclature for eligibility. The constraints exist partly because of political motivation to spread the money around and political pressure from local PIGs for "a piece of the action." In order to obtain political support for financial aid to needy governments, one must secure the support of those who are not so needy; to get money for

Fit:	General Revenues from Own Sources			Direct General Expenditures		
	Largest City	Local Overlying Units	State Gov't	Largest City	Local Overlying Units	State Gov't
Good ±10.0%	1	6	—	5	4	10
Fair ±10.1 to 25.0%	2	8	1	5	5	12
Poor ±25.1 to 50.0%	7	13	34	6	18	20
Bad ±50.1 to 100.0%	14	12	15	17	12	8
Worse ±100.0 to 200.0%	23	1	—	15	2	—
Miser- 200.1% or more able	3	3	—	2	2	—
Total	50	43	50	50	43	50

central cities, political support of suburban areas must be forthcoming. In crass terms, political support must be bought. Another partial explanation of formula constraints is failure by policymakers and those who construct these formulas to understand the complexity and extreme diversity of the fifty state/local systems. Even if one ignores the physical, demographic, and political differences, there is enough fiscal/service variation to keep formula-makers busy for a long time. Eligibility for GRS is based on nomenclature, and the nomenclature used is spurious. Many political subdivisions are not "general purpose" local governments and never will be. How can giving GRS funds to almost 11,000 municipalities and townships lacking even one full-time employee be justified? How viable are these governments if they do not engage the services of even one FTE employee?

In a recently published article, Robert D. Reischauer attributes part of the overall failure of the federal "grants strategy" to governmental complexity and diversity. To paraphrase him, a partial explanation of the failure of the grants strategy to solve or ameliorate the problems at which they are aimed, even with massive infusions of money, is the extreme diversity and complexity of state/local systems.[32] In discussing GRS and the state/local split, he notes:

> . . . what appears to policy-makers to be a neutral means of dividing resources between state and local governments was, in fact, far from that.[33]

Reischauer uses a number of different aid programs and proposals to illustrate the general level of ignorance about state/local systems by the nation's policymakers. It might also be added that the Carter Administration's "new ARFA" program not only eliminates the states from participation, but also compounds the problem by letting each recipient local government select one of four variables on which to base its entitlement (whichever one assures it the most money). This is then multiplied by the recipient unit's GRS entitlement.[34] Targeting is bad enough with GRS, but no one can even guess how bad it will be with recipient selection of variables in a multiplicative formula.

Policy Implications

Given the problems of targeting and the failure to recognize variability and complexity of state/local systems, it is perhaps fortunate that General Revenue Sharing never became a more important part of the federal grant package. The difficulty is, however, that these criticisms apply to many other federal grant programs as well. In view of the way policymakers and their advisors construct grant programs, one would surmise that state and local governments are not only alike from one state to the next, but also that they operate in isolation (state from local). Actually, most state and local governments are part of an interactive and interdependent state/local system.[35] By treating state and local governments as if they were all the same, federal policymakers are abrogating one of the distinct advantages of a federal system—allowing the states freedom to develop or evolve the kind of state/local systems appropriate to their own needs and desires. Federal aids have become such a large portion of state/local fiscal structures that they have the potential for forcing state/local systems into a common mold. As it now stands, federal aids often go not only to the wrong government but also to the wrong level of government.

If federal aids are to be given directly to local governments, they must recognize the different roles played by state and local governments and adjust funding accordingly. After saying this, there is a very real question as to whether it is possible to construct such a formula and have it work. The odds are against it. The task cannot be totally left to the formula-makers. Many politicians want to distribute the money without too much reference to need or the roles played by different state and local units. An alternative is to give all federal aids to the states with adjustments designed to achieve horizontal balance among them and let them either spend the money directly for state-administered activities or pass it on to local governments for local functions. There would have to be safeguards to insure that federal aids are passed through to the responsible local unit. Such a proposal would have a beneficial side effect—it would return the fight over the division of federal aids to the state capitol where it belongs in a federal system and where local governments do not lack political resources and influence. The states could in this way be held responsible for the achievement of horizontal balance among their political subdivisions as they should in a two-tier federal system. It would also be easier to insure conformity with fifty rather than 39,000 recipient units.

Opposition to the above proposal from local PIGs would be almost monumental. The usual complaint about how local governments, and especially cities, are imposed on by the states would be heard throughout the country. But states are no longer the "rotten boroughs" of American government. Over the past twenty or thirty years, they have gone through a metamorphosis in representation, legislative procedure, executive organization and administration, professionalization, court systems, and financial responsibility, not to mention solvency.[36] This statement, of course, applies more to some states than to others, but overall the change has been remarkable. As to the charge that the states preempt the federal aids they receive, this is simply not the case. The average state passes on nearly half (48 percent, fiscal year 1976) of all its federal aid to its political subdivisions; local governments receive not only three-fifths of this aid but also a large amount of state aid from the state's own revenue sources.[37] (In fiscal year 1976, local governments received $32.2 billion in direct and pass-through federal aid and $36.8 billion from state aids derived from the state's own-source revenues.)[38]

Prospects

The prospects for an improved or expanded General Revenue Sharing program are quite dim, but the possibility of making the same mistakes and miscalculations with other programs, such as the Carter Administration's "new ARFA" and with other elements of the new urban policy, is very real. Over the last twenty years, federal aids have doubled every five years, but there is very little chance that future increases will be of this magnitude except in inflated dollars— that is, unless the federal government finds a new, very large, revenue source. In constant dollars, between 1957 and 1972 federal aids increased 70 percent every half-decade, while the 1972 to 1977 increase was only 29 percent.[39] The services for which the federal government has primary responsibility (defense and international relations, Social Security and other retirement systems, income maintenance, the postal service, and health and medical care) all have escalating costs and demands. As a result, federal aid for other purposes is likely to be constricted for the foreseeable future. State revenue systems, on the other hand, are better able to collect greater dollar amounts than in the past. Sales and income taxes have benefitted from inflation as price increases raise sales tax receipts, and higher incomes put taxpayers in higher tax brackets. Furthermore, while services that account for three-fourths of state-local funding responsibility have escalated in cost, they have stable or declining demand populations—the principal services being education and roads. By periodically reducing federal income taxes, the central government has in effect indexed the income tax, although recent Social Security payroll taxes work in the opposite direction. Most states have not indexed their income taxes and therefore are reaping revenue benefits through both sales and income taxes as a result of inflation.

Local governments now receive seventy-five cents in state and federal subsidy for every dollar of own-source general revenues, thus becoming fiscal dependents of both the states and the federal government.[40] Massive increases in federal aids, particularly direct federal aid to local subsidies, have eased some of the pressure on the states for more state subventions and have therefore contributed to their relative solvency. As federal aid levels off or declines in real terms, local governments will be forced to cut back services, increase local taxes, or focus more attention on the states as a source of additional subsidy. Over the past decade, the federal government has been a "soft touch" for local governments, but that era has come to an end.

These developments highlight a critical need for better use and better targeting of the federal aid allocated by GRS and similar programs. The crunch is not coming—it is here.

NOTES

1. Will S. Meyers, "A Legislative History of Revenue Sharing." in *General Revenue Sharing and Federalism, Annals*, AAPSS, 419 (May 1975), pp. 1-11.

2. National League of Cities, *Revenue Sharing—A Guide to the State and Local Fiscal Assistance Act of 1976* (Washington, D.C.: National League of Cities, October 1976).

3. Advisory Commission on Intergovernmental Relations, *Categorical Grants: Their Role and Design* (Washington, D.C.: ACIR 1978), A-52, pp. 44-45.

4. Ibid., pp. 7-8.

5. U.S. Treasury Department, Office of Revenue Sharing, *EP-9 Entitlements*, 1977, pp. 435, 437, and 439; U.S. Department of Commerce, Bureau of the Census, Governments Division, Governmental Finances in 1975-1976, Table 17A.

6. Office of Revenue Sharing (ORS), *EP-9 Entitlements*, pp. 435-436.

7. A very good, though much simplified, diagram of how the GRS formula operates is given in a report, *General Revenue Sharing Data Study*, vol. II (Menlo Park, Calif.: Stanford Research Institute, August 1972). (See Appendix Figure A-4-1.). Volumes I and III of the National Science Foundation's (RANN) *General Revenue Sharing Research Utilization Project* (Washington, D.C.: 1975), summarize the findings of nine formula research grants. Volumes II and IV summarize the results for the research findings of nine other projects exploring the effect of GRS on local communities. Other relevant studies include books by Richard P. Nathan and others, *Monitoring Revenue Sharing* (Washington, D.C.: Brookings Institution, 1975) and *Revenue Sharing, the Second Round* (Washington, D.C.: Brookings Institution, 1977).

8. ACIR, *General Revenue Sharing*, (Washington, D.C.: 1974), A-48, pp. 1-17; J.H.S. Hunter, *Federalism and Fiscal Balance* (Hong Kong: Australian National University Press, Canberra, 1977), pp. 87-89; Graham W. Watt, "Goals and Objectives of General Revenue Sharing." *Annals*, 419, May 1975, pp. 12-22.

9. For a brief description of the allocation procedure for GRS, see Appendix Figure A-4-1.

10. These statements are made on the basis of two tables (not included in this paper) prepared for this study that analyze (1) total and per capita changes in GRS monies for state and local governments between fiscal year 1973 and fiscal year 1978 and (2) changes in GRS as a percent of state and local finances. U.S. Treasury, *Federal Aid to States*, 1973-1977; Bureau of the Census, GF No. 5 series, 1974-1976, and ORS Entitlements, EP-1 to EP-9.

11. ACIR, A-52, *Categorical Grants*, May 1977, p. 44. Block grants include funds for community development, comprehensive health services, comprehensive employment and training, criminal justice, local public works, ARFA, and school impact aid.

12. Ibid., pp. 43-45.

13. G. Ross Stephens and Gerald W. Olson, *State Responsibility for Public Services and General Revenue Sharing*, University of Missouri-Kansas City, June 15, 1975, Final Report, NSF-RANN Project 74-27, pp. 52-58; G. Ross Stephens, "State Centralization and the Erosion of Local Autonomy, "*Journal of Politics*, 36, 1 (February 1974), pp. 44-77.

14. These data are taken from tables (not included in this paper) developed for this study that analyze the proportions of GRS monies allocated to EP-9, numbers of recipient units and finances of state and local governments for fiscal year 1972 and fiscal year 1976. Bureau of the Census, GR No. 5 series for fiscal years 1972 and 1976.

15. Allocation of Places (Municipalities) and Townships, fiscal year 1975 (EP-5). Prepared by the Stanford Research Institute, General Revenue Sharing Data Study, vol. II (Meno Park, Calif.: August 1972), p. 20.

16. ACIR, A-48, *General Revenue Sharing*, pp. 3-4.

17. Stephens and Olson, *State Responsibility for Public Services;* Stephens, "State Centralization and the Erosion of Local Autonomy."

18. G. Ross Stephens and Gerald W. Olson, "The Interlevel Flow of Intergovernmental Payments and Pass-through Federal Aids," paper delivered to the Midwest Political Science Association Meeting, Chicago, April 20, 1978, pp. 14-28; NSF/APR 7700348 research grant, preliminary findings.

19. Preliminary data from the 1977 Census of Governments.

20. Office of Revenue Sharing, Department of the Treasury, *General Revenue Sharing Ninth Period Allocations*, (Washington, D.C.: July, 1977).

21. This same issue is approached from a different perspective by Norton Long in "A Lot of Our Knowledge is a Dangerous Thing," *Nation's Cities*, (May 1978), pp. 54-55.

22. See Figure 4-1, Typology of State Systems of Local Government, 1977.

23. G. Ross Stephens, "State Systems of Local Government," an unpublished paper revised July 7, 1978.

24. G. Ross Stephens, *American Fiscal Federalism*, a manuscript prepared for ACIR, 1978.

25. The data used to derive these comparisons are taken from the 1972 Census of Governments, vol. 4, no. 4, Table 22; vol. 4, no. 5, Tables 45, 46, and 53; Office of Revenue Sharing, U.S. Treasury Department, *Ninth Period Entitlements*, Washington, D. C., 1977.

26. General revenues own-sources and direct general expenditures.

27. The total local figure is the same as the city figure where there are no overlying local governments.

28. Stephens and Olson, *State Responsibility for Public Services*, pp. 8-20.

29. ACIR, A-48, *General Revenue Sharing*, p. 3.

30. Stephens and Olson, *State Responsibility for Public Services*, p. 46.

31. For more detail see Tables 4-2 and 4-3.

32. Governmental Diversity: Bane of the Grants Strategy in the United States," in Wallace E. Oates, ed., *The Political Economy of Fiscal Federalism*, (Lexington, Mass.: Lexington Books, 1977), pp. 115-127.

33. Ibid., p. 121.

34. The formula for distributing about $1.4 billion is really much more complex than indicated in this brief statement, but after the "appropriate" ratio is determined, it is multiplied by a multiplicative formula, that is, GRS.

35. With the possible exception of New Hampshire where a "layer-cake" model of state/local finances and services still persists.

36. ACIR, "The States in 1977," *Intergovernmental Perspective*, 4, 1 (Winter 1978), pp. 15-31.

37. G. Ross Stephens and Gerald W. Olson, "The Interlevel Flow of Intergovernmental Payments and Pass-through Federal Aid," a paper delivered to the Midwest Political Science Association, Chicago, April 20, 1978, pp. 16-17.

38. Ibid., pp. 16-17.

39. ACIR draft on *American Fiscal Federalism*, 1978, approx. 233 pp.

40. Ibid., Chapter 1.

Appendix Figure A-4-1. General Revenue Sharing Allocation Procedure

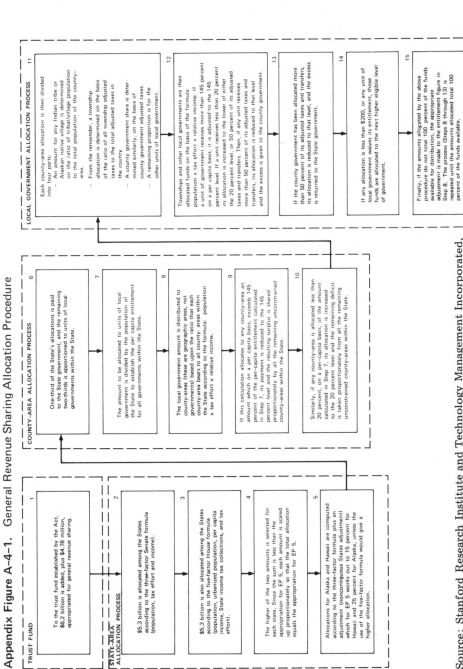

Source: Stanford Research Institute and Technology Management Incorporated, *General Revenue Sharing Data Study*, vol. 2, August 28, 1974, p. 16.

Chapter 5

The Fiscal Implications of Social Welfare Programs: Can They Help the Cities?

Alan Fechter

Expenditures from federal programs are an important source of revenues for most American cities. In recent years, revenues from federal intergovernmental grants have provided cities with a substantial proportion of the new resources available to them. A consequence of this has been a growing fear that cities may have become so dependent on federal aid that many would face dire fiscal circumstances—some would probably be forced into bankruptcy—in its absence.

An early form of this type of aid is the system of social insurance and welfare programs enacted in 1935 under the Social Security Act. This act, an omnibus measure containing the framework for cash payment programs—both insurance and assistance—together with federal grants-in-aid to support a variety of health and welfare services were the foundation for the vast system of social insurance and social welfare programs that now serve the old, the disabled, the unemployed, and the indigent. These income maintenance programs have grown from humble beginnings to become the largest single component of the federal budget.

The objectives of this chapter are (1) to survey these programs, describing their objectives and goals, their operation, and their impact on intended beneficiaries; (2) to examine their role as part of the federal response to the fiscal problems currently faced by many American cities; and (3) to discuss the public policy implications of the programs as they are currently structured and of proposed changes in these programs currently on the legislative drawing boards.

Unlike the other federal programs discussed in other chapters of this book, income maintenance programs are not regionally oriented. Rather than aiding local governments or depressed regions of the country, the purpose of these programs is to aid families or individuals with particular characteristics. Moreover, while most—if not all—of the other federal programs considered in this book derive their resources from general revenues of the federal government, several of the most important income maintenance programs—the Old Age, Survivors, Disability and Health Insurance (OASDHI) program and the Unemployment Insurance (UI) program—operate on quasi-insurance principles, deriving their revenues from trust funds supported by contributions from workers and employers. In addition, while the other federal programs discussed in the book represent federal intergovernmental grant programs that provide resources to local jurisdictions—many of the cities have more or less discretion over how they are to be allocated—the income maintenance programs either bypass local governments altogether—as in the case of the OASDHI program—or operate primarily through states and counties— as in the case of the welfare and the UI programs—and have virtually no discretion over how their resources are to be allocated. In effect, the state and county welfare agencies act as funnels through which federal and local dollars pass on their way to their ultimate destinations—the indigent or unemployed beneficiaries who are the target groups of these programs. These differences make the task of connecting the impact of income maintenance programs to the so-called fiscal crisis now being confronted by cities somewhat less than straightforward.

The next section of this chapter presents an overview of income maintenance programs—their general operating characteristics and their relative importance. The third section contains a brief discussion of the common goals and objectives of these programs and the issues that must be addressed in making them operational. The fourth section analyzes program performance in terms of goals and objectives. The fifth section discusses the fiscal implications of these programs for local governments. The sixth section describes current federal government initiatives for these programs and their potential fiscal impact on local government budgets.

AN OVERVIEW OF INCOME SUPPORT PROGRAMS

There are literally dozens of programs aimed at providing income support to families. These programs can be characterized as either social insurance or public aid programs. The former programs are distinguishable as providing benefits as a matter of right—generally earned on the basis of past contributions—rather than on the basis of needs or means. However, they are not pure insurance programs since no attempt is made to actuarially equate individual contributions with individual insurance. Included in these programs would be the OASDHI and UI as well as other retirement programs, such as those for state and local government employees, and other insurance programs, such as the temporary disability insurance programs operating in some states and the state workers compensation programs.

Public aid programs can be distinguished as programs providing benefits only to those who are categorically eligible for them. The criteria for eligibility are typically sociodemographic characteristics, such as age, family or disability status, and income. For example, the Supplemental Security Income (SSI) program pays benefits to the aged and the blind or disabled on the basis of their incomes, and the Aid to Families with Dependent Children (AFDC) program pays benefits to one-parent families (or two-parent families in which one adult is unemployed) on the basis of their incomes. Included in addition to the above are General Assistance, Medicaid, Food Stamps, and Social Services programs.

Most of these social insurance and public aid programs provide benefits in cash. But some, such as Medicare and Medicaid, reimburse providers for services rendered in kind or, as in the case of the Food Stamp program, provide beneficiaries with coupons that can be used to purchase food at discount.

Several of the programs—OASDHI and Food Stamps—have federal standards for eligibility and benefit payments. These programs are characterized by a form of horizontal equity in which families and individuals with identical characteristics, sociodemographic and economic, but living in different locations, will be treated equally. The remaining programs are governed by state standards of eligibility and benefit payments. These are characterized by a form of horizontal inequity in which families and individuals with identical sociodemographic and economic characteristics may be treated unequally. They may be eligible for the program in some states, but ineligible for the program in others; if eligible, they may receive different benefit payments in different states.

The SSI program is somewhat unique in that it operates under a federal standard for eligibility and benefit payments, but states may supplement the federal payment at their option. This program, which in 1974 replaced the state-administered, federally reimbursed programs of Old Age Assistance, Aid to the Permanently and Totally Disabled, Aid to the Blind, and Aid to the Aged, Blind and Disabled, permitted state supplementation to prevent reductions in incomes of recipients in states paying benefits that were higher than the federal standard and to encourage these states to pay new applicants to SSI a combined benefit comparable to the one paid under the earlier assistance programs.

Table 5-1 summarizes expenditures for all social insurance and

Table 5-1. Income Security Expenditures by Source (in millions of dollars)

	1975		
Program	*Federal*	*State &* *Local*	*Total*
Social Insurance	$114,580	$25,011	$139,582
Old-age, survivors, disability, health	78,430	NA	78,430
Health insurance (Medicare)	14,781	NA	14,781
Public employee retirement[a]	13,339	6,780	20,119
Railroad employee retirement	3,085	NA	3,085
Unemployment insurance and employment services[b]	3,465	10,407	13,863
Other railroad employee insurance[c]	75	NA	75
State temporary disability insurance[d]	NA	990	990
Workmen's compensation[e]	1,355	5,024	6,379
Hospital and medical benefits	50	1,810	1,860
Public Aid	36,228	20,090	56,318
Public assistance[f]	14,547	12,212	26,759
Vendor medical payments (Medicaid)[g]	7,056	5,928	12,984
Supplemental security income	4,802	1,290	2,623
Food stamps	4,694	NA	6,092
Other[h]	3,166	NA	4,694
Total Income Security Expenditures	150,808	45,101	195,900

Source: U.S. Bureau of the Census, *Statistical Abstract of the United States, 1977*, 98th ed. (Washington: U.S. Government Printing Office, 1977), pp. 318-319.

NA = Not applicable.

[a]Excludes refunds to those leaving service. Federal data include military retirement.

[b]Includes compensation for federal employees and ex-servicemen, trade adjustment and cash training allowance, and payments under extended, emergency, disaster, and special unemployment insurance programs.

[c]Unemployment and temporary disability insurance.

[d]Cash and medical benefits in five areas.

[e]Benefits by private insurance carriers, state funds, and self-insurers. Beginning 1970, federal includes black lung benefit programs.

[f]Beginning 1970, includes work incentive activities, not shown separately.

[g]Also includes payments under state general assistance programs. Medical vendor payments are those made directly to suppliers of medical care.

[h]Refuge assistance, surplus food for the needy, and work experience training programs under the Economic Opportunity Act and the Comprehensive Employment and Training Act.

public aid programs in 1975 by level of government and program. roughly $196 billion dollars were spent—most of it by the federal government. These expenditures constituted over 12 percent of GNP. Federal expenditures for these programs represented almost 46 percent of total federal expenditures; state and local expenditures, about 18 percent of total state and local expenditures.

Among the social insurance programs, OASDI was the largest, representing over one-half of the combined federal and stae-local expenditures. Expenditures for public employee retirement programs exceeded $20 billion in 1975. The Medicaid and UI programs involved almost $15 billion each. The remaining programs were considerably smaller. The next largest social insurance program was Workers' Compensation, which accounted for over $6 billion.

Among the public aid programs, Medicaid was the largest, accounting for $13 billion of expenditure. The combined public assistance programs, AFDC and General Assistance, involved over $11 billion. SSI accounted for slightly more than $6 billion, and Food Stamps contributed almost $5 billion to public aid expenditures.

GOALS AND OBJECTIVES

A common goal of these social insurance and public aid programs is the provision to families and individuals of a floor of support below which income cannot fall. Before objectives can be set to meet this goal, a number of issues must be taken into account. The first is what factors should be considered in setting this floor. The social insurance programs have typically opted for some concept of earnings replacement, basing benefits on past earnings. The public aid programs have typically opted to base the floor in their benefit formulas on some concept of "needs," making these benefits a function of family size with allowances for work-related expenses or minimal standards for food and housing.

A second consideration is whether or not the standard should be established in real or nominal terms. Setting the standards in real terms would imply that the amount paid should vary with the cost of living. Many programs typically adjust their benefits over time for changes in the cost of living as measured by the Consumer Price Index or the Bureau of Labor Statistics budget standards. One can argue that similar regional adjustments may be called for because of regional variations in the cost of living. The South, for example, may be considered a low-cost area of the country. If this is true, then benefit payments in the South can be lower and still be consistent with the goal of equality of real benefit payments.

Once the standard has been established, the major objective of such programs would then be to assure that all families and individuals covered by the program who have incomes *below* that standard be paid a benefit that would raise their incomes *to* that standard. Such an objective would be attained if all eligible program beneficiaries participated and if benefits were distributed in an equitable manner.

Since the standard could vary with sociodemographic as well as economic characteristics, equitable treatment would not necessarily be equated with equal payments to all families and individuals. Moreover, if the standard is established in real terms, then equitable treatment need not necessarily mean equal nominal payments to all families and individuals with given sociodemographic and economic characteristics.

PROGRAM PERFORMANCE

As noted earlier, the foundation of the social insurance and public aid programs discussed was laid in the Social Security Act of 1935. The founders of the programs authorized by this act were concerned with two overwhelming social problems that were being experienced at that time: old-age dependency and widespread unemployment. The aim of the program was therefore to provide social insurance against both risks. However, since the pensions, aimed at minimizing old-age dependency, would not be immediately available for those past the age of 65 and not working and since some industries were not covered under the new program, public assistance for the needy aged was established as a second line of defense.[1]

Thus the programs originally established under the Social Security Act sought to provide protection against income inadequacies. For those in the work force, this protection was purchased as a matter of right through contributions collected by means of payroll taxes. The funds collected from these taxes were used to provide retirement benefits to covered workers reaching the age of 65 and to provide unemployment insurance benefits to younger workers who might experience layoffs. For those out of the work force (the aged, the blind, dependent children), public assistance was provided from federal and state revenues with benefits designed to fill the gap between the needs and the resources of the indigent family or individual.

This two-pronged approach to income security—an insurance program for those in the work force to cover retirement, survivors, disability, health, and unemployment benefits and a public welfare program providing both cash and in-kind benefits for those who cannot (or should not) work, such as the aged, the disabled, dependent children—continues to serve as the basic organizing principle of our social welfare programs.

To assess the performance of these programs—since the objectives are to assure that no one remains below the floor of income established as adequate—it would be necessary to determine the number of families or individuals who are below the floor of income and the total number of families or individuals who *would be* below this floor in their absence.

A commonly used operational measure of this floor is the "poverty index," devised in 1964 by the Social Security Administration on the basis of income-food expenditure patterns and a nutritionally adequate food plan designed by the Department of Agriculture for emergency or temporary use when funds are low.[2] This index provides a range of income cutoffs, or "poverty income thresholds," adjusted for such factors as family size, sex and age of family head, number of children under age 18, and farm-nonfarm residence. It is also adjusted annually for price changes. Table 5-2 summarizes the 1975 thresholds for nonfarm families by size.

Given this definition of poverty, the Congressional Budget Office has examined the effect of social insurance and public aid programs on the number of families in poverty and the incidence of poverty in 1982. Table 5-3 summarizes their findings about the number of families in poverty; Table 5-4 summarizes their findings about the incidence of poverty.

Almost 19 million families, or 22 percent of all families, would have been classified as poor if they had not received benefits from social insurance and public aid programs. Over 14 million, or about

Table 5-2. Weighted Average Poverty Thresholds for Nonfarm Families of Specified Size, 1975

All unrelated individuals	$2,724
Under age 65	2,797
Aged 65 and over	2,581
Two persons	3,506
Head under age 65	3,617
Head aged 65 and over	3,257
Three persons	4,293
Four persons	5,500
Five persons	6,499
Six persons	7,316
Seven persons or more	9,022

Source: *Social Security Bulletin, Annual Statistical Supplement, 1975*, p. 46.

Table 5-3. Number of Families in Poverty by Family Type and Other Characteristics under Alternative Definitions of Income in Fiscal Year 1982: Families in Thousands[a]

Characteristics of Families in Poverty	Pretax, Pretransfer Income	Pretax, Postcash Social Insurance Income	Pretax, Postwelfare Transfer Income[b]	Posttax, Postwelfare Transfer Income[b]
Total Families	19,117	9,752	6,586	7,055
Family Type				
Single parent with children	3,512	3,013	1,692	1,749
Youngest child under 6	1,698	1,579	906	930
Youngest child 6 to 13	1,574	1,307	731	757
Youngest child 14 or older	239	127	56	63
Two parents with children	1,561	1,072	667	793
Other	14,044	5,667	4,227	4,512
Age of Head				
65 and over	9,527	2,506	1,520	1,528
Under 65	9,590	7,246	5,066	5,527
Health Status				
Disabled member	1,355	972	560	572
No disabled member	17,761	8,780	6,026	6,483
Employment Status of Head				
Working full-time	1,792	1,392	1,023	1,210
Working part-time	1,945	1,325	890	1,033
Unemployed	944	761	528	573
Not in labor force	14,436	6,274	4,146	4,238
Race of Head				
White	15,152	6,923	4,724	5,094
Nonwhite	3,965	2,828	1,862	1,961
Region of Residence				
South	6,755	3,673	2,701	2,941
West	3,533	1,944	1,198	1,285
Northeast	4,478	2,097	1,317	1,379
North Central	4,351	2,037	1,370	1,449

Source: Congressional Budget Office, *The Administration's Welfare Reform Proposal: An Analysis of the Programs for Better Jobs and Income*, (Washington, D.C.: U.S. Government Printing Office, April 1978), p. 64.

[a]Families are defined to include unrelated individuals as one-person families. Components may not add to totals because of rounding.

[b]In addition to AFDC, SSI, EA, food stamps, and general assistance, this includes the earned income tax credit, veteran pensions, child nutrition, and housing assistance, but excludes Medicaid benefits.

64 percent of the pretransfer poor, were in families in which the head was not in the labor force. The remainder were poor either because the head was unemployed or because the head was employed but did not earn enough to lift the family out of poverty. Among these pretransfer poor with heads in the labor force, almost 2 million

Table 5–4. Percent of Families in Poverty by Family Type and Other Characteristics under Alternative Definitions of Income in Fiscal Year 1982[a]

Characteristics of Families in Poverty	Pretax, Pretransfer Income	Pretax, Postcash Social Insurance Income	Pretax, Post-welfare Transfer Income[b]	Posttax, Post-welfare Transfer Income[b]
Total Families	22.0	11.2	7.6	8.1
Family Type				
Single parent with children	42.7	36.6	20.6	21.2
Youngest child under 6	57.8	53.9	30.8	31.7
Youngest child 6 to 13	39.3	32.7	18.3	18.9
Youngest child 14 or older	18.5	9.8	4.3	4.9
Two parents with children	5.2	3.6	2.2	2.6
Other	29.0	11.7	8.7	9.3
Age of Head				
65 and over	54.5	14.3	8.7	8.7
Under 65	13.8	10.5	7.3	8.0
Health Status				
Disabled member	54.2	38.9	22.4	22.9
No disabled member	21.1	10.4	7.1	7.7
Employment Status of Head				
Working full-time	3.9	3.1	2.2	2.7
Working part-time	16.8	11.4	7.7	8.9
Unemployed	21.1	17.0	11.8	12.8
Not in labor force	57.2	24.9	16.4	16.8
Race of Head				
White	19.9	9.1	6.2	6.7
Nonwhite	37.4	26.7	17.6	18.5
Region of Residence				
South	24.8	13.5	9.9	10.8
West	20.9	11.5	7.1	7.6
Northeast	22.6	10.6	6.6	7.0
North Central	19.0	8.9	6.0	6.3

Source: Congressional Budget Office, *Welfare Reform Proposal*, p. 65.

[a]The percent of families in poverty is calculated as a percent of all U.S. families in the respective categories. Components may not add to totals because of rounding.

[b]In addition to AFDC, SSI, EA, food stamps, and general assistance, this includes the earned income tax credit, veteran pensions, child nutrition, and housing assistance, but excludes Medicaid benefits.

were working full time, almost 2 million were working part-time, and almost 1 million were unemployed. The full-time employed poor workers have been characterized as the "working poor," while the part-time poor workers have been described as the "underemployed." The relatively small number of pretransfer poor heads who were unemployed is surprising, given the fact that in 1975 unemployment rates reached their highest levels in thirty years. However, it is interesting to note that almost one-half of all unemployed heads would have been classified as poor if they had not received benefits from these programs.

The regional concentration of pretransfer families in the South is also notable. Almost 7 million families, or 37 percent of all 'pretransfer poor families, were located in the South.

Social insurance benefits reduced the number of families that would have been classified as poor by 9.3 million or almost 50 percent. Once these benefits are taken into account, only 11.2 percent of all families are classified as poor. The decline is concentrated in families with aged heads, with heads not in the labor force, and heads who were disabled. Families with children—particularly single-parent families—and families with heads in the labor force were not as strongly affected by social insurance programs—although, among these families, the relative effect on poverty status is strongest for families with unemployed heads, reflecting the impact of the UI program. The regional distribution of the effect of social insurance programs on poverty is reasonably uniform with slightly larger relative reductions in numbers of families occurring in the Northeast and the north central regions.

Families with relatively high incidences of poverty other than those with aged heads—single-parent families with young children, families with disabled heads, families with nonwhite heads—are not as dramatically affected by social insurance programs. Table 5–4 shows that the relative incidence of poverty for some families with heads not expected to be in the labor force—single-parent families with young children and families with disabled heads—are not as dramatically affected by social insurance programs. The relative incidence of poverty falls most dramatically for families with aged heads and families with heads not in the labor force, suggesting that, in terms of the objectives stated earlier, social insurance programs have been more effective in providing income support for older workers covered under the Social Security retirement program.

Benefits from public aid programs further reduced the number of families that would have been classified as poor by 3.1 million, or 31 percent—not as dramatic an absolute reduction as for social insurance programs, but significant when measured relatively to the amount spent on benefits in the two programs. Once these benefits are accounted for, only 7.6 percent of all families are classified as poor. The declines are concentrated in single-parent families with children and families with disabled heads in which the incidence rates relative to those of other families fall dramatically. Since these families had the highest incidences of poverty, one can infer that the targeting of these public aid programs is reasonably consistent with their objectives, discussed earlier.

Note that the South did not benefit as much from these programs as the non-South. In the absence of the programs only 37 percent of poor families would have been living in the South. After adjusting for social insurance programs, 38 percent of the poor families would have been from the South. Surprisingly, the effect of adjusting for public aid programs is to raise this percentage from 38 to 41 percent, suggesting that a disproportionately large share of public aid expenditure is made outside the South. Since the incidence of poverty is systematically higher in the South than in other regions (see Table 5-4), this suggests that current public aid programs are not well targeted regionally. A principal reason for this poor targeting is that the major cash benefit public aid program, AFDC, has its benefit standards set by the states. Southern states tend to be conservative both in establishing eligibility criteria and in setting benefit payment standards.

Using the poverty index as a standard of adequacy, it can be concluded that the programs examined in Tables 5-3 and 5-4 work reasonably well, but do not provide enough support to lift all families above that particular income floor. The major reasons for this failure can be found in the level of benefit payments and the coverage of existing programs.

Benefit payments in many cases are not high enough to lift covered families out of poverty. This shortcoming is particularly relevant to the public aid programs since their objective is to provide an adequate level of income support to families according to their need.

An examination of the AFDC programs, the largest of the public aid programs providing cash benefits, can illustrate this point. In 1974 the poverty index for a nonfarm family of four was $5,038, or $419 per month.[3] The median of the maximum monthly amount payable to a family of four under AFDC benefit standards in all states was $262 in July 1974, and ranged from $60 in Mississippi to $403 in Wisconsin.[4] Only three states—Alaska, Michigan, and Wisconsin—paid more than $400. Only five states—Hawaii, Minnesota, New Jersey, New York, and Vermont—paid between $350 and $399. Southern states, as noted earlier, tended to be the low-benefit states.

The major area in which coverage appears to be inadequate is two-parent families with heads who can work. Table 5-5 summarizes the categorical (as opposed to income) standards for eligibility to the major federal cash public aid programs. Note that both two-parent

Table 5-5. Public Aid Programs by Characteristics on Covered Populations

	Single Parent with Children	*Intact with Children*	*Single Parent or Intact, No Children*
Aged	SSI[a]	SSI	SSI
Disabled	SSI	SSI	SSI
Nondisabled	AFDC[b]	AFDC-U[c]	

[a]Social Security income.
[b]Aid to Families with Dependent Children.
[c]Aid to Families with Dependent Children and an Unemployed Parent.

and single-parent families in which the head is nondisabled (and is therefore able to work) and in which there are no eligible children are not covered by any of these programs. Moreover, although many states provide AFDC benefits to two-parent families with children in which the head is unemployed, twenty-four states, located primarily in the South and the Southwest, exclude such families. Only 86,000 families received money payments under this program in July 1974.[5] Since there are approximately one million poor two-parent families with children (see Table 5-3), this coverage can certainly be considered quite low.

A major obstacle to reforming existing programs to eliminate poverty is the substantial budgetary cost such reforms might entail; estimates of these costs range in the billions of dollars.[6] Of course, it can be argued that these are not real social costs but merely constitute the redistribution of income from the nonpoor to the poor. Moreover, advocates of these reforms argue, such reforms could provide additional indirect benefits by eliminating some of the inequities and adverse incentives created by the existing programs.

The major adverse incentives created by existing programs include their effects on family stability, out of wedlock birth rates, and work behavior. It is argued that AFDC encourages family breakdown and out of wedlock births by making categorical eligibility dependent on being a single parent.

It is also argued that several factors combine to produce adverse work incentives. First, many programs have benefit provisions that result in high marginal tax rates on earnings. For example, both AFDC and SSI reduce benefits by $2 for every $3 in earnings received by the family head (beyond some minimum earnings determined by program regulations). A similar provision exists for beneficiaries under the Social Security program, in which benefits are reduced $1 for each $2 of monthly earnings exdeeding $250 (or $3,000 annually). Thus, the marginal tax on earnings can be as high as 50 to

67 percent, depending on the program and earnings level. It is believed that such a high tax rate can act as a powerful deterrent to work effort.

A second factor likely to produce adverse work incentives is commonly referred to as the "notch" effect, which arises from program interactions that produce combinations of benefits from several programs. The North is in the range of earnings increments (beyond the breakeven point) within which families could be financially worse off by working and leaving the welfare rolls than they would be by not working and remaining on these rolls. For example, families deemed eligible for cash benefits under the AFDC and SSI programs are also entitled to in-kind medical and social services benefits and food stamps. Thus, earnings increments that take families beyond the breakeven point (where computed benefits would be zero) and cause them to leave the welfare rolls could result in a substantial loss in in-kind income. Such potential loss in benefits by working raises the marginal tax rate on earnings in this range even higher than the 67 percent produced by the direct effect of earnings on cash benefits. Thus, to make working financially attractive at the breakeven point, earnings would have to be large enough to carry the family beyond the notch.

Most efforts to reform public aid programs have centered around removing the inequities in eligibility and payment standards and reducing the adverse incentives in existing programs summarized earlier. Proposed reforms have included federalization and consolidation of existing program as well as the "cashing out" of programs involving in-kind benefits. The proposals to federalize key public aid programs are most directly relevant to the fiscal circumstances of cities.

FISCAL IMPLICATIONS OF INCOME SUPPORT PROGRAMS FOR CITIES

As noted earlier, the fiscal implications of income support programs for cities are difficult to identify since most benefits are directed toward families and individuals rather than local governments, and in those cases where such funds flow to localities, it is usually states and counties that administer the funds. If "fiscal" is narrowly interpreted as budgetary components (i.e., revenues, expenditures, and deficits or surpluses), these programs have little direct impact. If states and localities had been relieved of their financial responsibilities for AFDC, the result would have been over $4 billion in fiscal relief. However, only a small fraction of that relief, 7 percent, would have gone to local jurisdictions.[7]

The major direct impact would have been concentrated in cities that administer and contribute to their state public aid programs. In these cities, the federal contribution to such income support programs represents a direct form of fiscal relief. Relatively few major cities administer and contribute to these programs—New York City, St. Louis, Columbus (Ohio), Richmond, and Norfolk, for example. However, while these programs have little direct impact on the fiscal circumstances of most cities, their effect can be critical, especially when one of those cities is New York. New York City spent $3.5 billion, more than 20 percent of its budget, on public welfare in fiscal year 1976. The state government contributed approximately $3.3 billion in intergovernmental grants. Given the current fiscal crisis in New York, these contributions have undoubtedly alleviated what is universally acknowledged as the city's fiscal burden.

In view of the nature of these income support programs, most of the fiscal implications are necessarily indirect, operating through such vehicles as the effect of expenditures of beneficiaries on local tax receipts and through what local expenditures on income support would have been if there had been no federal or state grant program.[8] These indirect effects could, however, conceivably be quite large. Expenditures by beneficiaries create tax revenues directly from local sales taxes and indirectly through any employment they might stimulate. Assuming that there is some fiscal substitution in the provision of income support to residents, cities would probably have assumed some of the fiscal burden of supporting these programs if the federal, state, and county governments had not. Similarly, states might have reduced their contributions to cities if the federal government had assumed a larger share of the burden. An examination of the urban share of federal income support dollars might shed some light on their fiscal impact on cities and the potential consequences for cities of changes in the federal role.

Tabulations of urban concentration ratios (i.e., the percentage share of federal outlays divided by the percentage share of population) have been constructed from data—on federal outlays in fiscal year 1976 by area—provided by the Community Services Administration (see Table 5-5). These ratios indicate whether an area (or group of areas) receives proportionately more or less federal dollars than its share of the population warrants. A ratio greater than one indicates that it receives disproportiontely more federal outlays; a ratio less than one indicates it receives disproportionately less federal outlays.

In principle, several factors can affect this ratio, assuming the population base accurately reflects the population eligible for the program. First, the ratio can reflect variations in program participation rates. Other things being equal, there should be a positive association between the participation rate and the concentration ratio. Second, the ratio can reflect variations in benefit payments per recipient. Other things being equal, there should also be a positive association between these benefit payments and the ratio. Localities with greater than average participation rates or benefit payments will have concentration ratios that are greater than one; localities with below average participation rates and benefit payments will have ratios that are less than one.

Since most of the federal income support programs operate at the federal, state, or county level, estimates of expenditures are derived by allocating expenditures to cities by the proportion of a particular state or county population in the city. For most of the programs—all but Food Stamps and Unemployment Insurance—expenditures are allocated on the basis of the state's program recipients in the city or county. For Food Stamps, expenditures are allocated by the proportion of the county's population in the city. Expenditures for Unemployment Insurance were actual expenditures.

Table 5-6 summarizes the urban concentration ratios nationally for cities by region for each type of program. At the national level, the urban concentration ratios for cities are 1.21 and 1.02 for OASDI and UI, respectively. The ratio is only 0.69 for public assistance and other income supplements. These ratios suggest that participation rates or average benefit payments in cities are higher than average for OASDI and lower than average for public assistance and other income supplements.

Lower OASDI participation rates might be expected in rural areas because of poorer program coverage. Self-employed farm workers were not covered prior to 1955, and regularly employed farm workers were not covered prior to 1951. Thus, lower average OASDI benefit payments could be expected in rural areas since benefit payments are determined by past earnings history and earnings in rural areas tend to be lower than those of comparable workers in urban areas. The concentration ratios of public assistance programs are biased downward because the Community Service Administration did not allocate expenditures from two of the larger cash public assistance programs—AFDC and SSI—to all cities. These expenditures were allocated only to cities operating their own programs (instead of those with county-operated programs). Studies of AFDC, the largest of the cash public assistance programs, suggest that both participation rates and average benefit payments are higher in central cities of Standard Metropolitan Statistical Areas than elsewhere.[9]

The low concentration ratio for public assistance programs in

Table 5-6. Urban Concentration Ratios of Federal Expenditures of Income Security Programs by Region, Fiscal Year 1976

Program	City Outlays Fiscal Year 1976 (millions)	All Cities	New England	Middle Atlantic	East North Central	West North Central	South Atlantic	East South Central	West South Central	Mountain	Pacific
Retirement and disability insurance	87,725.7	1.21	1.12	1.10	0.96	1.00	1.46	1.04	0.77	0.83	0.89
Unemployment insurance	2,162.0	1.02	1.29	1.48	0.80	0.84	0.76	1.01	0.56	0.81	1.01
Public Assistance and other income supplements	18,194.5	0.69	0.71	1.69	0.73	0.56	1.33	1.01	0.84	0.76	0.76

Source: The Rand Corporation and unpublished tabulations from data on federal outlays by geographical location provided by the Community Services Administration.

Note: Concentration ratio is the percentage share of each type of outlay divided by the percentage share of population in each type of area.

cities may also reflect lower participation rates and average monthly payments in smaller cities. This hypothesis is supported by evidence presented in Table 5-7, which shows urban concentration ratios greater than one for public assistance programs in large cities and in central cities and ratios less than one in smaller cities and in suburban cities. However, these observed tendencies may be biased estimates of true tendencies because expenditures for AFDC and SSI were allocated to only a few cities.

As Table 5-6 shows, there is a considerable amount of regional variation in these concentration ratios. For the OASDI program these ratios range from 0.77 in the west south central states to 1.46 in the south Atlantic states. Ratios of less than one are generally found in the western regions. For the UI program, these ratios range from 0.56 in the west south central states to 1.48 in the middle atlantic states. They are substantially greater than one in New England and the middle Atlantic states, are 1.01 in the east south central and Pacific states, and are substantially below one in the remaining states. For the public assistance programs, the ratios range from 0.56 in the west north central states to 1.69 in the middle Atlantic states. They are substantially greater than one in the middle and south Atlantic states, are 1.01 in the east south central states, and are substantially below one in the remaining states.

Table 5-7 summarizes urban concentration ratios by certain characteristics of cities for each type of program. Ratios tend to be higher in cities with high rates of unemployment, in cities with indexes of fiscal hardship that suggest more severe hardship, in larger cities, and in central (as opposed to suburban) cities. The ratio for OASDI is lower in high per capita income cities; the ratio for public assistance programs is higher in low per capita income cities.

The findings in Table 5-6 suggest that, while OASDI and UI may be programs that allocate disproportionate amounts of money to cities, the public assistance programs are oriented more specifically to rural areas. However, as noted above, the findings about public assistance programs must not be taken too seriously since expenditures in three of the larger programs—AFDC, Medicaid, and SSI—are allocated to only a few of the cities for which concentration ratios were constructed—presumably because they were allocated to counties instead.

The findings about fiscal hardship and unemployment suggest that, although these programs have other goals and objectives, they allocate proportionately more funds to cities that seem susceptible to fiscal difficulties. Again, these tendencies may be biased for public assistance programs because expenditures for AFDC and SSI were not allocated to many cities.

Table 5-7.   Urban Concentration Ratios of Federal Outlays of Income Security Programs by Type of City, Fiscal Year 1976

Program (Number of Cities in each category)	Per Capita Income 1970		Population Growth 1970-1975			Unemployment Rate 1976		Hardship Index		Size (000)			Central City (207)	Suburban City (144)
	≤$3304 (199)	>$3304 (151)	≤0 (182)	0-15.0 (135)	>15.0 (34)	<8.9 (168)	≥8.9 (183)	<100 (219)	>100 (128)	<100 (202)	100-300 (105)	>300 (44)		
Retirement and disability insurance	1.10	0.89	1.03	0.97	0.76	0.89	1.06	0.84	1.12	0.99	1.12	0.95	1.02	0.88
Unemployment insurance	1.00	1.00	1.13	0.74	0.57	0.69	1.17	0.70	1.24	0.79	0.93	1.10	1.06	0.71
Public assistance and other income supplements	0.87	1.12	1.05	0.81	1.10	0.79	1.11	0.75	1.20	0.69	0.82	1.19	1.10	0.51

Source: The Rand Corporation and unpublished tabulations from data on federal outlays by geographical location provided by the Community Services Administration.

Note: Concentration ratio is the percentage share of each type of outlay divided by the percentage share of population in each type of area.

CURRENT FEDERAL INITIATIVES AND THEIR IMPLICATIONS FOR FISCAL RELIEF

A number of proposals to reform the existing system of public aid programs were on the legislative agenda of Congress in 1977–1978. These include:

1. HR 9030, the Carter Administration's Program for Better Jobs and Income (PBJI)
2. A revised version of HR 9030 reported out by the Special House Subcommittee on Welfare Reform (the Subcommittee bill)
3. HR 10711, the Welfare Reform act of 1978 (the Ullman bill)
4. S.2777, the Job Opportunities and Family Security Program (the Baker-Bellmon bill)[10]

Each of these programs proposed to modify or replace elements of existing programs with a unified program of cash assistance and jobs for eligible families. The major existing programs proposed for modification or replacement were: AFDC, SSI, Food Stamps, the Earned Income Tax Credit (EITC), and public service employment programs currently funded under the Comprehensive Employment and Training Act (CETA). Each also includes measures to provide work opportunities for able-bodied family heads—either directly through public service employment or indirectly through tax incentives to private firms. Moreover, the proposals also attempt to make the financial return of choosing the work opportunities more rewarding than that of remaining on welfare without working. This attempt to link public assistance policy with job creation policy is a unique aspect of these proposals that was not as strongly considered in past efforts to reform the welfare system.

Major differences among these proposals can be highlighted by their federal budgetary costs. Table 5-8 summarizes these by type of cost:

1. New funds for cash assistance programs and Food Stamps
2. New funds for Public Service Jobs and Work Incentive Program (WIN)
3. New funds for the Earned Income Tax Credit (EITC) program
4. New funds for job creation in the private and nonprofit sector
5. New funds to provide fiscal relief to states

These cost estimates, produced originally by the Congressional Budget Office and the House Ways and Means Committee, should be interpreted with caution since they involve numerous assumptions including what the state of the economy will be in 1982, what states will do about supplementing the minimum federal payment, and so on. The costs are in 1982 dollars and represent net incremental 1982 costs; that is, the cost of these proposed programs over what the current programs would have cost in 1982.

Table 5-8 clearly reveals that the Carter Administration bill and the House Subcommittee bill are the more ambitious programs with estimated federal budgetary costs of nearly $20 billion, while the programs proposed by the other bills have estimated costs of around $9 billion. The major differences between these two sets of programs are in their costs for cash assistance and food stamps and their costs for Public Service Jobs and WIN.

The more ambitious programs—the administration bill and the subcommittee bill—proposed to extend the eligibility of existing cash assistance programs to all low-income families. Specifically, they proposed to extend coverage to include childless families. The less ambitious programs—the Ullman and the Baker-Bellmon bills—expand

Table 5-8. Breakdown of New Federal Program Costs for Alternative Welfare Reform Proposals, 1982 (billions of 1982 dollars)

	Administration Bill	Subcommittee Bill	Ullman Bill	Baker-Bellmon Bill
1) New funds in cash assistance and food stamps	$ 2.68	5.53	-.55 to -.95	-2.01[a]
2) New funds in Public Service Jobs and the WIN program	11.03	11.42	5.07	3.09
3) New funds in the Earned Income Tax Credit (EITC)	2.07	1.06	3.07	3.12
4) New funds in tax credits and wage subsidies for private sector job creation	—	—	.05	1.18
5) New fiscal relief	3.36	2.21	1.0 to 1.5	3.05
6) Total 1982 costs	$19.14	20.22	approx. 9.0	9.33

Source: Frank Levy, "The Harried Staffer's Guide to Current Welfare Reform Proposal," Urban Institute Working Paper No. 996-7 (Washington: The Urban Institute, May 1978), p. 11.

[a]This number will be lower (more negative) when benefit recoupment is taken into account.

AFDC coverage by establishing a federal benefit payment standard and by mandating Aid to Families with Dependent Children with an Unemployed Parent (AFDC-U) in all states. The net decrease in cash payments in these bills occurs because they move some AFDC recipients into public service jobs whereby the resultant cost saving outweighs the additional costs arising from expanded coverage.

The difference in costs between the two sets of programs for Public Sector Jobs and WIN can be attributed to differences in job search requirements. The more ambitious programs stipulate that an eligible person can be placed in a public service job after searching for private sector work for five weeks; the less ambitious programs require anywhere from ninety days to sixteen weeks of job search. The longer job search requirement of the latter programs cuts the number of public jobs that are necessary.

Each of the four programs offers the prospect of instantaneous fiscal relief to state governments when they first become operational in 1982. Estimates of fiscal relief in 1982 are substantial, ranging from $1.0 to $3.6 billion. Recall, however, that these estimates are based on assumptions including, for example, one about the strength of the economy and, most relevant to this estimate, one about what the states will do about supplementing the minimum federal payment. Thus, any projections of fiscal relief beyond this instantaneous estimate for 1982 would have to be used cautiously.

The amount of fiscal relief provided by these programs is affected by two provisions: state supplementation and the "hold-harmless" provision. State supplementation offers federal matching funds to states that are willing to pay benefits in excess of the federal minimum standard. The "hold-harmless" provision places a ceiling on what states are required to spend.

The federal minimum standard provided for does not vary much among programs. The administration and the subcommittee bills adopt essentially the same program, providing a minimum benefit of $4,200 to a family of four. The Ullman bill retains separate AFDC and Food Stamp programs and provides a combined benefit of $4,200 from both of these programs. The Baker-Bellmon bill also retains separate AFDC and Food Stamp programs and defines the minimum federal standard as 60 percent of the poverty index. This would provide a family of four with $3,875 in benefits from these two programs, slightly below the other three proposals. However, the Baker-Bellmon bill also specifies that the standard minimum benefit should rise in 1985 to 65 percent of the poverty index, bringing it approximately into line with the other proposals. Thus, differences in fiscal relief among the bills must flow from the nature of the federal match required.

Under PBJI, the federal government would pay states that opt to supplement 75 percent of supplements up to 112.32 percent of the federal benefit plus 25 percent of supplements up to the poverty line or the current AFDC-Food Stamp benefit, whichever is greater, for families with children. The subcommittee bill provides approximately the same match. The Ullman bill requires that a state contribute only an amount equal to 85 percent of its 1977 AFDC cost. This share will not be adjusted for inflation and would therefore provide for an increasing amount of fiscal relief as AFDC benefits rise over time. However, offsetting this projected trend, the bill provides for AFDC-U payments for only sixteen weeks at which time the head would be expected to accept a public sector job. If no job were available, the family would continue on AFDC-U for an additional thirty-seven weeks, but the costs associated with this additional time would be borne by the state. This provision could saddle states with additional costs, particularly in periods of high unemployment. Under the Baker-Bellmon bill, fiscal relief would come through a modification of the AFDC and the AFDC-U federal matching requirement. This matching rate would be based on the Medicaid matching rate in that year. This rate would be increased by 20, 40, and 60 percent, respectively, in the years 1980–1982, providing ever-increasing amounts of fiscal relief to states for those years.

The hold-harmless provision applies only to the administration and the subcommittee bills. It is designed to protect the states from incurring increased expenditures from the transition to the new program. It does this by placing a ceiling—the "hold-harmless limit"— on what states will be obliged to spend.

This hold-harmless limit includes: (a) 90 percent of all nonfederal expenditure for payments in the AFDC, SSI, state supplement, emergency assistance, and general assistance programs; and (b) 100 percent of the state's emergency needs allotment. This limit would be adjusted upward for inflation since 1977 in both programs. However, the administration bill would adjust the limit still further upward by increasing the inflation-adjusted limit by an additional 10, 30, and 50 percent in the years 1983–1985.

In contrast, the subcommittee bill decreases the inflation-adjusted limit downward by 5 percent in the years 1983–1985. It also extends the inflation-adjusted hold-harmless limit beyond 1985 while PBJI specifies no hold-harmless limit beyond 1985. This difference in hold-harmless limits would result in a larger amount of fiscal relief from the subcommittee bill, other things being equal.

Allowable expenditures, from which the hold-harmless limit is deducted to determine the federal hold-harmless payment, include:

1. The state contribution toward supplementation of the minimum federal payment
2. State payments toward wage supplements in the jobs program
3. State payments to "grandfather" AFDC and SSI beneficiaries so that they do not lose benefits under the new program—either because they lose eligibility or because they get paid smaller benefits
4. State expenditures for emergency needs

The Congressional Budget Office prepared detailed estimates of the impact of the administration's program on the state and local share of the costs of relevant public aid programs, delineating the effects of various provisions of the bill (Table 5-9). Fiscal relief is defined as the difference between the state and local share of costs under the current system and the state and local share of costs under PBJI. The major elements operating to reduce fiscal relief are the requirements for localities to match federal supplements and to

Table 5-9. Fiscal Impact of PBJI on State and Local Governments under Alternative Supplementation Assumptions in Fiscal Year 1982: In Billions of Dollars

	Costs under Assumption of:		
State and Local Share of:	*No Supplementation* [a]	*Matching Supplementation Only*	*Matching and Grandfathering Supplementation*
Current Welfare System	11.91	11.91	11.91
PBJI Program			
10% basic federal benefit [b]	1.79	1.96	2.03
Matching supplements	—	3.66	3.67
Wage supplements	—	0.62	0.58
SSI and AFDC grandfathering	—	—	3.04
Administrative costs	—	—	0.33
Federal tax reimbursements	—	0.06	0.06
Federal hold-harmless payments	—	(0.18)	(1.08)
Offsets [c]	0.17	(0.01)	(0.14)
Total State and Local PBJI Costs	1.96	6.11	8.49
Fiscal Relief [d]	9.95	5.80	3.42

Source: Congressional Budget Office, *Welfare Reform Proposal*, p. 52.
[a] Assumes no maintenance of effort requirement.
[b] Except for states in which 10 percent of the basic federal benefit exceeds 90 percent of the state's current maintenance of effort inflated to fiscal year 1982.
[c] Offsets include indirect cost offsets and changes in revenue sources.
[d] Estimates assume no substitution of special public service employment expenditure for other state and local spending.

"grandfathering" former AFDC and SSI recipients who would lose benefits under the new program. Federal assumption of these responsibilities would increase fiscal relief from $3.4 billion to almost $10 billion, leaving localities with slightly less than $2 billion in expenditure burden.

The regional distribution of fiscal relief is summarized in Table 5–10. It shows that the major beneficiaries of the fiscal relief provided

Table 5-10. Fiscal Impact of PBJI on State and Local Governments by Region under Alternative Supplementation Assumptions in Fiscal Year 1982: In Billions of Dollars[a]

Region[b]	Costs under Assumption of:		
	No Supplementation[c]	Matching Supplementation Only	Matching and Grandfathering Supplementation
Current State and Local Welfare Expenditures			
South	1.45	1.45	1.45
West	3.58	3.58	3.58
Northeast	4.05	4.05	4.05
North Central	2.83	2.83	2.83
Total	11.91	11.91	11.91
State and Local PBJI Costs			
South	0.69	0.84	1.08
West	0.36	1.84	2.65
Northeast	0.49	2.15	2.83
Northeast Central	0.42	1.29	1.92
Total	1.96	6.11	8.49
Fiscal Relief			
South	0.76	0.61	0.37
West	3.22	1.74	0.93
Northeast	3.56	1.90	1.22
North Central	2.41	1.54	0.91
Total	9.95	5.80	3.42

Source: Congressional Budget Office, *Welfare Reform Proposal*, p. 54.
[a]Figures may not add to totals because of rounding.
[b]Regions of the country are the four major census regions as follows: Northeast—Connecticut, Maine, Massachusetts, New Hampshire, Rhode Island, Vermont, New Jersey, New York, Pennsylvania. North Central—Illinois, Indiana, Michigan, Ohio, Wisconsin, Iowa, Kansas, Minnesota, Missouri, Nebraska, North Dakota, South Dakota. South—Delaware, District of Columbia, Florida, Georgia, Maryland, North Carolina, South Carolina, Virginia, West Virginia, Alabama, Kentucky, Mississippi, Tennessee, Arkansas, Louisiana, Oklahoma, Texas. West—Arizona, Colorado, Idaho, Montana, Nevada, New Mexico, Utah, Wyoming, Alaska, California, Hawaii, Oregon, Washington.
[c]Assumes no maintenance of effort requirement.

by PBJI would be governments located outside of the South. It also shows that further federal assumption of the welfare burden (by assuming the local costs of grandfathering and state supplementation) would further benefit governments located in the North and West. Governments in the South stand to gain little from federalization of welfare for a number of reasons: (a) their share of costs are relatively low under the current program; (b) their incentives to provide state supplementation will be low since most currently pay less than the federal standard; and for the same reason, (c) their need to grandfather will be small.

Two aspects of proposals to reform the welfare system by complete federal takeover are critical in assessing their fiscal impact for states and localities: (1) the levels at which federal eligibility and payment standards are set, compared to those currently prevailing in the individual states; and (2) the nature of the requirements established and the kinds of opportunities and incentives offered for state supplementation.[11] A high basic federal benefit would provide little incentive to supplement for states that currently pay generous benefits—primarily, large, industrial states—and therefore would offer these states substantial amounts of fiscal relief. A low basic federal benefit might force these high-benefit states to supplement and maintain a substantial part of their current welfare spending to prevent their current beneficiaries from losing, thus providing these states little fiscal relief. Any plan to establish a national benefit standard at or above the average benefit level under current state programs would provide large sums of new federal money to states with below-average benefit standards—mainly Southern states. It does not seem likely that Congress will enact a plan providing for full federal assumption of the costs of the high-benefit programs in the urban Northeast without providing similar benefits to poor people in other states. It also seems unlikely that Congress would be willing to assume the costs of a high-benefit program for the entire nation. Under these circumstances, complete federal asumption of costs seems unlikely and some role for state supplementation seems inevitable, implying that the fiscal relief for the northern urban states that might be derived from welfare reform will be only some fraction of the current state and local costs of these programs. The four proposals discussed earlier seem to confirm this prognosis.

Currently, welfare reform efforts were abandoned by Congress for the remainder of the 1977–1978 session after an attempt to construct a coalition of support around the Ullman bill failed. Residual efforts persist, however, efforts such as the proposal by Senators Moynihan and Cranston for a federal takeover of the AFDC program, an act that would redound to the great benefit of high-payment states such as New York and California. However, it appears likely that efforts will be made to resurrect the Ullman bill in the 1978–1979 session of Congress.

The amount of fiscal relief that welfare reform would provide to cities would depend on decisions made in each state about the division of total fiscal relief between the state and the locality. It has been shown that full federal takeover would provide substantial relief to six major cities: Baltimore, Denver, New York, Philadelphia, San Francisco, and Washington, D.C.[12] It would also provide relief to a scattering of smaller cities and to certain urban counties. However, these gains would be conditional, depending on the reactions of their respective state governments. The relief would be smaller if states cut back on their own aid to localities, if they imposed the costs of supplementation onto cities, or if they lowered the taxing authority of cities by an amount commensurate with the reduced local responsibility to finance welfare.

To conclude, current federal initiatives to reform the welfare program, while providing for valuable improvements by a more equitable distribution of benefits and better incentives for work behavior and family stability, do not offer much in potential fiscal relief to cities as reduced expenditure burdens for public assistance programs. Since this is not the major objective of these programs, it should not raise obstacles to the enactment of such reforms. Fiscal relief for cities, however, will have to be generated through other programs.

NOTES

1. Philip Booth, *Social Security in America*, 3rd ed., Policy Papers in Human Resources and Industrial Relations, No. 19 (Ann Arbor: Institute of Labor and Industrial Relations, The University of Michigan-Wayne State University, March 1976), pp. 9–14.

2. For a discussion of other poverty measures, see U.S. Department of Health, Education, and Welfare, The Measure of Poverty, April 1976.

3. *Social Security Bulletin, Annual Statistical Supplement*, 1975, p. 46.

4. U.S. Congress, Joint Economic Committee, Subcommittee on Fiscal Policy, *Handbook on Public Income Transfer Programs: 1975*, Studies in Public Welfare, Paper No. 20 (Washington, D.C.: U.S. Government Printing Office, December 1974), pp. 151, 165.

5. Ibid.

6. The 1971 costs of a program providing a guarantee of $5,500 for a family of four with a 19 percent marginal tax rate on earnings was estimated to be $71 billion, including some $20 billion in tax loss. Jodie T. Allen, *Perspectives on Income Maintenance: Where Do We Go From Here and How Far?* Urban Institute Paper No. 805-2 (Washington, D.C.: The Urban Institute, April 1972), p 3.

7. Edward K. Hamilton and Francine Rabinovitz, "Federalization of Welfare: The Financial Effects," in George Peterson, ed., *Fiscal Choices* (Washington, D.C.: U.S. Government Printing Office, 1977), p. 106.

8. Stephen M. Barro, *The Urban Impacts of Federal Policies*, Rand Corporation Report, R-2114-KF/HEW (Santa Monica, Calif.: The Rand Corporation, April 1978), pp. 74-75, 86-87; Hamilton and Rabinovitz, "Federalization of Welfare."

9. Barbara Boland, "Participation in the Aid to Families with Dependent Children Program (AFDC)," in *The Family, Poverty, and Welfare Programs: Factors Influencing Family Instability*, Studies in Public Welfare, Subcommittee on Fiscal Policy of the Joint Economic Committee, Paper, No. 12 (Part I) (Washington, D.C.: U.S. Government Printing Office, November 1973), pp. 139-179. See especially p. 153.

10. Frank Levy, "The Harried Staffer's Guide to Current Welfare Reform Proposals," Urban Institute Working Paper, No. 996-7 (Washington, D.C.: The Urban Institute, May 1978).

11. Barro, *Urban Impacts*, pp. 95-96.

12. Hamilton and Rabinovitz, "Federalization of Welfare."

Chapter 6

Countercyclical Public Works Programs

Georges Vernez
Roger J. Vaughan

Increased public expenditures on construction activities have long been part of governments' response to cyclical increases in the unemployment rate or to persistent pockets of high unemployment. Imperial Rome may have been the first to increase spending on road and aqueduct building to alleviate the impact of economic recessions. In the United States, the 1930s depression marked the first use of federal public works expenditures to provide temporary work relief to needy unemployed people. The Local Public Works (LPW) program implemented in response to the national recession that began in late 1973 is the most recent example of a public works program designed to stimulate the national economy.

This chapter reviews the extensive national experience with countercyclical public works programs. It summarizes what is known about the effectiveness of these programs in providing jobs for the cyclically unemployed, identifies possible adverse effects, and compares their performances with other types of countercyclical fiscal policies, particularly public service employment programs. Knowledge about these programs is often fragmented and sometimes contradictory. Systematic evaluation efforts have only recently been undertaken, but the full effects of the ongoing Local Public Works program will not be felt for some years.

The remainder of this section provides a brief historical account of countercyclical public works programs, their provisions, and objectives. The second section documents the distribution of countercyclical public works funds among states and assesses the extent to which it matches the distribution of cyclical unemployed. The effectiveness of public works programs in creating jobs is discussed in the third section. The last section focuses on five issues relevant to the use of public works in national stabilization policy: displacement of local capital expenditures by federal funds; delays in program formulation and implementation; targeting on the disadvantaged; value of services provided; and likelihood of encountering bottlenecks in the supply of labor or materials.

Brief History[1]

The 1930s depression marked the beginning of federal assistance for those unemployed because of a reduction in the level of aggregate economic activity. From 1933 to 1942, a decade during which the national unemployment rate did not fall below 13 percent, the federal government spent about $19 billion in the form of countercyclical public works and public service employment programs (see Table 6-1).[2] Two of these programs—the Emergency Administration of Public Works (PWA), aimed at job creation through construction of public facilities, and the Works Progress Administration (WPA), aimed at reducing relief rolls by giving unemployed workers temporary jobs—have been the most extensive public hiring programs ever. The PWA program employed some 600,000 workers at its peak in 1934, and the WPA employed over three million at its peak in 1936.[3]

Since the end of World War II in 1945, the national economy has experienced five classical cycles with troughs in 1948, 1954, 1961, 1970, and 1975[4] (Mintz, 1974; Vernez et al., 1977). However, it was not until the recession in early 1960 that the first postwar countercyclical public works program was implemented. During 1962 and 1963 about $1.7 billion was expended by the Accelerated Public Works program (APW). The first postwar countercyclical public employment program, the Public Employment Program (PEP), created by the Emergency Employment Act, was not implemented until 1971. The 1970-1971 recession also marks the first time since World War II that federal countercyclical policies provided for a combination of public works and public service employment programs, a strategy repeated during the latest recession. Table 6-1 shows that the outlays in these programs were generally proportional with the amplitude of the cycles. But in no postwar cycle were the outlays sufficient to provide job opportunities for more than 10 percent of those idled by reduction in the levels of aggregated economic activity.

Post-World War II expenditures on countercyclical public works or public service employment programs have been a small component of total .countercyclical expenditures. For example, during the recent recession of 1974-1975, countercyclical public works outlays have constituted about 5 percent of estimated total countercyclical outlays. As Table 6-2 shows, the bulk of these outlays have been in the form of tax reductions and automatic stabilizers such as unemployment compensation and public assistance.

Annual outlays on countercyclical public works programs have also been small compared to regular outlays in public construction. APW spent a total $1.7 billion by 1964 compared to $20 billion in public construction in 1964 alone. Similarly, the Public Works Impact Program (PWIP) spent $69 million in 1972 compared to more than $30 billion spent on regular public construction during the same year.[5]

There are a number of possible reasons for the sporadic reliance on public works and public service employment programs. First, despite the real achievement of the 1930s programs,[6] their popular image remains as an inefficient "make work" activity. Second, the use of macroeconomic policies—the control of the total stock of money and the aggregate federal deficit—has been preferred. Third, there has been a rapid increase in the importance of automatic countercyclical relief programs, including Social Security, unemployment insurance, and welfare, which has reduced the political pressure for direct job creation programs. Fourth, postwar recessions have been comparatively mild and of short duration, leading to a concern that public works programs could not be implemented rapidly enough to provide countercyclical stimuli.

Program Provisions

Over the years, the federal share of public works investments has increased. The first program, the Emergency Relief and Construction Act of 1933, provided only low-interest loans to state and local governments. As the depression grew longer and deeper, the federal government assumed greater financing responsibility both by undertaking direct federal construction and by increasing the federal share of locally financed construction projects from 30 percent to 45 percent. The federal share increased to 50-75 percent under the APW program during the early 1960s and to 80-100 percent under the PWIP in the early 1970s; it finally reached 100 percent under the present LPW program.

The responsibility for the administration and implementation of countercyclical public works programs has been decentralized over time. The early public works programs of the 1930s were controlled,

Table 6-1. Major Countercyclical PW and PSE Programs Since 1930

Recession Years	Annual Average Amplitude[a]	Public Works		Public Service Employment	
		Description	Outlays ($billions)	Description	Outlays
1933–1942 (Depression)	9.3	Emergency Relief and Construction Act (fiscal year 1933)	0.30[b]		
		Federal Civil Works Administration (CWA, fiscal year 1934)	0.95		
		Emergency Work Relief Program (EWRP, fiscal years 1934–1935)	1.30		
		Emergency Administration of Public Works (PWA, fiscal years 1934–1938)	6.08[c]	Works Progress Administration (WPA, fiscal years 1936–1942)	9.58[d]
1960–1961	2.5	Accelerated Public Works Program (APW, fiscal years 1962–1963)	1.70[e]		
1970–1971	2.5	Public Works Impact Program (PWIP, fiscal years 1972–1973)	0.13	Emergency Employment Act (PEP, fiscal years 1972–1974)	1.62
1974–Present	NA	Local Public Works Program (LPWP, fiscal year 1977)	2.00[f]	Comprehensive Employment and Training Act[g]	
				CETA I, II, III (fiscal years 1975–1977)	1.94
				CETA VI (fiscal years 1975–1977)	4.00

Sources: William J. Tobin, *Public Works and Unemployment: A History of Federally Funded Programs*, U.S. Economic Development Administration, January 1975; *Special Analyses Budget of the United States Government*, Office of Management and Budget, fiscal year 1974, fiscal year 1975, fiscal year 1977, fiscal year 1978; Georges Vernez et al., *Regional Cycles and Employment Effects of Public Works Investments*, The Rand Corporation, R–2052–EDA, January 1977.

Note: NA means not available.

[a] Defined as

$$\frac{1}{2} \left(\frac{\text{Employment at Initial Downturn minus Employment at Upturn}}{\text{Number of Years of Decline}} + \frac{\text{Employment at End Peak minus Employment at Upturn}}{\text{Number of Years of Rise}} \right) \Big/ \text{Cycle Base}$$

where cycle base is defined as the average monthly employment over the cycle.

[b] Another $1–1/2 billion was also made available for financing self-liquidating PW projects—i.e., projects whose costs could be recouped within a reasonable period through use changes. This fund was not used and eventually transferred to other uses.

[c] Include state and local share. Federal share was approximately $.82 billion.

[d] Include federal and state and local shares. The initial fiscal year 1936 allocation was $4.38 billion.

[e] Include an initial fiscal year 1973 allocation of $3.3 billion.

[f] Allocation. An estimated $0.8 billion is expected to be outlayed in fiscal year 1977.

[g] Include only outlays in the public service employment component of the CETA.

Table 6-2. Estimated Outlays of Planned and Automatic Countercyclical Programs: 1974 to 1977 (in billions)

Program Type	Expansion Year 1974	Recession Years			Increase from 1974		
		1975	1976	1977[a]	1975	1976	1977[a]
Planned Countercyclical Programs							
Public works[b]	0.04	—	—	1.28	—	—	1.24
Public service employment[c]	0.55	1.26	2.75	2.83	0.71	2.20	2.28
Tax deductions[d]	—	10.56	10.70	—	10.50	10.70	—
Revenue sharing[e]	—	—	—	1.25	—	—	—
Subtotal	0.59	11.76	13.45	5.36	11.21	12.90	4.77
Automatic Countercyclical Programs							
Unemployment insurance	5.21	12.22	17.61	14.28	7.01	12.40	9.07
Public assistance[f]	6.83	8.67	9.80	10.18	1.84	2.97	3.35
Food stamps	2.73	4.36	5.27	4.39	1.63	2.54	1.66
Subtotal	14.77	25.25	32.68	28.85	10.48	17.91	14.08
Manpower Programs[g]	3.44	4.60	5.48	6.18	1.16	2.04	2.74
Total	18.80	41.61	51.61	40.39	22.81	32.81	21.59

Sources: *Special Analyses Budget of the United States Government,* Office of Management and Budget, fiscal year 1977, fiscal year 1978; *The Budget of the United States Government,* Office of Management and Budget, fiscal year 1975, fiscal year 1977, and fiscal year 1978; *Summary of Administration's Economic Stimulus Program and Summary of Tax Deductions in 1976 and 1976,* Joint Committee on Taxation for the Committee on Ways and Means, February 1, 1977.

Notes: Figures may not add to totals because of rounding.

[a] Estimated outlays.

[b] Includes the Public Works Impact Program (1974 appropriation), the Local Public Works Program, and additional grants for construction of waste treatment plants under the Environmental Protection Agency (1977 estimated outlays).

[c] Includes the public service employment portion of the Emergency Employment Assistance (1974, 1975); Comprehensive Manpower Assistance, CETA Titles I, II, III (1975, 1976, 1977); Temporary Employment Assistance, CETA VI (1975, 1976, 1977); Job Opportunities Program (1975, 1976, 1977); and Work Incentives (1974 to 1977).

[d] Includes the refund of 1974 taxes to individuals (1975), increase in standard deductions (1975, 1976), general tax credit (1975, 1976); earned income credit (1976); tax credit for home purchase (1976); investment tax credit (1975, 1976); and corporate tax rate deductions (1975, 1976).

[e] "Countercyclical" revenue-sharing assistance to state and local governments (1977 appropriations).

[f] Includes AFDC, AFDC-UF, and SSI.

[g] Includes all federal training and employment programs other than public service employment: on-the-job training; institutional training; vocational rehabilitation; work experience; and labor market services.

coordinated, and administered by specially created federal agencies —mainly the PWA and WPA[7]—with the authority to implement their own projects as well as to make grants to state and local governments. Implementation of these programs was the sole responsibility of these special agencies. Under the post-World War II public works program, legislated authority for implementation of direct federal construction projects was limited (APW) or nonexistent (PWIP and LPW). Only projects sponsored by state and local governments were implemented. Coordination and administration control were the responsibility of federal agencies (Area Redevelopment Administration for APW, Economic Development Administration for the PWIP and LPW programs) with other responsibilities.

Participation in prewar programs was restricted to those unemployed and on relief, a restriction eventually relaxed to include those unemployed not on relief. In the postwar period, there has been no restriction on those eligible to work on public works programs. Construction has typically been subcontracted to private contractors subject to no special restrictions on hirees.

Most past programs have placed some form of wage limitations on participants. Programs in the early 1930s set wages and number of work hours in such a way as to make up for each individual's means-tested deficit. Later, a minimum wage was set low enough not to be competitive with private sector wages but high enough to provide earnings above a minimum living standard.[8] Consistent with the Davis-Bacon Act, the wages provided for in postwar programs have been commensurate with the prevailing wages in the areas where projects were implemented. No maximum wage ceiling was imposed on public works program participants.

Some provisions remain unchanged. Except for a short period during the 1930 recession, all programs have emphasized that "to the extent possible" jobs should be created in occupations or activities for which private and public demand was expanding. They were not to be "make work" or "dead-end" jobs. Jobs were also not to compete with private sector jobs. Finally, they were not to replace jobs or activities that would have been undertaken by state and local governments without the programs. Maintenance of effort provisions were included in most of the legislative enabling acts although these provisions are nearly impossible to enforce.

Goals
Generally, there is agreement that the main objective of counter-cyclical public works programs has been to provide jobs for those who are underemployed or unemployed because of economic re-

cession (Bakke, 1972; NPA, 1974; Tobin, 1975; Wiseman, 1976). This objective underlines the temporary nature of such programs. In addition to this primary objective, these programs have sought to meet other secondary objectives: providing productive jobs from the point of view of both the economy and the workers involved (Bakke, 1972; NPA, 1974); maintaining and developing human resources in readiness for the renewal of economic growth; increasing the quantity and quality of public infrastructure; and targeting on areas and social groups most affected by recessions— the disadvantaged or the unskilled. These objectives are not necessarily compatible. For instance, the creation of jobs that are productive may be relatively expensive and require skilled rather than unskilled labor.

Undesirable effects arise because the goals of countercyclical programs may conflict with the national goal of efficiency. First, financing the program may divert funds from private use. Second, because these programs stress rapid job creation, projects with a low benefit-to-cost ratio may be selected. And third, the demand for labor, materials, and supplies required by the programs may impose excessive demands on certain occupational groups and industries leading to "bottlenecks" and price or wage increases. This chapter explores the degree to which past countercyclical public works programs have met the above objectives and to what degree they have resulted in undesirable effects.

DISTRIBUTION OF COUNTERCYCLICAL PUBLIC WORKS FUNDS

The incidence of cyclical unemployment varies among states, labor market areas, cities, and neighborhoods. The extent to which the distribution of countercyclical public works targets on areas with relatively high cyclical unemployment is of interest from three viewpoints. First, the social cost of the program will tend to be lower; second, the probability of encountering bottlenecks in the availability of labor and materials will be less; and, finally, the equity of the program may be perceived to be greater if the jobs generated are distributed in proportion to local cyclical unemployment.

Unfortunately, there is no general agreement about how to measure cyclical unemployment. The difficulty is that cyclical unemment must be separated from three other types of unemployment: structural, frictional, and institutional (Vaughan, 1976). Three approaches to this separating of cyclical unemployment have been used. The first has been to define a "full employment rate of unemployment" and to measure cyclical unemployment as the difference between this benchmark and the actual rate. However, there is no consensus about the full employment rate. The second approach has been to assume that cyclical unemployment is proportional to total unemployment. This concept has been used in allocating funds under all countercyclical public works programs. The third approach has been to measure cyclical unemployment as the deviation of actual employment levels at cycle trough from the level at preceding cycle peak or from a long-term moving average. It is shown below that the allocation of countercyclical funds would differ substantially depending on whether the second or third approach to measuring cyclical unemployment is used. As background to this discussion, the nature of the variations in cyclical behavior among geographical areas is addressed first.

Geographical Distribution of
Cyclical Unemployment[9]

Although all regions are affected by the national business cycle, they differ according to the timing of their cycles, their amplitude, and responsiveness.

Timing.   There is some evidence of consistent lead and lag behavior in local areas for changes in local and national monthly employment growth rates. Labor market areas (LMAs) in the Northeast and North Central regions tend to lag behind the nation, while LMAs in the South Central and West are inclined to lead the nation. Large urban areas tend to coincide more closely with the nation than do small areas. For actual turning points, however, there is no distinct regional pattern. Neither is there consistency from cycle to cycle in the states and LMAs that have led or lagged the nation at upturn and downturn.

Amplitude.   The extent or amplitude of regional cyclical response may be measured by the absolute change in local employment from peak to trough. Analysis of the past cyclical behavior of states and LMAs reveals a number of facts.

The amplitude of local cycles and the variation among areas have declined steadily since the beginning of this century (Borts, 1960). The latest 1974–1977 cycle represents a deviation from this trend. There is no consistent regional pattern from cycle to cycle. A region that experiences a relatively large relative amplitude in one cycle may not do so in the following cycle. Overall, however, areas experiencing high relative amplitudes tend to be located in the Northeast and the west north central regions.

Responsiveness. Responsiveness measures the extent to which local employment growth changes in response to a change in the national rate of employment growth. For this measure, there is also a distinct regional pattern. LMAs located in the Northeast tend to be highly responsive to changes in the national employment growth rate. For these areas, a change of 1 percent in the national growth rate of employment will lead to a greater than 1 percent change in local growth. Unresponsive areas are clustered in the mountain, western, and west north central regions.

Reasons for Regional Variation. Regions differ in their cyclical response for a number of reasons. First, the higher the share of regional employment in consumer durables, the greater the tendency for that region to lead the national cycle and to experience a large cycle amplitude. However, differences in industrial composition among regions have played a diminishing role in explaining inter-areas differences in cyclical behavior. Differences in the behavior of a given industry in different regions—intraindustry variations—are of much greater importance. Second, a high growth region tends to experience less severe contractions, to be less responsive to national changes, and to enjoy a low average unemployment rate. However, the theory of the mechanism by which secular growth affects cyclical behavior has not been developed. Third, in areas with high secular employment growth and with low average unemployment, cyclical fluctuations tend to be lower.

Distribution of Public Works
Program Expenditures

The regional effects of a countercyclical program depend, first, upon how the funds are allocated among regions, and second, upon how the jobs—including induced jobs—created by the program are distributed among regions. While the first issue is relatively simple to answer, the second cannot be answered with precision.

In Table 6-3, the allocation of funds by states for the three most recent countercyclical public works programs—Public Works Impact Program (PWIP) and local Public Works program (LPW), Rounds I and II—is compared with (1) the number of cyclically unemployed, to determine how well the distribution has matched cyclical unemployment problems; and (2) the total number of employed, to determine how well the distribution has matched local aggregate unemployment problems. State means and standard deviations have been calculated for each of these measures.

There are considerable variations among states in the dollar amounts allocated per unemployed. As may be seen in Table 6-3,

Table 6-3. Allocation of Public Works Funds Per Cyclically Unemployed and Unemployed Persons by State, 1972 and 1976

Region[a] and State	PWIP Project Cost Per Cyclically Unemployed Person[b]	PWIP Project Cost Per Unemployed person, 1971[c]	LPW I Obligations Per Cyclically Unemployed Person[b]	LPW I Obligations Per Unemployed Person, 1975[c]	LPW II Allocation Per Cyclically Unemployed Person[d]	LPW II Allocation Per Unemployed Person
Region I						
Connecticut	39	16	676	356	1120	580
Maine	87	16	507	227	1503	716
Massachusetts	67	24	1049	153	2672	508
New Hampshire	115	47	887	394	2727	1200
Rhode Island	30	11	668	246	1314	901
Vermont	32	8	1188	435	3750	1579
Region II[e]						
New Jersey	46	7	577	306	1262	633
New York	11	6	719	296	1548	622
Region III						
Delaware	82	33	618	434	1878	1307
Maryland	S	15	843	149	1637	307
Pennsylvania	28	15	473	184	1031	449
Virginia	S	12	489	149	879	297
West Virginia	S	58	771	202	2308	588
Washington, D.C.	S	28	S	369	S	400
Region IV						
Alabama	353	29	391	145	696	334
Florida	S	10	575	66	670	501
Georgia	S	15	281	123	661	428
Kentucky	S	23	603	140	1154	370
Mississippi	S	33	296	143	911	514
North Carolina	S	8	301	122	489	286
South Carolina	S	42	208	105	458	348
Tennessee	302	36	380	159	464	278

Region V						
Illinois	11	5	330	155	463	270
Indiana	7	S	151	109	266	270
Michigan	26	12	775	282	1048	572
Minnesota	25	5	290	159	529	279
Ohio	12	5	285	146	1274	425
Wisconsin	49	22	619	147	995	285
Region VI						
Arkansas	S	55	245	136	714	484
Louisiana	73	14	1241	215	1733	343
New Mexico	S	37	S	300	S	957
Oklahoma	108	19	S	230	S	784
Texas	S	11	1115	171	1825	287
Region VII						
Iowa	14	3	735	153	1875	566
Kansas	13	7	387	193	1164	658
Missouri	72	17	275	128	523	275
Nebraska	S	6	S	256	S	1272
Region VIII						
Colorado	S	20	440	198	1092	431
Montana	S	54	S	376	S	1649
North Dakota	na	20	na	700	na	3000
South Dakota	S	68	1495	738	4971	3163
Wyoming	S	102	4968	1263	15,000	4286
Utah	76	11	1771	269	5047	1044
Region IX						
Arizona	S	14	412	145	2532	671
California	27	6	1589	269	3057	540
Hawaii	f	f	na	375	na	771
Nevada	S	10	S	348	S	1169
Region X						
Alaska	na	54	na	464	na	3507
Idaho	S	24	S	379	S	1456
Oregon	64	15	1176	275	2269	556
Washington	22	11	4628	284	6802	578

Table 6-3.   continued

Region[a] and State	PWIP		LPW I		LPW II	
	Project Cost Per Cyclically Unemployed Person[b]	Project Cost Per Unemployed person, 1971[c]	Obligations Per Cyclically Unemployed Person[b]	Obligations Per Unemployed Person, 1975[c]	Allocation Per Cyclically Unemployed Person[d]	Allocation Per Unemployed Person
National mean	62	13	740	223	2381	1799
Mean for states	66.3	22.6	869.0	274.5	2008	857
Standard deviation for states	82.6	19.7	982.1	204.2	2497	865
Ratio standard deviation to mean	1.23	0.87	1.13	0.74	1.24	1.01

Sources: Georges Vernez et al., *Regional Cycles and Employment Effects of Public Works Investments*, The Rand Corporation, R-2052-EDA, January 1977; *Employment and Training Report of the President 1976*, Washington, D.C., 1976; *Federal Register*, Vol. 41, No. 248, December 1976; Anthony J. Sulvetta and Norman L. Thompson, *An Evaluation of the Public Works Impact Program (PWIP) Final Report*, Economic Development Administration, U.S. Department of Commerce, April 1975.

Notes: na means data unavailable on state absolute amplitude; S means state skipped cycle.

[a] Regions correspond to CETA region definitions.

[b] Total project cost (PWIP) or obligations (LPWP) divided by the number of cyclically unemployed. Cyclically unemployed defined by absolute amplitude of employment cycle, 1970–1971 for PWIP, 1974–1975 for LPWP, from Vernez et al. (1977), Table C.5.

[c] Total project cost (PWIP) or obligations (LPWP) divided by the number of unemployed, defined as the annual average level of unemployment for each state (ETRP, 1976).

[d] Weighted by the state's share of total national cyclical unemployment or by state's share of total national unemployment.

[e] Excludes Puerto Rico.

[f] Hawaii received no PWIP funds.

under the PWIP program $62 was allocated per cyclically unemployed person nationally and $13 per unemployed person. The corresponding allocations of LPW I obligations are $740 per cyclically unemployed and $223 per unemployed, and for LPW II, $2,381 and $1,799. The range among states is considerable—Hawaii received no PWIP allocations, while Alabama received $353 per cyclically unemployed. Wyoming received $1,263 per unemployed person under LPW I and $4,286 under LPW II, while Florida received only $66 and $501, respectively. The allocation among states is more uniform for total unemployed than for cyclically unemployed for PWIP and both rounds of the LPW program. For instance, the ratio of standard deviation to mean equals 0.74 per total unemployed compared to 1.13 per cyclically unemployed for LPW I, and 1.24 per cyclically unemployed compared to 1.01 per unemployed for LPW II. This is to be expected since total unemployment rather than cyclical unemployment was considered in fund allocation.

PWIP projects were concentrated in small towns and rural areas. Towns with populations of less than 25,000 and rural areas received over 60 percent of total funds allocated although they comprised less than 48 percent of the population (Table 6-4). By contrast, large cities with populations in excess of 100,000, in which nearly 28 percent of the nation's populations lived, received only 12 percent of the funds.

The Local Public Works program was much more heavily concentrated in larger areas: those with populations in excess of 100,000 received 30.3 percent of the allocations under LPW I and 35.4 percent under LPW II. By contrast, areas with populations less than 25,000 received only 40.7 percent of LPW I funds and 32.8 percent of LPW II funds (Table 6-4).

Spillover Effects. Not all public works funds allocated to a specific area benefit this area. The demand for materials as well as the induced demand for goods and services will be felt in other areas where the supplying industries are located. The distribution of these demands is difficult to anticipate.[10] Some measure of the degree of such spillover effects can be inferred from the employment multipliers calculated by Vernez and others (1977). While they estimated that there would be 0.2 job created within a labor market area for each on-site job created, there would be three jobs created in the nation as a whole. Thus, contrary to widely accepted belief, the ability of public works to serve local cyclical needs may be limited. To some extent, indirect jobs may be created in the high cyclical amplitude supplying industries, which tend to be concentrated in the Northeast and in the north central regions.

Table 6-4.   Distribution of PWIP, LPWI, and LPW II by Population of Recipient Area

Population (thousands)	Percent of U.S. Population 1970[a]	PWIP		LPW I		LPW II	
		Percent of EDA Funds	Concentration[b]	Percent of EDA Funds[c]	Concentration[b]	Percent of EDA Funds[c]	Concentration[b]
< 2.5	26.9[d]	12.6	0.47	10.8	0.40	6.6	0.24
2.5–24.9	20.8	48.2	2.32	29.9	1.44	26.2	1.26
25.0–49.9	8.8	15.8	0.79	10.8	1.23	10.6	1.20
50.0–97.7	8.2	11.9	1.45	8.1	0.99	11.7	1.42
> 100	27.8	12.2	0.44	30.3	1.09	35.4	1.27

Source: Anthony J. Sulvetta and Norman L. Thompson, *An Evaluation of the Public Works Impact Program*, U.S. Department of Commerce, Washington, D.C., April 1975, p. AP. B-12; Bureau of the Census, *Statistical Abstract of the United States, 1975*, U.S. Department of Commerce, Washington, D.C., 1976; and Economic Development Administration, *Local Public Works Program: Status Report*, U.S. Department of Commerce, January 1978.

[a]Total does not add to 100 because of omission of those living in unincorporated parts of urban areas.

[b]Defined as the percent of EDA costs divided by percent of U.S. population.

[c]Excludes funds allocated to Multiareas or for which no data were available (6.0 percent for LPW I; 6.5 percent for LPW II) and also Indian and territorial projects.

[d]Percent of U.S. population living in urban areas with populations less than 3,000 and entire U.S. rural population.

JOB CREATION

Gross short-run employment generated by a countercyclical public works program is the sum of three types of jobs:

Direct employment is created by the expenditure of public funds in the form of wages to on-site labor for public works (PW) and to public employees for public service employment (PSE).

Indirect employment is created in industries supplying the program with materials, supplies, and services.

Induced employment results from the consumption expenditures by those workers directly and indirectly employed by the projects and by the major supplying industries.[11]

Distinction between these three types of employment effects is important for several reasons. First, each type of job will be created with a different lag following program implementation. Direct and indirect jobs will be the first created, and the speed of their creation can be in part controlled by program administrators.

Second, as suggested in the preceding section, the geographical distribution of the jobs is likely to differ among the three types. Direct jobs are more likely to be filled by labor located in the area in which the public funds are spent. Indirect and induced jobs will be generated in areas where the industries producing the goods and services necessary for the projects are located.

Third, while eligibility for direct jobs can be influenced by federal hiring guidelines, other types of jobs are less amenable to selective hiring. Thus, specific groups of unemployed can best be reached by programs with large direct job creation. Fourth, it is possible to anticipate possible bottlenecks in the supply of labor and materials by identifying the indirect employment generated in supplying industries. Projects differ in their demands for materials and supplies. Finally, there is a difference in the degree of accuracy with which the magnitude of different types of job creation may be predicted. Direct employment may be predicted with greater accuracy than indirect and induced employment.

Net job creation may differ from gross job creation if federal borrowing to finance the program results in a reduction of private investments or if state-local governments reduce their own levels of expenditures on receipt of the federal funds. Thus, the net employment created is equal to gross job creation less (a) the decrease in private employment resulting from raising the necessary public funds and (b) the decrease in state and local public employment resulting from the displacement of state and local funds by federal funds.

This section reviews a number of empirical estimates of the direct, indirect, and total short-run employment effects of alternative countercyclical fiscal programs.

Direct and Indirect Job Creation

Direct jobs are those created on site for public works projects. Indirect jobs are those created in industries that provide the goods and services demanded by the public works activities.

Direct Job Creation. Estimates of gross direct job creation per $1 billion of expenditures on public works projects by types are shown in Table 6-5. New public works construction generated an average of between 1.8 and 3.3 on-site jobs per $100,000 of expenditure, while public works projects involving repair and rehabilitation generated between 1.9 and 3.9 jobs per $100,000 of expenditure. Between 20 and 40 percent of expenditures are spent on wages for on-site labor.

There are wide variations in the number of on-site jobs created by different types of new public works construction. On-site labor requirements differ, depending on whether private contractors (bid projects) or local government agencies (force account projects)[12] build the projects. Among PWIP projects, the average force account project generated nearly twice as many on-site jobs (3.2 per $100,000) as the average big project (1.8 per $100,000). This relationship appears to hold for most project types (Sulvetta and Thompson, 1975).

Estimates of the number of jobs that would be created by a specific project type vary widely among the studies reported in Table 6-5. For example, Thompson and Sulvetta (1975) estimated 1.8 jobs per $100,000 would be created by school construction while Vernez and others (1977), estimated 2.7 jobs would be created. The discrepancies are attributable to differences in the way the two studies converted on-site labor requirements into estimates in man-years. Sulvetta and Thompson (1975) divided total hours worked by the average annual number of hours worked in all industries,[13] while Vernez and others (1977) divided the total on-site earnings bill by the average annual wage in the construction industry.[14] Since annual earnings implicitly reflect the number of hours worked in the construction industry, the estimates by Vernez and others do reflect the average annual number of years worked in the construction industry, which is below 1,400 hours a year, well below the average for all industries.[15] If Vernez and others had used the same procedure as Sulvetta and Thompson, the discrepancies in estimated number of man-years created per $1 billion would be small: 18,970 versus

Table 6-5. Estimated Gross Direct and Indirect Employment Effects per $1 Billion of Expenditures on PW or PSE Programs by Type of Projects (in man-years)

Type of Program or Project	Direct Employment[a]			Indirect Employment[b]
	Vernez et al. (1977)	Sulvetta and Thompson (1975)	National Council for UED ((1975)	Vernez et al. (1977)
PUBLIC WORKS, NEW CONSTRUCTION				
Building Construction				
Private-one family housing	19,076			9,022
Public housing	31,947			8,644
Schools	26,987	18,970		10,935
Medical buildings	30,062	24,372		10,178
Nursing homes	29,573			10,404
College housing	33,547			10,564
Federal office buildings	33,280			10,161
Municipal office buildings		18,600		
Multi-purpose municipal buildings		13,754		
Jails and police stations		11,220		
Fire, ambulance or rescue vehicle stations		19,633		
Municipal airport buildings and passenger terminals		25,736		
Heavy Construction				
Highway or roads	20,089	18,595		10,484
Water and sewer lines		21,372		
Water lines		14,080		
Sewer lines	27,295	16,079		10,617
Water/sewer system		27,098		
Sewer plants	29,404			479
Civil works				
Large earth-fill dams	38,578			8,673
Small earth-fill dams	39,271			10,370
Local flood protection	45,396			9,806
Pile dikes	36,987			13,372
Levers	42,991			4,528
Revetments	17,120			24,941
Powerhouse construction	26,444			13,665
Medium concrete dams	43,227			8,442
Lock and concrete dams	32,773			14,621
Large multiple purpose projects	49,351			9,174
Dredging	45,484			6,642
Miscellaneous	34,836			10,240
Others				
Recreational facilities		16,207		
Conservation, beautification		19,992		
Industrial site or parks		14,787		
Sample Average	33,387	18,278	28,150[c]	10,725

PUBLIC WORKS, REPAIRS
AND ADDITIONS

Building additions	15,861	
Building renovations,	17,360	39,050[c]
remodeling and restorations		

Sources: Georgez Vernez et al., *Regional Cycles and Employment Effects of Public Works Investments*, The Rand Corporation, 2-2052-EDA, January 1977; Anthony J. Sulvetta and Norman L. Thompson, *An Evaluation of the Public Works Impact Program (PWIP), Final Report;* Economic Development Administration, U.S. Department of Commerce, April 1975; National Council for Urban Economic Development, "Sample Projects to be Undertaken in Cities if Federal Accelerated Public Works Legislation is Enacted," mimeo, July 14, 1975; Westat, Inc., *Longitudinal Evaluation of the Public Employment Program and Validation of the PEP Data Bank, Final Report,* prepared for the Office of Policy Evaluation and Research, U.S. Department of Labor, April 1975; Congressional Budget Office, *Temporary Measures to Stimulate Employment An Evaluation of Some Alternatives,* U.S. Government Printing Office, September 1975.

Notes: All estimates are of gross employment accounting for no employment substitution due to either the mode of financing or the displacement of state and local expenditures by federal expenditures. Blank means not available.

[a]Direct employment is defined as number of jobs created on site for public works and public service employment.

[b]Indirect employment is defined as number of jobs created in major supplying industries of materials for public works construction. Estimates shown are estimates of jobs increase over present levels (marginal) rather than increase of jobs in average.

[c]From survey of 46 public works projects proposed by eight cities under the Public Works Impact Program.

19,840 for schools; 24,372 versus 21,919 for medical buildings; and 18,595 versus 18,535 for highways and roads. This methodological point highlights the importance of using standard assumptions when converting on-site labor requirements—measured in wages or number of hours worked per $1,000—into equivalents in man-years.

The number of persons that will hold a job under the program is larger than the number of man-years because the average worker may hold a job for less than a year—a man-year could provide jobs for twelve persons working one month each. Under the PWIP program the average duration of employment was one month.[16] Because of the nature of the jobs on public works projects, more than half the workers (58 percent) on the projects sampled held jobs for no more than eighty hours (two weeks) (Sulvetta and Thompson, 1975). High labor turnover on public works projects undermines the ability of a public works program to assure income or skill maintenance during an economic slowdown.

Indirect Job Creation. Estimates of the number of jobs created in major supplying industries, presented in Table 6–5, are available only for new public works construction. The national input-output table was used to convert on-site demands into final demands for the output of major supplying industries. These final demands were then converted into demands for labor, using industry specific marginal ratios of output to employment.[17] The average project generates an estimated 1.1 man-year in supplying industries per $100,000 of expenditure with a range of from 0.9 to 2.4 man-years, depending on the project considered. About one-third of this employment is in manufacturing, one-third in the transportation sector, and one-third in the wholesale and retail trade sector.

In interpreting these estimates, two considerations should be kept in mind. First, little is known about the relationship between a *marginal increase* in output and the *marginal change* in employment in industry at various stages of the business cycle. During a recession, companies may hoard labor or acculumate higher than a "normal" inventory, which permits an increase in output during the recovery with very little corresponding increase in employment. Second, a man-year of indirect employment will not necessarily translate into a full-time job for an unemployed person. Portions of the increased demand for labor may be translated into additional work hours for part-time workers or into overtime for full-time workers. The earnings of these workers would be increased, but no additional employee would be hired. Further research, therefore, is indicated.

Total Job Creation

On-site and indirect employment represent between one-third to one-half of the total gross employment generated by increased public works investments. The remaining jobs results from consumption expenditures of participants and investment expenditures of businesses in response to increased demands.

Estimates of the total number of jobs created per $1 billion of expenditures in public works and four alternative programs—public service employment, government purchases, personal tax cuts, and revenue sharing—are presented in Table 6-6. Also presented is the timing of job creation following initiation of outlays; the initial impact shown is spread over three to six months. For each of these programs there are two, sometimes three, estimates that were based on the use of different models and assumptions. Bezdek and Hannon (1974) calculated the job-creating potential of a number of federal programs using input-output analysis. Their estimates are likely to be too large because they ignore the probability of labor hoarding in material supply industries. The estimates of Vernez and others (1977) are based on a simple forty-five-sector quarterly econometric model

Table 6-6. Estimates of Total Employment Generated by Selected Countercyclical Programs (in man-years)

Type of Program	Source	Increase in Jobs Per $1 Billion		
		Initial Effect	12 Months	24 Months
Public Works				
Corps of Engineers	Bezdek and Hannon (1974)	NA	NA	65,000
Highway				81,000
Railroad and mass transit				84,000
Educational facilities				85,000
Water and waste treatment				82,000
Sewer plant	Vernez et al., (1977)	NA	90,600	108,000
Flood protection			127,000	183,000
Federal office building			42,300	131,000
Accelerated public works[c]	CBO (1975)	16–46,000	56–70,000	64–80,000
	CBO (1975)	80–125,000	90–145,000	90–150,000
Public Service Employment[b]	Johnson and Tomola (1975)	17–111,000	31–126,000	77–162,000
	CBO (1975)	20–50,000	40–70,000	60–80,000
Government Purchases	Johnson and Tomola (1975)	6,000	54,000	99,000
	Bezdek and Hannon (1974)	NA	NA	87,000
Tax Cut[c]	CBO (1975)	12–22,000	39–52,000	45–60,000

	Johnson and Tomola (1975)	CBO (1975)
	51,000	72–100,000
	15,000	70–97,000
Revenue sharing to state and local governments	200	40–77,000

Sources: Roger H. Bezdek and Bruce Hannon, "Energy, Manpower and The Highway Trust Fund," *Science*, Vol. 185, No. 4152, August 1974, pp. 669–675; Congressional Budget Office, *Temporary Measures to Stimulate Employment*, Congress of the United States, U.S. Government Printing Office, Washington, D.C., September 1975; George E. Johnson and James D. Tomola, *The Efficacy of Public Service Employment Programs*, Office of Evaluation, U.S. Department of Labor, Technical Analysis Paper #17A, June 1975; Georges Vernez et al., *Regional Cycles and Employment Effects of Public Works Investments*, The Rand Corporation, R–2052–EDA, January 1977.

Note: NA means not available.

[a]The range shown reflects alternative assumptions on the mix of public works projects that might be implemented.

[b]The range shown reflects alternative assumptions on displacement of state and local funds by federal funds. The higher figure reflects no displacement, while the lower figures reflect moderate displacement (CBO) or large displacement (Johnson and Tomola).

[c]In all estimates the tax cut is assumed to be entirely on personal taxes. If the tax cut were to be one-third corporate and two-thirds personal, job creation would be about 50 percent smaller (CBO, 1975).

relating changes in national employment by sector to changes in construction employment. Because this model was calibrated using time series data for projects with relatively low on-site labor intensity, the estimates of effects for public works projects with high on-site labor intensity—flood protection and federal office buildings—will be overestimated.[18] Because neither study takes into account the effects of substitution and displacement, they provide estimates of *gross* rather than net employment.

In contrast, the Congressional Budget Office (1975) and Tomola and Johnson (1975) attempted to estimate the *net* total employment effects. Congressional Budget Office (CBO) based its estimates on the forecasts of changes in the rate of unemployment from three quarterly econometric models of the economy constructed by Chase Econometric Associates, Inc., Data Resources, Inc., and Wharton Econometric Forecasting Associates, Inc. The change in unemployment was converted into employment changes by assuming that the first represents only 60 percent of the actual number of jobs created by the policy.[19] Johnson and Tomola estimates were derived from an aggregate econometric model of the economy developed by Liu and Hwa (1974). Both studies account for the effects of increased interest rates (substitution). Ranges in estimates reflect different assumptions. For public works, they reflect different combinations in the types of public works project constituting the program.[20] For public service employment, they reflect a moderate to high displacement of federal for state and local expenditures.

Because of these limitations, the estimates presented in Table 6-6 are order of magnitude rather than precise measures of total short-run employment generated by alternative fiscal policies. Comparing programs, a public service employment program that includes provisions for a wage ceiling and a requirement for funds to be spent mostly on participants' wages creates the most jobs, particularly during the first year. However, if displacement of local by federal funds is high, reflected in the lower figure in the range, public service employment has no clear advantage over the other programs.

Uncertainty about the size of the displacement effect and about the use of funds by local government (see following section) makes it difficult to estimate reliably the number of jobs created not only by public service employment, but also by any fiscal program, such as public works and antirecessionary revenue sharing, that channels funds through state and local governments. In short, available estimates of total job creation provide no strong evidence that fiscal policies differ widely in the number of jobs they would create per dollar of expenditure.

ISSUES WITH THE USE OF PUBLIC WORKS
AS A COUNTERCYCLICAL DEVICE

The countercyclical effectiveness of public works programs may be undermined for several reasons. First, the increased flow of federal funds may encourage local governments to reduce their own expenditures. When this is so, the federal grant may provide local fiscal relief but its overall expansionary effect will be reduced. Second, the jobs may not be generated while the recession is most critical. Instead, legislative or executive delays may result in program effects being felt well into the recovery period and in possible price or wage increases. Third, those employed by the projects may not be those in need of employment—the disadvantaged that the program may be specifically designed to assist. Fourth, the projects selected may be of little social value. Fifth, the increased federal expenditures on public works may result in excessive demand of labor for specific skills or for materials and supplies from some industries. A further result may be inflationary pressures on prices and wages. This section examines these potential problems.

Displacement of Local by Federal Funds
Countercyclical federal funds channeled through state and local governments may induce state and local governments to reduce their own expenditures. In this case, *total* public spending—federal plus local—would not increase by the full amount of the federal grant.[21] The policy importance of this problem depends on the objective. If the objective is to increase the volume of public construction, then displacement reduces the effectiveness of the program. However, if the primary objective is to create jobs—either in the public or private sector—the level of displacement is less important than the use made of the displaced funds. If these funds are used for other public purposes or find their way back into the private sector through tax relief, some jobs will be created. However, the level, speed, and type of jobs created would differ from those without displacement.

Countercyclical federal grants to state and local governments are generally of two types. *Close-ended lump sum transfers* involve unconditional grants to local governments that simply augment the local public revenues. Countercyclical revenue-sharing grants that broadly define eligible spending are of this kind. The second type of grant, *close-ended categorical grants*, restricts the use of the money. These grants may include matching grants in which the federal government pays only some portion of the cost of the program with the balance funded from state or local revenues. Countercyclical public works programs are of the second type since grants are limited to specific projects.

Theory suggests that displacement will be greater for unconditional grants than for categorical grants. However, the distinction between unconditional and categorical grants is not as clear as it may initially appear. For example, many types of public construction are eligible under public works programs. State and local governments may regard countercyclical grants simply as additional revenues rather than as incentives to implement a specific additional project.

Only a few empirical studies of the size and time path of displacement of revenue sharing and public service employment programs have been made.[22] They indicate that displacement under countercyclical public service employment programs increases over time from less than 30 percent in the first and second quarters after implementation to 40 to 60 percent after a year and to between 80 and 100 percent in the long run—in a year and a half to two years.[23] Onsite observers of the implementation of the Public Employment Program (PEP) confirm that short-run displacement is small. For example, Levitan and Taggard (1974) conclude from such a process evaluation that "at the outset, the level of PEP jobs represented net additions to the total number of public employment opportunities."

There are no equivalent empirical estimates of the displacement effect of a countercyclical public works program. However, recent data about the Local Public Works program suggest displacement may be expected to be large. The program was debated in Congress for nearly fourteen months, and Congress had to override a presidential veto. Despite the Ford Administration opposition to the program, the mood in Congress was such that local officials—anticipating the program would eventually be enacted—may have delayed regular construction spending. Gramlich (1978) shows that capital expenditures by states and local governments dropped from $32.8 to $28.8 billion between the second and third quarters of 1976 when the Local Public Works Act was debated and eventually passed by Congress. They dropped further in the fourth quarter of 1976 and then again in the first quarter of 1977 (to $26.6 billion). By that time, LPW funds had been allocated to specific projects, and in the second quarter of 1977, state and local capital expenditure increased to $30.0 billion.

The possibility of total displacement in the long run is a mixed blessing. On the one hand, it can be argued that it implies automatic phasing out. If the policy horizon does not exceed two years, displacement insures that the effect of the program is not extended beyond the intended horizon. On the other hand, as federal subsidies are reduced, local political problems are exacerbated. Once local governments have used federal monies to finance local investments, when federal subsidies are cut back they are faced with the unpleasant option of either seeking additional revenues to maintain the level of capital investments or of cutting back. However, increased revenues generated by the economic recovery partially offset the need to raise taxes.

From the standpoint of net job creation, the size of the displacement effect is only one-half of the issue. The other half concerns the use that is made of the displaced funds and how fast these are recirculated in the economy, thereby also creating jobs, albeit not in the public sector. Displaced funds can be used for any one of the following purposes: (1) tax reduction; (2) tax stabilization, that is, avoidance of a local tax increase; (3) avoidance of borrowing; (4) increased reserve balances; (5) increase in pay and benefits. In addition to these uses, displaced public works funds may be used for increasing local operating expenditures.

The use of displaced funds to increase fund balances or wages or to avoid borrowing would have no or only a modest effect on job creation. The latter would simply be a transfer of debt from the local to the federal government. Using displaced funds for increased local government purchases or operating expenditures would result in job creation roughly equal to federal government purchases or in public service employment programs of a size equal to the displaced funds, respectively.[24] Finally, using displaced funds for local tax reduction or stabilization would result in a net job creation roughly equal to that of a federal income tax cut.[25]

Little is known about the local use of displaced funds. One study of the revenue-sharing program, however, may be illustrative. Nathan and others (1975) estimated that nearly half of displaced shared revenues were used for tax relief and about one-quarter were used for avoidance of borrowing and increased fund balance, neither of which would be creating jobs. The remaining funds could not be allocated to any specific category. The large size of the unallocated component illustrates the difficulty of tracing displaced funds.

Timing of Job Creation

The elapsed time between an economic downturn and actual job creation by a countercyclical program is an important determinant of its effectiveness in accomplishing its objectives and in minimizing adverse consequences on price stability. If this interval is long, jobs may not be generated until economic recovery is well under way, a situation that may lead to excess demand for materials and labor.[26] Delays in the formulation and implementation of a countercyclical program may occur at any one of three stages: (1) initiation of legislative action; (2) program legislative enactment; or (3) program implementation. Table 6-7 identifies the lags that have been experienced under three countercyclical public works programs implemented in response to three national recessions: 1960-1962, 1970-1971, and 1974-1977.

Lag in Initiation of Legislative Action. The time elapsing between the begining of a national recession and the introduction of countercyclical legislation in Congress has been long, ranging from eight to twenty-two months for public works.[27] These delays resulted in the spending of countercyclical funds when the economy was already recovering. In the early 1960s, the Kennedy Administration delayed until February 1962—twelve months after the trough of the 1960 recession—its request to Congress for standby authority to commit $2 billion in Federal funds to stimulate the economy.[28] Similarly, congressional countercyclical public works action was not initiated until three months after the trough of the 1970-1971 recession (PWIP),[29] and it coincided roughly with the trough of the most recent recession (LPW).

One reason the initiation of countercyclical policy is slow is the difficulty of not only anticipating a forthcoming recession, but also of predicting its duration and severity. Little progress has been made toward anticipation, and present techniques are not reliable in predicting severity or duration. Leading indicators or leading index cannot yet be regarded as reliable predictors of immiment cyclical downturn because the timing relationships are derived from data analysis rather than a complete econometric model; at most it gives an indication of something to look for as new observations arrive (CBO, 1975). Given present forecasting capabilities, some delay in the initiation of countercyclical policy action is unavoidable, making it imperative that program legislative enactment be rapid.

Lag in Legislative Enactment. The lag between the initiation of policy action in Congress and actual program legislative enactment ranged between six and fourteen months for public works program.[30] These delays occur whether or not the program had executive support and reflect the need to reconcile conflicting interests about the size of the program and the distribution of benefits among areas. For example, it took six months to enact the Public Works Acceleration Act of 1962 proposed and supported by the Kennedy Administration, while it took five months for legislative enactment of the Public

Works Impact Program passed in August 1971, and more than twelve months for enactment of the Local Public Works program in July 1976, the latter two in the face of executive opposition.

In addition to the lag in initiation of legislative action noted above, legislative lags have had important repercussions for the counter-cyclical effectiveness of the programs. When national cycles have been mild and of short duration—as has typically been the case in the postwar period, excepting the present recession[31] —these delays have meant that the programs were actually enacted well into the recovery period.

Lags in Program Implementation. Lags in program implementation reflect the time required after legislative enactment to (1) draw up regulations by the appropriate federal implementing agency; (2) prepare project applications; (3) process and review project applications; and (4) allocate funds among sponsoring agencies. This is often referred to as the inside lag. In addition, there is an outside lag as allocated funds are spent.

The inside lag for a public works program can be as long as five months, and the outside lag—until at least half the total on-site public works jobs are created—averages about twelve months (Table 6-7).

Variations in inside lag among these programs have been due to differences in administrative requirements and in allocation procedures. Under the APW program, less than one month elapsed until the first project approval was made, while four and five months elapsed under the PWIP and LPW programs, respectively. Two factors appear to account for the faster allocation under Accelerated Public Works (APW). First, coordination for the implementation of the APW program was entrusted to the Area Development Administration (ARA) in the Department of Commerce, created especially to carry out the Area Redevelopment Act (ARA) of May 1961. By September 1962, the agency was experienced and since the areas eligible for the APW program included those already designated to receive assistance under the ARA, project approvals proceeded swiftly.[32] In contrast, the PWIP and LWP were implemented by the Economic Development Administration (EDA), being added on to its regular activities and using guidelines developed by the EDA in Washington, D.C., but with EDA regional field offices responsible for implementation in the field. Local applications were made first to the field offices, and if approved, were forwarded to the EDA office of Public Works in Washington, D.C., for review and executive approval. The time period from project application to approval, which takes an average of 200 days for regular projects, was con-

Table 6-7.   Lags in Job Creation (in months)

Lag In	Accelerated Public Works 1962	Public Works Impact Program 1971	Local Public Works 1976 (Round 1)
Initiation of legislative action[a]	22	8	19
Program enactment[b]	6	6	14
Subtotal	28	14	33
Federal administrative action[c]	1	4	5
Outlays until half the jobs have been created[d]	12	12	12
Total	41	30	50

Sources: Ilse Mintz, "Dating United States Growth Cycles," *Explorations in Economic Research*, National Bureau of Economic Research, vol. 1, no. 1, Summer 1974, Tables 3 and 7. Public Law 92-54, *Emergency Employment Act of 1971*, Public Law 93-203, *Comprehensive Employment and Training Act of 1973*, Public Law 93-567, *Emergency Jobs and Unemployment Assistance Act of 1974*, Public Law 94-369, *Public Works Employment Act of 1976*, and information provided by: House Committee on Education and Labor; House Committee on Public Works and Transportation; Senate Committee on Human Resources (formerly the Senate Committee on Labor and Public Welfare); Senate Committee on Environment and Public Works (formerly the Senate Committee on Public Works); and the House Documents Office. Also, Economic Development Administration, *Local Public Works Program: Status Report*, U.S. Department of Commerce, January 1978.

[a]Time lag between date of recessionary downturn—as dated by the National Bureau of Economic Research (NBER)—and date the legislation was first introduced in Congress.
[b]Time lag between introduction of initial legislation and presidential signing of passed legislation.
[c]Time lag between the presidential signing of passed legislation and the allocations of funds to state and local governments.
[d]Time lag between obligations of funds to state and local governments and half the number of *direct* jobs have been created or half of actual outlays have taken place. For public works, it includes any lag occurring between project selection and start of construction.

siderably accelerated under PWIP, but it still required an average of 68 days (Tobin, 1974, p. 155).

The second and perhaps more important factor was the procedure adopted for the allocation of funds. APW funds were allocated on a continuing basis as applications came in on a project by project basis, rather than under the "once-for-all" procedure used under PWIP and LPW Round I. APW project selection was made using a two-tier approach. (1) Funds were tentatively earmarked to eligible areas on the basis of readily available data provided by the Department of Labor; (2) area projects meeting prespecified criteria—ready to begin and high ratio of on-site employment costs to total costs—were approved on a continuous basis until the amount earmarked for the area was reached. No comparison was made of the projects' economic merits with those of projects in other areas (Levitan, 1964).

Under PWIP, no funds could be allocated to federal projects, and a deliberate decision was made not to develop a priority list of special impact areas.[33] Instead, PWIP funds were allocated on a "project first, designation after" basis (Tobin, 1975, p. 125). Since eligible areas could be communities or neighborhoods, defined without regard to political or other subdivision or boundary, it was difficult to make any allocation before all eligible special impact areas had been identified. Since such areas could not be identified from readily available data, regional offices were to attach convincing evidence supplied by a "reliable source" that the target area(s) met at least one of the four PWIP designated criteria.[34]

Finally, under the LPW (Round I), EDA opted for a simultaneous "area-project" allocation procedure. Funds were allocated among states (65 percent based on each state's share of the number of unemployed in the nation and 35 percent to twenty-one states whose unemployment rates exceeded the national rate). Projects within states were selected on the basis of a number of area and project characteristics (number of unemployed, rate of unemployment, per capita income, and project on-site labor intensity).[35] As with PWIP, LPW areas were defined without regard to political or other subdivision or boundary, and thus the selection of projects could not be made until all applications providing the necessary area information had been made and screened. Allocation rules such as those used under LPW Round I and PWIP significantly increased the inside lag. As under APW, LWP Round II area planning targets were determined from readily available area unemployment data with project selection left to state and local officials within certain basic guidelines. Under this procedure, the inside lag was considerably shorter as state and local government allocations were completed in two months, and projects were approved on a continuing basis in the following ten weeks.

Once the fund allocation was made, jobs were created at a comparable speed under all programs—40 to 50 percent of total on-site jobs were created in four quarters.[36] This delay includes the time between project approval and beginning of construction.[37] Most projects under both APW and PWIP programs were completed two years after initial allocation. Under PWIP, the average time from start of construction to completion was 308 days.

Accelerating the implementation of a countercyclical public works program is difficult. The time necessary to plan the projects, to process and review the local applications, to request and review the bids from contractors, and to start construction cannot be compressed easily. However, past experience suggests that administrative lags in implementation may be shortened by: (1) allocating funds on a continuing rather than a onetime basis; (2) entrusting responsibility for implementation to a separate agency not burdened with other responsibilities; and (3) determining eligible areas from readily available data rather than from locally provided data. There are opportunities for shortening the outside lag if a portion of total appropriations may be used to implement federal public works projects.

Targeting

In a preceding section, the extent to which countercyclical public works funds were targeted to areas most affected by cyclical unemployment was examined. Below, the extent to which the programs have targeted on those sectors, occupations, and socioeconomic groups most affected by national recessions is investigated.

Sectors and Industries. Public works have targeted effectively on industries most affected by national recessions: the construction and durable goods industries. Approximately one-third of the expenditures on public works projects is spent on on-site labor in the construction sector, and about one job in four created by a public works program is in the construction sector. This is compatible with the large relative cyclical amplitude of this sector.

In addition, between 40 percent and 60 percent of public works project cost is for material supplies although the amount varied considerably among projects. The dollar demands per $1,000 of expenditure for the output of selected industries by the project making the heaviest demand are shown in Table 6-8. Public works projects make relatively heavy demands on the output of the lumber and wood product industry (SIC 24) and the primary metals industry (SIC 33). Both of these industries experience high cyclical amplitude. Some heavy construction projects make intensive demands on the transportation equipment industry (SIC 37), which also exhibits high cyclical amplitude. On the other hand, heavy construction projects also draw upon the output of the mining sector (SIC 14), which exhibits low cyclical amplitude and therefore raises the possibility of supply constraints.

Table 6-8. Dollar Requirements for Selected Material Supplies Resulting from Expenditure of $1,000 on Local Public Services and Selected Public Works Projects[a]

Supplying Industries [b]		*Dollar Requirements from Expenditure of $1,000 on Selected Public Works Projects* [c]	
SIC	Description	Amount	Project
14†	Mining	219	Revetments
15,17*	Construction	377	College housing
24*	Lumber and Wood Products	165	One-family housing
27	Printing and Publishing	—	
28†	Chemicals	23	One-family housing
29†	Petroleum and Related Products	70	Highway construction
32	Stone, Clay and Glass Products	141	Sewer lines
33	Primary Metal Products	157	Lock and concrete dams
34	Fabricated Metal Products	119	Local flood protection
35	Nonelectrical Machinery (excluding construction machinery)	297	Powerhouses
36	Electrical Equipment	217	Powerhouses
37*	Transportation Equipment	117	Dredging
49	Electric, Gas, Water, and Sanitary Service	—	
40-48	Transportation and Warehousing	300	Revetments
50-51	Wholesale and Retail Trade	302	Federal office buildings
60-63†	Finance and Insurance	—	
65,66†	Real Estate and Rental	—	
73,76†	Business Services	—	

Sources: Georges Vernez et al., *Regional Cycles and Employment Effects of Public Works Investments*, R-2052-EDA, The Rand Corporation, January 1977; Bureau of Economic Analysis, *Survey of Current Business*, vol. 54, no. 2, 1974, U.S. Department of Commerce, Washington, D.C., 1974.

Notes: — means that dollar requirements are negligible.
　　　　* indicates high cyclical amplitude industry.
　　　　† indicates low cyclical amplitude industry.
　　　　NA means not available.

[a]Requirements include some induced demands since interindustry purchases are included.

[b]These are identified initially through input-output sectors. Where there is a simple, corresponding SIC code definition, this is given.

[c]Project with the highest dollar requirement per $1,000 is listed. For a full list of dollar requirements for twenty-two types of projects, see Vernez et al., Table 4-2 and 4-3.

Occupations. The construction sector has a high concentration of workers in occupations that exhibit high cyclical amplitude: laborers, operatives, and craft and kindred workers (Vernez and Vaughan, 1978). Of course, the distribution of demands for labor of different skills for construction work will depend upon the type of project undertaken. The demand for material supplies by public works projects generates jobs in the manufacturing sector, which also contains a high concentration of operatives and craft workers. Overall, public works projects require labor from occupational groups that experience high cyclical amplitudes in employment.

Socioeconomic Groups. Except for one study (Sulvetta and Thompson, 1975), there have been no systematic analyses of the sex, age, race, educational, and other socioeconomic characteristics of those employed on countercyclical public works projects. However, some conclusions can be drawn from a review of the work force characteristics of the construction industry.

It can be expected that public works projects would target effectively on male workers who are more prone than female workers to cyclical unemployment. Males constitute 95 percent of the labor force in the construction industry and 80 percent in the durable goods industry. Less than 10 percent of the jobs in public works projects are expected to go to youths because the construction industry has relatively high job skill or experience requirements (Vernez et al., 1977). Workers over 45, who tend to be less affected by recessions than other age groups, comprise more than a third of the labor force in the construction industry and will benefit from the program.

More than half of cyclical unemployment appears to be due to a worsening of the unemployment experience of those typically prone to spells of unemployment even during expansionary years—the young and the less educated. To reach these groups effectively requires the inclusion of a training component in countercyclical public service employment programs or an increase in the size of manpower programs during recessionary years rather than a countercyclical public works program.

Countercyclical public works programs have provided minority employment although less effectively than manpower programs. The high concentration of minority employment under the Public Works Impact Program is surprising, given that public works projects were built by private contractors and that the proportion of blacks employed in the construction industry is equivalent to that in the total labor force—about 11 percent. But the program was small and was implemented during expansionary years when there were relatively few nonminority workers available. A comparable targeting on minority groups is unlikely under a larger countercyclical program implemented in a recessionary period without eligibility restriction.

Sixty-five percent of PWIP participants were reported as having been employed on the day prior to program entry.[38] Whether this affects the number of jobs created is difficult to assess. On the one hand, when entering the program, a previously employed worker may vacate a job (presumably less attractive) that will be filled by another person. Although net job creation is not altered, the vacated job may not be filled immediately. On the other hand, the participant may have lost his or her job had he or she not been enrolled in the program. There is no information on the prior public assistance status and unemployment insurance participation of participants in public works programs, and thus potential budgetary savings in the two first programs cannot be assessed.

Finally, public works programs do not seem to be able to assure income maintenance. Although many benefit, they do so for only a short time.

Supply Constraints

Concern has been expressed that an extensive countercyclical job-creating program may drive up wage rates and lead to inflation (Cook and Frank, 1971; Bailey and Tobin, 1977). These concerns arise from the presumed tradeoff between reducing unemployment and maintaining a stable price level that is reflected in the Phillips curve (Phillips, 1958; Wiseman, 1976).[39] Increased federal expenditures for public works might result in excess demand for certain materials and supplies, and yet the literature provides inconclusive evidence to support these concerns. Any adverse effects will be minimized the smaller the size of the program relative to the number of unemployed, the speedier the implementation of the program during the recession trough, the more accurate the targeting of funds, and the greater the extent to which participants are hired from the ranks of the unemployed rather than from the employed in the private sector. The evidence presented in this chapter indicates that past countercyclical public works programs scored unevenly on each of these considerations. First, they provided relatively few jobs compared with the number of unemployed—at most, 5 percent of the unemployed—and are unlikely to generate labor supply constraints in supplying industries. Moreover, a study by the Advisory Commission on Intergovernmental Relations (1977) found only a weak relationship between federal aid and state-local wage rates. Second, public works target fairly effectively on the industries and occupational and demographic groups most affected by cyclical unemployment. However, public works funds have not been concentrated in heavily urbanized areas that typically experience cycles of larger amplitude than do smaller, less urbanized areas. There is some evidence that in certain areas countercyclical funds might exert some pressure in the market for construction workers with highly specialized skills. Finally, programs have been implemented slowly.

Value of Output

The costs and long-term benefits from countercyclical public works projects have typically not been assessed. The value of services will be greater the more efficiently inputs are used, less if inputs are drawn from the private sector, and greater if the types of infrastructure provided are useful.

The choice of inputs—labor and materials and equipment—used to build the projects affect the efficiency of the program. The main factor affecting the efficiency of construction projects appears to be the mode of construction. Typically, post-World War II countercyclical public works projects have been built under contract by private contractors. Because there have been no limitations on labor inputs and only limited restrictions on the use of materials, [40] input choices for these projects are expected to be similar to those exhibited by regular projects. "Force account" projects, however, may be less efficient than those built by the contract method. While there is no recent evidence, one study of WPA construction projects found their costs to be about 13 percent greater than estimates of construction costs under contract (U.S. National Resources Planning Board, 1942).

Public works projects do not typically compete with the output of private industries. Although the programs can draw resources away from the private economy by attracting workers from private industry, there is no direct evidence of such substitution having taken place in past countercyclical public work programs. The existence of high unemployment coupled with the small size of the programs lessens the possibility of substitution.

CONCLUSIONS

This discussion of the effects of past countercyclical public works programs has cast doubts upon their effectiveness. First, the economic stimulus they provide is questionable. When channeled through state and local governments, significant portions of these federal grants appear to be used in lieu of local funds. Net job creation may not be greater than that achieved by an equivalent federal personal income tax cut and may be less if displaced funds are used for rebuilding local surplus. Second, their ability to target on the disadvantaged, youths, and unskilled, who are most affected by national recessions, appears to be limited. And so is their ability to target on the areas—labor market areas, cities, neighborhoods—most affected by national recessions. Only jobs created on site will necessarily be created in target areas. Indirect jobs are created in areas where the supplying industries are located. Third, their ability to assure income maintenance to those employed by the projects is limited because the jobs are of short duration—averaging one month. And fourth, they are slow to begin operations. During mild national recessions, jobs will not be created until well into the recovery. However, it must be emphasized that past lags were caused primarily by legislative delays that affect all types of discretionary countercyclical programs.

On the positive side, countercyclical public works programs target effectively on two sectors of the economy typically severely affected by national recessions: construction and durable goods manufacturing. Furthermore, the literature provides no evidence that these programs—small relative to the number of unemployed—have exercised inflationary pressures on labor wages or prices of materials although these problems may occur in some areas.

In many cases, the local construction industry cycle does not overlap with the local cycle in total employment, or the severity of the construction industry cycle is not proportional to severity of the local cycle in total employment. To ignore, as has been done in the past, the behavior of the local construction industry in allocating countercyclical public works funds may have resulted in adverse effects in some areas.

If a public works program continues to be a component of national stabilization policy, its effectiveness may be increased by a number of design improvements. To reduce the long delay between the beginning of a national recession and legislative enactment, the release of countercyclical public works funds should be made automatic. This could be accomplished by congressional enactment granting executive standby authority to release countercyclical funds when prespecified economic indicators reach certain specified values. Complementary measures might accelerate executive implementation of the programs. First, responsibility for implementation should be entrusted to a separate agency not burdened with other responsibilities. Second, allocation of funds among projects should be made on a continuing rather than a onetime basis. Allocation of funds on this basis would require establishing areawide funding ceilings and allocating funds within each area on a project by project basis until the ceilings are met. The ceilings should be defined by local data routinely collected by the Bureau of Labor Statistics. Allocation procedures requiring locally provided data should be avoided. Third, a portion of total countercyclical public works appropriations should be available for use in carrying out federal public works projects already authorized by Congress. Lastly, preference should be given to public works projects that are of short duration and that concentrate on-site labor demand in the early stage of construction.

To minimize possible adverse local effects, the allocation of funds among areas should take into account the stage in the local business cycle. There is evidence of substantial variations in the timing of the response of local areas to national recessions. Local monthly employment time series are available to determine whether an area is in its contraction or expansion phase at the time of funds allocation. Proportionately, more funds might be directed to areas that are in their contraction phase. Similarly, allocation of countercyclical public works funds should be based in part on the local availability of construction workers. In addition, building construction projects should be preferred to heavy construction projects.

NOTES

1. A number of detailed historical accounts of countercyclical public works and public service employment programs are available. For instance, see Tobin (1975); Briscoe (1972); and *Manpower Report of the President* (1975).

2. At today's cost of living, this is equivalent to an expenditure of $80 billion, or nearly $8 billion per year.

3. At a time when nearly nine million workers were out of work.

4. A classical cycle consists of a period of contractions in many economic activities, followed by a period of expansions.

5. Tobin (1975) and Bureau of the Census, *Value of New Construction Put in Place, 1947 to 1974*, C30074S (Washington, D.C.: U.S. Department of Commerce, December 1975).

6. Under the WPA program alone, some 651,000 miles of road, 16,000 miles of water and sewer systems, 85,000 public buildings, 2,877 utility plants, 3,085 playgrounds, and an equal number of athletic fields were built (Briscoe, 1972).

7. They coordinated the activities of ten federal agencies under PWA and 40 federal agencies under WPA (Tobin, 1975).

8. The Davis-Bacon Act passed in 1931 required that wages prevailing in the local construction industry be paid on public works projects. For a detailed discussion of wage policy during the depression, see Mitchell (1962).

9. Important work in the area of regional analysis has been conducted by Basset and Haggert (1971); Borts (1960); Brechling (1967); King, Casetti, and Jeffrey (1972); Tideman (1973); and Vernez et al. (1977). For a review and summary of earlier studies, see Vaughan (1976). This subsection summarizes the results of a study by Vernez et al. 1977).

10. For an attempt to estimate the regional distribution of final demand from public works projects, see Haveman and Krutilla (1968).

11. In addition to short-run job creation, public works, public service employment, and other fiscal programs may lead to the creation of jobs in the *long run*. For instance, the construction of public facilities—libraries, hospitals, or parks—will generate jobs for maintenance and operation and may attract new firms to the area. These effects result from induced structural changes that stimulate local economic development. Studies of long-run employment effects of public works are not reviewed in this report; for such a review, see Vaughan (1976, pp. 62–69).

12. Force account projects are projects for which the local government acts as contractor.

13. They used man-months, assumed to be about 165 hours or 1,980 hours in a year (p. 50).

14. In 1974, the average annual earnings for construction workers was $11,250.

15. No national estimate of average number of hours worked by construction workers is available. However, a survey for specific construction trade in Detroit, Omaha, Milwaukee, and Southern California indicates that in most occupations more than 50 percent worked less than 1,200 hours yearly and more than 75 percent worked less than 1,600 hours.

16. The Economic Development Administration expected the average length of employment per employee would be three months (Sulvetta and Thompson, 1975, p. 50).

17. They were computed using 1971-1972 data for the value of shipments and employment by industry. See Bureau of the Census, *Census of Manufactures, 1972*, (Washington, D.C.: U.S. Department of Commerce, 1975). For further details see Vernez et al. (1977, Chapter V).

18. In 1972, the weighted average on-site labor generated by all projects was 2.5 workers per $100,000. Sewer plant, flood protection, and federal office buildings projects generate an average of 2.9, 4.5, and 3.3 on-site jobs per $100,000, respectively.

19. This is because an unemployment rate change reflects both changes in employment and changes in labor force participation. It is typically assumed that if employment is increased by ten jobs the labor force will increase by four workers.

20. Displacement of local by federal funds is a problem unique to the countercyclical fiscal programs that channel funds through state and local governments: public works, public service employment, and antirecessionary revenue sharing.

21. For a recent review of the theoretical and empirical literature on intergovernmental grants, see Gramlich (1976).

22. See Johnson and Tomola (1975 and 1976); Fechter (1974); National

Planning Association (1974); Nathan, Manvel, and Calkins (1975); and Gramlich and Galper (1973).

23. These estimates should be used with caution. They may be subject to a fairly wide margin of error; there are inaccuracies in estimating procedures; no account is made of severity and length of recession; and they are sensitive to program design features and local variations.

24. Subject to the conditions that local purchases are comparable to federal purchases and that local operating expenditures are predominantly used for wages.

25. Subject to the condition that local tax cuts have the same distributional effects as a federal tax cut. Since local revenues are mainly raised from the property tax rather than income tax, this is unlikely to be the case.

26. For example, it is reported that construction projects on the West Coast are experiencing a chronic shortage of cement during 1978 as a result of the expansion of private construction during the economic recovery since early 1976.

27. By comparison, past delays in legislative initiation of countercyclical public service employment ranged from seven to eleven months.

28. This proposal resulted in the Public Works Acceleration Act (PWA) of 1962, signed by President Kennedy in September of 1962, authorizing an appropriation of $0.9 billion.

29. For evidence under the Public Works Impact Program (PWIP), see Sulvetta and Thompson (1975).

30. By comparison, the legislative enactment lag for public service employment programs has ranged between four and eight months (Vernez and Vaughan, 1978); and for tax cut legislation in 1962, it was eighteen months (Portney, 1976).

31. For an analysis of the duration of post-1960 cycles, see Vernez et al. (1977). This study indicated that the return to peak duration of the national employment cycle was twenty-one months in 1960–1962 and eighteen months in 1970–1971.

32. Areas eligible for the APW program were designated under ARA, and areas were chosen that the Secretary of Labor determined to have suffered from substantial unemployment for at least nine of the preceding twelve months (Tobin, p. 103).

33. The small size of the appropriation—$47 million in fiscal year 1972—and the desire to spread funding as widely as possible appear to have been at the root of this decision.

34. These criteria were (Tobin, 1974, p. 121):

1. Large concentration of low-income persons operationally interpreted to mean an area identified by OEO as an urban or rural special impact area or an area in which a majority of the families were living in poverty, as defined by OEO.
2. Rural areas having substantial outmigration, that is, 25 percent or more during the most recent quarter for which data were available.
3. Substantial unemployment, that is, an average unemployment rate of 8.5 percent during the most recent quarter for which data were available.

4. An actual or abrupt rise of unemployment due to the closing or curtailment of a major source of employment.

35. For a detailed description of the LPW allocation procedures, see GAO (1977, pp. 4-8).

36. Quarterly on-site jobs accounts have not been published for PWIP. However, since outlays reflect payments made upon receipt of requests for payments only for completed work, they can be used as proxy indicators of jobs produced prior to the time when outlays were recorded.

37. An econometric study of the timing of the response of employment to residential construction authorization by Adams and Spiro (1972) confirms the order of magnitude of this outside lag. They found that once a project is authorized and a contract is let, 90 percent of the employees needed will have been hired within five months. Adding to this this the startup time that can reach six months or more, the estimated outside lag derived by this study would equal about eleven months.

38. It is not certain whether those employed immediately prior to program entry were working part-time.

39. For example, Friedman (1968) and Phelps (1967) have argued that the tradeoff is only a short-run phenomenon.

40. Such as exclusive use of U.S.-made materials and supplies, or use of a specified share—10 percent—of construction funds or materials inputs built or produced by minority firms. There is at this time no evidence that such rules affect construction efficiency.

BIBLIOGRAPHY

Adams, E.W., and Spiro, M.H. "The Timing of the Response of Employment to Construction Authorization." *Applied Economics* 4 (1972): 125-133.

Advisory Commission on Intergovernmental Relations. *Federal Grants: Their Effects on State-Local Expenditures, Employment Levels and Wage Rates*, A-61. Washington, D.C.; February 1977.

Bailey, M., and Tobin, J. "Inflation, Unemployment and Direct Job Creation." Paper for Brookings conference on Direct Job Creation, April 1977.

Bakke, W.E. "Manpower Policy During a Recession," in Ivar Berg, ed., *Human Resources and Economic Welfare, Essays in Honor of Eli Ginzberg*. N.Y., N.Y: Columbia University Press, 1971, pp. 89-127.

Bassett, K. and Haggert, P. "Towards Short-Term Forecasting for Cyclic Behavior in a Regional System of Cities," in M. Chisholm, A.E. Frey, and P. Haggert, eds., *Regional Forecasting*. London: Buttersworth, 1971, pp. 389-413.

Bezdek, R.H., and Hannon, B. "Energy, Manpower and the Highway Trust Fund." *Science* 185, 4152 (August 23, 1974): 669-675.

Borts, G.H. "Regional Cycles of Manufacturing Employment in the United States, 1914-1953." *Journal of American Statistical Association* 55 (1960): 151-211.

Brechling, F. "Trends and Cycles in British Regional Unemployment." *Oxford Economic Papers* 19 (1967): 1-21.

Briscoe, A.T. "Public Service Employment in the 1930s: The WPA," in H.L. Sheppard et al., eds., *The Political Economy of Public Service Employment.* Lexington, Mass.: Lexington Books, 1972.

Congressional Budget Office. *Temporary Measures to Stimulate Employment.* Washington, D.C.: Congress of the United States, U.S. Government Printing Office, September 1975.

Cook, P.J., and Frank, R.H. *The Inflationary Effects of Public Service Employment.* Prepared for U.S. Department of Labor, Manpower Administration, Washington, D.C., June 1971.

Fechter, A. "Public Employment Programs: An Evaluative Study." *Studies in Public Welfare.* Washington, D.C.: U.S. Government Printing Office, December 30, 1974.

Friedman, M. "The Role of Monetary Policy." *American Economic Review* 58, 1 (March 1968): 1-17.

Gramlich, Edward M. "Impact of Minimum Wages on Other Wages, Employment, and Family Incomes." in Arthur M. Okun and George L. Perry, eds., *Brookings Papers on Economic Activity* 2 (1976): 459-461.

———. "State and Local Budgets the Day After It Rained: Why is the Surplus So High?" *Brookings Papers on Economic Activity* 1 (1978): 191-214.

Gramlich, E.M., and Galper, H. "State and Local Fiscal Behavior and Federal Grant Policy." *Brookings Papers on Economic Activity* 1 (1973): 15-58.

Haveman, R.H., and Krutilla, J.V. *Unemployment, Idle Capacity and the Evaluation of Public Expenditures.* Prepared for Resources for the Future, Inc. Baltimore: Johns Hopkins University Press, 1968.

Johnson, G.E., and Tomola, J.D. *The Fiscal Substitution Effects of Alternative Approaches to Public Service Employment.* Technical Analysis Paper 41, U.S. Department of Labor, September 1976.

———. *The Efficacy of Public Service Employment Programs.* Technical Analysis Paper 17A, U.S. Department of Labor, June 1975.

King, L., Casetti, E., and Jeffrey, D. "Cyclical Fluctuations in Unemployment Levels in U.S. Metropolitan Areas." *Tijdschrift Voor Econ. En Soc. Geografie* (September-October), 1972.

Levitan, S.A. *Federal Aid to Depressed Areas: An Evalution of the Area Development Administration.* Baltimore: Johns Hopkins University Press, 1964.

Levitan, S.A., and Taggart, R., eds. *Emergency Employment Act: The PEP Generation.* Salt Lake City: Olympus, 1974.

Liu, T.C., and Hwa, E.C. "A Monthly Econometric Model of the U.S. Economy." *International Economic Review* 15, 2 (June 1974): 328-365.

Manpower Report of the President, Washington, D.C., 1975.

Mintz, I. "Dating United States Growth Cycles." *Explorations in Economic Research* 1, 1 (Summer 1974): 12-47.

Mitchell, B. *The Economic History of the United States.* New York: Holt, Rinehart and Winston, 1962, vol. 9, ch. 9.

Nathan, R.P., Manvel, A.D., and Calkins, S.E. *Monitoring Revenue Sharing.* Washington, D.C.: The Brookings Institution, 1975.

National Planning Association. *An Evaluation of the Economic Impact Project of the Public Employment Program, Final Report,* vol. 1, May 22, 1974.

Phelps, E.S. "Phillips Curves, Expectations of Inflation and Optimal Unemployment Over Time." *Economica* 34, 135 (August 1967): 254-281.

Phillips, A.W. "The Relation Between Unemployment and the Rate of Change of Money Wages in the U.K., 1862-1957." *Economica* 26, (November 1958): 283-299.

Portney, P.R. "Congressional Delays in U.S. Fiscal Policymaking." *Journal of Public Economics* 5 (1976): 237-247.

Sulvetta, A.J., and Thompson, N.L. *An Evaluation of the Public Works Impact Program.* Washington, D.C.: U.S. Department of Commerce, April 1975.

Tideman, T. "Defining Area Distress in Unemployment." *Public Policy* 21, 4 (Fall 1973): 441-492.

Tobin, W.J. *Public Works and Unemployment: A History of Federally Funded Programs.* Washington, D.C.: Economic Development Administration, U.S. Department of Commerce, April 1975.

U.S. General Accounting Office. *Observations Concerning the Local Public Works Program,* Comptroller General of the United States, CED-77-48. Washington, D.C.: U.S. Government Printing Office, February 1977.

U.S. National Resources Planning Board. *Security, Work and Relief Policies.* Washington, D.C.: U.S. Government Printing Office, 1942.

Vaughan, R.J. *The Use of Public Works as a Countercyclical Device: A Review of the Issues,* R-1990-EFA. Santa Monica, Calif.: Rand Corporation, July 1976.

Vernez, G. *Public Works as Countercyclical Fiscal Policy,* P-5859. Santa Monica, Calif.: Rand Corporation, April 1977.

Vernez, G. and Vaughan, R.J. *Assessment of Countercyclical Public Works and Public Service Employment Programs,* R-2214-EDA. Washington, D.C.: U.S. Department of Commerce, April 1978.

Vernez, G. et al. *Regional Cycles and Employment Effects of Public Works Investments,* R-2052-EDA. Washington, D.C.: U.S. Department of Commerce, January 1977.

Wiseman, M. "Public Employment on Fiscal Policy." *Brookings Papers on Economic Activity* 1 (1976): 67-114.

✻ *Chapter 7*

Fiscal Implications of CETA
Public Service Employment

Robert F. Cook

Public Service Employment (PSE), the provision of federally subsidized jobs in the state and local public sector, has now been in effect continuously since the begining of fiscal year 1972. Funding has grown from $1 billion in 1972 to roughly $6 billion in fiscal year 1978, and employment levels have varied from 50,000 in 1974 to the mid-1978 level of some 750,000. The emphasis of the program has gone from countercyclical to structural and back at least once. In the last year the size of the program has more than doubled as the major part of the administration's 1977–1978 Economic Stimulus Package.

In line with the focus of this book, the purpose of this chapter is to look at the impact of PSE on cities, in particular the fiscal impact. The chapter relies heavily on the Brookings Monitoring Study of PSE and, in particular, on the efforts and judgments of twenty-six Brookings associates who observed the operation of the program in a sample of forty-two state and local government jurisdictions across the country in July and December 1977. These individuals, mostly economists and political scientists, are resident of the area they are examining and are familiar in an ongoing way with the local government and the operation of the program on which they are reporting. The findings as of July 1977 have been published.[1] This chapter contains some of these results as well as preliminary information from the December observations, which are currently being analyzed.

History of the Program

Public service employment was first used as national policy by the Roosevelt Administration with the establishment of the Works Progress Administration (WPA) in 1935. The WPA was directed at relieving the high unemployment rates of the Depression; it served as an alternative to charity in the absence of unemployment compensation. The WPA employed over three million workers at its peak (at a time when more than nine million were unemployed out of a labor force slightly more than one half what it is currently) and averaged about $1.4 billion annually in wage payments from 1935 to its termination in 1943.[2]

With the recovery of the economy after the Depression, major federal employment and training programs were not widely used again until the 1960s. The focus of the programs in the early 1960s was again on mitigating the effects of cyclical unemployment although with particular emphasis on the needs of distressed areas.[3] The Area Redevelopment Act (ARA) of 1961 and the Public Works and Economic Development Act (PWED) of 1965 sought to generate employment in designated geographical areas such as Appalachia. The Manpower Development and Training Act (MDTA) of 1962 was enacted as a broader program providing skill training and work experience, especially to workers displaced as a result of technological change.

Civil rights legislation and the social ferment that developed in the mid-1960s dramatically shifted the focus of employment and training programs to structural unemployment. These programs placed heavy emphasis on training, job placement, and work experience for the disadvantaged. The MDTA program, which had barely become operational, was reoriented to target on minorities and the disadvantaged. The Community Work and Training Program (CWTP), which had been established in 1962 to provide jobs to recipients of public assistance, was expanded and renamed the Work Experience and Training Program. In 1967, the program was superseded by the Work Incentive Program (WIN). It is administered jointly by the Department of Labor and the Department of Health, Education, and Welfare.

The number of categorical programs for employment and training increased significantly under the authority of the Economic Opportunity Act (EOA) of 1964. The Job Corps, unique in its use of residential centers, was authorized by Title I-A of the act to provide training and education for disadvantaged youths between the ages of 16 and 21. The Neighborhood Youth Corps (NYC) was established under Title I-B of the act to provide part-time work experience, remedial education, and limited job training for disadvantaged youths who either did not complete high school or were potential high school dropouts; it functioned as a combination income maintenance and maturation program.

Operation Mainstream was authorized in 1965 by an amendment to Title II of the Economic Opportunity Act to meet the special needs of workers over 55 years old in rural communities. This program also provided income maintenance for its participants.

One year later another amendment to the Economic Opportunity Act established the New Careers Program (NCP), primarily to aid disadvantaged adults and out of school youths in becoming paraprofessionals in various public sevice fields such as health, education, welfare, neighborhood redevelopment, and public safety. In 1970, through amendments to both the Economic Opportunity Act and the MDTA, the New Careers program was subsumed and expanded by the Public Service Careers program. In addition to the goals of the New Careers program, it focused on facilitating placement and eliminating barriers to employment.

Various work experience programs have also been attempted in the private sector. The Opportunities Industrialization Center (OIC) was founded in Philadelphia in 1964 by the Reverend Leon H. Sullivan. The OIC is a private, nonprofit training and work experience program supported by both federal and private funds. It was developed in response to the plight of urban minorities and is distinguished by its grass roots, community-based support and its self-help doctrine.

The JOBS (Job Opportunities in the Business Sector) program was established in 1967 as a joint effort of the public and private sectors to assist businesses in developing jobs and training programs. By July 1968, 165,000 permanent jobs had been pledged, a number far surpassing the original goal. The economic slowdown that began in 1970, however, had an immediate impact on this program. Workers were laid off; employers became reluctant to meet their outstanding commitments and declined to make further pledges.[4]

Rising unemployment rates in the 1970s brought a renewed emphasis on countercyclical public employment programs. The Emergency Employment Act of 1971 authorized the Public Employment Program (PEP), which was designed as a two-year program aimed primarily at reducing aggregate unemployment rates. PEP operated as a decentralized program with employment provided by state and local governments. The program was funded at $1 billion in 1972, $1.25 billion in 1973, and $250 million in 1974. Funding was triggered automatically by local unemployment rates in excess of

4.5 percent with additional allocations to areas with unemployment rates of 6 percent or more. As would be expected of a counter-cyclical program, the participants were better educated and less disadvantaged than participants in the previous, more structurally oriented programs, and fewer were from minority groups. Although training was authorized, little of the total funding was spent in this way; it was estimated that 94 percent of all PEP funds was spent on compensation of participants.[5]

The Comprehensive Employment and Training Act (CETA) was passed in December 1973 and took effect in July 1974. The purpose of the act was to decentralize and decategorize many of the previously enacted federal employment and training programs. Title II, the Public Service Employment (PSE) portion of the act, was initially designed as a structural rather than a countercyclical policy measure. The $250 million appropriated for PEP in 1974 was to be used to provide a transition to CETA Title II, which had a total authorization of $370 million for 1974. Funding was provided only for areas of "substantial unemployment," defined as having 6.5 percent unemployment for three consecutive months, and participants had to be unemployed or underemployed to enter the program. Under-employed was defined as working part-time but seeking full-time work or working full-time but earning less than a poverty level income.

With the rise in unemployment that accompanied the recession in 1974, Congress in December of that year passed the Emergency Jobs and Unemployment Assistance Act of 1974, which established Title VI of CETA as a countercyclical public service employment program. The authority was temporary, providing for only eighteen months of operation. Funding was distributed primarily according to the level of unemployment of the area. To be eligible under Title VI, an individual had to have been unemployed for thirty days, or fifteen days if the local unemployment rate was over 7 percent. Under the 1974 legislation, $875 million was provided for Title VI and an additional $400 million for Title II. By June 1975 enrollment in Title II had reached 155,000, and the total for Titles II and VI, plus the remainder of PEP enrollment, stood at 310,000.

Authorization for Title VI expired on June 30, 1976. Extension of the program was held up by Senate insistence on major changes in the program aimed at reducing what was alleged to be the high displacement of local employment under this program and the substitution of federal funding for local revenue. However, given continuing high unemployment rates, Congress on April 15, 1976, passed an Emergency Supplemental Appropriations Act that provided for a continuation of the employment of Title VI participants by transferring them to Title II funding.

On October 1, 1976, Congress passed the Emergency Jobs Program Extension Act of 1976, which provided a Title VI appropriation retroactive to June 30, 1976, and Title VI funds for fiscal year 1977. As of October 1976 there were approximately 50,000 enrollees in Title II and 260,000 in Title VI. The addition of $6.6 billion in funding for Title II and VI in the May 13, 1977, economic stimulus package was to raise the number of participants to 125,000 under Title II and to 600,000 under Title VI in fiscal year 1978.

Two major changes were included in the extension of the Title VI program. One was the introduction of the project approach. The additional Title VI funding was to be used first to sustain the level of PSE employment that had existed previously under the PSE program in the area. Remaining funds were to be used for positions in locally designed public service projects. A project was defined as a specific task or group of related tasks with a public service objective that could be completed in less than a year and would not be undertaken by the local area without PSE funds.

The second change was that the eligibility requirements were made more restrictive, targeting the program on the long-term unemployed, low-income individuals, and the recipients of AFDC (Aid to Families with Dependent Children).[6] These requirements were to be applied to all positions created under the project approach and to one-half of the vacancies filled among the "sustainment" positions.

The intent of both changes was to reduce job displacement and the attendant fiscal substitution effects. The eligibility changes were designed to more narrowly target employment on the economically disadvantaged. The result, however, is that the initially countercyclical Title VI program now has the eligibility requirements of a more structurally oriented program, and the initially structurally oriented Title II program now has the minimal eligibility requirements more characteristic of a countercyclical program.

All of the various Titles of CETA expire on September 30, 1978. As of this writing, there are both House and Senate versions of the reauthorization bill and the final legislation is yet to be passed. Both the House and Senate bills create a separate structural PSE program under the training title of CETA (new Title II) and a countercyclical PSE program under Title VI. The eligibility for the Title II PSE jobs would remain essentially that of the current Title I, that is, economically disadvantaged and unemployed, underemployed, or in school. Four billion dollars is appropriated for this program; this translates into approximately 200,000 PSE jobs (on the assumption that a maximum of 50 percent will be used for PSE). This is 100,000 jobs below the level of the prestimulus PSE program but four times the level of the "old" Title II. Although there is no project requirement on these jobs, there is, however, a limit on the tenure of an individual in a PSE job to eighteen months out of a three-year period.

The cyclical PSE program under Title VI would be triggered by a national unemployment rate in excess of 4 or 4.5 percent with the possibility that funding would be provided to absorb 25 percent of the unemployed in excess of 4 percent. This would translate into approximately 500,000 jobs if the national unemployment rate were 6 percent. Eligibility would be limited to those unemployed eight weeks and with a family income below the Bureau of Labor Statistics (BLS) lower living standard. Tenure in the program would be limited to eighteen months out of a three-year period; 50 percent of the jobs must be employed in projects as is also true under the existing Title VI program.

The change in the eligibility under the proposed Title II PSE program is more restrictive in that it requires that individuals be unemployed *and* economically disadvantaged as opposed to the current Title II, which requires that the individual be unemployed *or* economically disadvantaged. The proposed eligibility requirements for Title VI as a countercyclical program are less tightly targeted than those of the existing Title VI. However, they remain more restrictive than those of the existing Title I.

Legislative Objectives

Public service employment programs can and do have a variety of and sometimes conflicting objectives. Some employment and training programs of the federal government are primarily employment programs; others stress training and placement; most, however, have multiple purposes. The fact that goals have often shifted in emphasis, plus the potential for conflict among them, is necessarily a central theme of the examination of any federal program, and PSE is no exception.

- *Decentralization and Decategorization.* CETA represented a change in policy in that it provided for a "flexible system of Federal, State, and local programs" in place of the federally run categorical programs that dominated the 1960s. For PSE, this means that local governments are the program operators under a fairly broad set of guidelines from the federal government.
- *Training.* CETA attempts to upgrade the skill levels of the labor force through work experience or the provision of other training services otherwise not available.

- *Transition.* PSE is to provide for transitional employment and for improvement in the earning capacity of the participants by enabling them to move into unsubsidized employment.
- *Public Service Provision.* Participants are to provide needed public sector services. This, in turn, leads to the "hidden objective" of fiscal assistance.
- *Job Creation.* The provision of transitional employment in the public sector is designed to aid the unemployed and underemployed and to reduce unemployment.
- *Economic Stimulus.* PSE is intended to produce countercyclical stimulus for the economy in addition to the provision of direct jobs. It is important for this objective that the program be capable of building up and phasing down rapidly so that the stimulative expenditure of the funds takes place when desired.
- *Targeting.* The eligibility requirements of the legislation emphasize concentration on certain groups within the population, particularly on the unemployed and economically disadvantaged.

The decentralization objective conflicts with the ability of the federal government to guarantee that the other objectives of the program are met. A later section will detail how the programs stand in relation to the stated objectives. However, two cases of conflict are illustrative.

An early concern with PSE was about its service to the target groups. Reports on the Public Empoyment Program and CETA indicated that the characteristics of the individuals served differed from those of the categorical program participants. Table 7-1 compares the distribution of characteristics of enrollees in the categorical manpower programs of the 1960s with those of PEP enrollees and CETA enrollees in training programs and PSE. These differences are largely the result of the shift from training to PSE. To a certain extent, however, they are a function of decentralization in that, with the passage of CETA and the establishment of local governments as the program operators, a substantial number of governments—most specifically, counties—for the first time became involved in employment and training programs. The categorical programs had been operated primarily in urban areas. While the characteristics of the participants in urban programs remained similar, the broadening of the program to smaller metropolitan and rural areas resulted in a change in the mix of people served. In addition, for PEP and PSE the countercyclical emphasis on the unemployed results in a distribution of characteristics that comes even closer to that of the general population.

The greatest difference between larger and smaller jurisdictions is

Table 7-1.   Characteristics of Categorical Programs, PEP, and CETA II and VI Enrollees, and U.S. Unemployed Populations

Characteristic	Categorical Programs Fiscal Year 1974	PEP Fiscal Year 1974	Title I Fiscal Year 1975	Title I Fiscal Year 1976	Title I Fiscal Year 1977	Fiscal Year 1975
Total	100	100	100	100	100	100
Sex						
Male	57.7	66.1	54.4	54.1	51.5	65.8
Female	42.3	33.9	45.6	45.9	48.5	34.2
Age						
Under 22 years	63.1	22.8	61.7	56.7	51.7	23.7
22–44 years	30.5	66.5	32.1	36.5	40.8	62.9
45 years and over	6.2	10.7	6.1	6.8	7.4	13.4
Race						
White	54.9	68.8	54.6	55.3	56.7	65.1
Black	37.0	22.9	38.5	37.1	34.7	21.8
Other	8.1	8.3	5.6	6.2	7.2	13.1
Education						
8 years or less	15.1	3.0[a]	13.3	11.9	10.0	9.4
9 to 11 years	51.1	20.0	47.6	42.9	39.8	18.3
12 years or over	33.8	77.0	39.1	45.2	50.2	72.3
Economically disadvantaged	86.7	38.0	77.3	75.7	78.3	48.3
Veteran	15.1	39.2	9.6	8.1	10.1	23.9

Sources: *Continuous Longitudinal Manpower Survey*, report 4 (U.S. Department of Labor, November 1976); *Employment and Training Report of the President* (U.S. Department of Labor and U.S. Department of Health, Education and Welfare, 1978).

[a]Figure not statistically reliable due to small number of cases.

[b]Based on March 1977 only.

[c]Not strictly comparable, definition changed to include either poverty level or 70 percent of BLS lower-living standard.

[d]NA indicates not available.

in the percentage of minority participation. Almost three-fourths of the participants in the large cities are members of minority groups, compared with one-fourth in smaller jurisdictions. However, when these findings are compared with the relative proportions of minorities in the population in 1970 (Table 7-2), two important observations emerge. First, in all types of government in the Brookings sample, the percentage of PSE participants from minority groups was considerably higher than the minority percentage in the general population, using 1970 as the base year. Second, small cities and

CETA					U.S. Unemployed Population		
Title II		*Title VI*					
Fiscal Year 1976	*Fiscal Year 1977*	*Fiscal Year 1975*	*Fiscal Year 1976*	*Fiscal Year 1977*	*Fiscal Year 1975*	*Fiscal Year 1976*	*Fiscal Year 1977*
100	100	100	100	100	100	100	100
63.8	60.0	70.2	65.1	64.1	54.9	55.5	53.2
36.2	40.0	29.8	34.9	35.9	45.1	44.5	46.8
21.9	20.3	21.4	22.0	20.3	34.8	33.6	34.2
64.0	64.2	64.8	64.1	64.9	46.0	46.6	47.2
14.1	15.5	13.8	13.9	14.8	19.1	19.8	18.6
61.4	70.6	71.1	68.2	66.2	81.1	80.7	79.2
26.5	22.9	22.9	23.0	25.9	18.9	19.3	20.8
12.1	6.4	6.0	8.8	7.9			
8.0	7.3	8.4	8.1	8.2	15.1	12.9	13.0[b]
17.9	15.2	18.2	17.7	18.9	38.9	28.7	29.9[b]
74.1	77.5	73.3	74.2	72.8	46.0	58.4	57.1[b]
46.5	48.9	43.6	44.1	66.6[c]	NA[d]	NA[d]	NA[d]
21.5	22.6	27.1	20.7	24.9	16.9	17.7	15.9

suburban areas actually served the highest proportion of minorities relative to their minority population.

To date, the primary concern of Congress has had to do with conflict among decentralization, job creation, and the provision of needed public services. The federal objective is the creation of as many new jobs as possible and therefore a maximum reduction in the number of unemployed. To the extent that local program operators are concerned with the provision of needed public services and view the program as fiscal assistance, they may use PSE as a way of providing desired service levels with federal rather than local funds. This possibility is referred to as the displacement of regular local government employees and the substitution of federal for local funding. Oddly, the federal response to this has been to increase the categorization of PSE through tightened eligibility, project requirements, and so on.

EMPLOYMENT AND FISCAL EFFECTS
ON CITIES

In public discussions of PSE, considerable interest has focused on the program's relative share of local government employees as the level of PSE rises. The terms reliance, dependence, and "federal aid junkies" have been used to describe the extent to which local governments, particularly cities, utilize federal programs for the provision of governmental services. For PSE, this takes two forms: the number of PSE employees in relation to the regular local government work force and what Harry Katz and Michael Wiseman call the "hidden objective" of PSE—fiscal relief.[7]

Often these discussions fail to take into account the outstationing and contracting out of participants, which can be appreciable under PSE.[8] Outstationing refers to the practice of paying people through the personnel, manpower, or some other office of a local government that receives an allocation of PSE positions, but then assigns the participant to work in a different organization—a school, a hospital, a Social Security office. Contracting out, on the other hand, refers to cases in which a jurisdiction receiving a PSE allocation does not itself expend some portion of its CETA-PSE funds, but instead contracts with another organization to use these funds to hire additional employees.

Table 7–3 shows the PSE enrollments as of the end of December 1977 for the sixteen large cities included in the Brookings Monitoring Study of PSE. The second column of the table indicates the number of PSE workers in the city government. On average, the cities in this study retain 59 percent of their PSE positions. The rest are outstationed or subcontracted to nonprofit agencies or to other local governments. Assuming that a government retained all of its Title II and Title VI substainment positions, it could retain a maximum of 86 percent of its PSE positions. The regulations recommend that 35 percent of the project positions be assigned to nonprofit organizations; in December, the project Title VI positions accounted for 40 percent of all PSE positions, both nationally and in the Brookings sample.

The percentages shown in the third column are for the PSE positions as a proportion of the 1976 Census figures on noneducational employment in these cities. On average, in the sample cities the December PSE enrollment amounted to 21 percent of the regular employment in the city. These figures would be somewhat higher now since the enrollment in PSE nationally at that time was 663,000 and current enrollment levels are closer to 763,000.

Table 7-2. Minority Group Representation among PSE Participants and in the General Population by Type of Government

	Large Distressed Cities	Other Large Cities	Small Cities and Suburban Areas	Rural Areas
Percent minority PSE participants July 1977	74	74	26	22
Percent minority, 1970 census	37	20	6	12

Sources: Field research data; U.S. Bureau of the Census, *County and City Data Book, 1972,* Statistical Abstract Supplement (Washington, D.C.: U.S. Government Printing Office, 1973).

If allowance is made for the fact that 41 percent of the positions are allocated to other local governments and noprofit agencies, PSE employment in these cities declines to 12 percent of the 1976 local government employment. While roughly 12 percent of local government is not insubstantial, it is neither the 30 nor the 40 percent that one reads in the newspapers. It is also true that cities, particularly large distressed cities, are assigned relatively more PSE positions because of their higher unemployment rates. At the peak of the PSE enrollment in March 1978, 763,000 PSE enrollees represented 6 percent of the 12.8 million employees of state and local governments.[9]

On the other hand, depending upon how the jurisdiction elects to utilize the PSE positions it retains, it is possible for PSE to account for a large part of the employment in certain departments. To the extent that these are high-priority service areas, this fact lends support to the dependence hypothesis. For example, in one of these cities PSE accounts for one-fourth of the fire department; in another, PSE represents 71 percent of the employment in parks and recreation but only 9 percent of the police department. In still another city PSE represents 2 percent of the police, 39 percent of the street maintenance, 38 percent of the parks and recreation, and 58 percent of the municipal arts department. The overall percentages of employment accounted for by PSE in these cities are all within a range of 2 percent. However, depending upon how the city ranks police in relation to municipal arts and recreation, the extent of dependence varies substantially.

Another point illustrated by the table is that the jurisdictional spreading of PSE funds is greater than has been assumed in other analyses. While it is reasonable to talk about providing service to

Table 7-3. PSE Grant and Employment in Relation to City Revenue and Employment

	December 31, 1977, PSE Enrollments[a]	December PSE in City Government[a]	Percent Retained by City[a]	1976 City Employment[b]	Fiscal Year 1978 PSE Grant[c] ($000)	Fiscal Year 1978 Retained PSE Funds[d] ($000)	Estimated 1977–1978 Own-Source Revenue[e] ($000)
St. Louis	4,160 (31)	2,006 (15)	48	13,325	5,177 (2)	2,496 (1)	208,161
Rochester	980 (26)	421 (11)	43	3,778	12,518 (12)	5,378 (5)	102,969
Cleveland	1,500 (15)	1,332 (13)	89	10,049	45,487 (24)	40,392 (21)	189,919
Boston	2,856 (17)	2,197 (13)	77	16,485	31,549 (7)	24,269 (5)	465,652
Baltimore	2,578 (12)	1,967 (9)	76	21,003	63,889 (16)	48,747 (12)	411,144
Philadelphia	5,194 (16)	4,087 (13)	79	32,274	60,866 (9)	47,894 (7)	686,527
Detroit	4,044 (20)	2,985 (15)	74	20,059	56,631 (12)	41,801 (9)	467,524
Chicago	9,117 (19)	3,821 (8)	42	48,799	108,727 (13)	45,568 (5)	859,061
Los Angeles	10,494 (24)	6,456 (15)	62	44,503	122,775 (14)	75,532 (9)	871,802
Houston	2,621 (17)	1,285 (9)	49	15,082	26,822 (8)	13,150 (4)	349,672
Phoenix	2,650 (34)	1,302 (17)	49	7,792	29,824 (23)	14,653 (12)	127,410
San Francisco	3,587 (17)	2,273 (11)	63	21,599	38,071 (8)	24,125 (5)	470,132
Kansas City	1,735 (26)	900 (14)	52	6,569	17,217 (9)	8,931 (5)	194,660
St. Paul	837	271	32	3,288	9,835	3,184	74,719

Tulsa	(25) 630	(8) 390	62	3,507	(13) 7,178	(4) 4,444	94,831
New Orleans	(18) 2,319	(11) 1,016	44	10,544	(8) 19,242	(5) 8,430	166,684
Unweighted mean	(22) (21)	(10) (12)	59		(12) (12)	(5) (7)	

Note: Numbers in parentheses are percentages of city employment or own source revenue.

[a] Brookings field research data.

[b] U.S. Census Bureau, Local Government Employment in Selected Areas and Large Counties, 1976.

[c] 1977–1978 allocations less outlays to September 30, 1977.

[d] 1978 PSE grant multiplied by the percentage of the December PSE enrollment retained by the city.

[e] U.S. Census Bureau, City Government Finances, 1970–1971 to 1975–1976. Figures are estimated by taking the average annual change from 1971–1976 forward to 1978 for general revenue from own sources.

a target population within an area, given the residency requirements of the legislation, it is difficult to assess the fiscal effects upon a particular jurisdiction without knowing the distribution of funding below the prime sponsor level.

Fiscal Magnitude

The second part of Table 7-3 relates to the fiscal magnitude of the PSE program in the large cities in the Brookings sample. Column 5 contains the 1978 allocation for each city, both absolute and as a proportion of estimated 1978 own-source revenue for the city. Column 6 shows the part of that grant that is estimated (using the proportions of PSE positions retained) to be used by the city itself. While the 1978 PSE grant varies from 2 to 24 percent of the city's own-raised revenue, the average for the sixteen cities is 12 percent. The comparable figures for that part of the grant retained by the city governments are 1 and 9 percent, respectively, with an average for the group of 7 percent.

Overall, PSE accounted for $6.6 billion or 35 percent of the $18.7 billion stimulus package. In fiscal year 1979 the relative importance of PSE will rise. The Congressional Budget Office estimates that expenditure under Local Public Works (LPW) and Antirecession Fiscal Assistance (ARFA) will decline in fiscal year 1979 while that of PSE will rise. This is a function of funding the peak enrollment through the year. The Department of Labor estimates that sponsor governments began the new fiscal year with $6.7 billion to spend. Of this amount the sixteen sample governments accounted for $656 million or 10 percent. What the figures in the table as well as the aggregate figures indicate is that PSE employment and funding, even for the portion of the positions and funding actually utilized directly by cities, represent a substantial minority of their employment and have a fiscal effect equal to between one in $8 and one in $14 of the revenues that they raise directly.

Another perspective on the relative magnitude of PSE is indicated in Table 7-4, which presents estimated outlays under General Revenue Sharing (GRS) and CETA Titles II and VI for fiscal years 1976 through 1979. The striking thing is that since the prestimulus period, PSE has increased from slightly under 40 percent of the magnitude of GRS to slightly under 90 percent in fiscal year 1979. PSE in fiscal years 1978 and 1979 will be second only to GRS in its fiscal impact on state and local government. A more speculative picture is presented in the last two columns of the table. In these columns 50 percent of the state share (one-third) of GRS is taken out on the assumption that only half of the state's share is passed through to

Table 7-4. Estimated Outlays under General Revenue Sharing and CETA/ PSE for Fiscal Years 1976-1979 (in billions of dollars)

	Estimated Total Outlays				*Estimated Local Government Share*	
	Fiscal Year 1976	*Fiscal Year 1977*	*Fiscal Year 1978*	*Fiscal Year 1979*	*Fiscal Year 1978*	*Fiscal Year 1979*
General Revenue Sharing[a]	6.240	6.760	6.827	6.852	5.6	5.6
CETA, Title II and Title VI (PSE)[b]	2.431	2.738	5.580	6.036	4.6	5.0

Source: Budget of the United States Government, Fiscal Year 1979, 1978, Special Analyses Office of Management and Budget, Washington, D.C. "Results of CETA Economic Stimulus Survey," National Governors Conference, December, 1977.

[a]The General Revenue Sharing figures include 50 percent of the state share. The PSE figures include 86 percent of the allocations to state sponsors but exclude 14 percent of the total allocations.

[b]CETA Title II refers to the funds released under the 1974 Emergency Jobs and Unemployment Assistance Act. Title VI represents outlays for PSE.

local governments. For PSE, Balance of State and Statewide Consortia prime sponsors received 30 percent of the allocation. However, according to a survey taken in December 1977, state agencies retain only 14 percent of the money. Therefore, 86 percent of the state's share is included in the PSE figures in these columns. Some of the PSR funds are in turn subcontracted to nonprofit agencies. Consequently 14 percent (35 percent of the projects that account for 40 percent of the PSE program) of the remaining funds are subtracted to represent that proportion of the funds passed through to nonprofit agencies. While these numbers are tentative, they suggest that in fiscal years 1978 and 1979 the magnitude of PSE funding will approximate 80 to 90 percent of GRS for local governments.

OBJECTIVES AND RESULTS

Employment Effects

As indicated in the introduction to this chapter, the federal objective of reducing unemployment may conflict with the local objective of fiscal relief. To the extent that local governments utilize PSE to provide governmental services that would have been provided anyway, there is no addition to total employment and the countercyclical objective of creating jobs is less likely to be achieved.

Previous studies of the employment effects of Public Service Employment programs have reported considerable variation in the rates of displacement. In econometric studies of the Public Employment Program, George Johnson and James Tomola estimated that the displacement rate rose from 39 percent in the first quarter to 67 percent after two years.[10] Alan Fechter estimated displacement at 50 to 90 percent after one year.[11] In reexamining the Johnson and Tomola data, Michael Wiseman estimated that, depending upon the assumptions used, the rate of displacement after one year varied from zero to 80 percent.[12] The National Planning Association examined the results of the PEP in twelve demonstration sites that received sufficient federal funding to absorb 8 percent of local unemployment; it estimated displacement for the demonstration sites at 46 percent after one year.[13]

Estimates of displacement under the CETA program show a similar range. A study by Johnson and Tomola, covering public employment under the PEP (1971–1974) and its continuation through the end of 1975 under CETA, estimated displacement at 0 percent after one quarter, 58 percent after one year, and 100 percent after one and a half years.[14] The Congressional Budget Office (CBO) assumed displacement rates under CETA of 60 percent after one year and 90 to 100 percent after two years.[15] A later study done by the CBO when the Carter Administration's economic stimulus package was being considered assumed a first-year displacement rate of 25 percent and a second-year rate of 40 percent based on program operation at a rate of 30,000 new positions per month.[16]

In the view of those concerned about the problems of the cities, a Public Service Employment program that concentrates on these jurisdictions can provide fiscal relief where it is most needed. To the extent that this happens, PSE operates in effect as a form of counter-cyclical revenue sharing by relieving the pressure on the local tax base. Where the resulting fiscal effect of such displacement is to cut or stabilize local taxes, PSE still has a stimulus impact, but it is in the private sector.

Likewise, displacement is not incompatible with other objectives of the PSE program such as the targeting of assistance on disadvantaged persons. For disadvantaged persons, PSE can mean increased employment opportunities even if displacement occurs. The program can change the composition of the recipient government's work force by adding employees from groups that were not represented as heavily in the preexisting work force. Under these conditions, the PSE program can be thought of as a hybrid, having the attributes of both a revenue-sharing program and an affirmative action program to promote the hiring of minority and disadvantaged persons.

Net Employment Effects

Table 7-5 shows the allocation of PSE participants by title and according to type of organization in which they were employed in July 1977. Participants employed by the Brookings sample governments are shown in column A; columns B through F show PSE participants employed by other organizations under subcontracting or outstanding agreements with the sample governments. Overall, 70 percent of the positions shown were retained by the sample governments. The share of positions retained was higher for Titles II and VI sustainment (79 percent) than for Title VI projects (59 percent). Nonprofit organizations account for 24 percent of Title VI positions and 10 percent of Title II and VI sustainment positions, making them the largest recipients of PSE positions outside of the sample governments themselves.

Table 7-5 also provides figures for job creation and displacement, broken down by title and type of employing organization. Three important findings stand out. First, according to these figures the displacement rate for PSE employment is considerably lower than that reported by other researchers. For all titles and for the sample as a whole, 18 percent of the positions were judged by the associates to represent displacement and 82 percent job creation. If the results in the jurisdictions where the sampling procedure was used are weighted to reflect the relative size of the program in these jurisdictions, the extent of displacement for the sample as a whole rises to 20 percent. This is still well below the results reported by other researchers.[17] There are several possible reasons for this difference, one being that the other estimates were for PEP or the prestimulus PSE program with its projects and heavy involvement of nonprofit organizations. Moreover, as of July 1977, a substantial number of the positions examined had not been in place very long—and most of the evidence indicates that displacement increases over time. Finally, a substantial number of the positions (31 percent), primarily accounted for by distressed large cities, were judged to be job creation in the sense that they represented positions that would have been cut in the absence of the PSE program. Most of the other studies do not include a cyclical variable.

Second, the displacement rate varies depending on the employing organization. The rates for sample governments (21 percent), school

Table 7-5. PSE Positions Classified as Job Creation and Displacement by Title and Type of Employing Organization July 1977

	Sample Governments (A)	Other School Districts (B)	Other Local Governments (C)	State Agencies (D)	Federal Agencies (E)	Nonprofit Organizations (F)	Total (G)
II and VI Sustainment							
Job Creation	8,458 (76)	874 (84)	631 (76)	508 (93)	24 (96)	1,453 (99)	11,948 (79)
Displacement	2,738 (24)	163 (16)	199 (24)	41 (7)	1 (4)	18 (1)	3,160 (21)
Total	11,196	1,037	830	549	25	1,471	15,108
Percent	(79)	(7)	(5)	(4)	(a)	(10)	(100)
VI Project							
Job creation	2,865 (93)	278 (74)	389 (89)	95 (93)	—	1,188 (96)	4,815 (92)
Displacement	205 (7)	99 (26)	47 (11)	7 (7)	—	53 (4)	411 (8)
Total	3,070	377	436	102		1,241	5,226
Percent	(59)	(7)	(8)	(2)		(24)	(100)
All Titles							
Job creation	11,323 (79)	1,152 (81)	1,020 (81)	603 (93)	24 (96)	2,641 (97)	16,763 (82)
Displacement	2,943 (21)	262 (19)	246 (19)	48 (7)	1 (4)	71 (3)	3,571 (18)
Total	14,266	1,414	1,266	651	25	2,712	20,334
Percent	(70)	(7)	(6)	(3)	(a)	(13)	(100)

Source: Field research data gathered in Brookings Monitoring Study of PSE, July 1977.
Note: Figures in parentheses are percentages.
[a]Less than 0.5 percent.

districts (19 percent), and other local governments (19 percent) were slightly higher than the displacement rate for all employing organizations combined. By contrast, the rates for state and federal agencies and for nonprofit organizations were lower than the overall rate. Some qualifying comments are needed here. Federal agencies received such a small number of positions (25 out of a total of 20,000) that the extent of job creation and displacement cannot really be determined. As for nonprofit organizations, their low displacement rate undoubtedly reflects the fact that many of the agencies involved had very few employees prior to the application for PSE funds and used PSE to expand operations. In such cases, all positions represent new employment and new expenditures. In addition, some nonprofit organizations used PSE funds to monetize existing volunteer work that was not classified as displacement.

A third important finding is that the displacement rate was substantially higher for Title II and VI sustainment positions (21 percent) than for Title VI project positions (8 percent). These figures also vary depending on the employing organization involved. Nonprofit organizations had the lowest rate of displacement in both sustainment and project categories.

Among positions retained by the sample governments, nearly one-fourth of the sustainment positions were judged to be displacement as opposed to only 7 percent of the project positions. The figures for other local governments were similar to those for sample governments. Among positions filled by school districts, on the other hand, the displacement rate was higher for project than for sustainment positions.

Employment Effects by Type
of Jurisdiction

Table 7-6 presents a breakdown of job creation and displacement by type of jurisdiction and six of the larger subcontracting governments or "subgovernments" studied as well as for all of the state agencies for which data are available. Since the concern here is with differences between types of jurisdictions, only the positions retained by the sample governments and subgovernments are included in the analysis. The governments and subgovernments are grouped in the following categories:

Large city, including central cities over 250,000 in population.
Suburban, including smaller cities (the largest being a suburban city
    of 111,000) and suburban counties
Rural, including rural towns (with a population of less than 50,000)

Table 7-6. PSE Positions Classified as Job Creation and Displacement by Type of Jurisdiction and Title for Sample Governments, Six Subcontracting Governments, and State Agencies July 1977

	Title II and VI Sustainment			Title VI Project			Total		
	Job Creation	Displacement	Total	Job Creation	Displacement	Total	Job Creation	Displacement	Total
Large city	7,553 (75)	2,490 (25)	10,043	2,466 (93)	195 (7)	2,661	10,019 (79)	2,685 (21)	12,704
Suburban	620 (71)	254 (29)	874	458 (94)	29 (6)	487	1,078 (79)	283 (21)	1,361
Rural	349 (98)	7 (2)	356	37 (100)	0	37	386 (98)	7 (2)	393
State	572 (83)	120 (17)	692	142 (95)	7 (5)	149	714 (85)	127 (15)	841

Source: Field research data gathered in Brookings Monitoring Study of PSE, July 1977.

Note: Figures in parentheses are percentages.

and counties outside SMSAs
State agencies

For Title II and VI sustainment PSE, one-fourth of the positions in large cities were categorized as displacement. These jurisdicitons were divided into distressed and other cities, but there was virtually no difference between the two groups.[18] Suburban jurisdictions had the highest level of displacement—29 percent. Displacement was lower among positions assigned to state agencies (17 percent); it was almost nonexistent in rural jurisdictions.

For Title VI project employment, the extent of displacement was generally lower. In the large cities displacement averaged 7 percent— 10 percent in the distressed large cities and 4 percent in the other large cities. Six percent of the project employment in the suburban jurisdictions and 5 percent in state agencies represented displacements. There was no displacement in Project VI employment in the rural areas. However, the number of positions involved was very small for two reasons. In some cases the overlying sponsor allocated only sustainment positions to rural county governments; in other cases the rural county governments had project positions but subcontracted most of them to other organizations, which meant that the positions were not included in this section of the analysis.

There are reasons to believe that these results will have changed by the December 1977 observation. First, the positions will have been in place longer, and most evidence indicates that displacement increases with time. Second, economic conditions will have improved in many of the jurisdictions, and what was job creation in July 1977 may have become displacement if the government has later funded a position out of its own revenues. Third, PSE has become a major source of federal funds, and if it is perceived as a primary source of fiscal assistance, increased displacement would result. Finally, and operating counter to the first three considerations, the project portion of the program has increased from 25 to 40 percent of the total program. Since there appears to be less displacement in this part of the program, this would lower the overall rate of displacement.

Stimulus, Speed of Buildup, and Expenditure

Leaving aside the question of any slippage resulting from displacement, there is evidence that enrollment levels can be built up fairly rapidly and expenditure can increase fairly quickly. Enrollment in the PEP started in August 1971, and by December of that year 89,000 of the 132,000 planned positions were filled. The experience of the PSE stimulus program is given in Table 7-7.

Table 7-7. PSE Enrollment May 1977 to February 1978 (in thousands)

End of Month	Total	Title II	Title VI
May 1977	329.2	64.7	264.5
June	363.7	71.2	292.5
July	438.4	77.9	360.5
August	512.5	88.3	424.2
September	543.4	94.0	449.4
October	571.5	100.4	471.1
November	602.7	105.8	496.9
December	626.9	110.3	516.7
January 1978	674.1	118.3	555.8
February	753.2	129.2	624.0

Source: Department of Labor program data.

Sponsors managed to fill 424,000 positions in a ten-month period from May 1977 through February 1978. It should be noted that the enabling legislation was passed in October 1976, the regulations governing the buildup were published in January 1977, and sponsors were notified of the need to have a pool of eligibles and approved projects well ahead of the appropriation in May. Without the preexisting legislation and the lead time provided, it is not clear that these results could have been achieved.[19] There is, however, some evidence that the rapid buildup of enrollees is at the expense of concentrating on certain target groups and program design. Responding to pressure from the sponsors, the Department of Labor had to relax the eligibility requirements on unemployment as well as modify the definition of what constituted a project. Under pressure from the regional offices to meet hiring targets or face loss of part of their funding, sponsors sometimes relied on such other creative solutions as transferring all PSE eligible Title I participants or allowing termination data to lag.

According to the 1979 budget, outlays were $2.7 billion in fiscal year 1977; future estimates are $5.6 billion in fiscal year 1978 and $6.0 billion in fiscal year 1979. Determination of the fiscal impact depends upon the use that is made of the funds. If the expenditure is for employment or administrative purposes under PSE, funds to displace someone who otherwise would have been employed by that government, this substitutes federal money for local resources, which can then be used for other purposes.

Such substitution effects can occur in one of three ways. First, local taxes can be cut or stabilized, transferring the direct PSE stimulus from the public sector to the private sector.

The second substitution effect would have the local government maintaining a higher level of fund balances than otherwise would have been the case. As there is no stimulus impact in the public sector and to the extent that fund balances accumulate, any private sector economic stimulus occurs through the monetary system. In any case, the economic stimulus effect is delayed or dissipated.

The third substitution effect involves cases in which the recipient government uses the freed resources to expand other programs. It is possible for displacement and substitution to occur and still witness a direct (or nearly so) stimulus effect in the public sector, either for capital or operating purposes.

Table 7-8 summarizes the fiscal effects data for both titles for all of the sample units in the Brookings study in July 1977. More than four-fifths of the funds included in this analysis were assigned to direct stimulus effects through increased employment by local governments and other sponsoring organizations. Among substitution effects, tax stabilization was by far the most important fiscal effect of displacement on the finances of the governments and agencies receiving funds for PSE positions.

Targeting

The eligibility criteria, both existing and proposed, were mentioned in the introductory section of this chapter, and the characteristics of participants are included in Table 7-1. In this section the effects of some of the proposed changes are examined.

William Barnes of the National Commission for Manpower Policy (NCMP) has estimated that under the existing eligibility requirements, within the course of a year the eligible populations for the various Titles are Title I, 26.7 million; Title II, 20.6 million; Title VI sustainment, 20.6 million; and Title VI projects, 6.8 million.[20] One unmistakable observation that results from such data is that the countercyclical part of the current program, project Title VI, has eligibility requirements like a structureal program and the structural PSE program, Title II, has the eligibility requirements of a countercyclical program. Furthermore, the structural training title has the largest eligible population although the people served in that title tend to be more disadvantaged than those in either Title II or Title VI.

Another observation gathered from the characteristics data in Table 7-1 is that the Title VI project eligibility requirements have had an effect on the characteristics of the individuals served, not only for those in projects but also for those served in the sustainment Title VI. Those enrolling now are more disadvantaged than was true in previous years.

The effect of the proposed shift of the structural PSE to the

Table 7-8.   Fiscal Effects Data for the Sample Units

Effect	Amount	Percent
Direct PSE stimulus		
Job creation	$12,166,300	73.0
Administration	1,920,900	11.5
Substitution	2,583,700	15.6
Tax reduction	209,300	1.3
Tax stabilization	1,730,900	10.4
Increased fund balances	69,400	.4
Operating expenditures	65,000	.4
Capital expenditures	29,000	.2
Unallocated (displacement)	480,100	2.9
Total	$16,671,000	100.0

Source: Field research data gathered in Brookings Monitoring Study of PSE, July 1977.

training title (the new Title II) and of the application of the joint income and unemployment eligibility requirements to the PSE program is that the size of the eligible population will be reduced to roughly that of the current Title VI projects. The application of the joint criteria to the countercyclical Title VI will bring the eligible population for that title closer to the existing Title VI projects. The reduction in the duration of unemployment will expand that population slightly. However, unless the current Title I or II definitions of unemployed (which include AFDC, SSI, and public assistance recipients who are willing to work) were carried over to Title VI, the eligibile population would be reduced by the number of these individuals.

Provision of Needed Public Services

PSE assists participants by providing them with employment and income. As Baily and Solow point out, from a macroeconomic perspective a dollar spent on PSE contributes a dollar to GNP, since the output of government is calculated on the cost of the inputs rather than on the value of the output produced unless there is displacement of local employment and the substitution of federal for local expenditure.[21] Questions about who is employed and what is produced are relevant only in the sense of determining the relative inflationary impact of the expenditure. From the perspective of the budgetary cost of providing income maintenance, the concern would be with who is receiving the assistance and what the offsets are in terms of reduction in other transfer payments and the increase in taxes paid by PSE participants. From a structural perspective, the concerns are over who is being served by the program, the extent of training involved, and the value of what they do only in the sense of whether it contributes to their later employability. However, to the extent that the provision of public services is one of the objectives of the PSE program, the kinds of services produced by PSE employees and their productivity relative to that of regular local government employees are fairly important elements in discussing the value of PSE. Relatively little current information is available about the types of services provided under the PSE program. The lack of such information can be attributed in part to the fact that the legislation and regulations focus more on who is to be employed than on the services to be provided. The result is that recipient governments can tailor their PSE programs to their particular needs in the functional areas in which participants are employed and the type of work in which they are engaged. The amount of latitude that recipient governments are afforded is very broad. The Department of Labor (DOL) currently requires sponsor reports on the functional areas in which PSE participants are employed only for Title VI projects.

In the analysis, nine functional areas, grouped into four major categories, are examined. The categories are described below and are illustrated in Table 7-9.

1. *Primary services* These four functional areas—protective services, public works, utilities and sanitation, and general administration—generally parallel the Census Bureau definitions of common functions for municipalities.
2. *Social and cultural services* This category includes functions that may or may not be provided by cities and counties. They are considered to be variable functions in the analyses of local public finances.
3. *Parks and recreation.* This category combines both park building and maintenance functions as well as more socially oriented recreational functions.
4. *Education* Education is classified separately in this analysis because in most cases this function is provided by school districts, many of which are independent.

Table 7-9 shows the distribution of positions by functional area and by title for jurisdictions in the Brookings sample. An examination of the four main categories demonstrates that the overall distribution does not vary significantly by title. The data suggest that the functional areas of public works and utilities and sanitation within the primary services category are particularly amenable to the project

Table 7-9. Percentage Distribution of PSE Participants by Functional Area and Title, July 1977

Functional Area	Title II, VI Sustainment	Title VI Projects	All Titles
Primary services	50	44	48
Protective services	19	2	14
Public works	14	27	18
Utilities and sanitation	5	11	7
General administration	12	4	9
Social and cultural services	19	24	21
Social services	13	19	15
Health	4	2	3
Culture and arts	2	3	3
Parks and recreation	12	16	13
Education	11	10	11
Unallocated	8	7	8
Total	100	101	101
Number of participants	12,071	5,161	17,232

Source: Field research data gathered in Brookings Monitoring Study of PSE, July 1977.

approach. One reason for this may be time constraints. Because of the pressure to develop projects and spend money quickly, the easiest solution often is to assign PSE positions to activities that require the least amount of planning. Public works and utilities and sanitation frequently have a workshelf of planned but unfunded projects, some of which involve relatively limited capital costs. Together the two functions account for nearly 40 percent of all Title VI projects in the sample.

There was also a tendency among some jurisdictions to segregate Title VI projects so that if and when the level of federal funding for PSE was reduced, jurisdictions could disengage relatively easily.

It should be pointed out, however, that the distribution shown for Title VI projects may be due to the seasonal nature of many public works and utility and sanitation activities. These activities generally involve outdoor work, which is presumably most easily performed during the summer.

Another important factor in considering the overall functional area distribution is the fact that the midsummer observations were made when school was not in session. For this reason, the distribution for education appeared smaller than otherwise would be the case for both sustainment and project PSE.

A Comparison with Regular
Government Employment

One approach to an analysis of the overall distribution of PSE positions by functional area is to compare the distribution for PSE with that for regular employment by local governments. As shown in Table 7-10, the proportion of PSE positions in the primary services category is similar to that of regular governments workers—in both cases over half. In the other three main categories, however, there are considerable differences between PSE and regular government employment. PSE employment is proportionately much higher in parks and recreation and much lower in social services and education (though the qualifications stated earlier about midsummer findings on PSE employment in education apply here too).

Table 7-10. Percentage Distribution of PSE Positions and Regular Government Positions by Functional Area

Functional Area	Sample Government and School District PSE Positions July 1977[a]	Regular Positions within Cities and Counties[b]
Primary services	56	51
Protective services	17	21
Public works	21	8
Utilities and sanitation	7	10
General administration	11	12
Social and cultural services	10	17
Social services	5	5
Health	3	12
Culture and arts	2	NA
Parks and recreation	15	5
Education[c]	13	21
Unallocated	5	8

Sources: Field research data gathered in Brookings Monitoring Study of PSE, July 1977; U.S. Bureau of the Census, *Public Employment in 1976*, Ser. GE76-no. 1 (Washington, D.C.: U.S. Government Printing Office, 1977).

[a]Sample government positions and school district positions are combined to provide greater comparability with U.S. Census Bureau data.

[b]Data on major cities and counties only. U.S. Census Bureau functional areas were changed to provide greater comparability with Brookings field data.

[c]PSE positions include those for both independent and dependent school districts. Regular city and county positions include only those for dependent school districts.

There is also considerable variation within the four main categories of functional areas. Public works has the largest proportion of PSE participants within primary services and yet is the smallest functional area under this heading within the regular government work force. Similarly, within the category of social and cultural services, health accounts for a much higher percentage of regular government employment than of PSE.

To summarize, it appears that PSE, compared with regular public employment, is more oriented toward the project type of activities that can be organized quickly and toward functions that involve a relatively low level of capital intensity. This is demonstrated by the considerably higher proportion of PSE workers in social services than in health services.

The Brookings PSE Associates were asked to comment on the productivity of PSE participants relative to that of regular local government workers. The results of this inquiry are clouded by the inclusion of judgments on the priority of the tasks performed by PSE in their evaluations of productivity. They generally view PSE activities as lower in priority than those of regular local government workers. Nevertheless, the productivity of PSE participants appears to be similar to that of regular local government workers although this is less clear for project PSE.

Training and Transition

Both Title II and Title VI are designed to provide transitional public service employment to the unemployed. Aside from the income maintenance provided, the value of public service employment can be measured by the placement of participants in unsubsidized employment, the improvement in the stability of their labor force status (improvement in the duration of their employment), or the improvement in their earnings levels following their experience in the program. The answers to most of these questions are not yet determined. However, reliable data are becoming available from the Continuous Longitudinal Manpower Survey (CLMS) being conducted for the DOL. Table 7-11 presents data on the labor force status of PSE enrollees prior to program entry and following termination for those enrolled between January and June 1975. While some caveats are in order, this information is certainly superior to the termination data obtained from sponsor reports. Overall, 64 percent of those enrolled in PSE had terminated eighteen months after entry. In fact, the termination rate is even somewhat higher because the nonterminees include significant numbers of participants who were out of the program but had no termination information in their files.

Table 7-11. Percent of 88,500 January to June 1975 CETA-PSE Enrollees—Terminated and Out at Least Twelve Months to Eighteen Months after Entry in Various Labor Force States at Selected Points in Time

	Employed	Unemployed	Not in the Labor Force
Prior to entry			
12 months	55	17	28
9 months	59	18	22
6 months	53	24	23
3 months	42	37	21
1 month	25	54	21
1 day	27	55	19
After termination			
1 day	62	20	18
1 month	57	28	15
3 months	60	23	17
6 months	60	22	18
9 months	63	21	16
12 months	65	21	14

Source: *Continuous Longitudinal Manpower Survey: Follow-Up Report No. 1,* Westat, Inc., Office of Program Evaluation, U.S. Department of Labor, Washington, D.C., July 1978, Tables A-57 to A-59.

In order to make an exact assessment of the effect of the program on subsequent labor force status, it would be necessary to have the experience of a similar group of individuals with the same prior labor force history but no program experience. However, a rough approximation can be described by assuming that the twelve-month prior status was typical of the experience of this cohort. If this assumption is plausible, several tentative points can be made. First, a substantial proportion of the participants are placed in or otherwise find jobs after termination from the program. From twelve months prior to the program to twelve months after the program, there is a 10 percent gain in the number employed, although there is no offsetting reduction in unemployment. The decline in the proportion out of the labor force both prior to entry and following termination suggests that a significant number of individuals utilize PSE to enter or reenter the labor force. In considering these conclusions, particularly with regard to the percent unemployed following termination from the program, it should be noted that the twelve-month prior period included January through June 1974, when the national unemployment rate was 5.9 to 5.3 percent, while the postprogram period covered June 1975 to December 1976, when the national unemployment rate ranged from 7.4 to 9.1 percent. Therefore, some deterioration in labor force status would have been expected for this cohort in the absence of the program. On the other hand, it should be remembered that this cohort of PSE is dominated by the original buildup under Title VI when there was substantial skimming of the eligible population, and thus these individuals may have been more employable than later cohorts of participants. Furthermore, the post-program period for these individuals approached the expiration of Title VI so there would have been more effort to place them—and also to transfer them to Title II, in which case they would also show up as employed. This suggests that the more recent experience, when the emphasis was on hiring rather than placement, may not be as favorable.

It should be noted that there are disincentives to the placement of participants in unsubsidized jobs. The requirement of wages similar to those prevailing on similar public sector jobs and the benefit of regular work and income may create a disincentive for the individual participants to look for other employment, particularly if the alternate job would involve a pay cut. From the perspective of the sponsor, the emphasis for the last year has been on hiring rather than placement. This emphasis on the buildup has diverted resources that might otherwise have been used for job development and has created a disincentive for the sponsor since each person terminated represents one more person who must be hired to maintain the enrollment levels.

Although all the results are not in, the data that we have suggest that with a few exceptions the only training that takes place in PSE, other than possible orientation, is informal on-the-job training. Given the nature of the majority of PSE positions, plus the fact that for the more skilled jobs the individual must have those skills to get the job, it appears that the training component of the PSE program is rather limited. The major benefits are probably the achievement of the credential of a continuous work history and possibly the acquisition of regularized work habits.

POLICY IMPLICATIONS OF PSE

PSE as Countercyclical Policy

There is evidence that PSE programs can be phased up rather rapidly and that the funds can begin to be expended almost immediately. The PEP and stimulus program figures have been cited previously. Title VI was initiated in January 1975, and by the end of March the enrollment level had reached 102,000. If displacement is low, at least initially, PSE has a substantial employment effect. However, the unemployment-reducing effect is somewhat smaller than the employment effect because some part of the employment is represented by people coming in from outside the labor force. Under the proposed eligibility requirements there is an attempt to exclude these people (e.g., students, women not in the labor force) from participation, particularly in the countercyclical Title VI.

In comparison with other income maintenance programs (e.g., UI, AFDC), the gross cost of PSE is high—currently about $8,500 per direct position per year. However, in relation to other employment stimulus programs (e.g., LPW), it is relatively low. PSE differs from countercyclical revenue sharing in that it is possible to control the amount devoted to wages and to target employment upon particular groups. However, as a general proposition, the tighter the eligibility standards the longer it takes to meet employment goals. Furthermore, if employment is directed to groups of people who are less likely to be employed and if wages are kept lower than available private sector wages (which is generally not the case in the cities), then PSE may have less of an inflationary impact than other federal government spending—or, for that matter, than countercyclical revenue sharing.

Another aspect of a countercyclical program is that it should also be able to be dismantled as conditions warrant. In this regard, potential problems with PSE may arise. A phasedown should occur either automatically, as in UI, or through some sort of triggering mechanism. The history on this, however, is mixed. The WPA ended in 1943 in the middle of the Second World War. The PEP was to begin phasedown in October of 1973. Between that time and July 1974, when it was phased into CETA, the size of the program dropped from 102,000 to 43,000. During the period of the phasedown the unemployment rate nationally hovered between 4.5 and 5.5 percent. Meanwhile, program agents were to move 50 percent of the participants into unsubsidized employment. Title VI of CETA expired in June of 1976; however, there was an emergency supplemental appropriation under Title II and subsequent reauthorization of Title VI at the end of December of that year. During that time, enrollment declined from 301,000 to 271,000. Currently, although the unemployment rate has been declining, the administration has asked for full funding of the 725,000 jobs through fiscal year 1979.

The results of the Brookings monitoring study of PSE indicated that in distressed large cities PSE was being used to maintain programs that would have been cut back in the absence of the program. Indeed, data presented earlier in the paper suggest that there may be a significant degree of dependence upon services provided by PSE in the cities examined. In addition, there has now been a new and potentially more dependent constituency developed in the form of the nonprofit agencies that are the present employers of PSE participants. All of this suggests the possibility of some political difficulty in reducing the size of the program as changing economic conditions warrant. This is particularly true in cities, in which the underlying employment problem is structural as well as cyclical.

Still another aspect is the requirement that PSE participants be employed in projects of limited duration (although the Brookings data indicate that less than half the Title VI project employment is in what are defined as limited duration one-time projects). This requirement, combined with the limit on individual tenure to eighteen months of participation, makes it possible for funding to be reduced as projects are completed and as enrollments are reduced through attrition.

PSE as Structural Policy

The buildup in PSE that was noted earlier proceeded despite the fact that the eligibility requirements for Title VI participation were more restrictive than they were for PEP or the early Title VI. Furthermore, there is evidence that the new eligibility requirements are having an effect on the characteristics distribution of sustainment Title VI as well as the project VI participants. Although we await studies on the effect of participation in PSE on the labor market status and earnings, it would appear that there has been relatively little training associated with PSE other than that obtained on the job—which in some cases may be substantial (emergency medical service is a case in point). While the provision of training and other services is permitted under Title II and VI, it is possible that moving the structural PSE program into the training title may make it easier to provide these services.

As far as near-term measures are concerned, the recent experience with transition to unsubsidized employment may not be encouraging—although, in all fairness, the objective over the last year was to build enrollments, not to move participants to unsubsidized employment. It is possible that the new private sector initiative, with incentives to hire from the group eligible for the training title, may assist in improving transition to unsubsidized jobs in the private sector.

At the same time, the issue of displacement does not loom so large for structural PSE programs. In this case displacement might be the assurance of at least eventual transition to the public sector. Furthermore, in addition to consideration of the benefits accruing to the individual participant, as in the case of a pure training program, there is the value of the provision of needed public services by those in the program, at least by those that do not represent displacement.

The issue that remains is targeting. At the current level of 725,000, the program can service only 10 percent of the eligible Title VI project population at any one time. Even with the tightened eligibility of the proposed structural program, at a level of 200,000 positions it will serve only 3 percent of the eligible population at any one time. It remains to be seen whether sponsors will be as selective in choosing participants for PSE as they are for training under the current Title I. There are at least two ways to assure that this occurs. One would be to further tighten the eligibility requirements or to reduce the desirability of the jobs. An example of this would be the Better Jobs and Income approach, which would select eligible welfare persons who had a labor market attachment, would require a period of job search prior to entry into the program, and would pay the minimum wage. The second, an eighteen-month limit on tenure in the program, would serve an equity purpose. Eighteen months are sufficient for most on-the-job training programs as well as for the provision of a work history. It is also possible that the limit on tenure would provide an incentive for transition since participants and employers would know that they faced the necessity of placing or terminating the individual after eighteen months. This could have the effect of reducing the wage disincentive effect of some PSE jobs. That is, an individual currently in a $5 per hour PSE job has little interest in looking for a $4 per hour unsubsidized job. The same individual who knows he or she has only two months left in the $5 per hour PSE job might view the possibility of an unsubsidized $4 per hour job quite differently.

PSE as Fiscal Assistance

As outlined earlier, PSE is *and may* become an even *more* substantial part of the stimulus funding to local governments, particularly to cities. Until now, concern has been expressed about the physical size of the PSE program, the ability of program managers to handle an expanded program, and the limits on the number of jobs that can be created. It is possible that the true limit on the size of the program is somewhat different. In recent weeks at least three people have used Gresham's law to describe the increase in the size of the PSE program.[22] That is, it is said that training and transition objectives have been lost in the rush to build enrollments and expend money lest it be reallocated to some other jurisdiction. As the fiscal assistance aspect of PSE grows, it is likely that it will generate pressure to relax the requirements in eligibility, salary maximums, local supplementation of wage levels, necessity of utilizing projects, placement, and so on. Furthermore, under these circumstances it is also likely (almost by definition) that displacement will increase. Then, too, there is the current uncertainty about continuation of the program at present levels.

It appears there are several reasons why PSE is not well suited as a program of fiscal assistance to local governments other than as an incidental aspect of a program of public service employment for the unemployed and disadvantaged.

The first is that PSE is targeted to individuals—unemployed, economically disadvantaged—within a jurisdiction rather than to the fiscal condition of the jurisdiction itself. It is possible, however, to change the funding formula to direct the funding increasingly to jurisdictions in need of fiscal assistance. For example, the use of annual rather than three-month unemployment rates in the funding formula would divert more funds to areas with structurally high rather than cyclically high unemployment rates and would, therefore, benefit urban areas.[23]

A second reason is that there is substantially more spreading of the funding than has been assumed under CETA. Table 7-3 indicates that for the cities in the Brookings sample, 59 percent of the funding will be passed through, via subcontracting and outstationing agreements, to other local governmental units and to nonprofit organizations in fiscal year 1978. While the amount of the 1978 funding retained by these jurisdictions is substantial, there is no assurance that the other governments and agencies resemble the granting one. For example, Maricopa County, Arizona, may be a candidate for fiscal assistance, but it is doubtful that its subarea, the city of Scottsdale, is. New York City may be eligible for fiscal assistance, but such a strong case cannot be made for the New York Port Authority.

Finally, if the authors of the previous references are correct—that emphasis on fiscal assistance and the provision of governmental services do indeed dispel concerns over servicing the disadvantaged and the provision of training and placement—then we are left with a poorly functioning employment and training program and a poorly functioning fiscal assistance program. Although the proposed Fiscal Adjustment Assistance Act may not be a good example, since it would increase the number of recipient governments to 26,000 compared to 17,000 in the April 1978 quarter under Antirecession Fiscal Assistance (countercyclical revenue sharing), it should be possible to devise a fiscal assistance program that would focus on distressed jurisdictions. This would leave employment and training programs to focus on the unemployed and disadvantaged.

NOTES

1. Richard Nathan, Robert Coo, Janet Galchick, and Richard Long, *Monitoring the Public Service Employment Program*, (Washington, D.C.: The Brookings Institution, 1978).

2. *Manpower Report of the President* (Washington, D.C.: Department of Labor and Department of Health, Education, and Welfare, 1975), p. 40.

3. Cyclical unemployment refers to unemployment that results from changed economic conditions whereas structural unemployment refers to the chronic difficulty of persons with limited education, skills, and work experience to become, and remain, employed.

4. Charles R. Perry et al., *The Impact of Government Manpower Programs* (Philadelphia: The Wharton School, University of Pennsylvania, 1975), p. 187.

5. Sar A. Levitan and Robert Taggart, eds., *Emergency Employment Act: The PEP Generation* (Salt Lake City: Olympus, 1974), p. 16.

6. To be eligible an individual must be economically disadvantaged or a member of a family with an income below 70 percent of the Bureau of Labor Statistics lower living standard and:

1. Be unemployed for fifteen of the prior twenty weeks
2. Be a UI exhaustee
3. Be an AFDC recipient.

7. Harry Katz and Michael Wiseman, "An Essay on Subsidized Employment in the Public Sector," *Job Creation Through Public Service Employment* (Washington, D.C.: National Commission for Manpower Policy, 1978), vol. 3, pp. 151-234.

8. *Report on the Fiscal Impact of the Economic Stimulus Package on 48 Large Urban Governments* (Washington, D.C.: U.S. Department of the Treasury, 1978).

9. State and local government employment figure is for the March 1978 *Survey of Current Business* (Washington, D.C.: U.S. Department of Commerce, May, 1978), vol. 58, no. 5.

10. George Johnson and James Tomola, "The Efficacy of Public Service Employment Programs," Technical Analysis Paper No. 17A, Office of the Assistant for Policy, Evaluation, and Research, Department of Labor, June 1975; processed.

11. Alan Fechter, *Public Employment Programs: An Evaluation Study* (Washington, D.C.: The Urban Institute, September 1974).

12. Michael Wiseman, "Public Employment as Fiscal Policy," *Brookings Papers on Economic Activity* 1 (1976), pp. 67-114.

13. *An Evaluation of the Economic Impact Project of the Public Employment Program*, Final Report (Washington, D.C.: National Planning Association, 1974).

14. George Johnson and James Tomola, "The Fiscal Substitution Effect of Alternative Approaches to Public Service Employment Policy," *The Journal of Human Resources* 12(1) (Winter 1977), pp. 3-26.

15. *Public Employment and Training Assistance: Alternative Federal Approaches* (Washington, D.C.: Congressional Budget Office, February 1977).

16. *Short Run Measures to Stimulate the Economy* (Washington, D.C.: Congressional Budget Office, March 1977). These estimates rise to 46 percent and 60 percent, respectively, if a buildup rate of 60,000 jobs per month is assumed.

17. The sample data were also adjusted in relation to the CETA-PSE program overall. Since there is no national distribution of PSE positions by type of government, displacement rates were generated for the governments within each sponsor type (balance of state and statewide, consortium, county, city) and weighted by the percent of the 1977-1978 funding allocated to each sponsor type. The weighted displacement rate that resulted is also 20 percent.

18. For a discussion of the urban conditions index used to rate urban distress, see Paul R. Dommel et al., *Decentralizing Community Development* (Washington, D.C.: The Brookings Institution, 1978), appendix 2. For this analysis, a cutoff of 250 was adopted.

19. Credit to due to Patrick O'Keefe for pointing out this fact.

20. William Barnes, "Target Groups," in *CETA: An Analysis of the Issues* (Washington, D.C.: National Commission for Manpower Policy, April 1978).

21. Martin Neil Baily and Robert M. Solow, "Public Service Employment as Macroeconomic Policy," in *Job Creation Through Public Service Employment* (Washington, D.C.: National Commission for Manpower Policy, March 1978), vol. 3, pp. 21-88.

22. See, for example, Harry Katz and Michael Wiseman, "An Essay on Subsidized Employment in the Public Sector," in *Job Creation Through Public Service Employment* (Washington, D.C.: National Commission for Manpower Policy, March 1978), vol. 3, p. 172, or William Mirengoff, Statement Before the Subcommittee on Employment, Poverty and Migratory Labor, Committee on Human Resources, U.S. Senate, March 1, 1978, p. 4.

23. For a discussion of the effects of formula alternatives and the effects of the proposed formula changes, see "Evaluating Funding Formulas," Robert Coltrane, Christopher King, and Burt Barnow, in *CETA: An Analysis of the Issues* (Washington, D.C.: National Commission for Manpower Policy, April 1978).

✳ *Chapter 8*

Block Grants for Community Development: Decentralized Decisionmaking

Paul R. Dommel

Enactment of the Housing and Community Development Act of 1974 ran counter to two important forces:

1. It took money from those who had been accustomed to getting it.
2. It took power from those who had been accustomed to having and using it.

In the first instance, the legislation meant directing money away from cities that had been receiving the bulk of money from the urban renewal and model cities programs, the two major programs consolidated into the law's Community Development Block Grant (CDBG) program. On the second point, the establishment of the block grant meant diminished power for those congressmen and bureaucrats who had exercised considerable control in deciding who got grants under the older programs.

How was it politically and legislatively possible to create a program with such important losers?

Two important interacting currents provided the backdrop for the enactment of the CDBG program in 1974. The first was a general unhappiness with the overall federal aid system as it had evolved

This paper is based on the first two years research of a six-year monitoring research program being carried out by the Brookings Institution under contract with the U.S. Department of Housing and Urban Development. The views presented in this chapter are the sole responsibility of the author; they do not represent the position of the officers, trustees, or other staff members of the Brookings Institution.

in the post-World War II period. The second was more specific discontent with the two approaches that had been tried to deal with the growing physical, economic, and social problems of cities.

New Federalism: Political and Legislative History

The CDBG program is an important part of the story of New Federalism, a move by President Nixon to decentralize a number of functions that over time had led to complaints about more and more decisionmaking at the federal level at the expense of state and local officials. New Federalism crystallized as policy in 1971 with Nixon's revised general revenue-sharing program flanked by six special revenue-sharing plans.[1] This discussion will focus on Nixon's plan for special revenue sharing for urban development that eventually became the CDBG program.[2]

By the mid-1960s there had evolved growing discontentment with many federal aid programs as they continued to increase in number and specialization and as planning and application requirements became increasingly overlapping and complex. The amount of available federal aid had been growing rapidly, particularly in the 1960s, but it was argued that it was becoming more and more difficult to get and spend the money because of federal red tape. General revenue sharing was one response to this discont by distributing new funds with virtually no strings attached to their use. Special revenue sharing was a second response, seeking to consolidate a number of the narrow purpose categorical grants into broad functional grants that would be given through automatic formula entitlements with greatly reduced requirements on their use.

Nixon's urban development program proposed to consolidate three discretionary project grants—urban renewal, model cities, and neighborhood facilities—and rehabilitation loans into a formula grant to go to central cities and other metropolitan cities with populations over 50,000. Funds would also go to cities—"hold-harmless" funds—to assure that they would not receive less than they had from the categorical programs. The formula funds were to be automatically distributed on the basis of population, overcrowded housing, housing deficiencies, and the number of persons below the poverty line.[3]

Initially the proposal received a cool reception in Congress, where special revenue sharing was seen as likely to disrupt a multitude of complex, vested relationships that had grown up between congressional committees responsible for the grants, federal and local bureaucrats, and interest groups. However, the pressure for grant reform was strong and Congress (both House and Senate) wrote their own versions of a block grant that had the overall effect of providing more federal controls over the distribution and use of money then proposed by Nixon. The Senate passed its bill in 1972, but the House failed to take any action before adjournment.

In March 1973, the Nixon Administration repackaged the program into the Better Communities Act. The new version expanded the list of programs to be consolidated to include grants for open spaces and water and sewer facilities and the public facilities loan program. Politically, the proposal was expanded to include urban counties and states as well as cities.

An important new ingredient in the 1973-1974 policy environment of block grants was the freezing by Nixon in January 1973 of a number of housing and urban aid programs, including those proposed for consolidation. This freeze put additional pressure on Congress to act on the block grant, particularly that from local officials who feared an end to federal funding once projects already in the pipeline were completed. Congress responded with enactment of the Housing and Community Development Act of 1974, which included a substantially modified form of the Nixon block grant.

Development Approaches

While the complaints against the complexity of the grant system and federal control generally shaped the categorical block grant controversy, the urban development approach incorporated into the CDBG program was more specifically shaped by past experience.

Two programs—urban renewal and model cities—were the focal points of this experience since they represented two major and distinctive approaches taken to deal with the problems of cities. They also represented 90 percent of the funds folded into the CDBG program.

The urban renewal program was adopted in the Housing Act of 1949. Its emphasis was on slum clearance and new construction, thus concentrating on physical redevelopment with visible and tangible results. It was supported by businesses and the construction unions because both stood to benefit directly from redevelopment activities. In addition, local governments saw such redevelopment as a means to improve their tax base by concentrating redevelopment on commercial and upper income residential projects.

By the 1960s, however, urban development had started to run into resistance. It had very frequently led to the displacement of lower income groups, often minorities, when their dwellings were torn down to make way for other kinds of projects yielding them few or no benefits. Renewal projects also started to fall into disfavor among local officials and business interests as planned projects went uncompleted and citizen participation requirements brought new damands into the decisionmaking process.

These factors, plus the urban riots of the mid-1960s, resulted in a broader conceptualization of urban development, encompassing social considerations as well as physical development. An important product of these broader concerns was the model cities program created under the Demonstration Cities and Metropolitan Development Act of 1966. Model cities borrowed from some of the planning and citizen participation approaches of both urban renewal and the war on poverty legislation. It also stressed the coordination of federal grant programs. But it differed from urban renewal by focusing on combined physical, social, and economic planning for model neighborhoods composed of low-income residents. In terms of citizen participation, it expanded on the urban renewal requirement, but it did not go as far as the war on poverty program under which citizen groups frequently received the aid directly and operated the programs.

The model cities program resulted in a greater federal role in urban development activities and consequently became part of the ensuing debate about how big this role should be. The program contributed to some extent to the disillusionment with the effectiveness of federal involvement in the cities. The program, like the war on poverty, had generated considerable hopes and expectations among those in the model neighborhoods who saw the program as a means of improving their living conditions. However, again like the war on poverty, the model cities program almost immediately suffered funding problems because of congressional resistance and the costs of the war in Vietnam and because the money that was appropriated was spread among too many (147) participating communities. Furthermore, the coordination of other federal aid programs to target projects into the model neighborhood did not succeed. The end result was that while the model cities program made some important contributions, particularly social services, and while it maintained citizen activism, it was never able to achieve many of the expectations it had generated.

By the latter part of the 1960s, both urban renewal and model cities had become linked with the increasing demands for grant reform and reexamination of the role of the federal government in state and local decisionmaking. This was reflected in the 1968 platforms of both the Republican and Democratic parties. The Republicans, more politically and philosophically linked to decentralized decisionmaking (and in a number of cases opposed to the grant programs themselves), pledged a "complete overhaul and restructuring of the competing and overlapping jumble of Federal programs to enable state and local governments to focus on priority objectives." The Democrats, the creators of many of the programs under scrutiny, were more constrained but nonetheless sensitive to the issue. They promised to "give priority to simplifying and streamlining the processes of government, particularly in the management of the great innovative programs enacted in the 1960s."

Thus, by the time Nixon took office in 1969, the issue of the grant system as a whole became mixed with that of the urban programs and set the context for the passage of the CDBG program in 1974.

Enactment of the Program

As noted earlier, the CDBG program as finally enacted had its origins in 1971 in the urban development special revenue-sharing plan of Nixon, but this underwent major change in Congress before final enactment in 1974. The central issue in the legislative controversy was how far to go in decentralization. The Nixon Administration took the most decentralist position, proposing to convert the categorical grants into automatic formula entitlements, requiring no application and only minimum federal oversight of what was done with the money. The Senate, on the other hand, took the side of more federal controls by making funding subject to federal approval of an application and by establishing several federal program objectives that communities would have to meet. The House of Representatives took a middle ground position on decentralization, setting out only general national objectives and establishing a procedure giving HUD the power to reject an application within a limited time (if not disapproved, the application was automatically approved).

The allocation system, while an important issue, was secondary to the decentralization controversy. In 1972 both the House and Senate committees, with little dispute, had gone along with the Nixon proposal for a formula distribution system. In 1973 the Senate reversed itself and proposed a system of "hold-harmless" grants for communities with previous HUD funding, combined with discretionary grants for other jurisdictions. The House retained a formula distribution system. In the end, the House-administration position on formula allocations prevailed. The allocation system will be discussed further in the next section.

Overall, the final 1974 legislation represented a compromise between the administration and congressional positions, the block grant compromise being tied to compromises on the housing sections of the legislation. The compromise was largely fashioned by the House and was facilitated by the Watergate affair, which enabled Secretary James T. Lynn of the Department of Housing and Urban Development to come to terms more readily than might have been possible had White House officials been more involved. Generally, the decentralization issue was resolved by combining the more specific national objectives of the Senate with the more general ones of the House; the application procedure followed the House "veto" approach, and the formula allocation system was close to what the administration had wanted.

DISTRIBUTIONAL ANALYSIS

Who gets the money is a central question in analyzing the effects of a federal aid program; this issue has become more contentious as policy discussions focus increasingly on the concept of "targeting." Analysis of the CDBG formula and its distributional impacts is particularly interesting because that program directly raised the issue of targeting toward distressed communities and significantly shaped the politics of formula writing and rewriting. To more fully understand both the distributional and political effects of the CDBG formula, it is necessary to go back to the pre-CDBG period and note the distributional history of the categorical grants.

Who Gets the Money

As stated earlier, the CDBG program was created by consolidating seven categorical programs; however, as also noted earlier, 90 percent of the consolidated money came from urban renewal and model cities. Both were discretionary grant programs, with federal officials deciding who got the money. For model cities, 147 jurisdictions received this money, while 1,200 communities received urban renewal between 1949 when the program was first created and 1974 when it was folded into the block grant.

Overall, the number of communities that received the bulk of the categorical funds was relatively small. In part, this accounted for one of the political weaknesses of the categoricals—too much money was going to too few places. This fact, combined with the other pressures to alter the federal grant system, contributed to the establishment of the formula distribution system for the CDBG program.

For analysis, the formula distribution system must be divided into two components: (1) the eligibility element—who may participate in the program; and (2) the allocation system—how much money goes to the eligible jurisdictions.[4] For the CDBG program, all general purpose units of government (about 40,000) are eligible for funds, but only relative few, 640 in 1978, are entitled to funding, and these entitlement jurisdictions receive about 75 percent of the money. It is also important to note that while only 640 jurisdictions had entitlement grants in 1978, 309 of these had received little or no funding under the categoricals and thus were major winners under the formula system. The remaining jurisdictions compete for the other 25 percent of CDBG funds, which are distributed by HUD on a discretionary basis. In the first year of the CDBG program, 1,818 communities received discretionary funds, 1,965 in the second year, and 1,950 in the third. The overall result is that far more communities receive funds under the block grant than under the categoricals. This fact was an important part of the political acceptability of the block grant system. It meant shifting from what could be characterized as a "nothing for some" system under the categoricals to a "something for all" system through the formula approach.

Since the combined urban renewal and model cities total represented the bulk of the consolidated categoricals, it was obvious that cities having extensive experience with these programs were the most likely to be disadvantaged under any allocation system that redistributed the funds to a larger number of recipients. For the cities that did well under the categoricals the problem of expanded eligibility was aggravated by the problem of the formula itself. As enacted in 1974, the CDBG formula allocated the funds on the basis of three formula elements—population, overcrowded housing, and poverty (double weighted). An analysis by the Brookings Institution of the impact of the distribution system raised several critical issues:[5]

1. The eligibility test presented a problem. By giving entitlement grants to all central cities, to suburban cities with populations of 50,000 or more, and to certain urban counties, substantial sums of money were going to some well-off, growing communities.
2. The allocation formula reinforced the eligibility problem. The population criterion put a premium on growth, directing funds away from older, declining cities to newer, growing communities. Poverty and overcrowded housing were highly correlated factors, weighting distributions toward poverty and providing no measure of physical development needs despite the emphasis of the law on physical development objectives. The poverty bias had the effect of directing large allocations to Southern jurisdictions where the level of poverty tends to be higher than in communities of other regions.

3. While the law provided that 20 percent of CDBG funds go for discretionary grants to nonmetropolitan communities, too large a share of the metropolitan funds were earmarked for discretionary grants to small metropolitan communities. The 1974 law provided that, after the allocation of grants to formula and hold-harmless (for the first three years no community would receive less than its average grant under the folded-in programs for the period 1968–72) entitlement jurisdictions, the remainder of the metropolitan funds were to go for discretionary grants to other communities within metropolitan areas. The Brookings study projected that by 1980, almost 30 percent of CDBG metropolitan funds would go to small communities as discretionary grants and the major portion of this money redirected from central cities, particularly older, declining ones.[6]

Table 8-1 compares the distribution of shares of funds between the allocations under the categorical system, the 1974 CDBG formula, and 1977 formula amendments. The CDBG distributions were projected to 1980 when the formula system would be fully in effect.

As can be seen, the 1974 formula resulted in a shift in shares out of the regions of the northeast quadrant into the southern and western regions. The four northeastern regions lost 10 percentage points. A greater shift among shares impacted adversely on the central cities whose share dropped from nearly 72 percent under the consolidated categorical programs to just over 42 percent under the block grant formula, a decline of nearly 30 percentage points.

Urban Distress and Urban Aid

While the regional shifts are important to the politics of formula change, the more crucial issue concerns the impact of the formula on distressed cities wherever they are located. Not all cities are in trouble, and there is no simple generalization to characterize distressed cities.[7] There are many indicators one can use to analyze distress, but generally the characteristics include declining population, concentrations of poverty, and deteriorating physical environments. These three properties are frequently found in combination in older, declining industrial cities in all regions; some smaller southern cities are more likely to suffer from problems caused by extremely high poverty rates. Such general conditions in turn place a heavy burden on a city's fiscal ability to cope with its problems. As population declines the tax base shrinks while expenditures range between fixed and increasing, usually the latter. This means an increasing tax

Table 8-1. Projected Distribution of CDBG Allocations by Region and Type of Jurisdiction

	Categorical Share (percent)	1974 Formula Share (percent)	1977 Dual Formula Share (percent)
Region-Northeast Quadrant			
New England	9.9%	4.7%	5.6%
Middle Atlantic	22.7	17.4	21.9
East North Central	15.9	17.2	19.9
West North Central	7.7	6.7	7.4
Regional Total	56.2%	46.0%	54.8%
Region-South and West			
South Atlantic	15.0	16.5	13.5
East South Central	6.0	7.9	6.1
West South Central	8.2	12.4	9.9
Mountain	3.6	3.9	3.2
Pacific	11.0	13.3	12.5
Regional Total	43.8%	54.0%	45.2%
Types of Jurisdictions			
Central Cities	71.8%	42.2%	57.6%
Satellite Cities	4.5	5.0	5.8
Urban Counties	3.2	10.3	11.2
Metropolitan Discretionary	7.9	22.5	6.8
Nonmetropolitan Discretionary	12.6	20.0	18.6[a]

Source: The data for entitlement jurisdiction was adapted from Tables 2-5 and 2-6, Paul R. Dommel, Richard P. Nathan, Sarah F. Liebschultz, and Margaret T. Wrightson, *Decentralizing Community Development* (scheduled for publication by the U.S. Department of Housing and Urban Development, Summer 1978). Nonmetropolitan allocations were added to the entitlement allocations of the two tables to compute the total regional and jurisdictional shares.

[a]Because of the method of setting aside the metropolitan discretionary fund, the nonmetropolitan share falls below the 20 percent provision of the 1974 act.

burden for those who live in the city; they are faced with the choice of either paying higher taxes (usually without accompanying improvement in services) or moving out and adding further to the city's fiscal pressure. In some cities a return of better-off residents has begun but this is still in the early stages, and it is likely to be some time before the impact of such a return can be measured.

The factors of community age, population decline, and poverty have been consolidated into an index to measure the relative differences in urban distress between the CDBG entitlement jurisdictions.[8] The mean index number was standardized at 100, with the most distressed cities having an index greater than 200 and the better-off communities an index below 100. As Table 8-2 shows, urban distress is found in all regions although disproportionately in the northeast quadrant. Among the types of jurisdictions, central cities have the highest incidence of distress although some satellite (suburban) cities have developed problems similar to those of the central cities. The table also shows that distress cuts across community size and is not confined to large cities. Thus, since urban distress cuts across region, type, and size, distributional analysis of the CDBG formula based on distress and need must be viewed in these terms.

For the distressed cities the 1974 CDBG formula did not adequately incorporate two important characteristics of distress—population lag and community age—with the result that the allocations were not well targeted toward many distressed jurisdictions.

In its first report, Brookings recommended major changes in the allocation system—specifically, the establishment of a dual

Table 8-2. Distribution of CDBG Recipients on the Brookings Urban Conditions Index by Region, Type, and Population Size

	Number of CDBG Recipients	Number Below 100	Number 100–200	Number Above 200	Percent Above 200
Region					
New England	53	22	17	14	26%
Middle Atlantic	99	43	21	35	36
East North Central	121	74	27	20	17
West North Central	33	20	9	4	12
South Atlantic	77	44	24	9	12
East South Central	27	14	9	4	15
West South Central	65	43	17	5	8
Mountain	26	22	4	0	0
Pacific	107	97	7	3	3
	608	379	135	94	16%
Type					
Central Cities	372	175	110	87	23%
Satellite Cities	158	133	18	7	5
Urban Counties	78	71	7	0	0
	608	379	135	94	16
Population Size					
Above 1,000,000	8	4	0	4	50%
500,000–1,000,000	30	20	4	6	20
250,000–500,000	80	59	12	9	11
100,000–250,000	122	67	39	16	13
Below 100,000	368	229	80	59	16
	608	379	135	94	16

Source: Dommel et al., *Decentralizing Community Development*, Table 2-3, p. 38.

formula system that would recognize the development needs of the old, declining cities as well as the needs of cities with problems based on growth or poverty. Both the Ford and Carter Administrations adopted the dual formula approach; this led to congressional passage in 1977 of a dual formula system that retained the original formula and added a second allocation system based on the factors of community age (using pre-1940 housing stock as the measure of age and infrastructure needs), poverty, and growth lag (declining population or slow population growth). Each entitlement community receives the greater of the amounts computed under the two formulas. This means that no jurisdiction receives less than its allocation under the original 1974 formula.

Politically, the no-loss characteristic did not prevent the outbreak of a sharp regional battle in the House of Representatives when the formula change was proposed.[9] As can be seen from Table 8-1, the dual formula resulted in boosting the share of funds going to regions of the northeast quadrant while reducing the share going to southern and western regions although all regions received increased funding in dollar terms. Alert to the impact of the proposed shift to a dual formula system, congressmen from the northeast quadrant voted as a block to adopt the change, while southern and western lawmakers were nearly as united in their opposition to it. On an amendment proposed by two California House members to kill the dual formula, eastern and midwestern congressmen voted 215 to 8 to keep the dual formula while southern and western congressmen voted 132 to 18 to eliminate it.

Analysis shows, however, that the interregional effects of the dual formula are not simply a matter of Frostbelt cities gaining while Sunbelt cities remain the same. There are Sunbelt jurisdictions that also benefit from the dual formula, as may be seen in Table 8-3, while some specific examples of gains by cities over 100,000 in the South and West are shown in Table 8-4.

As shown in Table 8-3, a large number of central and satellite cities—and some urban counties—gain by the dual formula. It should be noted, however, that those central cities gaining tend to be found most frequently in the northeast quadrant. Their aggregated allocations increase approximately 73 percent, and their share of all entitlement aid to central cities increases from 50 to 60 percent (Table 8-5). Southern and western central cities combined increase their dollar allocations by about 14 percent, but their share of total central city allocations declines from 50 to 40 percent.

A significant result of the dual formula system was that the added cost of the second formula came from the metropolitan

Table 8-3. Communities Benefiting from the Dual Formula by Region and Type

	Number of Jurisdictions	Number Benefiting	Percent Benefiting
Region-Northeast Quadrant			
New England	53	44	83%
Middle Atlantic	99	74	75
East North Central	121	70	58
West North Central	33	17	52
Regional Total	306	205	67
Region-South and West			
South Atlantic	77	19	25%
East South Central	27	5	19
West South Central	65	7	11
Mountain	26	3	12
Pacific	107	20	19
Regional Total	302	54	18
Types of Jurisdictions			
Central Cities	372	183	49%
Satellite Cities	158	61	39
Urban Counties	78	15	19
	608	259	43

Source: Adapted from Dommel et al., *Decentralizing Community Development* (Report to the U.S. Department of Housing and Urban Development, scheduled for publication Summer 1978), Table 2-4, p. 40.

discretionary fund (see Table 8-1), thus sharply reducing the amount available for discretionary grants for small metropolitan communities from nearly 30 percent of the metropolitan total to less than 10 percent.

When examining the above distributional analysis on the urban conditions index it can be concluded that the 1977 formula changes more effectively target CDBG funds toward distressed cities than was true under the original single formula allocation system. Table 8-6 divides the entitlement jurisdictions into quintiles ranked by the urban conditions index. As can be seen, there is a much greater difference in the mean per capita grant between the first and fifth quintiles under the dual formula system than under the original single formula approach. Under the original legislation the mean per capita ratio between the worst off communities (first quintile) and the best off (fifth quintile) is only 1.9:1 while under the dual formula this ratio increases to 3.4:1. As was shown in Table 8-2, the incidence of distress was greater among central cities than any other type of entitlement jurisdiction. Under the dual formula the central

Table 8-4. Southern and Western Cities with Populations over 100,000 Gaining under the Dual Formula

Region	Grant Under Single Formula ($000)	Grant Under Dual Formula ($000)	Percent Gain
Southern			
Atlanta, Ga.	12,774	14,650	15%
Baltimore, Md.	20,952	32,338	54
Birmingham, Ala.	8,286	12,440	50
Louisville, Ky.	8,415	13,673	63
New Orleans, La.	19,483	22,914	18
Norfolk, Va.	6,678	7,651	15
Savannah, Ga.	3,562	5,823	63
Washington, D.C.	18,389	23,451	28
Western			
Denver, Colo.	9,337	12,944	39%
Long Beach, Calif.	5,790	8,187	41
Oakland, Calif.	7,794	13,003	67
Portland, Ore.	6,173	12,016	95
Salt Lake City, Utah	3,352	6,036	80
San Francisco, Calif.	14,163	28,982	105
Seattle, Wash.	7,533	17,949	138
Spokane, Wash.	3,013	5,284	75

Source: Dommel et al., *Decentralizing Community Development* (Report to the U.S. Department of Housing and Urban Development, scheduled for publication Summer 1978), p. 47.

cities receive an average of $29.94 per capita compared with $20.84 under the original formula.[10]

IMPLEMENTING THE PROGRAM

Analysis of implementation of the CDBG program falls into two categories: programmatic and process objectives, and the relationship between the two. The principal programmatic objectives of the block grant are to "give maximum feasible priority to activities which will benefit low- or moderate-income families *or* aid in the prevention or elimination of slums or blight"[11] (emphasis added). At the process level, the principal objective is to decentralize more community development decisionmaking from federal to local officials. At the local level this is intended to mean more decision-making authority for chief executives and legislative officials (mayors, city managers, and councilmen) rather than specialist bureaucrats who dominated decisionmaking under the categorical programs. The process objectives also include citizen participation in the establishment of development priorities.

Table 8-5. Projected Distribution of CDBG Entitlement Allocations to Central Cities by Region

	Single Formula (millions of dollars)	Single Formula Share (percent)	Dual Formula (millions of dollars)	Dual Formula Share (percent)
Northeast Quadrant				
New England	61	4.4%	112	5.7%
Middle Atlantic	298	21.7	514	26.0
East North Central	252	18.3	434	22.0
West North Central	72	5.2	124	6.3
	(683)	49.6	(1184)	60.0
South and West				
South Atlantic	181	13.2%	214	10.8%
East South Central	82	6.0	93	4.7
West South Central	197	14.3	203	10.3
Mountain	51	3.7	59	2.9
Pacific	181	13.2	223	11.3
	(692)	50.4	(792)	40.0
Total	1,375	100.0	1,975	100.0

Source: Dommel et al., *Decentralizing Community Development* (Report to the U.S. Department of Housing and Urban Development, scheduled for publication Summer 1978), Table 2-7, p. 51.

Overall, the data for the first two program years suggest that local governments have used the flexibility of the block grant and their greater decisionmaking authority to take a different development approach than they did under the consolidated categoricals. At the same time, there have emerged some clear conflicts between objectives of the law.

Program Choices

Field research shows two trends: (1) a reduction in commitments to activities started under the urban renewal and model cities programs; and (2) a significant trend toward neighborhood conservation (housing rehabilitation and related neighborhood improvements).[12]

The shift to new kinds of programs was more evident in the second year than in the first, when communities had only five months in which to draw up a program and submit it for HUD approval. Largely as a result of this short time period and prior program commitments, communities with ongoing categorical programs tended to allocate more funds to continue these activities. In the second year the pattern started to change.

As shown in Table 8-7, communities with high or medium experi-

Table 8-6. Mean Per Capita Allocations Based on the Brookings Urban Conditions Index by Quintiles

Quintile[a]	Original Formula ($)	Dual Formula ($)
I	23.36	42.85
II	19.80	26.07
III	17.31	19.17
IV	14.26	15.29
V	12.34	12.54

Source: Computed from urban conditions index data, Dommel et al., *Decentralizing Community Development* (Report to the U.S. Department of Housing and Urban Development, scheduled for publication Summer 1978), Appendix II.

[a] A Pearson (Chi-square) correlation shows a coefficient of 0.6019 between the index and per capita allocation under the original formula. The coefficient increases to 0.9092 under the dual formula system although in part this is the result of the similarity of factors of the formula and the index.

Table 8-7. Second-Year Funding of New and Continued Programs by Level of Prior Experience; Overall Funding for New and Continued Programs, First and Second Years

Program Category	Level of Prior Experience[a]				Allocation Effects	
	High	Medium	Low	None	First Year	Second Year
New spending[b]	55.4%	60.8%	57.0%	93.6%	52.0%	60.1%
Program continuation[c]	36.4	37.3	10.6	.8	32.8	26.5
Substitution[d]	4.1	1.3	8.7	4.2	7.2	4.8
Other[e]	4.1	.6	23.7	1.4	.8	8.6
Number of jurisdictions	27	12	17	5		

Source: Adapted from Dommel et al., *Decentralizing Community Development* (Report to the U.S. Department of Housing and Urban Development, scheduled for publication Summer 1978), Table 5-3, p. 194.

[a] If a community's per capita grant under the categorical programs was more than 150 percent above the national mean of $17.63, it was considered to have a high level of prior experience; moderate is 50-150 percent of the mean; low is under 50 percent.

[b] New spending includes new capital and new operations.

[c] Program continuation includes community development program continuation and other program maintenance.

[d] Substitution includes avoidance of borrowing, tax reduction, tax stabilization, and increased fund balances.

[e] Allocations not categorized or funds passed through by urban counties to participating municipalities.

ence under the categorical grants allocated 36 and 37 percent, respectively, of their funds in the second year to continue programs started under the folded-in grants. What is significant, however, is that many of these communities had extensive urban renewal and model cities programs, and in spite of their heavy involvement, they allocated more than half of their block grant funds to new programs. Overall, the sample jurisdictions allocated 60.1 percent of their second year funds for new activities compared with 52 percent the first year.

Excluding urban counties (for which program data are limited), half of the sample jurisdictions in the Brookings study (twenty-five of fifty-one) allocated at least half of their money to new activities—neighborhood conservation (eighteen communities) or general development (seven communities).[13] General development includes communitywide planning and allocations for capital and operating projects intended to serve the entire community or individual projects in a neighborhood that is not a conservation target area.

Another significant finding was that twenty communities shifted from program concentrations under the categoricals to more mixed development programs in the second year, combining continuation activities with a variety of new programs. Of the twenty, most were central cities that had extensive experience in either urban renewal or model cities or both. These shifts from program concentration to a more mixed program are important in understanding the effects of decentralized decisionmaking. The legislative history of the CDBG program set an unofficial limit of 20 percent on social service spending, this limit emphasizing the physical orientation of the program. However, the data showed that many communities with model cities programs chose to reduce CDBG-funded social services below the 20 percent level. The data also showed that cities were shifting away from urban renewal, not simply because projects were completed but because they wanted to allocate funds for different kinds of development activities, frequently for housing rehabilitation.

Urban Distress and Program Choices

Under the categorical grants, program choices were significantly influenced by the fact that federal policy set priorities and established program goals. Local choices were influenced by the price effect of the grants; the availability of matching funds served to lower the price of certain programs. The block grant concept was adopted for community development in order to answer many of the complaints about the federal role and to decentralize decisionmaking. This process rearrangement has had the effect of substituting local preferences for federal preferences. Under the categorical grants, the competition for urban aid was to a great extent *between* communities; under block grants with formula entitlements the competition is primarily *within* the community.

Generally speaking, this intracommunity competition has two dimensions, particularly in the older, declining cities with extensive involvement in the categoricals. These are the cities that generally have undergone population losses, suffer from a variety of physical and social problems, and are experiencing a contraction of their tax bases. Thus, there is extensive competition among a variety of visible community needs. This competition among needs results in another form of competition—that among local government agencies and nongovernmental groups seeking support for their particular programs. This competition tends to be the greatest in those communities with extensive categorical experience and established decisionmaking processes. Now with the more flexible CDBG funds, new groups and interests are also competing for resources. This expanded demand structure (needs and groups) accounts in part for the shifting by the most hard-pressed jurisdictions to more mixed programs in order to meet a wider variety of community problems.

By contrast, in better-off communities there is a greater tendency to concentrate CDBG funds in a single program area. This is particularly true of suburban and nonmetropolitan communities, especially those without categorical grant experience. The explanation for this seems to be as follows. In jurisdictions with relatively few disadvantaged people, less physical decay, and therefore fewer problems, there is less pressure to fund a broad mix of programs. In the eleven sample jurisdictions with no prior grant experience, all chose to concentrate more than half of their funds in a single program area, either housing and neighborhood conservation or general development. Data from the field associates show that frequently these well-off communities use their CDBG funds to spread program benefits among better income neighborhoods or to undertake activities associated with growth rather than distress, for example, the installation of infrastructure to open up an area for new residential development.

The association between the type of development program undertaken—concentrated or mixed—and the level of distress is shown by the urban conditions index discussed earlier. Analyzing only central and satellite cities, there were twenty-two communities adopting a concentrated program in year two; of these, seven were above the index mean (less well off) and fifteen were below (better off).[14] Thus the concentrated programs were adopted by the better-off communities by a ratio of 2:1. On the other hand, the twenty communities choosing a mixed program were above the index mean by a ratio of 3:1. The range and severity of community problems thus appear to be importantly related to a community's overall approach to community development under the block grant.

Process and Program Uses

One of the objectives of the block grant approach was to give local chief executives, legislators, and citizens more control and influence over decisionmaking.[15] The data show that a significant amount of decentralized decisionmaking has occurred. Brookings field associates reported that jurisdictions with little or no HUD influence in CDBG decisionmaking were nearly three times as numerous as those where HUD was a major influence or determined the local program (see Table 8-8).

Considering only the forty-four sample jurisdictions (of the total of sixty-one shown in Table 8-8) with previous experience under HUD programs, thirty-eight of the units (or 86 percent) reported a reduced HUD role under CDBG.

An analysis of specific issues that arose between HUD and local jurisdictions in the first two years showed that local governments tended to prevail more frequently on substantive issues of development strategy and programs, whereas HUD did much better on procedural and on such compliance issues as equal opportuntiy and environmental requirements. The data suggest that local officials tended to be more willing to compromise on lower level issues, particularly on procedural issues where they could satisfy HUD without making basic changes in their plans. On the other hand, they were likely to resist HUD pressure on substantive issues where they felt it was necessary to defend their decisionmaking authority.

The above findings for the first two years of the program may be changing, however. Local officials expressed concern that HUD has been taking a more active role in decisionmaking as the program progresses. In part, this is attributable to the "aging" of the program. Beginning in the second year, HUD was required to initiate perfomance monitoring of local programs. Moreover, the rush of the first year application process was no longer necessary, giving HUD more time to consider the second-year applications. An important point for future research is to see whether the change from the Ford to the Carter Administration will alter the pattern of decentralization.

At the local level, the decisionmaking process in the first two

Table 8-8. HUD Influence in the First Two Years of CDBG

Level of Influence	*Number of Jurisdictions*
Local program determined by HUD	2
Major HUD influence	14
Minor HUD influence	34
No HUD influence	11
Total Number	61

Source: Dommel et al., *Decentralizing Community Development* (Report to the U.S. Department of Housing and Urban Development, scheduled for publication Summer 1978), Table 3-1, p. 69.

years of the program generally was dominated by local executives, but field reports showed that in the second program year local legislatures and citizens began to increase their influence in priority setting. As is the case in the characteristics of intergovernmental relations, it is still too soon to tell what patterns of local decision-making will finally occur. The strong executive dominance of the first year may have resulted from the necessity of getting an application together in a very short time. When the pressure of time eased and as legislators and citizens became more aware of the flexibility of the program, they made a greater effort to influence the decision process. It is not yet known whether legislative and citizen influence will continue to grow or whether such influence has already peaked and the process will give way to more institutionalized, bureaucratic decisionmaking.

One important effect that seems to accompany more active legislative and citizen participation is the tendency to spread the funds to meet the demands of more areas and more groups in a community. Indeed, in some jurisdictions local legislators have clearly adopted a policy of dividing the funds among legislative districts.

Social Targeting

A focal point for analysis of program objectives concerns the targeting of CDBG benefits to low- and moderate-income groups, one of the primary objectives of the law. This objective, referred to here as social targeting, has become a very controversial issue.[16]

Looking briefing at the legislative history of social targeting, the Nixon Administration in its block grant proposals emphasized decentralized decisionmaking and thus did not seek to introduce a federally mandated social targeting objective. The Senate has been the principal sponsor of social targeting language and of efforts to make this the primary goal of the CDBG program. The House, on the other hand, has accepted social targeting as a coequal goal with elimination or prevention of slums or blight but has resisted Senate attempts to elevate the former over the latter. The House has also tended to favor a more decentralizing role than the Senate; this in part explains the House resistance to imposing a rigorous social targeting requirement on local officials. Furthermore, the House takes the position that community development needs may require a strategy that focuses on objectives—such as keeping higher income groups in a community and improving the tax base through economic development—that are not oriented toward social targeting.

Three studies of low- and moderate-income benefits under the CDBG program have shown the level of benefits varying between 51 and 66 percent in the first year and between 44 and 70 percent in the second.[17] A large part of the difference in the levels of benefits among the three studies cited is the result of methodological and sample differences. A trend to be noted is that between the first and second year, both HUD and the National Association of Housing and Redevelopment Officials (NAHRO) found the level of benefits dropping. In its study, Brookings found that social targeting of CDBG funds had increased by the second year. Perhaps more significant than these changes, however, has been the great difficulty in devising a methodology to measure the program benefits that are going to various groups. Brookings has adopted a new methodology for its monitoring research of program years three and four but the results of the new approach are not yet available.

At the policy level, the Carter Administration, through HUD Secretary Patricia R. Harris, has sought to administratively tighten up the social targeting objectives of the law. In the fall of 1977 HUD proposed a set of regulations requiring block grant recipients to direct 75 percent of CDBG benefits to the lower income groups.[18] These proposed regulations met with opposition from local officials and from key members of the House subcommitte that has jurisdiction over the CDBG program, particularly from Representative Thomas L. Ashley, subcommittee chairman. Ashley took the position that legislatively the Congress had rejected all efforts to establish a percentage requirement on social targeting and therefore such limits should not be set by regulation. In its final specifications issued on March 1, 1978, HUD eased up substantially on its social targeting policy at least insofar as the regulations are concerned.

Social targeting of CDBG funds will continue to be a major focal point for analyzing and evaluating the block grant program, but that goal cannot be evaluated apart from other potentially conflicting goals. In addition to the goal to prevent or eliminate slums or blight, there is a third coequal goal in the legislation that permits a community to undertake activities of a "particular urgency"; in some cases this may involve development problems associated with community growth. These three and frequently conflicting goals increase the difficulty of measuring program effectiveness.

Conclusions

Measuring the results of the first two program years against the objectives, it seems reasonable to conclude that the decentralization objective has been met to a substantial degree. Local officials, while wary of the future, are taking advantage of the greater flexibility of the block grant to move into new program areas and to design specific programs to meet local conditions and demands.

It is less easy to assess the programmatic objectives, partly because of delays in getting some of the physical development projects under way. More important, however, is that the programmatic objectives have some significant built-in conflicts. For those seeking to maximize social targeting, the level and trend of benefits to lower income groups has been of concern, leading to pressure for more HUD attention to this objective. On the other hand, those who believe that community development encompasses wider objectives than social targeting argue that it is sometimes necessary to undertake activities that directly benefit higher income groups if it will help to keep them in or attract them back into the community. The social targeting goal also conflicts in some cases with the process goal to broaden local participation in CDBG decisionmaking. While such participation has expanded, it has also resulted at times in more pressure to spread the benefits.

Going one step beyond these goal conflicts, evaluating the effectiveness of the CDBG program is made much more difficult by the fact that the block grant is usually not the only development program under way in a community. The mix of private sector decisions, state and local spending, and other federal programs—such as transportation, housing, and environmental improvement expenditures—makes it difficult to sort out the independent development effects of the CDBG program.

POLICY ISSUES

This concluding section focuses on some of the continuing issues and larger urban policy implications of the CDBG program.

Formula

A major unresolved issue of the block grant is the distribution formula. In the 1974 legislation, Congress, uncertain about the ultimate impact of the formula, provided for a study of the grant distributions; in 1977 it adopted the dual formula system that, as stated earlier, had the effect of redirecting a significant amount of money back to old, declining cities, particularly those in the Northeast quadrant. As also noted earlier, this change did not come about without strong resistance from the southern and western states, which felt the dual system tilted the allocations too much against their areas.

Dissatisfaction with the formula, however, did not come only from the Sunbelt region; some discontentment came from Frostbelt senators who felt the formula did not go far enough in redirecting funds to their region.[19] They argued that distress should be measured by the "impaction" or concentration of a problem. They were particularly interested in structuring into the formula an adjustment for the percentage of houses built before 1940, an adjustment that would have added more money to the grants of the older cities. Firm House resistance in the conference committee prevented the impaction adjustment, but the final bill did call for still another study of the formula in order to consider the possibility of returning to some kind of single formula system and also to include the feasibility of using impaction data.

The use of impaction measurements merits some additional discussion. The current allocation system uses data factors based on absolute numbers. That is, the poverty factor is based on the number of poor persons in a community relative to the total number of poor persons in all entitlement communities; the same absolute numbers are also used for the overcrowded housing and pre-1940 housing factors. However, absolute numbers are not the best indicator of the degree of distress. For example, a city of 200,000 people may have 30,000 persons below the poverty level, whereas a city of 500,000 may have 50,000 in poverty. The latter city has more people in poverty and thus does better under the current system, but the poverty population represents only 10 percent of that city's population, while the smaller city, with a smaller poverty population, has a higher poverty impaction, 15 percent. Considering this factor alone, therefore, the smaller city has the greater poverty problem, but because the allocation is based on numbers rather than concentration, it does not fare as well. The same reasoning can be applied to the overcrowded housing and age of housing indicators. The use of impaction or concentration data thus seems to be justified if the purpose of the allocation system is to improve the targeting capability of the formula.

The biggest obstacle to altering the formula, however, lies in the political imperative that an entitlement once bestowed is extremely difficult to eliminate or reduce. By 1980, the time of the next renewal, the CDBG program will have been in operation for six years and all entitlement jurisdictions will be receiving their full allocations under the formula. It is difficult to imagine the formula being changed in any way that would result in any significant number of entitlement communities receiving reduced funds. It was this political imperative that led to the establishment of a dual formula in the first place—to make sure that no one would lose. This does not mean, however, that further formula changes in order to better target the CDBG money cannot be achieved. For example, a dual impaction formula may be possible in which both the impaction of poverty and pre-1940 housing are included, thus cutting across the regional bias of the 1977 Senate impaction proposal that included only the housing indicator.[20]

Through such an impaction approach it may be possible to deal with the regional politics, but the issue will then shift clearly to distressed versus well-off communities wherever they may be located. Poverty impaction would clearly benefit some cities of the South where concentrations of poverty are great, reaching the 30, 40, and 50 percent mark in some cases. Such high poverty concentrations are not found in northern cities. On the other hand, high percentages of older housing (in the 60, 70, and 80 percent range) are found generally in northern central cities and only infrequently in the South and West. The political problem arises, however, in the case of those well-off and growing jurisdictions that are not impacted by either poverty or older housing stock. They would be the new generation of losers under an impaction block grant, and it is doubtful if this is politically possible. Having included many well-off, growing areas as entitlement jurisdictions in the 1974 legislation, it is not likely that they can now be excluded. It may be possible to hold them harmless against any losses of grant money they receive under the current formula, but the combination of the dual impaction approach plus hold harmless for the well-off jurisdictions is likely to put the program cost well above the 1980 level of $3.8 billion.

Growing Communities

Expanding communities, found more frequently in the Sunbelt than the Frostbelt (although there is growth in northern suburban cities), take the position that the problems and burdens caused by growth ought to be treated similarly to those that accompany decline. Furthermore, southern spokesmen argue that that region, although experiencing economic growth, still lags behind the other regions in income; they reason, therefore, that the problem of lagging income should be given consideration equal to that given the distress of the older, declining cities. They have a point—to a point—but these concerns must be considered within the context of the larger pattern of federal aid and the intent of the CDBG program.

On the problems of community growth, there is no question that population and economic expansion bring new demands for community services and for a variety of amenities such as streets and sidewalks, parks, and other public facilities. These services and facilities require additional local revenues and frequently the issuance of local government bonds. On the other hand, growing communities are experiencing an expansion of their resource bases. The population moving in tends to be middle income; they require new housing and in turn pay additional property taxes. For many communities the expansion is not only people moving in for residence purposes, but also growth in industrial or commercial activities with further increments to the local tax base. Thus expansion generally results in additional resources with which to pay for the new services and facilities. It might, therefore, be possible to equate the problems of growth and decline on the cost side, but on the revenue side the growing communities are clearly in a better position to absorb increasing cost. Another important factor is that the CDBG program is not the only source of funds that deals with development problems. Other federal aid programs such as those for transportation and environmental facilities (water and sewer) are available.

Turning to the South, the per capita income in the region lags behind that of the other regions. The gap is closing, however, as the South experiences the continuing inmigration of both higher income population and new economic activity. But more to the point is the fact that CDBG program is oriented toward the physical and economic development problems of communities; it is not an income-oriented program. The problems of lagging personal income are better and more directly dealt with by an income transfer policy rather than through intergovernmental aid.

Taking a broader view, the issue of the CDBG allocation system frequently encompasses a range of arguments that often goes beyond the capacity and intent of the program. The block grant represents only a small part of overall federal aid, and the CDBG program is only one part of a recent large increase in federal aid to local governments generally. Federal aid to all cities, even the most well off, has increased within the past five years (see Table 8-9). For example, the percentage increases for two large, well-off Sunbelt cities, Houston and Phoenix, have been 591 and 689 percent, respectively, over the six-year period from 1972 to 1978. A spreading pattern of federal aid is observed from the Frostbelt cities which were the primary beneficiaries of the grants consolidated into the CDBG program to Sunbelt cities with less previous grant experience. This trend is likely to continue although at a less rapid rate.

Decentralization

A final issue that must be discussed is the continuing and overlapping question about decentralized decisionmaking under CDBG. Is there any means to assure achievement of CDBG legislative goals when key decisions are made among hundreds of autonomous local governments dealing with stated but conflicting national objectives? Or can the national objectives be viewed less as conflicting than as a range of possibilities that are designed to provide flexibility to deal with local problems?

The answer to these questions is not clear. The legislative history of the CDBG program shows that the House and Senate have taken different views on the decentralization and flexibility issues. It may be that the final arbiter is the federal bureaucracy administering the program. But even there a uniform view of the program is not yet evident. HUD area officials have taken different views on the application of the law in regard to such decisions as how far to allow communities to go in using CDBG funds for social services. There are indications that HUD under the Carter Administration is seeking a more uniform application of regulations and guidelines within a policy emphasizing social targeting and neighborhood renewal. But policy preferences are subject to change and the issue of decentralization is likely to continue.

NOTES

1. The six special revenue-sharing programs were transportation, law enforcement, urban development, rural development, education, and manpower.
2. For studies on the history of general revenue sharing, see David A. Caputo and Richard L. Cole, *Urban Politics and Decentralization* (Lexington, Mass.: D.C. Heath & Co., 1974); Paul R. Dommel, *The Politics of Revenue Sharing* (Bloomington: Indiana University Press, 1974); Richard P. Nathan et al., *Monitoring Revenue Sharing* (Washington, D.C.: The Brookings Institution, 1975),

Table 8-9.   Comparative Growth of Total Federal Grants to Selected Northeast and Sunbelt Cities, 1972-1978 (Thousands of Dollars)

City	Estimated Grants Fiscal Year 1978 (1)	Total Grants 1974-1975 (2)	Total Grants 1971-1972 (3)	Percent Increase 1975-1978 (4)	Percent Increase 1972-1978 (5)
Baltimore	181,394	108,015	43,835	68%	314%
Boston	120,885	66,782	61,249	81	97
Buffalo	80,947	31,744	15,346	154	427
Chicago	407,726	166,129	95,147	145	329
Cleveland	110,381	47,733	16,782	131	558
Detroit	311,142	166,183	132,071	87	136
Philadelphia	328,134	130,820	82,694	151	297
St. Louis	109,500	31,483	14,145	248	674
Mean, 8 Northeast Cities				133	354
Atlanta	58,994	38,548	10,435	53	465
Birmingham	31,643	14,458	3,240	119	877
Dallas	64,147	24,292	4,807	74	777
Houston	86,395	45,869	12,507	88	591
Jacksonville	40,886	30,619	6,247	34	554
Louisville	67,686	36,364	21,583	86	214
New Orleans	86,895	45,670	14,770	90	488
Oklahoma City	38,748	18,691	5,540	107	599
Phoenix	70,911	36,556	6,990	94	689
Mean, 9 Sunbelt Cities				83	584

Source: Computed by procedures described in Richard P. Nathan, Paul R. Dommel, and James W. Fossett, "Targeting Development Funds on Urban Hardship," Testimony before the Joint Economic Committee, July 28, 1977.

ch. 2. For background on the CDBG program, see Richard P. Nathan et al., *Block Grants for Community Development* (Washington, D.C.: U.S. Government Printing Office, January 1977), ch. 2.

3. The listing housing deficiencies was ultimately dropped from the formula.

4. For formula analyses, see Nathan et al., *Block Grants for Community Development*, chs. 3-6; Paul R. Dommel et al., *Decentralizing Community Development* (Report to the U.S. Department of Housing and Urban Development, scheduled for publication Summer 1978), ch. 2; U.S. Department of Housing and Urban Development, *An Evaluation of the Community Development Block Grant Formula* (unpublished study prepared by Harold Bunce, Office of Policy Development and Program Evaluation, December 1976); Richard DeLeon and Richard LeGates, "Community Development Block Grants: Redistribution Effects and Equity Issues," *Urban Lawyer* 9(2) (Spring 1977).

5. Nathan et al., *Block Grants for Community Development*, chs. 2-6.

6. Ibid., ch. 6.

7. Richard P. Nathan and Paul R. Dommel, "The Cities," in Joseph A. Pechman, ed., *Setting National Priorities: The 1978 Budget* (Washington, D.C.: The Brookings Institution, 1977), ch. 9.

8. See Dommel et al., *Decentralizing Community Development*, ch. 2.

9. Ibid.

10. Ibid., p. 38.

11. Public Law 93-383, Sec. 104 (b) (2), August 22, 1974.

12. For a discussion of program uses in the second program year, see Dommel et al., *Decentralizing Community Development*, ch. 5.

13. Ibid., p. 202.

14. Ibid., pp. 197-203.

15. For a discussion of the intergrovernmental and local decision processes, see ibid., chs. 3 and 4.

16. See Rochelle L. Stanfield, "The Latest Community Development Flap—Targeting on the Poor," *National Journal* 9, 49 (December 3, 1977), pp. 1877-1879.

17. Nathan et al., *Block Grants for Community Development*, ch. 8; *CommmunityDevelopment Block Grant Program: First Annual Report* (Washington, D.C.: U.S. Government Printing Office, December 1976), pp. 23-26 and 32-36; National Association of Housing and Redevelopment Officials, *Journal of Housing* 34, 4 (April 1977), p. 184.

18. "Community Development Block Grants," *Federal Register* 42(205), Part III, § 570,302 (October 25, 1977); p. 56454. For the final regulations, see ibid., 43(41), Part IV § 570.302 (March 1, 1978), pp. 8460-8462.

19. For a detailed discussion of this dispute, see Rochelle L. Stanfield, "Civil War Over Cities' Aid—The Battle No One Expected," *National Journal* 9, 32 (August 6, 1977), pp. 1226-1227.

20. For a discussion of one impaction formula possibility, see Richard DeLeon and Richard LeGates, "Beyond Cybernetic Federalism in Community Development," *Urban Lawyer* (scheduled for publication).

✳ *Chapter 9*

Countercyclical Revenue Sharing

John P. Ross

If one were asked to place a label on federal-state-local
fiscal relations for the 1976–1977 period, one might well
call it the era of countercyclical aid. During this period,
two new aid programs were enacted and two previously existing programs were expanded with the explicit purpose of providing anti-
recession aid to state and local governments. The total package had
three parts—a public works component, a general assistance component, and a public employment component.

Although the number of programs may not be sufficient to
warrant the suggested title for the period, the dollar amounts involved are substantial. From November 1976 to June 1978, almost
$13.9 billion has been allocated to state and local governments.[1]
This amounts to more than 19 percent of estimated total federal aid
to state and local governments in fiscal year 1977.

The purpose of this chapter is to examine one of those aid programs—Anti-Recession Fiscal Assistance (ARFA)—with special emphasis on its impact on cities. More specifically, the chapter reviews
the purpose of this program, how it works, and its potential impacts.
In the last section, special attention is given to the public policy
implications of general purpose countercyclical aid.

Purpose of the Program

Senator Edmund Muskie aptly stated the rationale of general
purpose countercyclical aid as:

The idea of emergency anti-recession budget assistance to State and local governments grew out of the concern of certain economists that during a recession, State and local governments experience a special budget squeeze and are often forced to make adjustments which run counter to Federal efforts to stimulate economic recovery. Such adjustments—which include tax increases, service cutbacks and reduced capital expenditures—become necessary because of revenue shortfalls due to the depressed local economy and a simultaneous increased demand for certain local services. In the past, such budget adjustments by State and local governments may not have been significant to the overall pace of economic recovery. But today, according to the theory of countercyclical assistance, State and local governments comprise a major sector of the U.S. economy, and thus the budget actions which they take can no longer be ignored in formulating national economic policy.[2]

Following this logic, the general purpose of the antirecession package is to ease "the general fiscal crisis of State and local governments during the recession and, thereby, contribute to the overall goal of economic recovery."[3] In the process, the package strengthens the hand of the federal government in stabilizing the national economy and promotes "greater coordination, during time of economic downturn, between national economic policy—as articulated at the Federal level—and budgetary actions of State and local governments."[4]

Thus, the program was originally passed as a countercyclical tool with two related but not necessarily consistent goals. The first objective is to counter the recession by using federal aid to make state and local governments agents of national stabilization policy. State and local governments are encouraged to accelerate their spending in order to hasten economic recovery.

The goal is to make the additional federal aid available to these jurisdictions that are in the best position to spend it quickly and to make sure that the federal aid supplements—not supplants—state and local funds.

The second objective of federal countercyclical aid is to provide fiscal support to replace the state and local revenue loss caused by the recession. Severe economic recessions have differential impacts on state and local jurisdictions. The degree of these impacts depends upon the geographic area occupied by the jurisdiction, the sensitivity of the jurisdiction's revenues and expenditures to changes in income, and the economic position of the jurisdiction prior to the recession. For example, a place already experiencing secular decline may be more severely hurt by a recession than a place that is experiencing rapid secular growth. The purpose of the aid would be to balance the impact of the recession across jurisdictions, cushioning those which would otherwise be most adversely affected. In essence, the program becomes a kind of state and local government insurance against recession.

These two purposes are not mutually exclusive and, therefore, can be blended into a mixed policy that includes both economic stabilization and fiscal support. To the extent that these objectives are compatible, the mix approach provides a workable political compromise for involving state and local governments in national stabilization policy and at the same time maintaining fiscal balance within the system.

However, a conflict between these objectives may occur as the recovery continues. First, different jurisdictions in different geographic areas will recover at different rates. While national stabilization concerns may call for the termination of additional antirecession aid, some jurisdictions will undoubtedly still need fiscal support. It is at this point that a distinction between these two general objectives becomes critical.

A second area of potential conflict between these two objectives concerns targeting. If the aid is targeted to places of high unemployment, the question is then raised as to whether such high unemployment is caused by a short-run or by a long-run decline. Under the national agent purpose, it may be argued that the funds should go to places with high cyclical unemployment. Under the fiscal support purpose, the distinction is not as important; the idea here is to provide a cushion regardless of the underlying cause of the problem.

The Anti-Recession Fiscal Assistance Program

Congressional interest in Anti-Recession Fiscal Assistance was given practical expression when, in May and June of 1975, the Subcommittee on Intergovernmental Relations of the Senate Committee on Government Operations held hearings on S.-1359, a bill sponsored by Senators Muskie, Humphrey, and Brock, "to coordinate State and local budget-related actions with Federal Government efforts to stimulate economic recovery by establishing a system of emergency support grants to State and local governments."[5]

The continued deterioration of the economic situation and pressures from state and local government officials who were experiencing the effects of the recession during 1975 and early 1976 led to the addition by the Senate of fiscal assistance aid as Title II of the Local Public Works Employment Act of 1976. The legislation was vetoed by President Ford on February 13, 1976, on the grounds that the bill was too costly for the number of jobs it would create. While there were sufficient votes to override the veto in the House, the Senate failed by three votes to do likewise.

In an attempt to tailor the legislation so that it would gain presidential approval or, failing such approval, gain sufficient votes to override a veto, Congress made substantial changes in the proposed allocation formula. The original version of the fiscal assistance grants had provided that the amounts due to the governments would be calculated on the basis of a formula using unemployment rates and state and local tax effort. The revised formula dropped any reference to tax effort and provided that payments would be determined by a formula using unemployment rates and general revenue-sharing payments (as determined by the Office of Revenue Sharing under the general revenue-sharing program). The effects of the change were to channel more funds to areas with relatively low state and local taxes and to provide more money to states with relatively high rates of chronic unemployment.

President Ford, as expected, vetoed the second version of the legislation in July 1976. This time there were sufficient votes to override the veto, and the new program of economic stimulants was passed over the President's veto to become P.L. 94–369 on July 22, 1976.

The Anti-Recession Fiscal Assistance Law

P.L. 94–369 authorized the Secretary of the Treasury to make grants in the total amount not to exceed $1.25 billion to help state and local governments maintain services, avert layoffs of public employees, and avoid tax increases. The program was to begin July 1, 1976, and run for five calendar quarters (ending September 30, 1977).

For each calendar quarter, the law authorized payments totaling $125 million plus $62.5 million for each 0.5 percent by which the national unemployment rate exceeded 6 percent for the quarter ending three months earlier. However, no funds were authorized if the national unemployment rate did not exceed 6 percent for the quarter ending three months earlier, or for the last month of the quarter.

One-third of the money was to be used for grants to states and two-thirds for grants to local governments. No state or local government would be entitled to a grant unless its own unemployment rate for the quarter ending three months earlier or the last month of that quarter exceeded 4.5 percent. Jurisdictions are also ineligible to receive payments if their quarterly allocation is less than $100.

Determination of the amount of payment to eligible state governments is based on a formula derived by comparing the state's fiscal year 1976 general revenue-sharing allocations and its "excess" (exceeding 4.5 percent) unemployment with similar data for all states. Payments to local governments are determined by the same formula. This system of formulas obliges states to compete with other states for a share of the one-third pot and local governments to compete with other units of local governments throughout the United States for their share of the two-thirds national pot.

To further antirecessionary goals, the legislation provided that the funds must be spent by recipients within six months of receipt. The only additional requirements were that eligible governments submit a series of eight assurances each fiscal year, the most important of these stipulating that funds would be used to maintain employment levels and basic services, and that the government in using the funds would comply with federal labor standards and antidiscrimination requirements.

For the first and second quarters, total payments of $562.5 million were made to 19,505 eligible governments (out of 39,000 who received general revenue-sharing payments). More than 4,000 governments failed to file the required assurances in time to receive the first payments.

As the program got under way, the major difficulties noted by participating governments were those encountered in (a) following normal budget processes as required by the law and still spending the funds within six months, and (b) the interpretation of the requirement that the funds be used only to "maintain customary basic services" and not be used for the acquisition of supplies and materials or for construction unless the supplies, materials, or construction are necessary to maintain basic services. (As jurisdictions continued to encounter difficulty in interpreting this requirement, it became known as the "leaky roof" provision because the repair of a leaky roof was always cited as an example of a permissible construction expenditure.)

The January quarter of 1977 payment of $312.5 million (on the basis of an unemployment rate of 7.8 percent) and the March quarter payment of an additional $312.5 million to 16,715 governments (on the basis of a 7.9 percent unemployment rate) left the program with only $62.7 million—obviously not enough to cover the expected payment for the fifth (July 1977) quarter.

President Carter, in his January 31, 1977, message proposing an economic recovery program, asked Congress to fund the program fully through fiscal year 1978 and to expand it further. He recommended that the program be authorized on a five-year basis (instead of the current one-year basis) and that the formula be made more sensitive to unemployment rate changes: each one-tenth of 1 percent unemployment over 6 percent would add $30 million to the basic $125 million available at 6 percent unemployment.

Congressional hearings, as well as views solicited from state governors, showed strong support for the extension. State and local officials testified that they found the program's simplicity and lack of red tape a great asset. The only difficulties apparently arose from problems jurisdictions faced in budgeting to meet the uncertain levels of quarterly allocations and the vagueness of guidelines about the use of funds, especially those relating to construction.

The Senate quickly approved an expansion and extension of the program when it was presented by Senator Muskie as a floor amendment to the stimulus tax bill, but cut the period of extension from five years, proposed by the Carter Administration, to one through fiscal 1978.

Opposition developed in hearings before the Subcommittee on Intergovernmental Relations and Human Resources of the House Committee on Government Operations. Testimony from government and research witnesses pointed out serious shortcomings of the first antirecession law. Major objections spelled out by the subcommittee[6] were that in allocating the grants, long-term decline of cities is confused with temporary effects of recession; that unemployment rates are neither reliable nor suitable for measuring governmental financial need; and that the program had not significantly increased employment or provided economic stimulation. The subcommittee's report concluded that if the program were to be extended through the first two quarters of fiscal 1978, it should be modified so that each government's tax collections and tax efforts would be substituted for unemployment rates in the allocation formula. The subcommittee recommended the establishment of a permanent antirecession program for future national recessions in which payments would be activated by two consecutive quarterly declines in private sector real wages and salaries, or in real gross national product. Allocations for the permanent program would be based on relative taxes and tax effort.

The subcommittee's substitute was rejected by a 23 to 19 vote by the full committee, which reported a revised bill authorizing an extension for one year, a higher funding level, and some additional minor changes.

The Intergovernmental Anti-Recession Act of 1977 (P.L. 95–30) extended the program for five quarters, beginning in July 1977 and ending on September 30, 1978, and provided a total new authorization of $2.25 billion. The Anti-Recession Fiscal Assistance program, during the last quarter under the old formula, had allocated $312.5 million for an unemployment rate of 7.9 percent. Under the new formula, the allocation would have been $695 million.

The Impact of the Program Upon State and Local Governments

The 1976 act provided that quarterly payments would be made to states and local governments when the unemployment rates for that government exceeded 4.5 percent for the quarter beginning three months before or the last month of the quarter.

As the employment situation improved, there was a decrease in the number and percent of recipients.

	First-third Quarter		Seventh Quarter	
	Eligible Governments	Recipients	Eligible Governments	Recipients
States, Territories	50	49	54	37
Counties	3,046	2,683	3,045	1,481
Municipalities	18,842	11,580	18,894	7,719
Townships	16,834	8,884	16,821	5,834
Indian tribes, and Alaska native village	335	193	332	163
	39,107	23,389	39,146	15,234
Total recipients as percent of eligible		59.8%		38.9%

Table A-9-1 in the appendix shows the Anti-Recession Fiscal Assistance allocations received by state areas (not by the state government alone but by all of the jurisdictions within the state) for the first, sixth, and seventh quarters (the latter ending March 31, 1978) as well as the cumulative allocations for the seven quarters.

The increase in the total national allocation, despite the drop in the unemployment rate from 7.6 percent in the first quarter to 7.0 in the sixth quarter and 6.9 percent in the seventh quarter, is attributable to the expanded funding provided under the extension of the legislation.

Changes in individual allocations are also influenced by changes in general revenue-sharing allocations—one of the two elements in the antirecession fiscal assistance formula—that are based on a complex formula ascertained from population, per capita income, and tax effort.

An analysis of the cumulative grants through the seventh quarter (beginning January 1, 1978) to states (all levels of government) shows that the funds are heavily concentrated in the most populous states. Six states received cumulative allocations through the seventh quarter exceeding $100 million or almost 57 percent of all antirecession fiscal assistance funds.

State (All governments)	State Unemployment Rate		Cumulative Allocation through the Seventh Quarter (000's)
	First Quarter	Seventh Quarter	
New York	10.2%	8.1%	$ 487,388
California	10.6	7.2	386,339
Michigan	11.8	6.6	158,263
Pennsylvania	9.2	6.3	155,969
New Jersey	10.8	8.2	147,064
Florida	10.9	6.9	104,970
Total, 6 states			$1,439,993

In contrast, twelve states—Idaho, Iowa, Kansas, Montana, Nebraska, Nevada, New Hampshire, North Dakota, South Dakota, Utah, Vermont, and Wyoming—received less than $10 million in cumulative allocations through the seventh quarter. States receiving the smaller amounts tend to be in the Rocky Mountain and Plains regions and have shown rapid recovery from the recession when

Region		Total Percent of Cumulative Allocation Through the Seventh Quarter
New England and Mideast		40.6
New England	7.0	
Mideast	33.6	
Midwest		17.0
Great Lakes	14.9	
Plains	2.1	
South		20.6
Southeast	16.0	
Southwest	4.6	
West		21.3
Rocky Mountains	1.2	
Far West	20.1	
Territories and Puerto Rico	.1	.1

measured by unemployment rates. In many cases, very few governments within these states are receiving allocations presently because most areas have unemployment rates below the 4.5 percent individual government cutoff.

When cumulative payments through the seventh quarter to all governments in a state are grouped by regions, it is noted that the Mideast states receive 34 percent of the funds with the Far West receiving the next greatest proportion, 20 percent.

Per Capita Allocations by Region and State

An examination of the per capita amounts given to all governments in each state shows a different pattern. When the cumulative allocation for the first seven quarters of the program are set up on a per capita basis (see Table A-9-2 in the appendix), Alaska receives the top amount of $28.68 followed by New York with $26.95. Six of the eight states receiving the highest per capita amounts are on the eastern seaboard. Five of the eight states receiving the lowest per capita allocations are in the plains region. States with high per capita cumulative allocations tend to be those with continued high unemployment, while those with low per capita allocations have, with one exception (New Hampshire), unemployment rates in the seventh quarter below the 4.5 percent individual jurisdiction cutoff rate.

State (all governments)	Unemployment Rate Seventh Quarter	Per Capita Cumulative Allocation through the Seventh Quarter
Highest		
Alaska	10.2%	$28.68
New York	8.1	26.95
Maine	7.8	21.83
New Jersey	8.2	20.05
Delaware	7.3	19.68
Vermont	6.4	19.58
District of Columbia	8.0	18.13
California	7.2	17.95
Lowest		
Wyoming	2.8	.36
Kansas	3.8	.84
South Dakota	2.7	.86
Iowa	2.8	1.16
Nebraska	2.3	1.25
North Dakota	2.9	1.65
New Hampshire	4.8	2.06
Indiana	4.5	3.32

Allocation to Cities

The figures on allocations to the largest cities in the United States (Table A–9–3 in the appendix) show that five cities consistently receive the highest allocation although their relative positions change slightly:

City	First Quarter		Seventh Quarter		Cumulative Allocation (000s)
	Unemployment Rate	Allocation (000s)	Unemployment Rate	Allocation (000s)	
New York	11.0%	$19,103	9.0%	$37,103	$196,923
Philadelphia	10.2	3,228	9.4	7,443	38,575
Detroit	15.8	4,928	9.4	5,662	37,527
Chicago	10.8	5,232	6.1	3,671	32,889
Los Angeles	11.1	3,028	7.9	4,189	25,127

These five cities, which make up approximately 8 percent of the total United States population, received about 13 percent of the cumulative Anti-Recession Fiscal Assistance funds. They received one-third of the cumulative funds going to municipal governments.

Per capita cumulative allocations through the seventh quarter for the forty-eight largest cities are shown in Table A–9–4 in the appendix. Newark, whose unemployment rate continued high (14.0 percent), leads the major cities with a per capita cumulative allocation of $39.34. Detroit and New York follow with per capita allocations of more than $25.00 each. These cities receive the highest per capita amounts because their unemployment rates and their allocations have remained high through the seventh quarter, indicating a persistent pattern more typical of structural than cyclical unemployment.

City	Unemployment Rate Seventh Quarter	Per Capita Cumulative Allocations through the Seventh Quarter
Newark	14.0%	$39.34
Detroit	9.4	28.11
New York	9.0	26.32
San Francisco	9.1	22.69
Philadelphia	9.4	21.25
St. Louis	10.1	20.18
New Orleans	9.0	20.25
Baltimore	8.7	19.71
Oakland	11.1	18.55
Boston	7.0	18.30

Most of the lowest per capita allocations go to cities of the Southwest and South. Dallas received only $0.04 for its per capita cumulative allocation, Fort Worth, $0.99, and Houston, $1.56.

Program Findings

For this chapter, two general categories of results of the Anti-Recession Fiscal Assistance program are important. These are concerned with purpose and effectiveness.[7]

Findings about Purpose. As discussed earlier, the ARFA program has two general purposes—economic stabilization and fiscal balance. The first objective—economic stabilization—has two components.

In its strongest form, it maintains that countercyclical assistance is necessary because without it state and local financial behavior is perverse with respect to national stabilization policy. This perversity hypothesis can be traced to the classic study by Hansen and Perloff of the behavior of state and local governments during the depression of the 1930s.[8] Although this hypothesis has been discredited by a number of empirical studies of state and local government behavior during recession,[9] it has continued to remain a part of conventional economic wisdom.[10]

Using the concept of fiscal leverage to measure the impact of state and local financial behavior on the economy, our own estimates also show countercyclical behavior by the state and local governments for the 1973-1975 recession, (Table A-9-5). Using the same measure since 1975, state and local government behaviors have been contractionary. Their impact on the economy has been to retard increases in aggregate demand.

In a somewhat less forceful manner, the national agent argument about economic stimulation maintains that regardless of what state and local governments are doing, they can be used as agents of the federal government to counter recession.

There are two problems with this position. First, it can be used to justify any action the federal government wishes to take. Second, state and local governments are difficult agents to control. Because of the possibilities of substitution and the difficulties involved in cutting off the aid, they may not work well as such agents.

The second component of economic stabilization concerns the effects of the recession on state and local governments. The combination of inflation and recession may lead to an erosion of the financial position of state and local governments, necessitating fiscal support assistance in order to prevent service level deterioration during recession.[11]

Under this justification, the effects of the combination of inflation and recession on state and local government finances become very important. However, even the course of these effects on expenditures is in doubt and needs much more study. On the revenue side at least the direction is clear. Recession should reduce revenues; inflation should increase revenues. If inflation-induced cost increases are greater than inflation-induced revenue gains, state and local governments may still lose from inflation.

Table 9-1 presents estimates of the impact of inflation on state and local governments. These estimates indicate that in the aggregate, state and local governments gained slightly from inflation.

Table 9-2 shows the net impact of both recession and inflation. What this table shows is that in fiscal year 1976, state and local governments lost about $10 billion because of the combination of recession and inflation. That loss amounted to about 5 percent of total own-source revenue. While not excessively severe, to a state or local government already under a great deal of financial stress that 5 percent could have been very important.[12]

While these findings are only estimates, they do provide a sense of the relative magnitude of the impact of inflation and recession on state and local governments. They indicate that while not devastating, the losses are sufficient to severely impact on those state and local governments already under financial stress.

In order to put these findings into perspective, it should be pointed out that the Council of Economic Advisors estimated that state and local government revenues would have increased by $17.2 billion had the economy been at full employment in 1976.[13] This compares with the $15.7 billion loss due to recession (Table 9-2).

Findings about Effectiveness. Early studies on the effectiveness of ARFA have generated mixed reviews. Perhaps the basic reason for the lack of consistency in determining the effectiveness of this program is duality of goals. Evaluations that emphasized the economic stimulus goal have tended to be much more critical than those that concentrated on fiscal impact. As an example of the problems involved, the question of which state and local governments should receive countercyclical assistance has been cloudy from the beginning of this program because the targeting mechanism, the unemployment rate, makes no distinction between areas with high unemployment caused by short-run (cyclical) fluctuations and areas with high unemployment caused by long-run (secular) changes. In fact, areas with both types of unemployment are aided by this program. Our own study indicates that the money goes to cities with high rates of unemployment and to cities that are high on Nathan's "urban conditions index."[14] However, the cloudiness between cyclical and secular unemployment remains and was considered such a drawback that GAO, in its study of antirecession fiscal assistance, strongly argued that if the program were to continue as a countercyclical measure a new targeting mechanism was necessary.

On the other hand, the dual objectives of the program to some extent require the use of the unemployment rate rather than the change in unemployment as suggested by those emphasizing only the economic stabilization aspects of the program. It is very difficult to separate cyclical from secular unemployment because the cycle does not affect all areas at the same time. Some feel the impact of a cyclical downturn long before others. As a result, trying to separate these two effects may well penalize those regions that lead the cycle. Second, regardless of the reasons, an area with a 10 percent rate of unemployment is in more difficult circumstances than one whose unemployment rate rises from 3 to 5 percent. On equity grounds, it would be impractical to aid the jurisdiction with the lower unemployment while ignoring the difficulties of the high unemployment jurisdiction. Choosing the appropriate targeting mechanism depends upon the purpose of the program. In this instance, there are multiple purposes, and as a result, a case can be made for any number of alternative targeting devices.

The 1975 CBO analysis of countercyclical programs gave high marks to antirecession grants. According to the CBO, such aid can be put into effect quickly and has a high potential for creating jobs. CBO estimated that expenditures of $1 billion annually would produce initially between 40,000 and 77,000 jobs at a net budget cost of $716 to $850 million and 72,000 to 100,000 jobs in twenty-four months at a net budget cost of $450 to $480 million.[15] The inflationary impact of antirecessionary aid was considered to be moderate, and the potential for targeting aid to governments especially hard hit by recession was good.[16]

The CBO did point out several disadvantages of such general antirecession grants. State and local governments would be subject to few, if any, restrictions on the use of the funds given to them. Therefore, in comparison with public service employment, a smaller proportion of payments might be used for wages. The average worker hired with "no strings" money would tend to be more skilled and more highly paid than the average public service worker. In addition, the study pointed out that antirecession grants could be criticized because they tend to increase the size of the state-local government

Table 9-1. Estimated Impact of Inflation on State and Local Revenues[a], Fiscal Years 1973–1976

	Inflationary[b] Increase in Revenues		Inflationary[c] Loss in Purchasing Power		Net Gain[d] From Inflation	
	Billions $	Percent of Revenues	Billions $	Percent of Revenue	Billions $	Percent of Revenues
Total State-Local						
1973	10.4	6.9	9.5	6.3	0.9	0.6
1974	18.9	11.4	12.4	7.5	6.5	3.9
1975	28.4	15.7	18.3	10.1	10.1	5.6
1976	19.4	9.7	13.8	6.9	5.6	2.8
State						
1973	6.2	7.7	5.0	6.3	1.2	1.5
1974	11.3	12.7	6.7	7.5	4.6	5.2
1975	16.9	17.5	9.8	10.1	7.1	7.3
1976	11.6	10.8	7.4	6.9	4.2	3.9
Local						
1973	4.2	6.0	4.4	6.3	-0.2	-0.3
1974	7.6	9.9	5.8	7.5	1.8	2.3
1975	11.4	13.5	8.5	10.1	2.9	3.4
1976	7.8	8.4	6.4	6.9	1.4	1.5

Source: ACIR staff calculations.

[a]Own-source general revenue.

[b]Based on regression analysis.

[c]Based on state and local government deflator in the National Income Accounts.

[d]Net loss equals inflationary increase in revenue minus inflationary loss in purchasing power, expressed in nominal dollars. Time series regression analysis was computed for each level of government using fiscal year data for the period 1957–1976. The model was specified as follows:

$R = \alpha + B_1 \Delta GAP\ \$ + B_2 \Delta DEFL + U.$ ΔR = Change in own-source general revenues. $\Delta GAP\$$ = Change in the nominal GNP GAP. $\Delta DEFL$ = Change in the implicit price deflator for GNP.

Regression Results	Constant	$\Delta GAP\$$	Coefficient estimated for: $\Delta DEFL$	$\bar{R}^2$	Durban Watson
Total	1.15	-0.12 (5.54)	236.42 (11.28)	0.883	1.35
State	0.33	-0.08 (5.91)	141.21 (10.31)	0.857	2.01
Local	0.82	-0.04 (3.53)	95.21 (9.59)	0.859	0.99

(T values are in parentheses)

Table 9-2.   Separating the Impact of Inflation and Recession on State and Local Own-Source General Revenues, Fiscal Years 1973–1976

	Net[a] Revenue Gain from Inflation		Net[b] Revenue Loss from Recession		Net Revenue Loss from Inflation and Recession	
	Billions $	Percent of Revenues	Billions $	Percent of Revenue	Billions $	Percent of Revenues
Total[c]						
State and Local						
1973	0.9	0.6	(0.3)[d]	(0.2)[d]	(1.2)[d]	(0.8)[d]
1974	6.5	3.9	2.4	1.4	(4.1)	(2.5)
1975	10.1	5.6	15.3	8.4	5.2	2.9
1976	5.6	2.8	15.7	7.8	10.1	5.0
State						
1973	1.2	1.5	(0.2)	(0.1)	(1.4)	(1.7)
1974	4.6	5.2	1.8	2.0	(2.8)	(3.1)
1975	7.1	7.3	11.2	11.6	4.1	4.2
1976	4.2	3.9	11.4	10.6	7.2	6.7
Local						
1973	-0.2	-0.3	(0.1)	(0.1)	0.1	0.1
1974	1.8	2.3	0.8	1.0	(1.0)	(1.3)
1975	2.9	3.4	4.8	5.7	1.9	2.3
1976	1.4	1.5	4.9	5.3	3.5	3.8

Source: ACIR staff calculations.

[a]Net revenue gain due to inflation is equal to estimated inflation related revenue increases minus the loss of purchasing power of revenues (see Table 9-1).

[b]Net revenue loss due to recession is the revenue shortfall state and local governments do not cover with tax rate increases.

[c]The total was estimated separately for the state and local sector. This explains why the parts do not add up to the total.

[d]Gains are reported in parentheses.

sector of the economy and because they also tend to a limited extent to protect state and local governments from the fiscal discipline to improve government performance exerted by recession-induced pressures.

A recent report by the Department of the Treasury on the economic impact of these three programs was also quite favorable. It found that the programs targeted well and provided most money to cities facing extreme financial stress.[17]

A study done by the General Accounting Office (GAO) examined the Anti-Recession Assistance Program. Its findings were not particularly favorable. For example, the report noted that many of the governments receiving payments under this program were not greatly affected by the recession, but rather that their problems resulted from long-term, secular declines in their economies. According to the GAO study, the reason for this distributional pattern was that "excess unemployment" is not a good measure of recessionary impacts. The study also found that some governments were not spending the money, and as a result, the effectiveness of the program as a countercyclical tool was reduced.[18]

The House of Representatives Intergovernmental Relations and Human Resources Subcommittee of the Committe on Government Operations took extended testimony on the antirecession fiscal assistance program. Like GAO they felt that the program could be greatly improved.[19]

A more recent evaluation done by Peat, Marwick, Mitchell and Company found that the program was producing significant fiscal and economic impacts.[20] The analysis noted that in 68 percent of the sample jurisdictions ARFA resulted in net additional purchases. In only 20 percent of the jurisdictions did ARFA result in tax reductions, and in 12 percent of the jurisdictions balances were increased. In addition, it was estimated that employment increased by 54,000 to 66,000 as a result of ARFA payments.

A New Proposal

The present program will end September 30, 1978. In anticipation of that event, the administration has introduced in Congress the Supplementary Fiscal Assistance Act of 1978. The new proposal changes the Anti-Recession Fiscal Assistance Program into a program with the explicit purpose of aiding local governments suffering severe secular economic decline. Emphasis is placed on fiscal support rather than on economic stimulation, and state governments can no longer receive the aid. The new proposal is being promoted as an essential component of a comprehensive urban policy.

In addition, the proposed bill changes the distribution formula. Local governments are divided into those within SMSAs and those outside SMSAs. A local jurisdiction's allocation is dependent on its revenue-sharing allocation times one of the following factors: (1) its excess unemployment (over 4.5 percent); (2) the difference between its rate of growth in employment and the average rate of growth in employment for all jurisdictions in its class; (3) the difference between its rate of growth in per capita income and the rate of growth in per capita income for all jurisdictions in its class; or (4) the difference between its rate of growth in population and the rate of growth in population for all jurisdictions in its class. The factor that makes the local jurisdiction's allocation the largest is the one that will be used. The total amount of money available is to be $1.04 billion in fiscal year 1979 and $1.0 billion in fiscal year 1980. The program is to be considered for renewal at the same time as general revenue sharing.

The administration's proposal for renewal eliminates state governments from the program and emphasizes the fiscal assistance rather than the economic stimulus aspects of the program. In addition, it greatly complicates the allocation formula.

General purpose aid formulas have a major distinct characteristic of increasing complexity. In the name of improved targeting, we began by multiplying together the levels of various factors as in the general revenue-sharing formula. From there we moved to multiplying levels by first differences. We are now taking the next step—levels times rates of changes. One may wonder what is measured by a formula that multiplies three factor levels by the rate of change of a fourth factor. If we are really interested in providing aid to financially hard-pressed cities, there must be a simpler formula that can both accomplish the desired purpose and also be understood.

It is very difficult to determine the net impact of these proposed changes. They increase the number of local jurisdictions eligible for aid and are supposed to improve the targeting of the aid to the most severely depressed places. Meanwhile, the cost in increased complexity is quite high. It is very difficult to determine, for example, how sensitive the allocation is to change in any of the formula factors. It is not even clear exactly what these factors, together with the factors continued in the general revenue-sharing formula, measure. Given these complexities, one may wonder if there is not a simpler way to target general purpose federal aid to hard-pressed urban areas.

CONCLUSION

The purpose of this chapter has been to examine the Anti-Recession Fiscal Assistance Program. The program had a dual purpose—to provide economic stimulation to the national economy and fiscal insurance to state and local governments suffering economic decline. Early evaluations of the effectiveness of the program have been mixed, with those evaluations that emphasized the fiscal support criteria in general more favorable than those that viewed the program primarily as a countercyclical tool. All of the evaluators, however, agree that the program does indeed target money to large declining central cities.

NOTES

1. The total authorization for these programs was $15.8 billion. Of that amount, $0.5 billion in Local Public Works funds were set aside for Indian tribes, Alaskan native villages, and U.S. territories. In addition, $1.4 billion in Anti-Recession Fiscal Assistance funds have not yet been allocated. Finally, while $13.9 billion has been allocated, much of that money has not yet been spent.

2. Senator Edmund S. Muskie, "Introduction and Summary," *The Countercyclical Assistance Program: An Analysis of Its Initial Impact*, prepared by the Subcommittee on Intergovernmental Relations of the Committee on Governmental Affairs, U.S. Senate, 95th Congress, 1st Session, February 28, 1977 (Washington, D.C.: U.S. Government Printing Office, 1977), p. 1.

3. Ibid., p. 1.

4. Legislative History of Title II of S.-3201 (Public Law 94-369): *Explanation of Anti-Recession Provisions*, prepared by the staff of the Subcommittee on Intergovernmental Relations of the Committee on Government Operations, U.S. Senate, 94th Congress, 2nd Session, August 1976 (Washington, D.C.: U.S. Government Printing Office, 1976), p. 1.

5. Hearing before the subcommittee on Intergovernmental Relations of the Senate Committee on Government Operations on S.-1359, May 6, 1975, p. 1.

6. See Dissenting Views printed in House Report No. 95-275 on the Intergovernmental Anti-Recession Act of 1977, May 9, 1977.

7. A number of other findings are interesting but not important to this paper. For example, it is possible for a jurisdiction's unemployment rate to decline and its allocation to increase because of the flexible total "pot". See ACIR, *Stabilization Policy: The Role of State and Local Government*, forthcoming.

8. Alvin H. Hansen and Harvey S. Perloff, *State and Local Finance in the National Economy* (New York: W.W. Norton and Company, 1944).

9. For example, see Robert W. Rafuse, "Cyclical Behavior of State-Local Finances," in Richard A. Musgrave, ed., *Essays in Fiscal Federalism*, Brookings Studies of Government Finance (Washington, D.C.: The Brookings Institution, 1965), pp. 63-121. For more detailed analysis, see Robert W. Rafuse, *State and Local Fiscal Behavior Over the Postwar Cycles*, unpublished Ph.D. dissertation, Princeton University, November 1963.

10. One of the reasons for the continued acceptance of this hypothesis is the problem associated with the definition of perversity. Perverse with respect to what? At least three different standards may be used to measure perverse behavior: (1) the business cycle of the national economy, (2) the full employment growth level, or (3) the business cycle of the region. In this study, the national business cycle is used as the standard.

11. For a detailed discussion of this position and a suggestion for the form such grants might take, see David Greytak and A. Dale Tussing, "Revenue Stabilizing Grants: A Proposal," *Proceedings of the Sixty-fourth Annual Conference*, National Tax Association, Kansas City, Missouri, 1971, pp. 47-54.

12. There are a number of other methods for estimating the impact of inflation and recession on state and local revenues. Thus the findings in these tables should be viewed as only preliminary estimates that give some idea of the magnitude of revenue loss. For a detailed discussion of this method, see Robert C. Vogel, "The Responsiveness of State and Local Receipts to Changes in Economic Activity: Extending the Concept of the Full Employment Budget," *Studies in Price Stability and Economic Growth*, Papers Nos. 6 and 7, The Impact of Inflation on the Full Employment Budget, prepared for the use of the Joint Economic Committee, Congress of the United States, 94th Congress, 1st Session (Washington, D.C.: U.S. Government Printing Office, 1975), pp. 21-35.

13. *Economic Report of the President*, January 1977, p. 76.

14. This study combines unemployment, income, poverty, dependency, education, and crowded housing into a single urban conditions index. See Richard P. Nathan and Charles Adams, "Understanding Central City Hardship," *Political Science Quarterly* 91, 1 (Spring 1976), pp. 47-62.

15. Net budget costs deducted budget savings due to increased tax payments and reduced unemployment compensation costs from the total expenditures for the program.

16. CBO, op. cit., 1975, p. V.

17. U.S. Department of the Treasury, Department of State and Local Finance, *Report on the Fiscal Impact of the Economic Stimulus Package on 48 Large Urban Governments* (Washington, D.C.: U.S. Government Printing Office, January 23, 1978).

18. The Comptroller General of the United States, *Anti-Recession Assistance is Helping but Distribution Formula Needs Reassessment* (Washington, D.C.: U.S. Government Printing Office, July 20, 1977).

19. Intergovernmental Relations and Human Resources Subcommittee of the Committee on Government Operations, House of Representatives, Report No. 95-275. Intergovernmental Anti-Recession Assistance Act of 1977. 95th Congress, 1st Session (Washington, D.C.: U.S. Government Printing Office, 1977).

20. Peat, Marwick, Mitchell and Company in association with Municipal Finance Officers Association, Phoenix Associates, Inc., and Harold A. Hovey, *An Analysis of the Anti-Recession Fiscal Assistance Program,* prepared for Office of Revenue Sharing, U.S. Department of the Treasury, April 1, 1978.

Appendix

Table A-9-1.   Anti-Recession Fiscal Assistance Allocations by State Areas

| States | First Quarter July 1–September 30, 1976 | | Sixth Quarter October 1–December 31, 1977 | | Seventh Quarter January 1–March 31, 1978 | | Cumulative Allocations (000's) |
	State Unemployment Rate[b]	Allocation (000's)	State Unemployment Rate[c]	Allocation (000's)	State Unemployment Rate	Allocation (000's)	
United States Total[a]	7.6%	$310,938	7.0	$424,351	5.9%	$408,066	$2,533,218
Alabama	7.3	3,271	5.8	4,306	5.9	5,178	28,415
Alaska	11.3	574	13.3	3,578	10.2	2,474	10,955
Arizona	9.1	3,247	7.1	4,797	7.0	5,352	28,261
Arkansas	7.4	2,166	5.6	2,677	5.3	2,232	16,424
California	10.6	45,674	7.8	68,554	7.2	62,782	386,339
Colorado	6.5	1,623	5.8	3,115	5.4	2,781	15,370
Connecticut	10.6	5,995	7.5	7,613	6.7	6,412	47,073
Delaware	8.1	849	7.8	2,175	7.3	2,116	11,451
Dist. of Col.	8.0	1,029	8.3	2,731	8.0	2,781	12,724
Florida	10.9	14,291	7.1	15,368	6.9	16,330	104,970
Georgia	7.8	4,681	6.4	8,230	6.2	8,471	44,588
Hawaii	8.6	1,323	7.6	1,811	7.5	3,143	15,843
Idaho	8.0	896	5.1	696	4.6	233	4,880
Illinois	8.5	15,584	5.0	8,677	4.8	6,505	84,495
Indiana	7.4	4,167	4.8	2,266	4.5	1,271	17,578
Iowa	6.5	1,838	2.9	64	2.8	41	3,342
Kansas	4.5	321	3.6	237	3.8	303	1,929
Kentucky	7.7	3,859	4.3	1,083	4.3	1,092	16,818
Louisiana	7.2	4,045	7.6	12,636	7.2	12,521	56,704
Maine	9.9	2,616	8.5	4,801	7.8	4,485	23,354
Maryland	7.3	4,224	5.5	5,752	5.3	5,532	36,280
Massachusetts	10.5	14,093	6.3	11,390	5.9	9,939	82,002
Michigan	11.8	22,928	6.9	22,317	6.6	21,538	158,263
Minnesota	7.1	3,926	5.0	2,757	4.2	831	18,638
Mississippi	6.2	1,778	5.9	4,735	5.8	5,067	22,801

Missouri	6.7	3,345	4.9	3,635	5.3	5,254	25,691
Montana	9.2	1,224	4.6	383	4.1	206	5,007
Nebraska	6.8	1,100	2.3	3	2.3	—	1,943
Nevada	10.1	949	7.1	1,189	6.3	984	7,103
New Hampshire	5.6	254	4.9	335	4.8	86	1,693
New Jersey	10.8	14,917	9.1	29,014	8.2	26,753	147,064
New Mexico	7.4	1,290	8.0	4,500	7.7	4,674	20,685
New York	10.2	47,598	8.6	89,531	8.1	90,361	487,388
North Carolina	6.9	4,149	5.3	4,890	5.0	3,872	32,443
North Dakota	6.6	517	3.8	48	2.9	16	1,059
Ohio	8.7	12,673	6.1	13,990	5.9	14,027	93,684
Oklahoma	7.8	2,641	4.8	1,418	4.5	971	13,308
Oregon	11.2	5,094	8.5	8,000	7.6	6,895	41,066
Pennsylvania	9.2	18,540	6.6	24,275	6.3	24,229	155,969
Rhode Island	12.6	2,513	6.8	1,881	6.9	2,217	14,502
South Carolina	7.1	2,584	5.3	2,455	5.3	2,750	17,449
South Dakota	5.4	261	3.1	66	2.7	73	591
Tennessee	7.6	4,087	5.2	3,028	4.9	1,793	23,582
Texas	5.5	4,232	5.0	9,207	5.1	12,131	54,592
Utah	7.2	1,104	4.9	497	4.4	224	4,895
Vermont	10.4	1,223	7.5	1,703	6.4	1,200	9,319
Virginia	5.9	2,297	5.5	5,018	5.1	4,080	23,214
Washington	10.4	6,212	7.2	7,783	6.5	6,526	46,628
West Virginia	7.2	1,652	6.2	2,766	6.2	3,298	18,099
Wisconsin	7.6	5,534	4.5	2,126	4.3	2,083	23,310
Wyoming	5.0	51	3.5	15	2.8	3	139
American Samoa	N.A.	a/	N.A.	37	N.A.	34	115
Guam	N.A.	a/	N.A.	115	N.A.	108	374
Puerto Rico	22.2	a/	22.2	3,960	20.4	3,699	12,442
Virgin Islands	N.A.	a/	N.A.	117	N.A.	109	372

Source: Office of Revenue Sharing, Department of the Treasury, ACIR staff.

[a] Totals include payments to Puerto Rico, Guam, American Samoa, and the Virgin Islands in the sixth and seventh quarter; they were not eligible until the law was extended in May 1977.

[b] First quarter allocations were made on the basis of the unemployment rate for the quarter beginning January 1, 1976.

[c] Seventh quarter allocations were made on the basis of the unemployment rate for the quarter beginning July 1, 1977.

Table A-9-2. Anti-Recession Fiscal Assistance Program Unemployment Rates and Per Capita Cumulative Allocations Through the Seventh Quarter by Region and State

State and Region	Unemployment Rate Seventh Data Quarter (Ending September 30, 1977)	Per Capita Cumulative Allocation Through Seventh Data Quarter (Ending March 31, 1978)
New England		$14.56
Maine	7.8%	$21.83
New Hampshire	4.8	2.06
Vermont	6.4	19.58
Massachusetts	5.9	14.12
Rhode Island	6.9	15.64
Connecticut	6.7	15.10
Mideast		19.92
New York	8.1	26.95
New Jersey	8.2	20.05
Pennsylvania	6.3	13.15
Delaware	7.3	19.68
Maryland	5.3	8.75
District of Columbia[a]	8.0	18.13
Great Lakes		9.22
Michigan	6.6	17.38
Ohio	5.9	8.76
Indiana	4.5	3.32
Illinois	4.8	7.52
Wisconsin	4.3	5.06
Plains		3.17
Minnesota	4.2	4.70
Iowa	2.8	1.16
Missouri	5.3	5.38
North Dakota	2.9	1.65
South Dakota	2.7	.86
Nebraska	2.3	1.25
Kansas	3.8	.84
Southeast		8.42
Virginia	5.1	4.61
West Virginia	6.2	9.94
Kentucky	4.3	4.91
Tennessee	4.9	5.60
North Carolina	5.0	5.93
South Carolina	5.3	6.13
Georgia	6.2	8.97
Florida	6.9	12.47
Alabama	5.9	7.75
Mississippi	5.8	9.69
Louisiana	7.2	14.76
Arkansas	5.3	7.70

Table A-9-2.   continued

State and Region	Unemployment Rate Seventh Data Quarter (Ending September 30, 1977)	Per Capita Cumulative Allocation Through Seventh Data Quarter (Ending March 31, 1978)
Southwest		6.25
Oklahoma	4.5	4.81
Texas	5.1	4.37
New Mexico	7.7	17.71
Arizona	7.0	12.45
Rocky Mountain		5.24
Montana	4.1	6.65
Idaho	4.6	5.87
Wyoming	2.8	.36
Colorado	5.4	5.95
Utah	4.4	3.99
Far West		17.31
Washington	6.5	12.91
Oregon	7.6	17.63
Nevada	6.3	11.64
California	7.2	17.95
Alaska	10.2	28.68
Hawaii	7.5	17.86
Total, 50 States and D.C.		11.74
Others (P.R., Guam, American Samoa, V.I.[b]	3.88	
Total, United States		11.11

Source: Office of Revenue Sharing, Department of the Treasury, and ACIR staff computations.

[a]For the Anti-Recession Fiscal Assistance Program, the District of Columbia is classified as a local government.

[b]Allotted an amount equal to 1 percent of the quarterly allocation, which is divided among them according to population.

Table A-9-3. Anti-Recession Fiscal Assistance Allocations to 48 Largest Cities

Cities	First Quarter July 1–September 30, 1976		Sixth Quarter October 1–December 31, 1977		Seventh Quarter January 1–March 31, 1978		Cumulative Allocations (000's)
	Unemployment Rate	Allocation (000's)	Unemployment Rate	Allocation (000's)	Unemployment Rate	Allocation (000's)	
New York	11.0%	$19,103	9.2%	$35,048	9.0%	$37,103	$196,923
Chicago	10.8	5,232	6.4	3,943	6.1	3,671	32,889
Los Angeles	11.1	3,028	8.4	4,345	7.9	4,189	25,127
Philadelphia	10.2	3,228	9.9	7,418	9.4	7,443	38,575
Detroit	15.8	4,928	9.9	5,644	9.4	5,662	37,527
Houston	5.2	137	5.1	323	5.0	297	2,073
Baltimore	9.8	1,531	8.8	3,073	8.7	3,319	16,783
Dallas	4.7	30	3.9	—	3.9	—	30
San Diego	12.6	685	10.6	1,310	9.9	1,282	6,933
San Antonio	7.6	318	7.5	797	7.9	999	3,948
Indianap.	6.6	279	6.1	596	5.6	453	2,515
Washington	8.0	1,029	8.3	2,731	8.0	2,781	12,723
Honolulu	8.2	554	7.3	1,158	7.3	1,280	6,704
Milwaukee	9.4	720	7.1	975	7.1	1,078	5,744
Phoenix	9.3	483	6.8	528	6.3	457	3,339
San Francisco	12.7	1,665	9.6	2,576	9.1	2,569	15,075
Memphis	7.1	345	5.1	191	5.0	176	1,994
Cleveland	11.4	1,189	7.8	1,353	7.2	1,224	8,384
Boston	11.9	1,794	7.4	1,685	7.0	1,606	11,651
New Orleans	8.3	771	9.3	2,473	9.0	2,564	11,337
San Jose	10.6	372	7.5	450	6.1	265	2,493
Columbus	8.3	378	5.9	347	5.9	384	2,626
Jacksonville	7.0	258	5.9	323	5.6	281	2,070
St. Louis	9.9	814	10.1	2,032	10.1	2,247	10,593
Seattle	9.8	549	6.9	629	6.5	580	4,189

City							
Denver	8.1	524	6.9	826	6.8	875	4,665
Kansas City	8.3	505	5.7	384	6.5	707	3,486
Pittsburgh	10.8	913	8.6	1,337	8.0	1,262	8,250
Atlanta	11.5	534	7.8	619	7.6	643	3,928
Nash.-David.	6.9	232	4.0	—	3.8	—	690
Cincinnati	10.6	670	8.9	1,174	8.8	1,269	6,541
Buffalo	15.2	935	10.0	1,183	9.9	1,285	7,570
El Paso	9.1	341	11.7	1,279	11.6	1,395	6,149
Minneapolis	8.0	263	6.1	295	5.6	224	1,861
Omaha	9.7	293	3.7	—	3.7	—	821
Toledo	8.8	253	7.1	368	6.8	375	2,176
Okla. City	8.5	274	4.9	69	4.3	—	1,189
Miami	13.1	802	8.4	899	8.1	918	5,946
Fort Worth	6.4	116	4.2	—	4.2	—	355
Portland	10.6	635	8.3	1,008	7.6	909	5,441
Newark	18.3	1,374	15.3	2,583	14.0	2,512	13,358
Louisville	10.6	679	4.8	84	4.8	92	2,681
Long Beach	10.0	215	7.5	312	7.1	299	1,784
Tulsa	7.6	220	4.7	35	4.6	—	862
Oakland	15.4	659	11.6	1,060	11.1	1,089	6,135
Norfolk	6.9	193	6.5	399	6.3	397	2,077
St. Paul	7.6	168	5.8	177	5.3	121	1,128
Birmingham	8.4	320	6.3	393	6.6	507	2,776

Source: Office of Revenue Sharing, Department of the Treasury, ACIR staff calculations.

Table A-9-4. Anti-Recession Fiscal Assistance Program Unemployment Rates and Per Capita Cumulative Allocations, 48 Largest Cities

City	Unemployment Rate Seventh Quarter	Per Capita Cumulative Allocation Through March 31, 1978
New York	9.0%	$26.32
Chicago	6.1	10.61
Los Angeles	7.9	9.21
Philadelphia	9.4	21.25
Detroit	9.4	28.11
Houston	5.0	1.56
Baltimore	8.7	19.71
Dallas	3.9	.04
San Diego	9.9	8.96
San Antonio	7.9	5.11
Indianapolis	5.6	3.52
Washington	8.0	17.88
Honolulu	7.3	9.50
Milwaukee	7.1	8.63
Phoenix	6.3	5.02
San Francisco	9.1	22.69
Memphis	5.0	3.02
Cleveland	7.2	13.13
Boston	7.0	18.30
New Orleans	9.0	20.25
San Jose	6.1	4.49
Columbus	5.9	4.90
Jacksonville	5.6	3.87
St. Louis	10.1	20.18
Seattle	6.5	8.60
Denver	6.8	9.63
Kansas City	6.5	7.38
Pittsburgh	8.0	17.99
Atlanta	7.6	9.01
Nashville-Davidson	3.8	1.63
Cincinnati	8.8	15.85
Buffalo	9.9	18.59
El Paso	11.6	15.94
Minneapolis	5.6	4.92
Omaha	3.7	2.21
Toledo	6.8	5.92
Oklahoma City	4.3	3.25
Miami	8.1	16.29
Fort Worth	4.2	.99
Portland	7.6	15.25
Newark	14.0	39.34
Louisville	4.8	7.98
Long Beach	7.1	5.32
Tulsa	4.6	2.60
Oakland	11.1	18.55

Table A-9-4 continued

City	Unemployment Rate Seventh Quarter	Per Capita Cumulative Allocation Through March 31, 1978
Norfolk	6.3	7.25
St. Paul	5.3	4.04
Birmingham	6.6	10.05

Source: Office of Revenue Sharing, Department of the Treasury, and ACIR staff computations.

Table A-9-5. State-Local Tax and Spending Policies—Estimates of Their Effects on the Economy During Periods of Recession and Expansion

	During Recessions			
	Change in State and Local Leverage[b] (billions of 1972 dollars)		Percent Contraction Intensified by State and Local Financial Behavior	
Contraction[a] (Peak–Trough)	Including Federal Aid	Excluding Federal Aid	Including Federal Aid	Excluding Federal Aid
1948IV–1949IV	8.7	7.9	-55.9	-53.7
1953II–1954III	6.0	6.6	-22.7	-24.2
1957III–1958I	4.7	3.4	-17.5	-13.3
1960I–1968IV	4.0	4.2	-32.5	-33.3
1969III–1970IV	11.9	5.2	-49.8	-30.2
1973IV–1975I	14.7	12.2	-16.8	-14.4

	During Recessions			
	Change in State and Local Leverage[b] (billions of 1972 dollars)		Percent Contraction Intensified by State and Local Financial Behavior	
Expansion (Trough–Peak)	Including Federal Aid	Excluding Federal Aid	Including Federal Aid	Excluding Federal Aid
1949IV–1953II	4.7	3.6	3.5	2.7
1954II–1957III	15.0	12.2	23.2	18.1
1958I–1960I	6.5	1.4	9.2	1.9
1960IV–1969III	69.0	44.6	24.4	14.5
1970IV–1973IV	19.4	0.1	12.8	0.0
1975I–1977II	-0.5	-11.4	-0.3	-6.6

Source: ACIR computation, based on U.S. Department of Commerce, Bureau of Economic Analysis, Survey of Current Business, various years.

Note:Leverage is an index of fiscal performance. For the following table, we used the formula.

$$L = 2\left[\frac{G}{P_2} + \frac{aR}{P_2} - \frac{bT}{P_2}\right] + CF \qquad CF = \frac{G}{P_1} - \frac{G}{P_2}$$

Where

L = leverage
G = government expenditures
R = transfer payments to persons
T = tax collections
P_1 = implicit price deflator for state-local purchases
P_2 = implicit price deflator for personal consumption
CF = correction factor for differential inflation rates
a = 0.7.
b = 0.5.

The leverage measure is lagged as follows:
Lagged leverage = $(1/2) L_t + (1/2)^2 L_t - 1 + \ldots (1/2)^5 L_t - 4$. The change in lagged leverage for the period is then estimated. While changing either the lag structure or the assumed multipliers within reasonable ranges changes the magnitude of the leverage estimates, it does not affect the direction of the impact.

[a]Peak and Trough Quarters are those selected by BEA for Real GNP.

[b]This form of leverage is adjusted for inflation and includes lag effect, thus the change in leverage represents the ultimate addition to real GNP due to present and past state and local fiscal behavior.

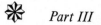 *Part III*

Possible New Directions

Chapter 10

Development Banking and Financial Incentives for the Private Sector

L. Kenneth Hubbell

Financial incentives designed to influence the spatial distribution of economic activity within a country are now widely employed by developed as well as by developing countries. Grants, loan guarantees, interest rate subsidies, tax credits, and depreciation allowances are now standard incentives to entice business firms to make site-specific investments in such countries as Canada, England, West Germany, Ireland, Israel, Italy, and Sweden. These investment incentives normally apply equally to domestic and foreign investors, but as one would expect for developing countries, foreign capital is the main target.

Regional policies have been adopted for a variety of reasons by these and other countries. In some cases, the reasons have been purely political, that is, to gain voter support or regional cohesion. In others, the regional policies have grown out of a desire to redress regional disparities in the allocation of economic resources. Moreover, some regional policymaking has been done to relocate strategic industries for national defense purposes, or to redistribute industry and people to deconcentrate a nation's population.

In the United States until just recently, financial incentives have been primarily viewed by policymakers as methods to stimulate aggregate private investment rather than as tools to eradicate poverty in distressed areas. This is due in large part to the emphasis in the post-World War II period on macroeconomic policies to combat regional and national unemployment problems. Thus, when the accelerated depreciation law was revised and the new investment tax credit established in 1962, little consideration was given to how these measures might be used to foster regional development or to the regional consequences of these two incentives. In contrast, federal grants, loan guarantees, and below-market interest loans have been regionally specific. Since 1965, firms locating in designated distressed areas have been eligible for subsidies, but due to the low level of funding and rather restrictive compliance rules, these instruments have not been extensively used.[1] This may not be the case in the future, however, inasmuch as one of the announced intents of President Carter's comprehensive urban policy is to make wider use of financial incentives as a means of attracting and increasing private investment in economically distressed areas.[2]

A major feature—or as some have called it, the "show piece"—of the urban policy is the proposed creation of a National Development Bank (NDB). Briefly stated, this new institution would encourage and assist the retention and further development of permanent private sector employment and private sector investment in areas with high unemployment, lagging economic growth, and significant poverty by lowering the operating costs of firms. Since the bank's structure and incentive policies for achieving this end are topics in subsequent sections, further discussion of the NDB is deferred until then.

The purpose of this chapter is to evaluate critically the possible or potential effectiveness of the proposed National Development Bank Act of 1978 and its various policy instruments. To this end, the justifications, objectives, and financial incentives of the NDB Act are discussed first. Next, the equity and efficiency implications of the bank's operation and its likely impact upon the allocation of resources are examined. This is in turn followed by a discussion of the factors that influenced firms to leave the core cities of many metropolitan areas and of the possible effectiveness of the NDB policies in reversing that trend. Finally, some concluding comments are offered on the public policy implications of establishing such an institution.

THE NATIONAL DEVELOPMENT BANK PROPOSAL[3]

Economic Rationale

It has been observed that while the economy as a whole is recovering from the worst recession since the 1929 crash, certain geographical areas, particularly the central cities of some of our larger metropolitan areas, still have unacceptably high levels of unemployment. The condition is thought to result from the declining job opportunities of central city residents due to slow growth, or even in some cases, to an absolute loss of private businesses. If this is indeed the underlying cause of the high unemployment, and there is growing evidence that it is, one way of reversing this trend is simply to induce private firms to expand employment opportunities in cities. Since the higher cost of doing business in urban centers must be a major reason for firms either stagnating or abandoning these centers altogether, then inducement must be offered to offset such debilitating costs. Those who support the NDB concept argue that new federal financial incentives are urgently needed and are justifiable on several grounds.

First, expanded job opportunities are essential if the structural unemployment that persists among certain groups and geographical areas is to be reduced substantially. Second, overall efficiency could increase while the total cost to the economy would drop if firms elect to expand or remain where they are rather than relocate and perhaps impose additional infrastructure costs on society. A third justification for the NDB concept is found in the multiplier effect that the expansion of an export industry has upon jobs, reducing welfare and unemployment costs, and strengthening the tax base of the local community at the same time. Finally, as formerly idle and underemployed workers are brought into the ranks of the employed, the social costs associated with crime, poor mental and physical health, and other such income-related social problems can be expected to fall.

Objectives and Policy Instruments

As suggested above, the NDB has two major policy goals, separate but clearly interrelated: to improve the permanent employment opportunities of workers and to strengthen the fiscal base of local jurisdictions that have been identified as chronically depressed. For accomplishing these ends, the NDB will have at its disposal four policy tools.

First, the bank is authorized to guarantee the payment of the principal amount of, and interest on, a portion of the long-term loans made by private financial institutions to finance the cost of eligible projects submitted by local development authorities (local DAs). Financing is to be conditional. At least 21 percent of the project's total cost (cost of land acquisition, construction or rehabilitation, and supporting public services) must be financed by private lenders. There is the further constraint that the loan guarantee for a single project cannot exceed $15 million or 75 percent of the amount to be financed by long-term debt. The principal amount guaranteed by the bank will bear interest at a rate determined by the bank after consultation with the Treasury Department as to the cost of comparable maturities guaranteed by the United States.[4]

Second, the NDB is empowered to make below-market interest rate loans. Firms qualifying for long-term loan guarantees are also eligible for an interest subsidy. At the bank's discretion, the interest rate may be reduced to as low as 2½ percent for particularly desirable projects.[5] In addition to subsidies for long-term loans to private firms, the bank is authorized to finance 35 percent of the annual interest payment on nontax-exempt long-term debt of local DAs.

Third, and perhaps the most important incentive in conjunction with the above financial inducements, the NDB will extend grants to local DAs or eligible business firms to defray investment costs. These grants will be limited to the lesser of 15 percent of a project's total cost or $3 million.[6]

Fourth, in an attempt to widen the financial base for development loans, the NDB establishes a liquidity facility for private loans made within designated areas. Loans made by commercial banks or other institutions to finance the required 21 percent (25 percent of the project's cost after the 15 percent grant) equity payment and loans by private lenders on eligible nonguaranteed long-term loans for capital improvements will qualify. Commercial lending institutions making use of this facility, however, will be required to pledge to the bank additional assets unrelated to the project. The market value of these additional debt securities (bonds, debentures, and notes) must have an aggregate value equal to at least 25 percent of the purchase price paid by the NDB for the original loan.

Structure and Eligibility Criteria

As indicated by the policy instruments delineated above, two separate institutional structures are called for in the NDB Act: a new federal lending entity and local development authorities. The administration's proposal specifies that the bank is to be established in the District of Columbia and that no offices are to be located outside the area. Thus, the bank is to be a national institution with a regional focus rather than a system of subnational banks with a regional orientation. It is to be governed by a board of directors consisting of the Secretary of Commerce, the Secretary of Housing and Urban Development, and the Secretary of the Treasury. The Secretary of Commerce and the Secretary of Housing and Urban Development will alternate on an annual basis as chairpersons of the board. The president and the executive vice president of the bank are to be appointed by the President of the United States with the advice and consent of the Senate. In general, the administration and management of the bank will be entrusted to these two bank officers.

Within some broad guidelines still to be defined, the bank provides financial incentives to businesses through local DAs. Under the NDB Act, the central responsibility for the identification, submission, and supervision of investment projects lies with the local DAs. This means that the local DAs have the principal responsibility for negotiating the terms and conditions of the loans with the management of the bank. By placing the primary responsibility for project selection with local authorities and by requiring a quasi-market test of profitability (the 21 percent rule), it is hoped the bank's administrative costs can be kept to a minimum.[7]

The designated local development authority in each distressed area is to be the municipality or the entity designed by the municipality as its agent.[8] In many cases, this means that existing development agencies will continue to plan and initiate local projects. For example, in cities like Boston, Detroit, and Pittsburg, the established, politically accountable, and professionally administered development agencies would most likely be designated as the local development authority.

Two significant restrictions are placed on aid to distressed areas. First, no more than 5 percent of each type of financial assistance that the bank agrees to provide each fiscal year is to go for projects in smaller areas (not defined). Unhealthy competition among distressed areas for financial assistance is ruled out. That is to say, any project that results in the removal of a plant facility or private sector jobs from one distressed area to another is prohibited.

Area eligibility criteria for NDB assistance is one of the most crucial and difficult issues connected with the establishment of the new financing entity. Although the act authorizing the bank specifies a method of determination, the question will not be resolved without great debate because of the political implications raised in any proposed set of criteria. As introduced, an eligible area is a geographical region within the boundaries of a local government jurisdiction that exhibits at least three of the following four symptoms of long-term distress:

1. In the jurisdiction, the annual average rate of unemployment over the past five years for which data are available is some percentage (to be specified) above the corresponding rate for the statistical group to which the local government unit belongs.

2. In the jurisdiction, the rate of growth of employment over the past five years (defined as the current period lagged one year) is some percent less than the rate of growth for the statistical grouping to which it belongs.
3. In the jurisdiction, the absolute growth in per capita income over the past five years (lagged one year) is some percent less than the absolute growth for the statistical grouping of which the unit is a part.
4. In the jurisdiction, the rate of growth in population over the past five years (lagged one year) is some percent less than the rate of growth for the statistical grouping of the local government unit.

To summarize, the stated goals of the NDB are to improve the fiscal base and private job opportunities in certain chronically depressed urban and rural areas by enticing the private sectior *(manufacturing and selected service industries)* to relocate, remain, or expand within these localities. The primary financial policy instruments to be used by the bank in moving toward these goals are: (1) guarantees of a portion of the long-term loans made by private financial institutions on eligible private sector projects, (2) interest rate subsidies for a portion of the interest on guaranteed loans, (3) the establishment of a liquidity facility for qualified long-term loans made by private banks and lending institutions in eligible areas, and (4) the extension of grants on eligible projects for land assembly and site preparation, rehabilitation, and equipment. To qualify for such assistance, the distressed area must meet certain long-term labor market, population, or income eligibility tests that basically compare conditions in the local jurisdiction to a benchmark statistical grouping.

FINANCIAL INCENTIVE SCHEMES: THEIR IMPACTS AND EFFECTIVENESS

As with all major policy issues, a considerable amount of controversy surrounds the NDB proposal. Before explicitly examining the possible effectiveness of the National Development Bank for its ability to entice businesses to invest in distressed areas, a few comments on the tools themselves are warranted.

Loan Guarantees
The principal attraction of the NDB's proposed loan guarantee is that it offers firms long-term financing at interest rates close to the Treasury Department's borrowing rate. This lower rate is possible

because in essence the bank assumes 100 percent of the risk on that portion of the investment submitted for long-term financing by the local DAs. The cost of guaranteeing the loans is to be borne by the bank and equals the administrative costs plus loan defaults that are not offset by any service charges the bank may impose.

Besides offering long-term financing at rates slightly below commercial interest rates, a potentially powerful inducement, the existence of a loan guarantee may encourage private investment in other ways. Small companies that are unable to borrow in the national money markets, but which must depend upon local lending institutions, may find it easier to obtain the nonguaranteed portion of the investment outlay if long-term financing is available through the bank. Furthermore, investments that are considered marginal by lending institutions may be viewed more favorably in light of the availability of such loan guarantees.

For the bank's policy, a major drawback is that, unlike other federal programs in this area, new, untested, and marginal businesses will in all probability not qualify because the majority of them will fail to meet the implicit market test of obtaining 25 percent outside funding. Without delving into the issue, most authorities agree that it is precisely this group of firms to which the terms "credit" or "structural gap" apply:[9] businessmen with economically feasible projects who cannot obtain adequate capital from private lending sources. Experts disagree on both the magnitude of the gap and the size of the firms that are most in need of financing, but they do agree that eliminating barriers to the flow of capital to firms that have been denied financing for structural reasons should be vigorously pursued.

Interest Subsidies

Long-term loans at subsidized rates of interest can be an important incentive to businesses, particularly to the new or small firm. And as in the case of loan guarantees, the availability of such financing may decide the fate of certain firms. The subsidy embodied in the NDB loans arises from two sources: (1) an interest rate lower than that available from commercial lenders and (2) the longer repayment period granted qualified borrowers.

As Stober[10] demonstrated, the present value of the difference in annual interest payments between a conventional loan and a government-financed loan varies inversely with the rate of interest charged by the government but directly with the terms of repayment of the subsidized loan. Over time the present value of interest payments rises as the loan repayment period is lengthened. However, the resulting cost increase is more than offset by delaying repayment. Furthermore, since annual interest payments are fully tax deductible, the present value of the cost saving to the firm varies inversely with the marginal income tax rate. It thus becomes apparent that a new or small firm faced with a low effective tax rate has more to gain from this subsidy than does a large corporation paying the maximum marginal tax rate.

From the standpoint of allocative efficiency, however, the use of below-market interest loans to encourage site-specific investment can be counterproductive. There are two points to be made here. Subsidizing private sector investment at rates below the social rate of discount (here defined as the yield on government debt), no matter how broadly supported the public policy objective may be, distorts the allocation of real investment capital. In an economy confronted with stagflation and tight monetary controls, funds raised by government borrowing reduce to some extent the amount of money capital available to nonsubsidized businesses. As a consequence, because of the reduced supply of funds for private sector investment, some goods that consumers demand either may not be produced or may bear higher prices if they are. Other products not in great demand, on the other hand, may be oversupplied. The degree of misallocation depends upon the depth of the assistance, the total amount provided, and the types of industries subsidized.

In addition, there are also offsetting effects to the desired employment and income changes. Failure to take account of possible job opportunities foregone elsewhere in the economy exaggerates the positive employment effects of the subsidy. Although the actual net gain in employment cannot be calculated, economic reason dictates that excluding foregone investment opportunities from the analysis, particularly during periods of near full employment or tight money, overstates the employment impact of interest subsidies. Actually, sorting out the effects would require extensive knowledge of the shapes of the labor demand schedules and the elasticities of the capital supply schedules of the affected industries.

A less theoretical but equally difficult issue is the fairness of the interest rate subsidy. Even though subsidized loans will be available to firms only within designated distressed areas, firms unable to avail themselves of such financial assistance are also affected. In particular, if the combined subsidies offered are large enough to attract new firms, they most likely will place some existing firms at a serious competitive disadvantage. A business within the area, for example, that has a newly constructed or renovated plant financed with a conventional loan would view any large financial concession to his or her competitor with alarm. Such potential conflicts, unfortunately, are unavoidable under any discriminatory subsidy program, but knowing this does not make them any less palatable as public policies to those who are adversely affected by their use.

Capital Grants

Capital grants represent an immediate improvement in the liquidity position of firms and are likely to be more attractive than any other incentive to firms facing large startup or other location-related costs. Given the considerable land price differentials between central city and suburban locations, grants appear to be an indispensable part of any policy to attract industry to distressed urban locations. In a study of six large U.S. cities, Hamer concluded that without a doubt suburban locations have an absolute advantage with regard to low-cost, accessible land. Depending on the type of land, in land-scarce cities the ratio of industrial land prices relative to those in the corresponding suburban areas falls between 2 to 3:1 and 5:1.[11]

While accepted as the traditional way of counterbalancing land and other locational cost differences, the capital grant incentive has all the drawbacks of a subsidized loan policy. In a sense, grants may be thought of as interest-free loans that never have to be repaid, which obviously makes them the form of financial incentive most preferred.

A rough idea of the effectiveness of cash grants in encouraging investment in distressed areas is provided from the experience of the Equalization of Industrial Opportunity (EIO) program in Canada. Under this plan, the government provides loans to manufacturing or tourist developments in expectation of increasing employment outside the industrialized southwest part of Ontario.

The scope of the program is small compared to what is proposed in the NDB Act. The maximum grant is $150,000, consisting of one-third of the first $250,000 of approved capital cost of new building and equipment, plus one-fourth of the remainder, up to $500,000. According to the officials of the Ontario Development Corporation, a review[12] of the firms receiving cash grants from 1967 to 1973 reflected the following:

1. Forty-six percent of the projects undertaken would not have proceeded without EIO assistance.
2. Twenty-eight percent of the firms involved in the program used the assistance to expand existing facilities.

3. Nine percent of the firms were induced by the grants to locate in the designated region instead of elsewhere.
4. Five percent of the firms both located in the designated region and increased the size of their investment.

While one can only speculate as to how relevant the Canadian experience might be for the United States, on the surface the results appear encouraging. Specifically, the data suggest that small firms may be particularly swayed by the granting of cash subsidies. This finding is in line with Stober's[13] contention that the cash grant is the most effective financial incentive for small businesses.

The Liquidity Facility

Little needs to be said about the establishment of the liquidity facility. The refinancing window is to serve as a mechanism for expanding the amount of loanable funds within the designated distressed areas by purchasing qualified loans from commercial lenders at a price that reflects a profit to the selling institution. The inducement to sell is weakened in some measure, however, by the requirement that additional marketable debt securities equal to 25 percent of the purchased loan be pledged by the sellers.

When qualifying loans are refinanced at or below the then existing commercial rate of interest, the bank in effect increases the excess reserves of the commercial institutions seeking the liquidity. Funds processed through the window must, however, be reinvested within the area for lenders to retain refinancing privileges. Assuming that the handling fees are kept low and that the commercial banks have adequate unpledged securities in their portfolios that they are willing to pledge, two big "ifs," the facility has the potential of substantially augmenting the supply of investment funds in capital-short distressed areas.

Tax-Exempt Industrial Development Bonds

A companion piece of legislation to the National Development Bank bill, also designed to encourage investment in economically distressed areas, is an amendment to the Revenue Act of 1978 allowing the maximum small issues exemption for tax-exempt Industrial Development Bonds (IDBs) to be raised from $5 million to $20 million. Briefly defined, IDBs are nominally issued obligations of state and local governments sold to finance the capital investments of firms. Most frequently, the proceeds of an issue of IDBs are sold to acquire or to construct a facility. When completed, the facility is then "leased" to a private firm for a rental fee that exactly covers the cost of the bond issue. At the end of the lease period, the tenant is normally allowed to purchase the facility for a nominal amount. In issuing tax-exempt IDBs, a state or local government essentially lends its tax exemption to private firms to enable them to finance structures at the lower interest rates prevailing in the tax-exempt market. In addition, the lease agreement is written in such a way that the lessee is able to obtain all the federal tax benefits associated with ownership of the property— investment tax credit and accelerated depreciation.

Under President Carter's tax proposal, the maximum amount of IDBs is to be quadrupled, but the employment of the small issue exemption will be more narrowly focused. Specifically, the proposal calls for limiting the issuance of IDBs only to local governments of economically distressed areas with eligibility to be determined under the same criteria imposed by the bank.

Two frequently heard arguments account for revising the legislation on IDBs. It is now recognized that because their use is universally available, the competitive benefit to any one locality in attracting investment is largely cancelled by the use of IDBs by other communities. Second, to an extent the issuance of tax-exempt IDBs by communities increases the total borrowing of local governments and thus drives up the cost of borrowing in the tax-exempt market to *all* state and local government borrowers.

To relieve the pressure on the tax-exempt market in general, President Carter's 1978 proposal also includes a Taxable Bond Option (TBO) for state and local governments. Under the TBO, state and local governments may elect to issue taxable—in lieu of tax-exempt—bonds and other debt obligations with the federal government paying a fixed percentage of the issue's interest expense. Obligations issued in 1979 and 1980 are to receive a 35 percent interest subsidy, while those issued after the latter date get a 40 percent subsidy. All state and local government obligations are to be elibible for TBO, including IDBs of qualifying communities.

From a public finance standpoint, reducing the supply of tax-exempt bonds by constraining the issuance of IDBs and the enactment of the TBO are correct policy choices. On equity grounds, they resist a further erosion of the progressive nature of the federal personal income tax, and on efficiency grounds, improve the allocation of real capital. To the extent that tax-exempt bonds aid the local community while reducing federal income tax liability, they also result in a shift of some financial burden from the local community to the nation as a whole. Rose suggests that the U.S. Treasury loses much more in foregone tax revenues than the local communities save in interest costs. This is still another sound reason for reducing the market for tax-exempt bonds.[14]

Other Macro Issues

Whether viewed as individual policy instruments or collectively as part of a new federal entity, the use of financial incentives to stimulate site-specific investment involves a number of economic tradeoffs. From a macroeconomic perspective, the most serious problem is a significant effort to stimulate investment in distressed communities, carrying with it the strong potential that private investment may be misallocated from its most productive use elsewhere in the economy. Some will be moved to treat this as a moot, theoretical point in light of the economy's poor performance over the past four years. This is a rather shortsighted view, however, since the bank is to be a permanent institution and economic activity has historically been cyclical in nature. Moreover, even in the best of times the fruits of a prosperous economy are never shared equally by all regions and communities. Consequently, regardless of the phase of the business cycle, some areas will always be eligible for subsidies.

In addition, over the long term, financial subsidies may cause income and employment shifts that run contrary to the bank's stated objectives. Direct subsidies to capital, as is well documented in the literature, can be expected to bias firms toward more capital-intensive production processes. The net result of the government's public policy intervention over the longer haul is to create fewer, not more, jobs for those judged least able to find employment. Disregarding the changes in the relative prices of the factors of production brought about by the subsidies to capital, the relative distribution of personal income would also be adversely affected. Specifically, the shift to capital-intensive methods of production could be expected to increase the demand for skilled labor and decrease the demand for the semiskilled and unskilled worker. Fewer job opportunities for the latter group of workers and a greater demand (increased wages) for the former group will make the poorer segments of our society relatively poorer.

Besides these longer term consequences, there is the strong possibility that in some cases the short-term gains in employment may be in part illusory. This occurs because some firms inevitably will receive financial assistance for making investment decisions that they would have made anyway. As soon as the incidence is low, those who support the bank would assume that the additional social costs (direct and indirect) introduced by this occurrence are more than offset by the social benefits to be derived from the bank's operation. On the other hand, if the practice turns out to be rather widespread, the basis for the public intervention in the private sector at best becomes very tenuous. A major question treated in the next section is whether the bank subsidies are sufficient to induce a firm that would otherwise locate or expand its facilities elsewhere to locate or expand in an economically distressed community. Only if the answer to this question is yes does it make sense to even attempt to compare and weigh the social costs and benefits of the NDB.

EFFECTIVENESS OF THE NATIONAL DEVELOPMENT BANK

Any attempt to prejudge the success of a policy instrument as complex as the NDB is bound to meet with criticism, irrespective of the conclusions. Those defending the bank will find little of substance in the criticisms, and those doubting its development potential will find little fault in them. Despite this no-win position, however, some overall assessment of its potential effectiveness is required. A logical starting point is an examination of the economic forces or conditions that lie behind the declining job opportunities and private investment in many urban areas. Such a study would seem fundamental both to the drafting of public policy measures to reverse the trends and to gauging the potential effectiveness of proposed policies.

Reasons for Employment Decline

The evidence as well as the reasons given for the shrinking number of jobs in our larger distressed cities are all too familiar. It is argued that central cities are losing their hold on manufacturing facilities and their relative attractiveness as places for expansion and new development because (1) movements in population have caused a shift in markets away from the older established central cities to the suburban rings and regionally to the Sunbelt states; (2) technological changes in transportation and communication have diminished the need for business firms to be in close proximity to markets, suppliers, and business services; (3) new production technology employs horizontal production processes that are very land-intensive and often require special design; (4) plant and equipment of firms located in the older, core cities tend to be outmoded and very costly to maintain and operate; (5) workers are now so spatially dispersed that firms often find it hard to retain a quality labor force; (6)

adequate land for expansion and growth is unavailable in core areas; and (7) political and socioeconomic conditions are perceived to be less favorable in the central cities than in suburban and ex-urban locations, that is, more bureaucratic red tape, congestion, crime, and neighborhood deterioration.

While urban experts may disagree on the relative importance of each of these factors, they would agree that each factor played some role in the malaise currently afflicting some cities. The reaction of firms to these social, economic, and demographic changes has been recorded in a number of recent empirical studies—Schmenner,[15] Birch,[16] Allaman and Birch,[17] Leone,[18] and Beckman.[19] From the evidence of these and other such studies, it is becoming clear that the decline in urban employment is directly traceable to three factors. First, in recent years the older central cities have failed to spawn new firms at a rate sufficient to offset the loss of business enterprises through attrition, for example, closures, failures, and movements. An unmistakeable shift in the population away from the northern and northeastern tier of states to the Sunbelt areas (West, Southwest, and South) is one explanation of this occurrence.[20] Another explanation is that the famous "incubator" role central cities have historically played apparently has shifted to the suburbs.[21] As in the past, new plants still value proximity to suppliers, business services, and customers, but the dispersal of population and economic activity within metropolitan areas has eroded the central cities' comparative advantage in this respect. Such a finding obviously has rather ominous implications for the beleaguered core cities.

Second, and perhaps more importantly, producers are apparently trimming their labor forces in the older, larger manufacturing plants of central cities.[22] This unsettling occurrence may in large part be the result of the development strategies pursued by the Fortune 500 manufacturers. The production facilities of many of these corporations were constructed a number of years ago, employing techniques that are outmoded by today's standards. As the demand for their output has increased over time, the prevailing practice has been to establish additional branch plants and to shift part of the production to them rather than to expand the original plant. These actions are evidently in line with a developmental strategy that has as its objective the establishment of a system of branch plants—market area, product, process, and general purpose plants—rather than an expansion of existing facilities. There is also a desire by corporations to develop a diversified "portfolio" of plants such that no one local jurisdiction is too heavily dependent upon the corporation for its revenues, nor is the corporation overly reliant upon a single city for its labor force.

Finally, a movement of firms away from the urban hub to the suburban ring, while a relatively insignificant factor, is responsible for some of the decline in jobs within the core city. At the risk of oversimplifying an admittedly complex issue, this loss is mainly the result of population movements[23] that in turn have been caused by rising incomes, improved transportation networks, and the pursuit of an improved environment.

Adequacy of the Financial Incentives

The bank's equivalency of the private sector's bottom-line profits rests in its effectiveness in producing new jobs in distressed areas. Clearly, this is not something one can measure beforehand. Some measurement of its success, however, is made possible by evaluating how well the NDB is equipped to assist firms that are most likely to take advantage of its incentives.

From the previous discussion of the sources of declining job opportunities in cities, unfortunately, the bank's policies appear to be slightly misdirected. As presently formulated, the policies of the NDB have in mind the older, well-established corporations. This is evident from the bank's emphasis on attracting financially sound corporations and the fact that subsidies are looked upon as inducements rather than compensation for capital market imperfections (risk). This emphasis upon solid, low-risk firms seems totally inappropriate.

Firms in this category are more apt to be swayed by real market considerations than by capital market subsidies. That is to say, large corporations can be expected to follow an overall corporate marketing and development strategy that is strongly influenced by population shifts. In fact, if they take advantage of financial incentives, there is a good chance they would have made the investment even without assistance.

The firms most likely to take advantage of the subsidies, on the other hand, are the newer, smaller, footloose producers with fifty employees or less. They are prime candidates for aid because they generally face chronic shortages of working capital and barriers to long-term financing at reasonable rates. In addition, they are the most active firms in expansion and relocation.

The significance of these firms to the expansion of urban employment is dramatically illustrated in a recent study by Birch of regional differences in factor costs.[24] He found that of the jobs created by the formation of a new establishment, approximately 90 percent are attributable to independent, free-standing entrepreneurs;

of those created through expansion, roughly 60 percent are due to independent firms. Moreover, as shown in Table 10–1, young firms (those less than four years old) and small firms (those with fewer than fifty employees) accounted for between 60 and 70 percent of all new jobs.

Thus, if the bank plans to fulfill its primary mission, it must place a greater emphasis upon wooing small producers. Failure to develop attractive investments for this group would most certainly severely limit the bank's effectiveness. Fortunately, with some changes this could be achieved within the proposed NDB framework. Under the planned structure, the loan guarantee part of the program could be expanded, and grants or loans for working capital and perhaps technical assistance programs could be introduced in the bank's portfolio of public policy instruments. Needless to say, the inclusion of these tools (particularly technical assistance) would greatly complicate and broaden the bank's administrative responsibilities, something which bank supporters have tried to limit but which would be necessary for reaching the firms most likely to take advantage of the incentives.[25]

Even if the NDB makes the suggested policy and firm-targeting adjustments, the bank can be expected to have a very limited impact upon the investment decisions of firms. This rather pessimistic view is based on two concluding observations. First, the impact of the grant and interest subsidy provisions of the NDB, as outlined in the Appendix may have little influence on a firm's location or expansion decision. Saving the details for the Appendix, the application of the present value model to a typical firm indicates that sizeable interest rate and grant subsidies are required to offset rather small city-suburban operating cost differentials. In the example used, a 15 percent capital grant ($816,000) for plant and equipment and a twenty-year loan at 6 percent (3 percent interest subsidy) are insufficient to neutralize a conservative 5 percent difference in operating costs between a central city and a suburban production site. If, however, the loan is made at 4 percent, the cost differential would swing to the advantage of the central city. On the other hand, even with a twenty-year loan, if the cost of doing business is raised to the more realistic rate of 15 percent, accounting for vandalism, congestion, higher insurance costs, government regulations, and labor-related costs, financial incentives are totally ineffective countermeasures. Reducing the interest rate to as low as 2 percent would still be insufficient to overcome such a differential in operating costs. That is to say, operating cost differences would more than swamp the interest subsidy extended. Thus, even ignoring or holding

Table 10-1. Percentage Distribution of New Jobs Created in Each Region Between 1974 and 1976 by Size and Age of Firm[a]

		Northeast				
						Age
		0–4	*5–8*	*9–12*	*13+*	*Total*
	0–10	25.7	3.5	1.8	1.6	32.6
	11–50	15.6	6.8	4.2	4.0	30.6
Size	51–250	9.1	6.3	5.1	4.5	25.0
	251+	3.2	3.0	3.1	2.6	11.9
	Total	53.6	19.6	14.2	12.7	100%

		Midwest				
						Age
		0–4	*5–8*	*9–12*	*13+*	*Total*
	0–10	29.1	3.9	2.1	1.8	36.9
	11–50	17.6	7.0	4.3	3.9	32.8
Size	51–250	8.0	5.2	4.0	3.3	20.5
	251+	3.1	2.2	2.7	1.7	9.7
	Total	57.8	18.3	13.1	10.7	100%

		South				
						Age
		0–4	*5–8*	*9–12*	*13+*	*Total*
	0–10	31.9	5.8	1.8	1.4	40.9
	11–50	17.4	6.0	3.6	2.9	29.9
Size	51–250	9.6	5.8	3.4	3.0	21.8
	251+	2.9	2.6	1.7	2.0	9.2
	Total	61.8	20.2	10.5	9.3	100%

		West				
						Age
		0–4	*5–8*	*9–12*	*13+*	*Total*
	0–10	32.8	3.7	1.8	1.5	39.8
	11–50	17.7	6.8	4.0	3.5	32.0
Size	51–250	8.9	5.5	3.4	3.0	20.8
	251+	1.8	2.0	1.9	1.8	7.5
	Total	61.2	18.0	11.1	9.8	100%

Source: U.S. Department of Commerce "Roundtable on Business Retention and Expansion in Cities," Washington, D.C., February 22, 1978.

[a]This table summarizes data for all businesses, manufacturing, trade and service, but similar results are obtained for the individual sectors.

market demand considerations constant, there is little reason to believe that the availability of grants and interest subsidies will induce many firms to expand or relocate in core cities. Many of those that would take advantage of such incentives, moreover, are firms that in all probability would have undertaken the core city investment without such subsidies.

A second and even more compelling reason for the gloomy outlook stems in large part from a recognition of the development changes that have been taking place in the United States. Briefly stated, the process of urban growth and decline is seen to follow growth curves that reflect the degree of adaptation of the cities to current technologies, tastes, and affluence, as well as the fact that present population densities were built up in response to tastes, technologies, incomes and costs of earlier periods.

Over time, there is a natural tendency toward lower densities, but the timing and extent vary, depending upon such factors as each city's original degree of adaptation, the age of its capital stock, and the proportion of the population in the age brackets most disposed to migration. Furthermore, within the metropolitan areas, there is a tendency toward suburbanization, that is the movement of people to surrounding areas of increasingly greater distances from the central cities, which over time become increasingly more self-sufficient. Superimposed on the urban process of growth and decline and suburbanization just described is a long-standing process of interregional competition that is causing a general, albeit slow, convergence of economic levels. As these changes have taken place, the growth in population in certain parts of the country and the economies associated with it have resulted in a number of relatively new and maturing cities.

If this scenario fairly well reflects the process of regional growth and urban changes, the sheer intensity and pervasiveness of long-term economic forces underlying these shifts will in all likelihood more than offset whatever positive incentives an NDB may offer. While this is a rather strong statement, there is considerable doubt as to the possibility of substantially preventing population and business declines by means of subsidies whose chief objective is to keep people working in areas whose urban structure is increasingly out of touch with the tastes and technology available to them outside the area.

CONCLUDING COMMENTS

Although clearly the above assessment will not be popular among many groups, the evidence appears incontrovertible that economic and population decline is inevitable for many cities. This decline should not be viewed as necessarily undesirable from a national perspective, however. Instead, it should be seen as a natural consequence of the changing pattern of economic growth. From a national vantage point, the ultimate objective of an urban policy should be how best to facilitate the adjustment process.

First, despite the difficulty in determining an objective standard to measure economic "distress" or "hardship," the limited amount of federal resources demands that priorities for distribution of urban assistance be established and that the list of cities qualifying be short. Extending funds to a large number of municipalities would in all likelihood result in spreading the monies without reducing the problem.

Second, as has also been suggested in the NDB proposal, it is essential that federal policy be directed at strengthening the employment opportunities for the urban poor as well as the fiscal base of the city. The federal policy must be flexible enough, however, to differentiate between the two types of assistance. The more successful approach would probably compensate the distressed cities for revenue losses due to employment declines through aid in the form of increased direct assistance, state or federal government assumption of certain public services (such as welfare and public education), and providing for job creation and manpower training programs specifically directed at low-income and unemployed persons. Although not without some limitations, a public policy strategy that attempts to aid targeted groups directly seems inherently superior to one that seeks to alleviate the problem through indirect measures.

Last, a national urban policy should support and fund the drafting of state urban economic policies. Many of the problems of central cities stem from the fragmented governmental and fiscal structures of metropolitan areas. Thus, state government urban policies that bring about a better balance of taxpaying capacity and expenditure requirements for local governments, such as tax-base sharing, regional financing, or areawide governance schemes, could do much to ease the financial plight of a number of distressed cities and should be strongly encouraged.[26]

NOTES

1. The federal government, under the Public Works and Economic Development Act of 1965 and the Rural Development Act of 1972, extends assistance to areas and regions of substantial and persistent unemployment and underemployment. In cooperation with the states, funds are made available for local planning and the financing of public works projects. In addition,

provision exists for the extension of grants, loan guarantees, and below-market interest rate loans to businesses.

2. President Carter announced a new comprehensive urban policy on March 27, 1978. The numerous components of the administration's proposal have subsequently been introduced in Congress under various bills.

3. There is considerable evidence that the proposed NDB Act of 1978 grew out of a concern by policymakers about the fiscal plight of the nation's largest cities. Thus, even though the NDB is designed to encourage business investments in economically distressed *rural* and *urban* areas, the emphasis of this chapter will be on the latter, the urban areas.

4. As introduced, the bank would be authorized to guarantee up to $2,175 million in loans in fiscal year 1979 and $2,900 million each year in fiscal years 1980 and 1981.

5. If the NDB Act is passed as proposed, $1,035 million in fiscal year 1979 and $1,380 million each year in fiscal years 1980 and 1981 will be available to subsidize loans of private firms.

6. Funds for grants are to come from two sources: $275 million in each of fiscal years 1979, 1980, and 1981 under the provisions of Title IX of the Economic Development Act of 1965, as amended, and $275 million for the same fiscal years through Title I of the Housing and Community Development Act of 1974.

7. The proposed NDB Act requests $50 million a year in each of the fiscal years 1979, 1980, and 1981 to facilitate the formation of the bank and to pay initial organizational and operating expenses.

8. In the proposed legislation, the terms "local government" and "statistical grouping" are precisely defined. The former term is interpreted to mean a municipality, township, or other political subdivision of a state (other than a county) that is specified as a unit of general government by the Bureau of the Census. What benchmark group a local government is measured against depends upon whether the jurisdiction is considered as a metropolitan or nonmetropolitan unit. If any part of a local government's land area lies within the boundaries of an SMSA, the corresponding grouping is considered to be all SMSAs. For local units that are totally outside the geographical boundaries of SMSAs, the appropriate grouping is all non-SMSA local governments.

9. See, for example, U.S. Congress, "Financing Small Business," Report to Committee on Banking and Currency and the Select Committee on Small Business by the Federal Reserve System, 1958; and "Small Business Financing: Corporate Manufacturers," *Federal Reserve Bulletin* 47 (January 1961): 8–22.

10. William J. Stober, *Taxes, Subsidies and Location Choice*, Discussion Paper No. 36, Program in the Role of Growth Centers Regional Economic Development, (Lexington: University of Kentucky, October 1970).

11. Andrew M. Hamer, *The Industrial Exodus from the Central City* (Lexington, Mass.: Lexington Books, 1974), p. 37.

12. Gordon D. Faye, *Recent Experience with Regional Industrial Subsidies in Ontario* (Chapel Hill, N.C.: University of North Carolina Graduate School of Business Administration, 1973).

13. Strober, *Taxes, Subsidies and Location Choice.*

14. Sanford Rose, "The Trouble with Municipal Bonds is Not Just New York," *Fortune*, (December 1975).

15. Roger W. Schmenner, *The Manufacturing Location Decision: Evidence from Cincinnati and New England*, Economic Development Research Report, (Cambridge, Mass.: The Harvard-MIT Joint Center for Urban Studies, March 1978).

16. David L. Birch, "U.S. Department of Commerce Round Table on Business Retention and Expansion in Cities," Washington, D.C., February 22, 1978; David L. Birch, "The Processes Causing Economic Change in Cities," MIT-Harvard Joint Center for Urban Studies, Program on Neighborhood and Regional Change, March 1977.

17. Peter M. Allaman and David L. Birch, "Components of Employment Changes for States by Industry Group, 1970-1972," MIT-Harvard Joint Center for Urban Studies, September 1975.

18. Robert A. Leone and Raymond J. Struyk, "The Incubator Hypothesis: Evidence from Five SMSA's," *Urban Studies* 13 (1976): 325-331.

19. John W. Beckman, *Industry in New York: A Time of Transition*, The 1974 Report of the Select Committee of the Economy, New York State Legislative Document, No. 12, 1974.

20. Richard Forstall, "Trends in Metropolitan and Nonmetropolitan Population Growth Since 1970," U.S. Bureau of the Census, May 20, 1975.

21. Schmenner, *The Manufacturing Location Decision.*

22. Schmenner (1978), in a survey of manufacturers located in Cincinnati between 1971 and 1975, found that retrenchment or cutbacks in stationary manufacturing plants was the single most important source of job losses, accounting for more than one-half of the decline in employment over the four-year period.

23. T.E. McMillan, Jr., "Why Manufacturers Choose Plant Location vs. Determinants of Plant Location," *Land Economics* 41 (1965): 239-246.

24. Birch, "U.S. Department of Commerce Round Table on Business Retention and Expansion in Cities."

25. An excellent review of capital development incentives in states, and state department finance institutions may be found in Martin Katzman and Beldon Daniels, *Development Incentives to Induce Efficiencies in Capital Markets*, report prepared for The NewEngland Regional Commission and The International Center for New England, Inc., January 15, 1976.

26. This point and the foregoing one are also stressed by Roy Bahl, Bernard Jump, Jr., and Larry Schroeder in "The Outlook for City Fiscal Performance in Declining Regions," Metropolitan Studies Program, (Syracuse: Maxwell School, Syracuse University, April 5, 1978).

Appendix

Present Value Model

The value of financial incentives to the firm and their effect upon location choice may be expressed by a simple present value model. Assuming a world of perfect certainty, the present value of an investment outlay (I) of a firm that seeks to maximize its after-tax net revenue stream is given by

$$Va = \int_0^n (1 - T) \, [R_t - A_t] \, e^{-rt} dt - K_0 \qquad \text{(A-10-1)}$$

where n = the economic life of the investment; T = the marginal federal and state income tax rate (for most states $T = T_f + Ts - T_f T_s$); R_t = a stream of revenue; A_t = a stream of operating, maintenance, processing, transportation, and other costs; r = the firm's cost of capital; and K_0 the amount of the capital outlay.

Both R_t and A_t in Equation (A-10-1) are locationally specific, which means that gross revenues and costs would normally vary with location. For convenience and without loss of generality, it will be assumed that R_t is geographically invariable. That is to say, revenue is constant because all transportation costs of the final product are borne by the producer, and consumer demand is assumed to be evenly distributed. By defining revenues in this way, the location decision is conceptually choosing a site where the present value of the cost stream is a minimum.

Taxes and Depreciation

Before rewriting expression (A-10-1) in light of these assumptions, several other changes need to be noted. Tax considerations complicate the investment decision and affect the firm's cost of doing business in three ways. First, the tax structure has a direct impact upon a firm's level of profits, since its tax liability is determined by applying the tax rate to net revenues after business cost deductions. Second, as is well known, the investment outlay is not totally deductible in the year in which it was incurred but must be depreciated over some minimum period defined by the Internal Revenue Service. As has been demonstrated elsewhere, (see S. Davidson and D. Drake, "Capital Budgeting and the Best Tax Depreciation Method" *Journal of Business*, Vol. 34, 1961, pp. 442-452), of the three most widely used methods of depreciation, the sum of the digits method creates a depreciation stream of highest present value for a given investment. The value of this depreciation stream per dollar of investment outlay, assuming no salvage value, is given by

$$D_t = \int_0^n \left[\frac{2(n-t)}{n^2} \right] e^{-rt} p K_0 \, dt \qquad \text{(A-10-2)}$$

where p represents the proportion of the initial expenditure K_0 that is depreciable and n the depreciable life of the asset.

Third, under current legislation an investment tax credit is allowed against depreciable assets other than buildings. Since the tax credit is deductible from taxes payable at the time the investment is made, the present value is simply

$$T_c = (cp)K_0 \qquad \text{(A-10-3)}$$

where c denotes the investment tax credit as a fraction of the total outlay on depreciable investment.

Financing

Funds to finance the outlay K_0 essentially come from one of three sources: a stock issue, retained earnings, or borrowing. Because debt financing represents an explicit cost to the firm, this source of financing affects present value. The cost to the firm in annual debt repayment (L) can be expressed as

$$K_0 = \int_0^n L e^{-it} \, dt \qquad \text{(A-10-4)}$$

where i is the loan rate of interest. Integrating and solving for L yields

$$L = \frac{K_0 i}{(1 - e^{-in})} \tag{A-10-5}$$

Expressing the location decision in terms of minimum costs and taking into account the effect of the existing tax structure, depreciation allowance, and investment tax credit, the present value of the cost stream at a given location (j) becomes

$$c_j = \int_0^n \left[(1 - T)A_t\right] e^{-rt} dt$$

$$+ \left[\frac{K_j i - K_j i T(1 - e^{-in} e^{it})}{(1 - e^{-in})}\right] e^{-rt} dt$$

$$- pTK_j^* \left[\frac{2(n - t)}{n^2}\right] e^{-rt} dt - cpK_j \tag{A-10-6}$$

where $K_j^* = (1 - cp) K_j$, the effect of the investment tax credit on depreciable capital at location j. Integrating Equation (A-10-6) yields the following general expression:

$$c_j = (1 - T)\frac{A}{r}(1 - e^{-m})$$

$$+ \frac{K_j i(1 - T)(1 - e^{-m})}{r(1 - e^{-in})} + \frac{K_j i T(e^{-m} - e^{-in})}{(i - r)(1 - e^{-in})}$$

$$- \frac{2pT}{rn}\left[1 - \frac{(1 - e^{-m})}{rn}\right] K_j^* - cpK_j \tag{A-10-7}$$

Comparing a producer's capital outlay and operating expenses at two alternative locations, j and h, we have

$$\Delta C_{jh} = C_j - C_h \tag{A-10-8}$$

Locational Cost Difference with an Interest Subsidy

Adapting Equation (A-10-7) the present value of a below-market loan on the location decision of a firm may be stated as

$$\Delta C_{jh} = C_{ji} - C_{hs} \tag{A-10-9}$$

where s is the subsidized interest rate at location h, and i the market rate of interest at j.

Empirical Results

Substituting the data contained in Table A-10-2 into expressions (A-10-7) and (A-10-9), an estimate can be made of the cost differences a typical producer is faced with when forced to choose between locating at a central city site (h) with subsidies or at a suburban site (j) without any incentives. The results under a number of assumptions concerning operating cost differences between city-suburban locations and the length and the rate (s) of the subsidized loan are shown in Table A-10-1.

It is implicitly assumed in the calculations that the depreciable life of the investment and the time of repayment of the debt coincide. Furthermore, it is assumed that the conventional financing rate (i) and the firm's cost of capital (r) are the same at j. The value of other variables is shown in Table A-10-2.

Table A-10-1. Values of City-Suburban Cost Differentials for Selected Interest Rate Subsidies and Operating Cost Differentials

Years	Subsidized Rate of Interest	City Suburban Cost Differential		
		0.05	*0.10*	*0.15*
$n = 10$	s = 0.06	-489,192	-1,627,657	-2,766,091
	s = 0.04	-203,675	-1,342,140	-2,480,604
	s = 0.02	64,761	-1,073,704	-1,212,168
$n = 20$	s = 0.06	-41,224	-1,642,364	-3,243,504
	s = 0.04	607,901	-993,239	-2,594,379
	s = 0.02	1,188,697	412,443	-2,780,197
$n = 30$	s = 0.06	798,437	-990,880	-2,780,197
	s = 0.04	1,875,168	85,851	-1,703,466
	s = 0.02	2,819,448	1,030,131	-759,186

Source: Figures computed by substituting capital and operating cost data of Table A-10-2 into expressions (7) and (9).

Table A-10-2. Capital and Operating Cost Data for Alternative Plant Sites Facing a Typical Manufacturer[a]

Required Capital	*City[b] Location (C_h)*	*Suburban[c] Location (C_j)*
(1) Land	$ 460,000	$ 288,000
(2) Building	2,240,000	2,240,000
(3) Machinery and Equipment	3,200,000	3,200,000
Totals	$5,900,000	$5,728,000
Annual Sales, Operating Costs, and Property Taxes		
Sales[d]	$8,000,000	$8,000,000
Operating Costs[e]	6,972,000[1]	6,640,000
Property Taxes[f]	64,800	30,336
Other Variables for Model		
r	0.09	0.09
c	0.10	0.10
p	0.78	0.95
grant[h]	$ 816,000	—
T	0.48	0.48

Source: Andrew M. Hamer, "The Impact of Federal Subsidies on Industrial Location Behavior: Preliminary Conclusions from a Case Study" (Atlanta, Georgia: Georgia State University, October 11, 1977).

[a]The establishment examined is a manufacturer of paper boxes, employing 200 persons, and requiring 800 square feet of plant space per employee.

[b]A new building in the city is estimated to cost $14 per square foot and to require a lot size of 2,000 square feet per employee. Land is estimated to cost $1.15 per square foot.

[c]A new building in the suburbs is estimated to cost $14 per square foot and to require a lot size of 2400 square feet per employee. Land is estimated to cost $0.60 per square foot.

[d]Sales per employee of $40,000 per year are assumed.

[e]Operating costs (materials, factory payroll, selling and marketing, and general administration) are assured to be 83 percent of sales.

[f]Effective property taxes are set at 2.4 percent in the city and 1.2 percent in the suburbs.

[g]Initially, it is assumed that operating costs in the city are 1.05 of those in the suburban location. In Table A-10-1, the values for 1.10 and 1.15 are also shown.

[h]The grant given to the central city manufacturer equals 15 percent of building, machinery, and equipment outlays.

Chapter 11

Tax Credits for Urban Revitalization

Richard McHugh
David Puryear

The spectacular fiscal brinksmanship of New York City has focused immense public attention on urban fiscal problems in the last three years. Congress has enacted a number of urban-related programs during this period, some aimed at fiscal relief and others aimed at unemployment, capital construction, and urban development. This chapter examines one type of federal response to urban problems, the use of federal tax credits to encourage urban revitalization.

The goals of these urban programs are frequently diffuse. This is best illustrated by the widely held assumption that capital subsidies will stimulate employment in urban areas. To avoid confusion about goals, this chapter will focus on three specific goals: employment, investment, and fiscal relief.

These three goals are clearly linked since both employment and investment have important fiscal benefits. Capital investment in urban areas generates property taxes and the creation of new jobs (or the retention of existing jobs). Employment in urban areas generates revenue from a variety of direct and indirect sources. For example, Roy Bahl and David Greytak have estimated that a manufacturing job in New York City in 1970 generated $815 in revenues to the city.[1] Through the production function, employment and investment are also linked to each other although their relationship is not as simple as the assumption that capital subsidies will stimulate employment.

The tax system has been used as a federal policy tool for some time so it is not surprising that it has been proposed as a tool for urban programs. It has two basic characteristics that dominate its impact on urban fiscal problems. First, a tax incentive tends to be a relatively blunt instrument. That is both a strength and a weakness. It allows private sector market mechanisms to respond "efficiently" to the distortions in relative prices introduced by the incentive, and it avoids the necessity for elaborate bureaucracies to allocate resources. On the other hand, it does not provide as much "bang for the buck" since it helps some beneficiaries whose behavior is not influenced, who would have done the same thing whether they got the tax break or not. Thus, tax credits do no allocate federal aid very efficiently.

The second dominant characteristic of tax incentives is that they do not provide direct fiscal relief to cities or other local governments. To the extent that they provide fiscal benefits to cities, they do so indirectly through their impacts on private sector activities, which in turn generate tax revenues or require public spending.

This chapter examines two types of tax subsidies, investment credits and employment credits. Both are discussed as general subsidies and then as targeted subsidies with specific urban goals. Because their impact comes almost entirely through their effects on employment and investment in the private sector, this chapter concentrates on employment and investment in discussing the impacts of alternative tax credit mechanisms.

The next section of this chapter examines two capital subsidy programs, the investment tax credit and the differential investment tax credit for distressed areas. The third section examines labor subsidies in the form of employment tax credits, particularly the highly targeted programs for disadvantaged workers. Finally, the fourth section contains a brief summary and offers conclusions.

CAPITAL SUBSIDIES

A variety of tax and subsidy mechanisms has been used in recent years to influence the aggregate level of capital formation in the U.S. economy. For the most part, these mechanisms have been employed to stimulate investment in periods of recession or to provide incentives for expansion of specific sectors of the economy. Whether they have taken the form of tax credits, accelerated depreciation, or some other special tax treatment, their influence has depended on the impact of changing the relative price of capital in the private capital market. Investment impacts have been determined by the responsiveness of capital markets to these price changes.

The secondary impacts of these investment stimuli include traditional macroeconomic multiplier effects and derived demand for such complementary factors as labor. The benefits of investment stimulus as a macroeconomic tool include its contribution to long-run productive capacity, which helps to avoid inflationary bottlenecks later on.

For all these reasons the use of capital subsidies as a macroeconomic tool has been generally accepted. Recently, however, attention has focused on allegations of uneven impacts of these incentives on central cities and suburbs. President Carter's 1978 Tax Program,[2] sent to Congress in January, contained several liberalizations of the Investment Tax Credit (ITC) that generated concern about effects on central city economic growth.[3] This section focuses on the ITC, its proposed liberalization, and the proposed Differential Investment Tax Credit (DITC) that was included in the President's March 27, 1978, National Urban Policy announcement. These tax credit mechanisms are examined for their aggregate investment and employment effects and for their effects on urban areas.

The Investment Tax Credit

Congress initially established the ITC in 1962. Except for brief periods, the credit has been a permanent feature of the tax code since that time. Originally set at 7 percent, the ITC was temporarily raised to 10 percent in 1975, and is scheduled to revert to 7 percent in 1981. The credit applies to purchases of new tangible property by firms, with the exception of expenditures for structures.

President Carter's 1978 Tax Program proposed three important changes in the ITC. First, the temporary 10 percent credit on equipment will be made permanent. Second, up to 90 percent of corporate tax liabilities may be offset, compared to the present limit of 50 percent. Third, the credit will be extended to the construction and rehabilitation of utility and industrial structures.

The purposes of this reform are to stimulate investment in general and to stimulate lagging investment in industrial structures in particular. The ITC is simultaneously a program to increase aggregate economic activity in the short run and manufacturing production capacity in the long run. The urban fisc stands to benefit from any expansion generated by this kind of stimulus. The true urban fiscal impact of such subsidies, however, depends first upon the degree to which the economy responds to these capital incentives, and second, upon the degree to which cities participate in any general expansion of the aggregate economy.

The estimation of the response to the national economy to capital subsidies, particularly the ITC, has generated a substantial scholarly literature. By examing the way in which the ITC has influenced capital accumulation to date, we may draw some conclusions as to the likely impact of the ITC in the future.

Aggregate Impacts. There exists a variety of studies of the impact of the ITC on capital formation and economic growth, but no consensus has emerged regarding these impacts. Agreement does exist, however, that federal tax policy can alter the price of capital and that the price of capital influences the level of investment, but the extent of this influence is still a focus of dispute in the literature.

The pure neo-classical view is that the optimal stock of capital is a function of the cost of capital and firms respond to changes in this cost by adjusting their investment behavior to achieve the new desired capital stock. The primary challenge to this view is that, while price matters in determining the level of investment, factors such as the liquidity position of the firm, recent changes in output or sales, and expected future profits are the most important determinants of the level of investment; the role of capital costs is therefore minimal.

Both views agree that the total impact of the reduction in the cost of capital via the ITC is a function of the price elasticity of capital plus whatever multiplier effects there may be on capital formation. The literature on this topic generally assumes a perfectly elastic supply capital, at least in the long run, and calculates estimates of the price elasticity of demand for capital. These estimates vary widely from nearly zero to more than one. (See, for example, Berndt and Christensen,[4] Coen,[5] Eisner,[6] and Kesselman, Williamson, and Berndt.[7])

Through its impact on the price of capital, the ITC also has an impact on the demand for labor. Because the ITC subsidizes investment in capital, firms have an incentive to substitute capital for labor. The extent of this impact depends in part on the ease with which firms are able to make this factor substitution. The measure used by economists to quantify this process is the elasticity of substitution. If this elasticity is relatively low, the impact of the ITC on employment will be smaller than if the elasticity is high because a low elasticity implies that the firm has a limited capability for substituting capital for labor.

There are a number of studies of the elasticity of substitution. A sample of results from these studies appears in Table 11-1. The estimates cluster around a value of 0.6 for the aggregate elasticity of substitution. Several cross-section studies have also estimated this elasticity and their results are generally higher, usually not significantly different from unity. (See Arrow, et al.,[8] and Nerlove.[9])

Table 11-1. Time Series Estimates of the Elasticity of Substitution

Author	Data	Estimated Elasticity
Arrow, et al.[a]	U.S. 1909–1949	0.57
Brown—de Cani[b]	U.S. 1938–1958	0.47
Ferguson[c]	U.S. 1929–1963	0.67
Kendrick[d]	U.S. 1933–1957	0.62
Kravis[e]	U.S. 1900–1957	0.64
Schaafsma[f]	Canada—1949–1972	0.63–0.71

Sources: See Bibliography.

[a]Arrow, K.J., Chenery, M.B., Minhas, B.S., and Solow, R.M. "Capital-Labor Substitution and Economic Efficiency." *Review of Economics and Statistics* Vol 43 (1961): 225–250.

[b]Brown, M. and deCani, J. "A Measure of Technological Employment." *Review of Economics and Statistics* Vol. 45, (1963): 386–94.

[c]Ferguson, C.E. "Time-Series Production Functions and Technological Progress in American Manufacturing Industry." *Journal of Political Economy* Vol. 71, No. 1, (1963): 135–147.

[d]Kendrick, J.W. "Comment on Solow, Capital, Labor and Income in Manufacturing," in J.W. Kendrick, *The Behavior of Income Shares: Selected Theoretical and Empirical Issues.* No. 27: *Studies in Income and Wealth.* Princeton: Princeton University Press, 1964.

[e]Kravis, I. "Relative Income Shares in Fact and Theory." *American Economic Review* Vol. 49, (1959): 917–949.

[f]Schaafsma, J. "On Estimating the Time Structure of Capital-Labor Substitution in the Manufacturing Sector: A Model Applied to 1949–1972 Canadian Data." *South Economic Journal* Vol. 44 (1978): 740–751.

The results reported in Table 11-1 are estimates of the long-run elasticity of substitution. Schaafsma[10] has recently estimated the rate at which this substitution occurs. His results indicate that the process of adjustment may be very slow. Initially, the response to changes in relative factor costs is sluggish, but it picks up after several years before slowing down again. The process of complete adjustment takes eight or nine years.

The factor substitution process is only part of the employment impact of capital subsidies, however. In general, there will also be an output effect on employment. The stimulus to the economy from a capital subsidy such as the ITC will generate additional production. At this higher level of productive activity, more of both factors, capital and labor, will usually be demanded. The net effect of these two components (output and substitution) of the employment response to a capital subsidy is an unresolved empirical issue. Substitution works to reduce employment, and higher output works to increase it. It is worth noting that Schaafsma's estimates of the rate of adjustment via substitution of capital for labor suggest a very long time horizon; in other words, the short-run elasticity of substitution is considerably lower than the long-run elasticity and does not rise very rapidly over time. Thus, the output effects of the ITC on employment are likely to dominate the substitution effects for the first few years following a change in the relative prices of capital and labor. This suggests the likelihood of an employment stimulus from the ITC. The impact of the ITC on urban areas, however, is still in question and we will turn to it shortly.

It is not our goal to review the literature for its own sake, but only to evaluate its usefulness in estimating the impacts of the ITC. Since there is no agreement on these impacts in the literature, its usefulness is limited to identifying a fairly wide range of parameter values for the key variables that influence ITC impacts. The literature indicates a wide discrepancy in estimates of the ITC's impact on aggregate capital accumulation (i.e., on the price elasticity of demand for capital) and a dichotomy between time series estimates and cross-section estimates of the elasticity of substitution of capital for labor. Thus, the investment and employment responses to the basic ITC are unclear.

Urban Impacts. When an urban dimension is added, the impacts are even less certain because the parameter estimates that do exist are no longer applicable. What is clear for older cities is their comparative disadvantage in attracting new investment in the first place, especially manufacturing investment. By stimulating such new investment, ITC accelerates the process of shutting down older factories that are more likely to be located in older central cities and to rebuild in the suburbs, the Sunbelt, or the Third World.

Despite their variation, the aggregate impact estimates reported in the previous section tell us something about the effects of ITC. For example, the estimates of the elasticity of substitution that appear in Table 11–1 represent in a sense a long-run upper limit on that variable, and that limit appears to be significantly less than unity. Unfortunately, not even these limited conclusions are applicable to urban areas in general or central cities in particular. There are at least three basic reasons for this incompatibility of national parameters and urban or central city impacts. First, the aggregate elasticity of substitution may disguise systematic differences between central cities and other areas. While factor proportions are variable ex ante, they may be fairly rigid ex post. This putty-clay hypothesis suggests that new equipment in old buildings may be less efficient than new equipment in new buildings, particularly if the new equipment embodies significant technological change. Since older central cities tend to have an older inventory of industrial structures, this sort of limit on flexibility is more likely to occur there. The most obvious result of this would be a disproportionately small share of new investment in older buildings and, therefore, a smaller share in older cities.

Second, new structures are more likely to be built outside older central cities. The price and availability of empty land (or costs of demolition where land is not empty), the decentralization of consumer demand and employee residential locations, the question of transport access in an increasingly highway-oriented economy, the demand for potential expansion space, and a number of other factors have insured that most new development and construction occur at the urban fringe or even further out.

Finally, recent evidence suggests that firms are more likely to move in order to exploit new technologies than for any other reason.[11] The existence of ITC encourages firms to relocate to exploit new technologies without delay. To the extent that these new technologies use relatively more capital per unit of labor, ITC makes them even more attractive. Viewed in this light, ITC represents a subsidy for decentralization as well as a macroeconomic stimulus.

Thus, there are several reasons why the estimated effects of ITC on capital accumulation may not be applicable to central city areas. Although a quantification of these differences is beyond this chapter, the response parameters reported here are likely to overstate the central city response. Since the aggregate elasticities in Table 11-1 are long-run estimates and, therefore, upper limits on the short-run elasticity of substitution, the short-run elasticity in central cities is likely to be very low indeed.

The proposed changes in ITC, particularly the extension of credits to industrial and utility structures, is not neutral in its effect on urban development in that it may accelerate job movement from central cities to suburbs and from built-up areas to areas in the process of development.

The provisions for a more liberal investment tax credit may not bring about industrial movement from central cities that would not have occurred anyway sooner or later. By lowering the relative price of capital and increasing the profitability of investment in plant construction, however, the ITC will certainly accelerate the decentralization of economic activity from the central city and increase the difficulty of central city adjustments. Although the extension of the credit to major rehabilitation may mitigate the antiurban impact of ITC to some extent, the lack of experience with major rehabilitation of industrial structures will minimize its use.

The extension of the ITC to structures also contains a bias against central cities in that it applies only to manufacturing and utility plant investment. The long-term decline of the manufacturing sector in central cities and the comparative disadvantages of central cities in attracting and holding manufacturing activities are well documented.[12] Unfortunately, investment in structures in the most important growth sectors of central city economies, services and commercial activities, is not eligible for the ITC.

One effect of ITC may be to foster a reallocation of investment funds from the service, commercial, and housing sectors of the economy to manufacturing and utility construction. Since the number of factors that determine the allocation of investment funds is large, the extent to which this is likely to occur is unknown. Any shifts to manufacturing will be limited by tax incentives and institutional rigidities in the other sectors and by the limited capacity of an economy to produce new industrial structures in the short run.

The differential impact of the liberalized ITC on investment in central city and noncentral city areas has implications for the impact of ITC on employment in the central city. To the extent that factor proportions are not as malleable in built-up areas, that is, the elasticity of substitution is lower, the impact of ITC on the substitution of capital for labor in central cities will be smaller for a given level of output. The primary influence of the ITC on employment may be through the output effect. The output response is also likely to be smaller in central cities. The net effect of these two relatively sluggish responses is unclear. It is possible that the general stimulus of ITC will generate some employment in central cities and it may be enough to overcome the influence of the lower relative price of capital.

The relative magnitudes of these two components of the response to ITC are not known with certainty for the national economy since the existing evidence does not agree. The uncertainty is even greater for central city impacts although there are reasons to believe the stimulus will be smaller in central cities.

The indirect impacts of ITC affect not only employment in cities, but also employment of city residents. If, as is often maintained, ghetto residents experience restricted mobility, the decentralization of employment will adversely affect employment of city residents. Furthermore, the capital-skill complementarity proposition that has received empirical support recently suggests the ITC will not improve the outlook for employment of relatively unskilled segments of the labor force.[13] The so-called "white-collar bias" in ITC is estimated to have caused a decrease in employment of unskilled individuals. To the extent that unskilled labor is concentrated in central city areas, these residents stand to suffer disproportionately from liberalized and increased capital subsidies such as ITC.

For a variety of reasons, therefore, it seems appropriate to adopt a federal policy toward investment that will have less potential danger for central city economies. One such proposal is an extension of ITC itself, the Differential Investment Tax Credit (DITC) that offers an extra tax credit to firms in distressed areas.

The Differential Investment Tax Credit

To address the potential antiurban impact of extending ITC to structures, as well as to channel capital into urban areas, a Differential Investment Tax Credit (DITC) for investment in distressed areas has been proposed as part of the President's National Urban Policy. The proposed DITC provides an additional 5 percent tax credit for investment in distressed areas. Thus, eligible investments in such distressed areas qualify for a total tax credit of 15 percent. The 5 percent add-on applies to the same set of investments as the regular ITC so that the extension to investment in industrial structures that is currently pending in Congress will be included automatically if it is enacted into law.

The proposed definition of distressed areas for the purposes of DITC is based on unemployment rates and the growth rates of employment, income, and population. Whatever Congress does with this formula, the focus of the program on distressed areas virtually insures that it will include the central cities that are generally considered to be in the most serious trouble. To control the macroeconomic impacts of this DITC, a limit of $200 million per year for two years has been proposed for the total credits available under this 5 percent add-on, with the Department of Commerce having responsibility for allocating the credits among investors in distressed urban areas by granting "Certificates of Necessity" to eligible firms. It is important to note that this certification procedure converts what is nominally a tax program into a discretionary grant program. Investors cannot simply claim the credit on their tax form but must formally apply for a certificate with no assurance that it will be granted. This chapter, however, will discuss DITC as if it were a genuine tax credit program with no application or approval procedure other than tax forms and IRS audits.

Unlike ITC, which is a nonurban program with urban impacts, DITC is explicity intended to have an urban focus. The extent to which DITC will generate incremental investment in distressed areas is the critical issue here.

There are several ways in which incremental investment in distressed areas can occur. For expository purposes, let us consider the decision to choose a location for a new plant. The substantive issue for DITC is the degree to which its 5 percent differential will induce firms to locate in these areas. Businesses will prefer a particular location if their stream of after-tax profits will be larger there than in another location. DITC has its impact by reducing the cost of capital acquisition. The question is whether or not the incremental 5 percent credit is sufficient to offset other existing cost differentials. The answer requires detailed data on the cost and revenue differentials between distressed and nondistressed areas.

If we assume revenues would be invariant with respect to plant location (e.g., the case of goods sold in a national market), we can focus attention on the relative costs of alternative locations. Information on cost differences of this nature is scarce, but Andrew Hamer[14] has provided some evidence on the magnitude of cost differentials between central city and suburban areas in a study of manufacturing production costs in the Boston metropolitan area.

Among the cost differentials, Hamer considers the relatively higher construction costs of multistory structures, the high costs of demolition that investment in denser areas may involve, and other problems, such as the allocation of space for parking, elevators, and storage, associated with investment in dense areas. Hamer finds that cost differences for identical facilities between Boston and its suburbs for an "average" manufacturer can be substantial, ranging from 23 percent to 100 percent higher in the city of Boston (see Table 11-2). While clearly not indicative of differences for all firms and locations, such data suggest a high probability that an incremental credit of only 5 percent of eligible investments is not likely to generate a massive flow of activity back into distressed areas.

Table 11-2. Percentage Differentials in Building Rentals: Central City-Suburb

	Range, Based upon Site Chosen
Low Density[a]	44-100%
High Density[a]	32- 70
Low Density in Suburbs Versus High Density in City[a]	23- 63

Source: Andrew Hamer, *Industrial Exodus from Central City* (Lexington, Mass.: D.C. Heath and Co., 1973).
[a]Low density is defined to be a 1:3 building to land ratio while high density is a 1:2 building to land ratio.

Hamer's study focuses on a "representative" industry. An estimate of the number and types of firms that the 5 percent DITC would be capable of attracting to particular areas requires a distribution of cost differentials over a number of industries—data that are not available. However, in light of the substantial differences for Hamer's representative industry, the proportion of firms whose location decisions DITC would influence appears to be small. This does not mean that 5 percent is too small a differential to have any effect but only that the available evidence suggests relatively few firms fall in the marginal group affected by a 5 percent differential.

The work of Roger Schmenner also provides some evidence on the implications of a differential tax credit for the location of firms. Specifically, firms prefer on-site expansion to total relocation or any other form of plant expansion, but such on-site expansion is often contingent upon the availability of contiguous open space. The central city-suburban differences in this factor suggest a lower response to tax credits in central cities. The question is whether those firms whose locational alternatives do include central city areas are likely to be swayed by the differential credit. The Schmenner approach is less precise than that of Hamer, but the attitude of business managers in a range of industries indicates DITC may have a relatively small effect. As noted earlier, firms that do move generally do not do so to exploit site-related cost differentials, the substance of DITC, but rather to exploit new technologies. Only if intensive land use is technologically desirable can urban locations hope to compete for these firms.

The most likely impact of DITC will be to subsidize firms that would have located in distressed areas in any event. Thus, the stimulative effects of DITC will occur primarily through whatever income effect these windfall gains generate. There is no reason to presume a large local multiplier.

To maximize the stimulation of DITC on investment and employment in distressed areas, we would like to target funds to those areas. One point is worth noting in this regard. As with any credit for expansion, there is a bias toward firms likely to have grown in the absence of the subsidy. Areas with many growing establishments are likely to share disproportionately in the initial allocation of tax expenditures under DITC, although such areas are less likely to be categorized as distressed. The net result may be maximum stimulus from DITC in the least distressed areas among the elibible places. Furthermore, the cost differences between central cities and suburbs are likely to vary from city to city, and the differentials are probably lower in areas with low density central cities. Since these areas are generally less severely distressed, this too contributes to the possibility that DITC may have its greatest impact on the least distressed areas.

Because the proposed DITC is limited to industrial structures (primarily manufacturing), it bypasses the most dynamic sectors of central city economies and concentrates on a sector that is growing very slowly nationally and declining rapidly in central cities. On the other hand, there are many kinds of manufacturing activity that are well suited to central cities and DITC would stimulate their growth. The rapid suburbanization of manufacturing in recent years is not an argument against the differential ITC but an indication that DITC cannot, in and of itself, cause major alterations in economic development patterns.

It is worth noting that DITC may be desirable from an economic efficiency standpoint. In many cases, the existing investment in place in central cities is being underutilized because of the rapid decentralization of recent years, and DITC may foster more efficient use of this stock of buildings and infrastructure.

In sum, DITC is a welcome offset to the bias of the liberalized ITC and may contribute to the tax base of cities, but its differential stimulus does not appear to be large enough to influence the vast majority of business location decisions.

Capital Subsidies and Urban Development

Urban fiscal problems are nearly always closely linked with declines in urban employment, declines that are most severe in periods of national recession. At first glance, therefore, any policy directed at simultaneously stimulating the economy, increasing the nation's capacity to produce, and minimizing the likelihood of inflationary bottlenecks would seem to benefit city economies and city governments substantially. It was argued above, however, that cities do not share proportionately in ITC-induced investment and employment growth and may even suffer net losses of activity as a result of ITC liberalization. Whether central cities suffer absolute losses of employment or only relative losses depends on the multiplier effects of the stimulus elsewhere rather than on increased investment in central cities.

By itself, the DITC proposal to deal with the anticity bias in the ITC is likely to have an impact on the locational decision of only a small number of firms. Market forces fostering decentralization are powerful, and enactment of a 5 percent differential credit for investment in distressed areas can at best be expected to slow the rate of exodus from these areas.

In sum, whatever aggregate impacts ITC and DITC may have on the national economy, distressed cities are not likely to enjoy a proportionate share of the benefits. Since the impact of ITC on employment is indirect, operating primarily through the output effects, it is equally unlikely that the impact of this form of capital subsidy will provide a major stimulus to central city employment.

LABOR SUBSIDIES

The basic labor subsidy mechanism considered in this chapter is the Employment Tax Credit (ETC). A general description of this mechanism is followed by a discussion of its potential impacts on the national economy and on cities. Since a general ETC has not been seriously proposed, this discussion serves as background for the two types of ETC that have received serious consideration, a marginal ETC and a targeted ETC. These are also described and their potential impacts discussed.

The Employment Tax Credit

A subsidy to a firm for the employment of any factor reduces the net price of that particular factor and increases demand. Given some elasticity in its supply, use of that factor increases. If unemployment of the labor force is viewed as a problem, the most direct way to use the tax system to address the problem is with an employment tax credit. ETC has stimulative macroeconomic effects, and this type of stimulus is the traditional rationale for such credits. Since it reduces production costs by lowering the net price of labor, it also has potential for beneficial impacts on inflation and unemployment. The unemployment impacts may be more concentrated in central cities than the benefits of ITC since unemployment rates are often higher there. The United States has yet to employ general employment tax credits, although they were originally proposed in the 1930s by Nicholas Kaldor. The idea has received a growing amount of attention in recent years, however, partly because of recent American experience with simultaneous inflation and unemployment. Given the adverse effects of both on city finances, city governments would appear to have a particular interest in such an idea.

The effectiveness of wage subsidies in increasing the employment level will depend upon the quantitative response of firms to the lower relative cost of labor. The potential effectiveness of ETC in achieving the goal of increased employment can be evaluated either through a direct examination of estimated employment demand elasticities or through estimates made with more general economic models. We turn first to the direct estimates of the wage elasticity of labor demand.

Hammermesh[15] has recently summarized the existing studies of labor demand and the responsiveness of employment to wage levels. While estimates and estimation methods vary from sample to sample, the degree of variance is surprisingly low. Nearly all of the estimates fall between 0 and 0.35, with a number clustered around 0.15 (see Table 11-3). That is, a 10 percent ETC would increase employment demand by 1.5 percent. It is important to note that limits on the total credit to any one firm or limits on the amount of subsidy per worker under an ETC program would bias these general elasticity estimates. This is discussed in greater detail in the following section.

Since the response of labor demand to a wage decrease is largely a result of substituting labor for other factors, the degree of responsiveness is a function of the elasticity of substitution. The easier it is to substitute labor for capital in production, the higher the elasticity of labor demand is likely to be and the greater the employment response to wage rate changes. The pure price elasticity of labor demand can be derived from the elasticity of substitution. Specifically, the elasticity of labor demand for wage decreases is equal to $(l - s)$ times the elasticity of technical substitution, where s is labor's share. As discussed in the section entitled "Capital Subsidies," this elasticity is generally in the range of 0.6 to 1.0 (see Table 11-1 and discussion). Hammermesh notes that the same basic estimates are obtained from entirely distinct literature.

Given the apparent inelasticity of labor demand for wage levels, ETC will be much like a lump sum grant to the firm, generating some increase in employment but a substantial windfall to the firm as well. The increased employment, to whatever degree, will increase the taxable capacity of local governments at the expense of the federal government, as will the windfall if local governments have a way of capturing the base. This is a relatively expensive form of fiscal relief.

Studies of the impact of various stimulative policies using more general economic models indicate that ETC will have a far greater impact on the overall employment level than would ITC, as would be expected, since labor is the factor made relatively less expensive. A second important finding of these studies is the absence of white-collar bias in ETC. Thus, the impact of ETC may be more favorable to the unskilled than a capital subsidy such as ITC would be.

Urban Impacts. While it appears likely that ETC will increase aggregate employment, urban areas may or may not enjoy a pro-

Table 11-3. Estimates of the Wage Elasticity of Employment

Author	Data	Estimated Elasticity
I. Private Sector		
A. Aggregate		
Brechling-Mortenson[a]	Manufacturing employment	.15
Brown-de Cani[b]	Nonfarm man-hours	.47
Chow-Moore[c]	Private man-hours	.37
Coen-Hickman[d]	Private man-hours	.18
David-van de Klendert[e]	Private man-hours	.32
McKinnon[f]	Manufacturing employment	.29
Nadiri[g]	Manufacturing employment	.15
Nadiri-Rosen[h]	Manufacturing employment	
	Production	.11
	Nonproduction	.14

	White Collar	*Blue Collar*
B. By Level of Skills		
Kesselman, Williamson, Berndt[i]	.19	.34
II. Public Sector		
Ashenfelter-Ehrenberg[j]	.75	
Johnson-Tomola[k]	.53	

Source: See bibliography.

[a]Brechling, F., and Mortenson, D. "Interrelated Investment and Employment Decisions." University of Essex, November, 1971. (Mimeo.)

[b]Brown, M., and deCani, J. "A Measure of Technological Employment." *Review of Economics and Statistics* Vol. 45, (1963): 386-94.

[c]Chow, G., and Moore, G. "An Econometric Model of Business Cycles," in Bert Hickman, ed., *Econometric Models of Cyclical Behavior.* New York: National Bureau of Economic Research, Vol. 2, 1972.

[d]Coen, R., and Hickman, B. "Constrained Joint Estimation of Factor Demand and Production Functions." *Review of Economics and Statistics* Vol. 52 (1970): 287-300.

[e]David, P., and van de Klendert, T. "Biased Efficiency Growth Capital-Labor Substitution in the United States, 1899-1960." *American Economic Review* Vol. 55, (1965): 357-394.

[f]McKinnon, R.I. "Wages, Capital Costs and Employment in Manufacturing: A Model Applied to 1947-58 U.S. Data." *Econometrica* Vol. 30, (1962): 501-521.

[g]Nadiri, M.I. "The Effect of Relative Prices and Capacity on the Demand for Labor in the U.S. Manufacturing Sector." *Review of Economic Studies* (1968): 273-288.

[h]Nadiri, M.I., and Rosen, S. *A Disequilibrium Model of Production.* New York: National Bureau of Economic Research, 1974.

[i]Kesselman, J.R., Williamson, S.H., and Berndt, E.R. "Tax Credits for Employment Rather than Investment." *American Economic Review* Vol. 67 (1977): 339-349.

[j]Ashenfelter, O., and Ehrenberg, R.G. "The Demand for Labor in the Public Sector," in Daniel S. Hammermesh, ed., *Labor in the Public Sector.* Princeton: Princeton University press, 1975.

[k]Johnson, G.E., and Tomola, J.D. "The Fiscal Substitution Effect of Alternative Approaches to Public Service Employment Policy." *The Journal of Human Resources* Vol. 12 (1977): 3-26.

portionate share of the employment growth generated by these credits. To the extent that urban areas have unused industrial capacity, the expansion in employment in cities can be readily accommodated. Thus, significant capital underutilization, or sufficient room for expansion, is likely to substantially increase the ability of individual urban areas to capture employment growth. Unfortunately, data on capacity utilization specific to urban areas are not available. When capacity must be increased, the relative costs of further expansion become an issue of importance. The plight of Boston and presumably of other similar urban areas as well has already been discussed (see Table 11-2).

The extent to which the central city labor force shares in overall employment growth will depend upon the labor force characteristics in urban areas. As noted above, Kesselman and others[16] find that ETC does not have the white-collar bias that characterizes ITC. Moreover, the simple wage elasticity of labor demand is generally estimated to be higher for blue-collar or unskilled workers than for white-collar workers (see Table 11-3). While the more favorable impact on unskilled labor does not necessarily have an impact on the *location* of employment, areas with concentrations of relatively unskilled blue-collar labor are likely to share more than proportionately in this employment growth provided these workers are sufficiently mobile or employers are willing to locate near such concentrations.

The Marginal Employment Tax Credit

The labor corollary to the investment tax credit is not the general employment tax credit but rather a credit for increments to the employment of labor. This is defined as a Marginal Employment Tax Credit (METC). Like the general ETC, this proposal has yet to receive official sanction, although it was considered as a possible alternative to the targeted ETC that was included in President Carter's National Urban Policy.

Under a marginal employment tax credit plan, a credit is given for employment over some base amount. For example, a credit may be given for the employment of labor in excess of 90 percent of the previous year's amount. In this sense, the general employment tax credit can be viewed as METC with a zero base. A fundamental relationship within the general category of marginal employment tax credits is that the higher the base employment or wage bill level is set, the greater the rate of subsidy, given a fixed tax expenditure cost. The implication of setting a nonzero base under the marginal programs is a greater price effect per dollar of federal cost. Kesselman and others[17] estimate that the employment generated by setting this base at 50 percent of the previous year's level is three times the amount generated by the zero-base general ETC for a given federal tax expenditure level.

The urban impacts of METC differ only slightly from those already discussed under the general ETC. The implicit allocation of benefits under METC to firms in proportion to their growth is likely to provide fewer benefits to older declining central cities. Incentives for retaining existing employment in central cities are weak since assistance is given to firms with declining employment only when the base employment level is set at a relatively low (and, therefore, costly) level.

The crucial urban tradeoff in comparing the general ETC with METC is between the general ETC's smaller stimulus per federal dollar and METC's bias toward growth areas.

Several caveats are in order in estimating the impacts of METC, especially if inferences are drawn from aggregate wage elasticities. Restrictions on total credits per firm or per worker are a likely part of any METC package. These restrictions distort the price effects of the tax credits and generally reduce the magnitude of the employment response. In the absence of the credit, firms that would have increased their employment by more than enough to receive the maximum credit per firm receive a windfall gain with no relative price effect. Thus, METC would tend to distribute a large share of the tax benefits to rapidly growing firms with no stimulative impact on employment.

Limits on the amount of credit per worker also distort the price effects and reduce the stimulative impact of METC. These limits favor low-wage workers and occupations. Their urban impact depends on the industry mix and labor force characteristics of individual urban labor markets. Some recent evidence suggests that central city-suburban wage differentials are not significant.[18]

The Targeted Employment Tax Credit

Tax credits for the employment of a specific portion of the labor force (TETC) are the only major form of private sector wage subsidy utilized to any significant extent in this country. In recent years, however, federal incentives for the employment and training of the hard-core unemployed have most often taken the form of direct public employment, as in the Public Employment Program (PEP) and Comprehensive Employment and Training Act (CETA) programs, rather than the form of wage subsidies.

One of the initial experiments with TETC came with the Job Opportunities in Business Sector (JOBS) program of the 1960s in which the federal government negotiated contracts with firms to hire and train welfare recipients. Employment subsidies in the private sector remained relatively small throughout this period, however.

More recently another version of TETC, the Work Incentive Program (WIN), has been used. In this program employment of eligible persons was subsidized by a 20 percent credit for payments in the first year of employment. To be eligible to receive the credit, the worker that the subsidy supported was required to remain employed at least one additional year. The WIN proposal was modified by the Talmadge Amendment of 1971, which required that all Aid to Families with Dependent Children (AFDC) recipients register for potential employment. This amendment also placed less emphasis on training and more on the job search process.

The use of targeted employment tax credits as an incentive for targeting hiring on particular groups of individuals is a central element of the President's National Urban Policy proposal. This version of TETC provides a tax credit to any employer for the employment of any eligible person. The program is specifically targeted on individuals between the ages of 18 and 24 from households in poverty (tentatively defined to be those having annual incomes lower than 70 percent of that needed for a low standard of living). A credit of 33 percent of salaries up to a $2,000 limit is given for the first year of employment, decreasing to 25 percent up to a $1,500 maximum for the second year. The total allowable annual credit is limited to a firm's tax liability.

The intent of these subsidies is to increase the demand for the targeted labor group by directly lowering the cost to the firm of hiring these persons. As for the general employment tax credit, the parameter that will determine the degree to which employment demand will increase as a result of the credit will be the wage elasticity of demand for the targeted group, in this case unskilled labor. However, unlike the general or the marginal tax credit, a further consideration is implied by the fact that the labor pool is divided into two distinct groups, subsidized and nonsubsidized laborers. The degree to which the targeted tax credit in fact increases the total level of employment will be a function of the degree to which targeted workers are substituted for, rather than added to, unsubsidized workers. In a sense, there is an implicit elasticity of substitution between skilled and unskilled workers, and the more easily a firm can substitute one type of labor for the other, the less likely it will be that TETC will increase total employment.

Employment Impacts. It is possible to draw some inferences about the likely response of manufacturers to TETC, based on experience in the public sector. Johnson and Tomola have estimated the impact of CETA and PEP on the level of public employment.[19] They demonstrate that despite a short-run employment increase, within one and one-half years the substitution of subsidized for unsubsidized employment was nearly total. For each new subsidized public employee hired, one unsubsidized employee left the payroll. Thus, the net effect on local government employment is close to zero in the long run. The actual role that this program has played is that of an affirmative action device, substituting disadvantaged for advantaged workers.

The differences between the existing subsidies and the proposed TETC include higher subsidy rates under PEP and CETA than under the proposed TETC, a potentially different elasticity of demand in the public sector from that in the private sector, local public officials who may be less likely to act as pure cost minimizers than would private employers, and finally, differences in geographical targeting because the funds under the public employment programs were allocated to areas with excess labor supply while the private subsidies will not necessarily be concentrated in these areas.

Data on the wage elasticity of labor demand in manufacturing and in the public sector were presented in Table 11–3. The responsiveness of labor demand to wages appears to be lower for manufacturing than for the public sector, implying that the initial response of employment to a private sector TETC would be smaller than for public employment. The long-term impact will depend on the extent to which the increment to employment is permanent and substitution is avoided. There is no hard evidence on the degree of substitution. However, manufacturing is believed to be generally less skill oriented than public sector employment.[20] This implies that after the two-year term of TETC has expired, the incentive to maintain the newly trained workers rather than replace them with new subsidized workers is less compelling in private sector manufacturing.

Urban Impacts. Central cities have a disproportionate share of the nation's low-skilled, hard-core unemployed. A credit targeted at this group of individuals would make central cities, to a greater extent than other parts of the country, attractive to firms seeking low-cost labor. The limited mobility of these workers may require firms to locate in areas more accessible to such a labor supply in order to exploit the tax credit, but the degree to which firms would move in response to the credit is still an unanswered empirical question.

Parameter estimates of the response of firm location to reduced labor costs do not exist. The essential question is whether or to what extent firms that are considering relocating or expanding will be influenced by a supply of cheap labor. Schmenner addresses this issue and finds, as noted above with regard to DITC, that firms that change their location are most likely to do so in order to employ new technologies, not to exploit site-related cost savings.[21] This implies that unless there are other reasons for firms to relocate in denser areas, the tax credit for unskilled labor is not likely to pull them in. Clearly, some firms would relocate in order to enjoy the temporary cost savings, but these are typically low-capital, footloose industries whose movement from area to area does not significantly affect their productivity. The disruptive impact of these firms on cities is another matter.

Another piece of evidence indicative of the locational implications of the targeted tax credit is a study by Somers on the hiring practices of firms that had moved into depressed areas.[22] Somers observed the degree to which these firms employed low-wage labor. He found no evidence that they substituted unskilled laborers for skilled workers, implying that the firms moved for other reasons.

In sum, the existence of TETC is not likely to have a significant impact on overall employment levels within urban areas although the supply of unskilled labor residing in central cities may benefit to a greater extent. Firms that can take advantage of the credit and employ the unskilled labor can very easily substitute the subsidized laborers for the unsubsidized, particularly when the program is permanent and the industry can plan on the credit. Furthermore, the influence of low-labor costs in location decisions of firms appears to be minimal.

Labor Subsidies and Urban Development

As a tool for stimulating employment, ETC and its variations are more effective than ITC and DITC because the stimulative effects of ETC programs are likely to be felt more rapidly and because the price effects are favorable in the long run. To the extent that central cities do not share in the economy's employment growth, they stand to gain less than growth areas from METC. The bias toward less skilled labor imparted by the credit limit per worker, on the other hand, may favor central cities.

TETC is clearly aimed at central city labor forces that have a disproportionate share of disadvantaged workers. It is less clear that TETC will increase employment in the city since targeted workers may work in the suburbs if firms are reluctant to relocate in the central city.

The demand for labor appears to be relatively wage inelastic. Although the employment response to ETC would be favorable, it would be small while the investment response to employment credits would be smaller still and much slower. Investment decisions are for a much longer term than employment decisions, and thus the investment impact of a short-term wage subsidy is likely to be very limited.

CONCLUSION

The previous sections of this chapter paint a somewhat discouraging picture for the use of tax credits to stimulate economic activity in cities. Not only do these credits have the potential for undesirable side effects such as reduced employment (in the case of ITC) and substitution of unskilled for skilled workers (in the case of the targeted ETC), but also by their very nature they bypass the entire nonprofit sector, which accounts for a steadily growing share of economic activity and is concentrated in central cities.

It is worth noting that the specific capital and labor subsidies discussed in this chapter must operate in a complex environment of dozens of other subsidies and taxes on the same two factors. This makes estimation of their responses to new subsidies extremely difficult, particularly when the other subsidies are quite large.

For example, ETC enacted to take effect concurrently with a substantial rise in Social Security taxes may have a very different impact than it would by itself. A targeted ETC, when combined with an increase in the minimum wage, may not reduce the cost of labor.

Despite this pessimistic evidence of uncertain and perhaps undesirable impacts, tax credits may well have an important function in a balanced urban policy. As was noted in the introduction, their weakness is their strength. They are blunt instruments so they are an expensive way to achieve some goals, but they also allow the market to make decisions about urban development while providing a slight push toward distressed areas and distressed people. This market test can help to avoid costly mistakes as well as expensive bureaucracies.

Furthermore, these credits may be put to work together, not individually, as they have been discussed in this chapter. The dual impact of targeted employment and investment tax credits may be greater than the sum of the separate effects and may constitute an effective tool with which to begin to address the serious problems facing our cities. In this chapter we have not argued that tax credits are not useful policy tools, but rather that the evidence suggests that by themselves they cannot be expected to have more than a minor impact on urban revitalization.

Finally, the urban-related tax credit programs are clearly identified as experimental for national urban policy. They therefore need to be evaluated carefully during the next several years so that our information on their impacts is more extensive a few years from now when it is time to reconsider their role in urban development.

NOTES

1. Roy Bahl and David Greytak, "The Response of City Government Revenues to Changes in Employment Structure," *Land Economics* Vol. 52 (1976), pp. 415-434.

2. U.S. Treasury Department, *The President's 1978 Tax Program* (Washington,D.C.: U.S. Government Printing Office, 1978).

3. Roy Bahl and David Puryear, "Impact of the President's 1978 Tax Program on Housing and Cities," Working Paper No. 1, Office of Policy Development and Research, U.S. Department of Housing and Urban Development (forthcoming).

4. E.L. Berndt and L.R. Christensen, "Testing for the Existence of a Consistent Aggregate Index for Labor Inputs," *American Economic Review*, Vol. 64, (June 1974), pp. 391-404.

5. Robert M. Coen, "Tax Policy and Investment Behavior: Comment," *American Economic Review*, Vol. 59, (June 1969), pp. 370-379.

6. Robert Eisner, "Tax Policy and Investment Behavior: Comment," *American Economic Review*, Vol. 59, (June 1969), pp. 379-388.

7. J.R. Kesselman, S.H. Williamson, and E.R. Berndt, "Tax Credits for Employment Rather than Investment," *American Economic Review*, Vol. 67, (June 1977), pp. 339-349.

8. K.J. Arrow, M.B. Chenery, B.S. Minhas, and R.M. Solow, "Capital-Labor Substitution and Economic Efficiency," *Review of Economics and Statistics* Vol. 43, (Oct. 1961), pp. 225-250.

9. Marc Nerlove, "Recent Empirical Studies of the C.E.S. and Related Production Functions," in Murray Brown, ed., *The Theory and Empirical Analysis of Production* (New York: National Bureau of Economic Research, 1962).

10. Joseph Schaafsma, "On Estimating the Time Structure of Capital-Labor Substitution in the Manufacturing Sector: A Model Applied to 1949-1972 Canadian Data," *Southern Economic Journal* Vol. 44 (April 1978), pp. 740-751.

11. Roger W. Schmenner, "Summary of Findings: The Manufacturing Location Decision: Evidence from Cincinnati and New England," Washington, D.C., 1978. (Mimeo.)

12. Seymour Sacks, "Trends in Large City Manufacturing Employment," Draft report to the Office of Economic Affairs, U.S. Department of Housing and Urban Development, June 1978.

13. Kesselman, Williamson, and Berndt, "Tax Credits for Employment Rather than Investment."

14. Andrew M. Hamer, *Industrial Exodus from Central City* (Lexington, Mass.: D.C. Heath and Co., 1973).

15. Daniel S. Hammermesh, "Econometric Studies of Labor Demand and Their Applications to Policy Analysis," *Journal of Human Resources* Vol. 11, (1976), pp. 507-525.

16. Kesselman, Williamson, and Berndt, "Tax Credits for Employment Rather than Investment."

17. Ibid.

18. Hamer, *Industrial Exodus from Central City.*

19. George E. Johnson and James D. Tomola, "The Fiscal Substitution Effect of Alternative Approaches to Public Service Employment Policy," *The Journal of Human Resources* Vol. 12, (1977), pp. 3-26.

20. Ibid.

21. Schmenner, "Summary of Findings: The Manufacturing Location Decision: Evidence from Cincinnati and New England."

22. Gerald Somers, "Labor Recruitment in a Rural Area," *Monthly Labor Review* Vol. 81, (Oct. 1958), pp. 1113-1120.

Index

About the Authors

Roy W. Bahl
Director of Metropolitan Studies Program
Maxwell School, Syracuse University

Robert F. Cook
Senior Fellow
The Brookings Institution

Paul R. Dommel
Senior Fellow
The Brookings Institution

Alan E. Fechter
Senior Research Associate
The Urban Institute

Richard D. Gustely
Chief, Analysis Branch
Regional Economic Analysis Division
Bureau of Economic Analysis, U.S. Department of Commerce

L. Kenneth Hubbell
Professor of Economics
University of Missouri—Kansas City

Bernard Jump, Jr.
The Maxwell School
Syracuse University

Richard McHugh
Assistant Professor of Economics
University of Missouri-Columbia

David Puryear
Acting Director
Public Finance Research Group
Department of Housing and Urban Development

John P. Ross
Associate Professor of Environmental and Urban Systems
Virginia Polytechnical Institute and State University

Larry Schroeder
The Maxwell School
Syracuse University

G. Ross Stephens
Professor of Political Science
University of Missouri-Kansas City

Roger J. Vaughan
Economist
Rand Corporation

Georges Vernez
Economist
Rand Corporation

David B. Walker
Assistant Director
Advisory Commission on Intergovernmental Relations